BUSH RUNNER

BUSH RUNNER

*The Adventures
of Pierre-Esprit Radisson*

MARK BOURRIE

BIBLIOASIS
WINDSOR, ONTARIO

FIRST EDITION

Library and Archives Canada Cataloguing in Publication

Bourrie, Mark, 1957–, author
    Bush runner : the adventures of Pierre-Esprit Radisson / Mark Bourrie.

(Untold lives)
Issued in print and electronic formats.
ISBN 978-1-77196-237-7 (softcover).—ISBN 978-1-77196-238-4 (ebook)

        1. Radisson, Pierre Esprit, approximately 1636–1710. 2. Fur traders—Canada—Biography.
3. Hudson's Bay Company. 4. Canada—History—1663–1713 (New France). I. Title.

FC3211.1.R33B68   2018   971.01092   C2018-901741-4   C2018-901742-2

Edited by Janice Zawerbny
Copy-edited by Emily Donaldson
Indexed and proofed by Allana Amlin
Typeset by Chris Andrechek
Cover designed by Michel Vrana

Published with the generous assistance of the Canada Council for the Arts, which last year invested $153 million to bring the arts to Canadians throughout the country, and the Government of Canada. Biblioasis also acknowledges the support of the Ontario Arts Council (OAC), an agency of the Government of Ontario, which last year funded 1,709 individual artists and 1,078 organizations in 204 communities across Ontario, for a total of $52.1 million, and the contribution of the Government of Ontario through the Ontario Book Publishing Tax Credit and the Ontario Media Development Corporation. This is one of the 200 exceptional projects funded through the Canada Council for the Arts' New Chapter program. With this $35M investment, the Council supports the creation and sharing of the arts in communities across Canada.

PRINTED AND BOUND IN CANADA

Contents

Timeline of Pierre-Esprit Radisson's Life

1636: LIKELY YEAR Radisson was born.

1650: The balance of power among First Nations of the Great Lakes region collapses with the conquest of the Huron (Wendat) Confederacy by Five Nations of the Iroquois. Most of what's now eastern Canada and the US Midwest is now a dangerous place of raids and counter-raids. At this point, Europeans are not important, direct military actors but are supplying weapons to Indigenous people.

1651: On May 24, Radisson, now an adolescent, arrives in Trois-Rivières, a tiny trading post between Montreal and Quebec City. It is under siege by the Iroquois. Radisson lives with his half-sisters.

1652: Less than a year after coming to Trois-Rivières, Radisson is captured by Mohawk (Iroquois) warriors, taken to their town in what's now northeastern New York State, and adopted by a wealthy and powerful family. In the fall, he escapes, is recaptured, and barely escapes being killed.

1653: Radisson is a member of a Mohawk party raiding into what's now Ohio, Indiana, and possibly as far west as Illinois. After the raid, he returns to the Iroquois country through the Ohio Valley. On October 19, he defects to the Dutch, who have a post at Fort Orange (Albany). Radisson is sent to Manhattan, then crosses the ocean to Holland.

1654: Radisson returns to Trois-Rivières, probably arriving in late spring. His half-sister, Marguérite, widowed in a Mohawk raid, has married Médard Chouart des Groseilliers, a fur trader about to leave on a trading trip to Lake Superior and Lake Michigan.

1654–1657: Radisson assists Jesuits priests with their missionary work in what is now southern Ontario. On one of these trips, he might have reached the northern end of Lake Michigan. Most, however, end badly until the Onondaga, members of the Iroquois Confederacy, allow the construction of a mission in their country (near what's now Syracuse).

1657: At the height of summer, Radisson travels with an Iroquois canoe flotilla up the St. Lawrence River and along the south shore of Lake Ontario to the Onondaga country.

1658: In early spring, Radisson and the French become anxious about their safety in the Onondaga country and abruptly flee.

1658–1660: Radisson and Groseilliers travel up the Ottawa River, along the north shore of Lake Huron and the south shore of Lake Superior, into present-day Wisconsin and central Minnesota. It's unclear if either saw the Mississippi, but they at least heard about it. Radisson may also have visited the area west of Chicago. Mostly, the two traders spend time in what's now the Upper Peninsula of Michigan and in the Duluth-Superior region.

1660: In May, a French-Huron force under Adam Dollard des Ormeaux attacks a large Iroquois war party on the Ottawa River northwest of Montreal. All the French and several Huron are killed.

1660: In the summer, Radisson and Groseilliers arrive in Montreal with a party of Indigenous traders with enough furs to ensure the temporary financial viability of the French colony on the St. Lawrence. They are heavily taxed and fined for illegal fur trading. Groseilliers goes to France and successfully appeals most of the fines.

1661: Groseilliers is back in New France, but the Ottawa River is controlled by the Iroquois and is far too unsafe for another trip west. Radisson and Groseilliers try to trade in Acadia, but are run off by other French traders and local farmers. They defect to the British, ending up in Boston.

1663: Radisson and Groseilliers help organize a New England fur-trading expedition to Hudson Bay. Storms off the coast of Labrador cause the ship to turn back.

1664: Radisson and Groseilliers befriend members of a delegation from England that arrive in Boston to negotiate the transfer of Dutch colonies in present-day New York and New Jersey to English control. Radisson and Groseilliers leave with one of the diplomats who has friends at the court of King Charles I. They are captured by Dutch pirates, who dump them on the coast of Spain.

1665: Radisson and Groseilliers arrive in England just after the Great Plague peaks in London. They live at the fringe of the King's court, first in Oxford, then Windsor. They befriend several powerful nobles and Radisson begins writing accounts of his adventures for Charles I.

1666: Radisson and Groseilliers have convinced the English to back their plan for a Hudson Bay fur trade. They are stuck in London because the Dutch have blockaded the English coast. London burns down.

1667: Another plan to sail to Hudson Bay is thwarted by Dutch naval successes in the English Channel. Radisson and Groseilliers are stalked and tempted by French and Dutch spies, one of whom steals Radisson's life story and convinces the French government to launch its own ill-fated Hudson Bay expeditions. Radisson probably finished the manuscripts of his Great Lakes adventures, which are given to the King and are not published for more than 200 years.

1668: Two fur-trading ships leave England for Hudson Bay. Groseilliers' ship arrives safely, but Radisson's turns back after hitting a storm south of Iceland.

1669: Groseilliers arrives in London in the fall with a shipload of furs, proving the Hudson Bay project's viability.

1670: Both the French traders make it to Hudson Bay. The Hudson's Bay Company is granted a royal charter, but Radisson and Groseilliers get no stock or options. They go back to Hudson Bay, spending the winter at Port Nelson.

1671: Radisson returns to England and spends several months buying trade goods for another expedition.

1672–1673: Radisson and Groseilliers spend another winter on Hudson Bay. Both men start to feel sidelined as British traders gain experience trading with the Cree.

1674: Radisson, back in London, marries Mary Kirke. Soon after, she has a child.

1675: Radisson defects to the French. He is sent to Quebec, where he fails to convince local merchants to finance a Hudson Bay trade.

1676: Radisson returns to France, then goes to England to try to reconnect with his wife. Her father refuses to let her and their child leave England. The Hudson's Bay Company refuses to give Radisson work. Discouraged and almost broke, Radisson joins a French military expedition to the Caribbean.

1677: Radisson is on the scene for French military successes in the Azores and Tobago.

1678: On May 11, Radisson is on one of the French ships that is destroyed when the fleet runs aground on Las Aves, off the coast of South America. Radisson survives but loses all his money.

1680–1681: Radisson goes back to Quebec, succeeds in convincing local merchants to open up a Hudson Bay trade, and leads an expedition to Fort Nelson.

Late 1670s–1680s: With the wars against the Dutch over, English xenophobia turns on the French. Foreign and English Catholics are also victims of mob violence and trumped-up plots.

1682–1683: Radisson returns to Quebec to find he has angered the French government by seizing English ships and men. He is sent back to France to explain himself. In Paris, he defects to the English lawyer sent to sue him.

1684: Radisson returns to Hudson Bay. He kidnaps and robs the French traders he left behind the previous spring.

1685: Mary Kirke dies.

1686: Radisson makes his last trip to Hudson Bay. On his return, he writes the stories of the Hudson Bay voyages for James, Duke of York, who, soon afterwards, ascends the throne as James II. Radisson marries Charlotte Godet.

1688: James II is overthrown. France and England go to war. As a Frenchman and supporter of the king, Radisson is effectively finished in London's business community at the age of 52, although he stays on a Hudson's Bay Company allowance.

1690: Hudson's Bay Company cuts Radisson's "gratuity."

1694–1695: Radisson successfully sues the Hudson's Bay Company for reinstatement of his "gratuity," but does not get paid for a shipload of furs that he robbed from his French former employees in 1684.

1697: Radisson gives evidence to a peace commission set up to determine European rights in Hudson Bay. Soon afterwards, he opposes the renewal of the Hudson's Bay Company charter unless he is credited with its founding. Radisson's demand is ignored.

1710: In July, Radisson dies in his house near Drury Lane at the age of 74. He is buried in St. Clement Danes Church.

1941: On May 10, St. Clement Danes is blown up by the Luftwaffe on the last day of the Blitz.

INTRODUCTION

His name is everywhere.

I noticed that when I was tying up my boat in the summer of 2018. There's a company that makes a "Radisson" brand of dock cleats. There are ships named after him. And, of course, a hotel chain.

Most students of American history have probably never heard of Radisson—the person, not the hotels—unless they live in Minnesota or parts of Wisconsin, where Radisson used to be honoured as the first European to explore the upper Mississippi. But there hasn't been a non-academic American biography of Radisson in eighty years.

In Canada, the situation is even more strange. Radisson is considered to be an "explorer," though I've come to the conclusion he never "discovered" anything that wasn't known to other Europeans, and he definitely never found anything the Indigenous people weren't already intimately familiar with. He's also credited with founding the Hudson's Bay Company. There's some truth to that, even though he was given almost no recognition by the company at the time and had to go to court to sue for the paltry amount it owed him. He would not recognize the chain of department stores that carries the company brand today, or comprehend its American hedge-fund owners.

So why write a book about Radisson?

Partly because he's everywhere in what's now the Western world that a time traveller to the 1600s would want to see. He's living with Indigenous people in North America. He's with Charles II of England and his court of scoundrels, traitors, and ex-pirates. He's in England during the Great Plague. He's in London during the Great Fire. He's set upon by spies. He's in the Arctic. Then he's with pirates in the Caribbean. After that, he's at Versailles. And then the Arctic again. Along the way, he crosses paths with the most interesting people of his day.

He's the Forrest Gump of his time. He's everywhere. And because he could read and write, he managed to tell us about it.

Radisson is also appealing because he was not a colonist or imperialist who wanted to remake North America into a European state. Stripped of the usual labels—"explorer," "fur trader," "adventurer"—Radisson is simply a hardware salesman with some of the most fascinating customers in the world. He lugged pots and pans, blankets, axes and guns all the way from Quebec to Lake Superior, and later shipped them across the Atlantic Ocean to Hudson Bay, because there was so much money to be made. Radisson was paid for this hardware in barter, furs that were torn into lint to make felt hats for men. It all seems so absurd now. But, except for the odd aspiration, that's all he wanted to do. He didn't want to turn the Indigenous North Americans into Christians. He didn't want to steal their land, except to build the odd fur trade fort (which the local Native people also wanted).

He discovered that Indigenous people—like the Mohawks, who guarded the eastern door of the Five Nations Confederacy—lived in a meritocracy, and that, for them a dynamic man can make something of himself no matter what his parents had or had not achieved. He learned this in a very dangerous way: by being taken captive as a teen by the Iroquois and quickly rising through their society. Then, like so many upstate New Yorkers do, he fled to Manhattan. But he never forgot the Mohawks, who were so good to him, and he wrote it down, too. This upward mobility was in sharp contrast to seventeenth-century Europe, where a man like Radisson would always be a peasant.

Radisson shows us North America through the eyes of a man willing to see everyone he encountered as a person. Reading the 350-year-old accounts of his travels, you come away feeling like you've finally found an early Euro-Indigenous contact history without the blatant racism that oozes from the writings of the Jesuit missionaries or from people like Champlain. Yes, Radisson was a man of his time, but he was also—much more than you'd expect—a man of ours, too.

He travels when almost no one else travels. He simply refuses to accept the limits placed upon him by class and demands the opportunity to prove himself as a business strategist. He is utterly without fear of anyone, whether it's Louis XIV of France, whom he double-crosses twice, or Charles I, whom he entertains with wilderness stories, and double-crosses only once. He has no fear of Caribbean pirates or Iroquois warriors. He lives all of Dale Carnegie's business maxims. Radisson is the kind of man who, after getting captured by a war party of Mohawks, the fiercest warriors known to the French, sizes up the situation, decides he'd like to see their country, and cooks them breakfast every morning on the canoe journey there.

So what's the great lesson of Radisson's life? Why write a publicly accessible biography of a man who is comfortably forgotten? Radisson is no hero. He was, at best, an eager hustler with no known scruples. Is there some other great, uplifting reason to let Radisson into your life?

Certainly, there's inspiration to be had from someone who simply would not quit. There's also a lesson in keeping an open mind for opportunities. And there's some proof, at least in the early part of Radisson's life, that fortune does, at least from time to time, favour the bold.

The real value of this book, I hope, is in the story it tells. My last two books were about creeping fascism and ISIS propaganda. After that, I found Radisson interesting company, despite his eating habits and untrustworthiness. Sometimes a story is just a story. And right now, I think everyone could use a good story.

First, though, a few acknowledgments, reflections, and confessions. To start, this book is Radisson's life story. It is told through the voice of someone of his culture, looking over a life that intersected with those of people from very different cultures. Radisson wrote down his observations of those cultures, and we're fortunate to have an observer who had no plans to colonize First Nations land, change their culture, or convert them to Christianity. Once, he muses about how much happier people from Europe's filthy, crowded cities might be in the wilds of what's now the Upper Peninsula of Michigan, and several times he puts his delusions of grandeur to paper, but Radisson never really saw Indigenous people as anything other than fur-trading partners. It was in his best interest to sell them what they wanted. Unfortunately, quite often what they wanted was guns.

Radisson arrived in North America at the worst time for the Indigenous people of the Great Lakes. Epidemics had already killed off vast numbers of people. The introduction of iron and steel weapons and tools was radically changing societies. Small-scale raids had evolved into wars of conquest. This brings up the issue of treatment of prisoners, which has always been seized on by those who would grind down North American Native people.

In 1650, no one treated any kind of prisoners well. Indigenous agricultural people killed many male prisoners taken in war. So did Oliver Cromwell, whose actions at Drogheda, in 1649, were as cruel as anything the Iroquois and Hurons did to their prisoners. The English of 1650 also had the option to jail prisoners and to ship them off to colonies, as Cromwell did with some of the Anglo-Irish. The North Americans had no jails. Imprisonment was not part of their system of justice. Nor were corporal and capital punishment. Societies like the Iroquois, who had used their technological advantage (guns) and superior organizational skills to wipe out all threats to their hegemony, were unable to cope with monitoring and assimilating hundreds or even thousands of young warriors. They did their best and adopted many, perhaps most, but they also used traditional religious practices and warrior culture to safeguard their country from men they could not trust. Radisson emerged from Iroquois torture initiated into the country's culture. In Western society, organizations like the Marines, fraternities, and even law schools have used hardship and hazing as ways to build loyalty: strip a person of everything, build them back up, and eventually welcome them as an equal, and you'll get lifelong loyalty from the right kind of candidate. In Radisson's case, it seems to have lasted all his life.

This book is not a deep examination of the culture and beliefs of Indigenous people. It does not expropriate their voices or their stories. I have tried to frame the descriptions of their civilizations through Radisson's eyes. We're fortunate that Radisson left behind very frank, although sometimes inconsistent, descriptions of his life in North America. Most were written for King Charles I and a very few people around him. They are mainly, I believe, stories for storytelling's sake. And that makes them unique.

Can we trust Radisson? Yes and no. His candidness about certain things shocked his reader, the King, and will likely still trouble us now. He is a self-admitted cannibal and murderer. He lies. He plunders people who, months earlier, were his business partners. And that's just the stuff he admits to.

He was often a lazy and sometimes dishonest writer. He took snippets from the stories of his travels to the Upper Lakes and plugged them into accounts of two voyages to what's now Illinois, even though it's clear he made only one trip that far. My own familiarity with the Great Lakes region helped me find some of his cheats and impostures. His description of southern Georgian Bay, for example, is utterly inaccurate. I don't believe he ever went there or saw the old Huron country. I also don't believe he saw the north shore of Lake Superior. His description of the canoe route from Montreal to Sault Ste. Marie and the region that's now northern and central Minnesota is, on the other hand, clear and accurate. A pattern emerges from his writing: when he tells the truth, there's plenty of detail. When he lies—like the claim he travelled from Lake Superior to Hudson Bay—there's almost none.

Lies, murder, and plunder aside, Radisson left us with the story of a remarkable man, a very free man in a time when they were rare, a traveller in a world where most people were tied to a village or farm, an ambitious man in an age when pedigree trumped all, and a brave man who must have been a tremendous dinner companion, as long as you weren't on the menu.

BOOK ONE:
LIFE WITH THE MOHAWKS (1639–1654)

IT STARTED WITH a nosebleed.

On a spring day in 1652, fifteen-year-old Pierre Radisson and two of his friends left the relative safety of the French fort and fur-trade post of Trois-Rivières to hunt ducks in the marshes along the St. Lawrence River, upstream from their small settlement. Each boy had a fowling piece—a sort of shotgun—and some, including Radisson, carried pistols. Radisson wore very light clothes so he could keep up with his friends and outrun any Iroquois raiders who might ambush them, but even with all those guns, the boys really had no chance against grown men who were experts in wilderness guerrilla warfare.

Radisson had arrived in the colony the year before, on May 24, 1651, possibly as a refugee from the most recent civil war in France. He was staying with his older half-sister, most likely because his family couldn't afford to keep him. France, like the rest of Europe, wasn't a good place to be living at the time. The Fronde, the violent revolts by the French aristocracy against the boy-king Louis XIV and his ministers, were still unfolding when Radisson was shipped to Quebec.

Scholars and historians have uncovered few details about Radisson's childhood. It is thought he was born in Paris in 1636, while his parents came from Avignon. Although later, the Hudson's Bay Company, the company he helped establish, claimed Pierre, too, was born in that southern French town.[1] We'll likely never be sure about his year of birth and the family's origins, since most baptismal records were destroyed during the French Revolution or when the Paris records office was burned in the Paris Commune violence of 1871.

If Radisson was born in Avignon, he did not stay there long. He was almost certainly taken to Paris as a baby or young child. Pierre survived to his teens, which is saying something considering the high infant-mortality rate and short lives of city people at the time. Families like the Radissons flowed in from the countryside to replace city workers, who rarely lived into their forties, and buried most of their children. At the time, one in four children in Paris was abandoned by their parents: the city had a form of dogcatcher whose full-time job was to round up the eight thousand or so children who were turned out on the street each year by their families.

While children were an asset on farms, they were a further expense in a costly place like Paris.[2] Some were hired out just before puberty as apprentices and labourers, and many found work in the army and navy. Others, like Radisson, were sent away with the expectation that they would never see their families again. There seems to have been no parental bond between Radisson and his father and stepmother: when Pierre returned to France just three years later, it seems he did not visit Paris or bother to try to contact his father.

Radisson had the proper handwriting and language of the French court, an ability very few laymen brought to New France in its early years.[3] Many people of that time could read enough to get by, but someone—and the picture is tantalizingly blank—saw potential in Radisson and taught him sophisticated communication skills. Whoever it was—it might have been Radisson's father, if he was more than the skilled labourer or tradesman he is speculated to have been—also taught him a bit about court life, knowledge that would come in very handy later in his career.

Whatever he was being groomed for, it's clear Radisson wasn't destined for a life in the civil service, the Church, or the military. Instead, he was packed off to New France, and we have no idea why. We can, however, fill in the gaps without lapsing into fiction. Paris in 1650 was a city on the verge of yet another civil war. Radisson's parents, either through real concern for the boy and his siblings, or because of their own problems, sent three of their children to the backwater of New France, where they ended up at the besieged frontier outpost of Trois-Rivières.

We don't know the name of Pierre's father, but we do know he married a widow named Madeleine Hayet after Pierre's birth mother died young. Hayet came to the marriage with a daughter, Marguérite, who was about fifteen years older than Pierre. Marguérite was either an adventurer or a woman with very few options, because, in about 1645, she married one of New France's first settlers and moved from Paris to the little fort at Trois-Rivières, where she ran the storehouse. About five years later, Pierre and his full sister Elizabeth joined her.

Marguérite had married well: Jean Véron, Sieur de Grandmesnil, was a minor noble, and, when she arrived in Canada, another petty aristocrat, John Godefroy, owner of the Lintot seigniory near Trois-Rivières, promised her forty acres of land. Soon after, however, the Iroquois began raiding the St. Lawrence Valley, making her land dangerous to farm and thus rendering it almost worthless. Her misfortunes were compounded when her husband was murdered by an Iroquois war party, leaving her with two young sons who were such hellions that the colonial authorities appointed special guardians for them. Given this situation, the arrival of her young half-siblings might well have been a burden too much to bear.

For Radisson, none of this made for a happy childhood. He wrote thousands of letters, books, and documents, heaped praise on those who helped him throughout his life, yet none contains a word about his parents or anyone else in his family except his brother-in-law, Médard Chouart des Groseilliers, who married Marguérite and then promptly left her to trade with the people of the upper Great Lakes. Groseilliers returned home periodically over the years, each time long enough to impregnate Marguérite, but he was no family man.

Radisson reached North America after a two- or three-month voyage from one of the French ports on the Atlantic. There was much danger for a young man like Radisson back in France. In the middle of the 1600s, France was so unsteady it could easily have fallen into a civil war like the one that had ravaged Germany for the previous thirty years or the one still tearing England and Ireland apart. Just two years before Radisson set out on his journey, England's Parliament had beheaded King Charles I. Now Charles I's two oldest sons, who would become important people in Radisson's life, were in exile on the continent.

New France was one of the worst places for a young man with ambition. Officially, it wasn't even a colony yet. The tiny settlements in Quebec—the entire population of which could easily fit into a modern high-rise apartment building—were owned by companies that bought their monopolies from the Crown. New France passed through the hands of several of these companies, none of which made a decent profit. The little bits of farmland around Quebec City, Montreal, and Trois-Rivières were owned by seigneurs, who were either petty nobles or clergy in the Church, and who rented the land to tenants. There was wealth all around, in the rich soil and mineral deposits of the Canadian Shield, but the companies were only interested in furs.

The Indigenous people of eastern North America, who far outnumbered the French, were going through their own agony of war, plague, and resistance to the encroachment of Europeans at the time. The settlers of Quebec, New England, New Netherland (parts of modern New York and adjacent states), and New Sweden (most of modern New Jersey) were in no position to take much Indigenous land, but the colonies were conveyers of cultural and physical viruses that would eventually destroy the Indigenous nations.

For more than a millennium, the people—mostly Iroquois and speakers of the Iroquoian language—in countries east of the Mississippi and south of the Canadian Shield had made their living farming corn, beans, squash, and tobacco.[4] The Indigenous people in the Great Lakes region lived together in towns with several thousand people. Since corn is very hard on soil, many of these communities moved once the land was exhausted. Whole towns and villages moved a few miles every twenty years.

Before the arrival of guns, Iroquoian warriors wore this kind of corn husk and bark armour. This illustration shows a Huron, but all Indigenous warriors in the southern Great Lakes region wore similar armour until the arrival of guns.

At first, these communities were evenly spread out along the shores of Lake Ontario and the St. Lawrence River, but by 1600, one group of Iroquoians, the Wendat Confederacy, had settled between Lake Simcoe and southern Georgian Bay. Two other nations, the Tobacco and the Neutral, lived between Georgian Bay and Lake Erie. The Haudenosaunee, or Iroquois Confederacy of Five Nations—the Mohawk, Cayuga, Onondaga, Oneida, and Seneca—farmed in the Finger Lakes area and Mohawk Valley of present-day upstate New York, roughly between the Hudson River and the Genesee Valley. In the last half of the 1500s—although some historians place the date a hundred years earlier—the Haudenosaunee were unified by Deganawida, a Huron who'd been adopted by the Mohawk, the nation living at the eastern end of the country. If the late 1500s date is correct, the federation of five old nations, each with its own language variants and customs, may have been forged as a reaction to European trade and the epidemics that came with it. If the league had indeed been formed a century earlier, the nations likely unified for their mutual benefit in the face of threats from other Indigenous groups.[5]

By the 1530s, these Indigenous people were trading with Europeans, who made summer visits to the Gulf of St. Lawrence, for tools and weapons. The archaeological record shows a swift change in the way the Great Lakes people lived during this time. Suddenly, Indigenous communities were building walls around their towns and settling in areas that were closer to the villages of their allies and much easier to defend.

There was a lot for these Indigenous communities to fear. First came the mysterious diseases, which would return, in waves, for a century. Jacques Cartier probably carried lethal viruses to the St. Lawrence Valley in the 1530s. Whole nations, including the Iroquoians living on the St. Lawrence River, "disappeared" in the 1500s, leaving farming and hunting territories that were fought over for almost two centuries. Simultaneously, waves of Spanish explorers brought pestilence to the big towns of what's now the American southeast. Hernando de Soto's men herded pigs on his expedition through the settled country of the south Mississippi Valley, Georgia, and Florida. Quite likely, he brought chickens as well. These animals are the two main incubators and carriers of influenza, a disease Indigenous people had never experienced and to which they had no immunity. Indigenous people died by the hundreds of thousands, maybe even millions, after the European invasion.

Then came war. Before the age of steel, war in eastern North America had been a relatively bloodless game. Warriors fought in wooden armour, wearing helmets of woven material, probably corn stalk. The armour and hat could stop, or at least slow, most arrows and cushion the blows of clubs, so it's unlikely many warriors died in battle. Until Europeans started trading guns in the Great Lakes, chivalry had been an important part of war. In Champlain's account of a fight between Algonkian, Huron, and Iroquois warriors near Lake Champlain in 1609—the only good written account of

An Iroquoian pipe effigy showing a warrior wearing a similar corn husk helmet to the one illustrated on page 20.

pre-gunpowder warfare in the region—both sides camped near each other but would not fight in the dark. Instead, warriors traded personal insults, showing at least some of them knew each other. But Champlain changed everything when he fired bullets into the Iroquois' battle line. The sound of the guns, and the sight of three important chiefs falling dead, frightened the Iroquois. For the French, however, it turned out to be an expensive display of power: in that moment the Iroquois learned the shock power of guns, something they would soon be teaching to their traditional enemies, the Mahicans (who were driven away from the Hudson River in the 1630s), the Huron, and the Algonkian hunting peoples of the Canadian Shield. Champlain started a century of warfare with the Five Nations that, several times, came close to driving the French out of Quebec, and cost the lives of thousands of Indigenous people from the Atlantic seaboard to the Great Plains.

Coincidentally, a few weeks after Champlain displayed his gun power, Henry Hudson, working for the Dutch, sailed up the Hudson Valley to within a hundred miles of Champlain's battlefield. The Dutch set up forts and went into the weapons trade on the eastern edge of the Five Nations country. An arms race, fuelled by fur profits, spread through North America. As the gun and steel-axe trade moved inland, country after country suffered massacre and assimilation at the hands of their better-armed enemies. The gun and axe were the most visible of the weapons turned against Indigenous people, deliberately or accidentally; other, less tangible ones were just as lethal: new diseases, the deliberate destruction of religion and culture, and, later, the trade in liquor.

17th-century French illustration showing warriors of the Great Lakes-St. Lawrence River region. (Johannis de Laet, 1633)

European farmers arrived with horses, pigs, chickens, and cattle, all of them carriers of diseases that were capable of being passed on to people. European children carried still other diseases, like mumps and measles. As these diseases moved along the trade routes, it was the youngest and the oldest of the Indigenous people—the future and the past—who died first. Smallpox was the worst of these diseases. When it devastated the Huron after a French trader carried it up the Ottawa River to Georgian Bay, the balance of power in the Great lakes region tilted toward the Iroquois.

As the religious wars in Europe wound down in the late 1640s, cheap war-surplus guns showed up in the Dutch and English trading posts south and east of the Great Lakes. In 1648 alone, the Dutch traded 1,200 guns to the Iroquois. The French, on the other hand, would sell guns only to Christian Indigenous people. Despite missionaries' boasting about saving thousands of souls, few of the latter seem to have been men of fighting age, even when a gun was their earthly reward. Very quickly, the Huron, Algonquins, Odawa, and Ojibwe[6] were outgunned by the Five Nations.

In late February 1649, about 1,200 Seneca and Mohawk warriors, who had left their Iroquois homeland the previous autumn, abandoned their campsites north of Lake Ontario and walked along the Huron deer-hunting trails from Rice Lake's drumlin country to the highlands south of Georgian Bay. On the evening of March 15, 1649, scouts in the vanguard of the Iroquois force reached the village of St. Ignace, the southernmost settlement in the Huron country, breached the wall, and seized the town. The nearby village of St. Louis also fell after a short fight. With that, the Huron Confederacy collapsed and all the Huron towns were deserted. As many as ten thousand Indigenous people had suddenly become refugees.

Several thousand Huron made a stand on Gahoendoe, now called Christian Island, in southern Georgian Bay. There wasn't nearly enough food to support these people. By the early winter, they were starving. Several thousand died of hunger over that winter, and hundreds more died when they fell through the ice trying to get to the mainland to collect acorns. On that island, Jesuits priests—who had lived among the Huron for forty years and had come close to taking power in their country—cruelly exploited the Huron. Having come to the island with several tons of corn and meat, which they kept for themselves and some converts through the winter, the Jesuits saw the Hurons' defeat, and the famine itself, as a great reaping of Huron souls. Jesuits cut copper cooking pots into tokens that could be used by devout Christian Huron to buy food from the French. Though the

Jesuit churches were filled day and night with people praying and chanting to earn the tokens, their acts of "piety" saved only a few lives.[7] Many Huron turned to cannibalizing their dead relatives. In contrast, not a single French priest, soldier, or lay worker died in that famine.

By early June, another Iroquois army had arrived and, outnumbered, the Jesuits gave up hope of staying in the Great Lakes country. With about five hundred Huron, the Jesuits and the rest of the French set out for Quebec, passing Trois-Rivières a year before Radisson arrived.

The Hurons' misery played an important role in Pierre Radisson's life. During the early years of the war, his future brother-in-law and trading partner, Médard Chouart des Groseilliers, was at the Jesuit post of Ste. Marie, near Georgian Bay, working as a hired labourer and armed guard. By 1651, Groseilliers was back in Trois-Rivières—along with dozens of Huron refugees, who lived in longhouses outside the town—and, with his knowledge of Indigenous languages and wilderness survival, ready to start his own fur-trading business.

By attacking the Iroquois and allying with the Algonkians and the Huron, the French had picked the losing side in a long, vicious war. The French couldn't protect the Huron refugees who, in 1650, had been driven from their Georgian Bay homeland to refugee villages in Quebec, nor could they protect themselves from a full-on Iroquois attack. While the Iroquois could put 1,500 warriors in the field, New France had fewer than three thousand men, women, and children colonists living in scattered pockets between Montreal and Quebec City. Trois-Rivières, like the other French settlements in the St. Lawrence Valley, was just a little fort surrounded by longhouses half-full of hungry Huron refugees. The Iroquois kept up a permanent siege at Trois-Rivières, but they were mostly unseen, as they rarely left the cover of the forest. There were only about forty French people in Trois-Rivières and, within a year, at least ten of them were dead, including Radisson's brother-in-law and the governor of the town. Many of the Huron were picked off, too, or gave up and handed themselves over to the Iroquois.

On May 10, 1652, just a few days after Radisson and his two friends had gone duck and goose hunting, Jesuit priest Jacques Buteaux and a French companion were killed on the St. Maurice River, just outside Trois-Rivières, and the Huron Christian warrior Thomas Tsondoutannen was captured. Despite the danger, people had to travel outside the walls of the fort. If no one could hunt, fish, and work the fields that summer, the settlement faced the threat of starvation the following winter.[8]

Radisson and his friends were well aware of the danger when they left Trois-Rivières, yet they were utterly reckless; willing, it seems, to risk their lives for some ducks. They decided two of them would walk through the woods to look for hidden Iroquois while one shot birds along the shore while keeping an eye out for anyone approaching by water. Talking tough, they promised each other they would rather die than allow themselves to be captured by the Iroquois.

They passed through some fields west of the town then took the high ground along the river for about a mile until they came across a Frenchman herding a few cattle in a clearing hacked out of the bush. The cowherd hadn't seen any Iroquois, but he warned the young hunters to stay away from the woods, where the Iroquois sometimes seemed to spring, fully formed, from the earth. The boys changed the ammunition in their guns. Two were packed with birdshot, which is effective on ducks but not on men, the other was loaded with heavier pellets. They also loaded some flintlock pistols. As they walked away from the farmer, Radisson's nose began to bleed.

He should have taken that as a sign. Instead, he and his friends moved down to the riverbank and worked their way through the marshland around l'île aux Sternes, a two-hour walk from the town. Radisson was an impetuous, adventurous, even reckless boy, but if he had seriously weighed the dangers against the benefits—his life for some ducks—he would never have made the trip. The quest for tasty, fresh food was, however, one of the driving forces of Radisson's life. The hunting was good, and Radisson's two friends were quickly satisfied that they had enough ducks. Radisson, however, wanted to keep going and get as many birds as he could drag back. The talk got nasty. Radisson told his friends they were timid, childish, and that he didn't like them anymore. He laughed at them as they turned back toward home.

Once alone, Radisson became even more careless, abandoning what seemed to be the safety of the marshes in search of something more, maybe some bigger game like deer or moose. But there were no big animals on that stretch of shore, so Radisson, with his bleeding nose, wandered farther and farther, picking off a bird or two here and there. He'd walked nine miles from Trois-Rivières, to what was then called the Ovamasis River (possibly the Yamachiche, the only river along that part of the shore than can't be easily crossed on foot). Along the way, he'd lightened his load by stashing his dead ducks in hollow trees, where, he hoped, they would be safe from eagles. Then, with the day more than half gone, he traced his way back, collecting three geese, ten ducks, a crane, and some teals that he'd hidden. He was about half a mile from where he'd left his friends, loaded down with his gun, two pistols (one of which was wet and useless), and all those birds when he heard a noise in the woods. He reached into his belt, felt the wet pistol, found the dry one, and fired it into the trees. He then loaded the gun again and went into the woods, about thirty paces from the riverbank and the marshes.

Radisson saw nothing in the forest. He collected more of his stashed birds and kept walking, oblivious to the Mohawk warriors shadowing him from the back of the treeline. They'd probably followed him for hours to see how he handled himself in the woods.

Nearer to the village, Radisson came across a flock of ducks. As he crawled through the rushes to get off a clear shot, he came across his two friends who lay naked and dead in the marsh grass, their hair standing on end. One had been hit by three bullets and struck twice with a hatchet.[9] The other had been run through several times with a sword, then brained with an axe. Radisson felt terror surge through his body, and his nose began to bleed again. He crouched down and tried to get through the mile-long marsh grass to the fields around Trois-Rivières. When he stopped to load his gun again, he heard the sound of gunfire close by, followed by war cries. Radisson kept moving. Suddenly, all around him, thirty Iroquois warriors rose from the grass and from behind the bushes. Radisson fired some bird-shot into them, slightly wounding a man, then shot his pistol, hitting no one. He had no time to reload before the warriors were on him. Some of the Iroquois tackled Radisson and dragged him into the woods, shoving him to the ground next to the heads of his friends.

But the Iroquois did not hurt Radisson. They just made him sit down. Several of them talked for a while, then one grabbed Radisson by the hair and pulled him along the river, back the way he had come, to a campsite four miles upstream. At the landing place, the Iroquois set up temporary bark tents and lit fires to boil some meat. Radisson was made to sit by the fire while the Iroquois stripped him, went through his things, took what they wanted, then tied a rope around the teen's waist that symbolized his captivity. They gave him back his shoes, and, presumably, some clothes, since he never complained of being naked and cold. Some of the Iroquois looked Radisson over and laughed, comparing their brown skin to his whiteness, but the fun was broken up by an alarm that the French and their Algonquin allies were coming. The Iroquois put out their fires and sent most of their men to see if the warning was true. By now, there were about seventy-five Iroquois warriors in the camp, but the French and Algonquins—who would have been outnumbered and outgunned—never came. When it was clear they were safe, the Iroquois began cooking stews of boiled meat and cornmeal. They gave some to their young captive, who didn't like the taste or the smell but kept his culinary opinions to himself. Some of the warriors began combing Radisson's hair and greasing it. They painted his face red, probably with a mixture of animal fat and ochre, and appeared quite thrilled with their work.

Radisson didn't know that the red paint identified him as a candidate for adoption. The Mohawks seemed to have liked what they saw: a brave and capable young hunter with enough spunk to shoot back, even when there was no hope of escaping capture or death. Radisson hadn't surrendered out of cowardice, but had gone down fighting. Radisson's charisma also attracted the Mohawks. Whether it came from his obvious bravery, his openness to Mohawk culture, or from a cheerfulness and eagerness to please, he quickly won his captors over and was treated as a special person. This was before Radisson learned their language and showed them that a persuasive, enthusiastic, open-minded and adventurous man was forming inside the boy.

There's no authentic picture of Radisson from this or any other time in his life. We can, however, draw an image with some accuracy. He was later described by an English writer as "swarty." He could pass for a Mohawk, at least on first glance, so he certainly had dark hair and brown eyes, like many people whose families came from Italy or the southern part of France. Radisson was also in excellent physical shape, but likely shorter than Mohawks of the same age, since the Iroquois, who grew up with better food, tended to tower over the French. There's also some evidence that Radisson looked younger than his years, but what he lacked in size he made up for in courage that bordered, and sometimes surpassed, the boundaries of recklessness. We can also assume he was attractive, since looks and personality were two very important qualities in the Iroquoians' calculations about whether to adopt.

He was also something of a fussbudget and a gourmand. Radisson, who complained all his life about various culinary assaults upon his mouth and stomach, couldn't keep down the food the Iroquois gave him. This seems to have disappointed and upset his captors, who were quickly morphing into hosts. One of them fetched clean water, heated some corn with hot sand, crushed the corn between some rocks, then boiled it with a bit of fresh meat. This new concoction suited Radisson's stomach, which was used to bread and gruel, and fresh or salted pork and beef. On the first night, Radisson was tucked in for bed, untied, between two Iroquois. He slept soundly, and dreamed of drinking beer with the Jesuits at Quebec. In fact, he slept so well that the Iroquois had to prod him at dawn to wake him up. Radisson wondered about the meaning of the dream. He gave it some thought and convinced himself it was a sort of prophecy. The Iroquois were friends of the Dutch, who had new settlements at Fort Orange and Manhattan. One of those places, he rightly predicted, was where he would get his next beer. Deep in his mind, he was already planning his escape.

Radisson's fixation with dream interpretation made him a kindred spirit to the Iroquois, although it would be some time before he could communicate that with them. The Iroquoians—the Five Nations of the Iroquois, Huron, Petun, Neutral, and smaller, corn-growing countries—were fixated on dreams, which they saw as the soul's communication medium. The soul expressed its desires through nighttime imagery, some of it direct, some requiring analysis by an *ocata*, a shaman with the gift of dream interpretation. The Iroquois believed unfulfilled desires of the soul caused serious harm to the body, both physically and psychologically, and could even cause death. When someone suffered, the community had a responsibility to determine and act on the messages being communicated through that individual's dreams, even if there was reason to believe the person was manipulating their descriptions of them.

Dreams could not always be taken literally, either, as some dream messages were false and could cause great harm if fulfilled. The *ocata*'s job was to determine which dreams were real and which were spurious. This was done through rituals that could involve staring into water, staying in a sweat lodge, or dancing until exhausted. Another way of fixing the soul's problems was through presents. Valuable things like fur robes, crafts, weapons, and beadwork could be offered to the person. Sometimes the dreamer—usually a man, but in some cases a woman—asked for something that might be harmful, such as subjecting themselves to ritualistic, though very real, torture. In those cases, the *ocata* had to come up with way of fulfilling the dream without killing the person. Once, when a Huron warrior asked to be tortured to death, his wish was fulfilled until he was in considerable pain, at which point the *ocata* had a dog killed in the man's place. Sometimes the dreamer asked for things beyond the power of the community to deliver, or that would cause too much trouble in structured, conformist Iroquoian society. In those situations, the *ocata* tried to work out a solution, though the community put more effort into helping popular and respected people; less important people were usually fobbed off with symbolic gifts.

If the soul's unfulfilled desire had already caused sickness, people worked even harder to make sure the dreamer's wish was sated. The *ocata* would aim to prevent the serious trouble that would arise if, say, the dreamer wanted someone killed. Other dreams were too expensive to be realized: if a person wanted a hundred presents, they might get ten, but the community would do what it could to oblige. If a dream involved a sexual fantasy, the dreamer might well get to sleep with the person of his dreams (apparently, and understandably, a common soul desire). Alternatively, the village might hold an *andacwander*, in which unmarried people would assemble in the longhouse of the sick person or dreamer and spend the night having sex with anyone they wanted while the sick person watched and two shamans stood by with rattles.[10] It was the kind of event that drove Jesuit priests to write at great length, and in angry detail, about the Iroquoians' sexuality.

So, back to Radisson's beer dream: if the boy had already been adopted by the Iroquois, who often visited Fort Orange on the eastern edge of their country in order to trade with the Dutch, they might well have made a special trip to that post to bring Radisson the beer he wanted. If Radisson's soul needed a beer or two to keep it happy and healthy, the Iroquois, being caring and community-minded toward their own people, would have tried very hard to oblige.

Despite being well cared for—Radisson's self-pitying account of his abduction makes clear he was never treated with anything but kindness during his first days as a prisoner, making his story a rarity among European and Indigenous survivors of Iroquoian captivity—he still felt lousy from eating strange food and being covered with grease and paint. The morning after Radisson's capture, the Iroquois raiding party left the Trois-Rivières shore in about forty big elm-bark war canoes, one of which contained Radisson, along with the scalps of his two friends.[11] Once the little fleet was offshore, presumably out of arrow and gunshot range of potential enemics, the warriors pulled their canoes closer together and the men began to sing loudly as they paddled. They stopped just once, to let out three loud cheers and to fire off some guns in a victory salute, but most of the time they chanted and sang and played pranks on each other. They also continued to take good care of their prisoner. One of the warriors offered Radisson some meat, but the teenager, either out of fear or due to an upset stomach, only drank water.

By sunset on the second day, the Iroquois had been joined by several other raiding parties and reached the mouth of the Richelieu River, near Sorel, where there was plenty of game. By now there were two hundred and fifty men in this new, big war party, enough to be a serious threat to the French settlements in the St. Lawrence Valley, had their intention been to exterminate and not just raid for prisoners. So far, the smaller war parties had been very successful at catching Hurons, but Radisson was the only Frenchman among the prisoners. As the army grew, Radisson worried that some of the Iroquois would not be as kind as his captors. "*Chagon,*" one of them said to Radisson, who didn't yet understand a word of Mohawk. Radisson would later find out that the word meant "cheer up."

Radisson did have the social skills to realize the Iroquois warriors preferred the company of happy people to that of whiners and complainers, so he did his best to smile. The youngest members of the Iroquois force were especially intrigued by Radisson. They kept grooming and painting him, and even tied his hair into a sort of double ponytail using a piece of red leather as a cord, a look that Radisson seems to have liked because he kept the style as his hair grew longer.

For someone who was supposed to be a prisoner, Radisson was having a pretty good time. It was clear within a few hours that his "brother," the man credited with capturing him, was protecting him from others in the group.

Samuel de Champlain fires the first shots of the Iroquois-French wars, Lake Champlain, 1609. The palm trees are bizarre but the woven fortification and warrior deployments are accurate. (Champlain, *Les voyages du sieur de Champlain*, 1613)

Within a couple of days, Radisson was roaming freely throughout the Iroquois camp, going into their bark houses and meeting people, including women, from the other war parties. Quickly realizing that Radisson had an ear for languages, the Iroquois began teaching him words and helped him practise until he could pronounce them properly. They also saw that Radisson had a European's taste for salty food, so they collected all the salt they had and gave it to him to season his meals. Nights were for feasting on fresh game and birds, daytime for canoe travel and singing as the Iroquois fleet moved upstream toward the Richelieu River through the flatland of the St. Lawrence Valley. The travelling band kept shrinking as small groups of men split off to return to their villages, some by continuing up the St. Lawrence toward Lake Ontario, the rest going south to Lake Champlain.

On the fourth day, Radisson's war party was on the Richelieu River, the great historic invasion route from the Hudson and Mohawk Rivers to the St. Lawrence Valley, moving upstream toward what's now Chambly and St. Jean en route to Lake Champlain. On the fourth or fifth day, Radisson's "brother," the Iroquois term for the boy's captor, signalled for Radisson to get into the canoe. This time he wasn't tied to anything. Someone gave Radisson a paddle, and the Iroquois watched him work until he was covered in sweat. He was working so hard because he was paddling sloppily. They let him know he could stop if he wanted, but Radisson kept paddling. It was only when one of the Iroquois showed the boy how to paddle correctly that Radisson was finally able to hold his own without becoming exhausted. He might not have known it, or he may have been uncommonly astute, but Radisson had done exactly what was needed to win the respect and admiration of his captors. He now had a very good chance of survival, but he was far from safe.

Somewhere on the calm water of the Richelieu below Chambly, Radisson's captors met members of another Iroquois war party, who were already on the riverbank. Radisson was made to stand up in the canoe as it closed in on the shore. In his first hours within this camp, the new group of warriors treated him as well as his "brother" and the rest of the men who had captured him had. But one man in the camp lurked around, glaring at Radisson, and the young Frenchman became worried this warrior would turn the rest of the camp against him, or strike him down with a club or hatchet. Radisson came up with a creative solution to his anxiety: he started cooking. There was plenty of fresh game in the camp, and Radisson rolled a piece of meat in finely powdered cornmeal with a little salt and fried it in a metal pot. He gave some to the menacing Mohawk, who liked it so much that he passed it around to his friends. He never bothered Radisson again.

The Iroquois also liked to hear Radisson sing. Having heard the singing of the Algonkians, who were allied with the French, he borrowed their cadence and tones and added French words. When Radisson sang his songs, the Iroquois warriors became silent. Sometimes there was dancing, an activity that, for Radisson, was marred somewhat by the sight of men swinging his former hunting partners' scalps around on sticks. The party lasted a day, then broke up as the various raiding groups went their respective ways. Before Radisson's canoe got far from the riverbank, a boat carrying a woman approached. She had her canoe pull alongside Radisson's so she could comb his hair with her fingers, then she tied a bracelet around one of his wrists, and quietly left. That night, the war party camped on a sandy beach, and, once again, the Iroquois went to work on Radisson's hair. They cut and shaved the front and crown of Radisson's head, thickened what hair was left on the back with grease so it stood upright in a sort of ponytail horn, and painted his face red and black. One of the warriors pulled out a mirror and showed Radisson their work. Except for the smell of the grease, he liked it. "I, viewing myself all in a pickle, smeared with red and black, with such a cap, and locks tied up with a piece of leather, and stunk horribly. I could not but fall in love with my new self, if not that I had had better instructions to shun the sin of pride."[12]

Radisson had been a prisoner for a week. Writing about this time fifteen years later, when he was in his early thirties, he never once mentioned missing his family or the people back in Trois-Rivières, nor expressed much horror at the fate of his two hunting friends. His description of his captivity among the Iroquois makes it clear that Radisson liked them, and that they, in turn, were both flattered and intrigued by the young man. The historic literature has many stories of seventeenth-century prisoner ordeals—of Indigenous people and Europeans captured in eastern North America—none of which involves captives having *fun*. Radisson did. His writings about life among the Iroquois have very few of the usual insults and slurs against Indigenous people that show up in the books written by Champlain, the Jesuits, and the few other Europeans who left a record of their time in the Great Lakes country. Radisson's accounts differ because it's obvious he respected the Iroquois, enjoyed their company, and didn't succumb to the depression that overwhelms most prisoners. The Iroquois applied psychological pressure and

Illustration of Iroquoian women working. Like many illustrations of this period, it was drawn from descriptions of European travellers. The tools are European but the women's clothes and fields are fairly accurately portrayed. (Joseph-François Lafitau, *Moeurs de sauvages*, 1724)

sometime great cruelty to coerce prisoners into conforming to the rigid cultural expectations of their society, and to dampen any resistance. Assimilation and adoption was the eventual reward for those deemed worthy. Radisson didn't need coercion. He leapt right in.

Whatever the situation back home, Radisson's life with the Iroquois had its advantages. After the first four or five days, Radisson could have tried to escape, but he wasn't sure he could elude his captors. He also knew that, if caught, he would face certain torture and death. "And moreover," he later wrote, "I was desirous to have seen their country."

In fact, he was so eager that he stopped sleeping in and woke up early every day to pester his captors to get moving. One morning, while his "brother" slept, he bided his time by playing with a sword. As he stuck it into the sand of the little beach on the Richelieu River where the war party had camped, another warrior called him over and taught him how to use it properly. The Iroquois soon let him carry a knife that one of the other warriors had given him. Later, as they got closer to the Mohawk country, his "brother" shot a stag from the canoe and wounded it. The warriors paddled over to the animal to let Radisson run it through before they cut it up and distributed the pieces. By now, they were almost at Lake Champlain and had to portage around a set of rapids. Once they got their heavy canoes, weapons, and travelling gear to the upper end of the portage, Radisson gathered dry wood for the fire. He was always useful, and always working just a little bit harder than everyone else.

Still, it was not clear, either to Radisson or to the Iroquois, whether Radisson would be allowed to live. This ambivalence is apparent in the way they painted his face: half black, half red. Radisson didn't know that black meant the prisoner was marked for death, while red meant life.

Radisson, like most first-time visitors to Lake Champlain, found the countryside beautiful. The canoe flotilla had crossed the forty-mile-wide flatlands of the St. Lawrence Valley, punctuated by half a dozen dead volcanoes that rise as steep hills from the forests and cedar swamps, and arrived in the Appalachian Mountains. Lake Champlain itself lies in a long finger valley, with mountains on its eastern shore and flatland on its western side that was, in Radisson's time, covered with great forests. This country, all the way down to the Saratoga Plain north of the junction of the Hudson and Mohawk Rivers, was the traditional hunting territory of the Mohawks, who saw their country as the eastern door of the Iroquois Confederacy.

On the first day, Radisson's party killed two bears, "one monstrous like for its bigness," but he did not like the taste of the meat.[13] The camping beach soon turned into a little village, complete with what Radisson called "cottages": houses made of bark or bulrushes tied over a pole frame. Radisson mentions the Iroquois "made places where prisoners were tied," but it's clear Radisson himself was not one of those prisoners, nor was he particularly concerned with their well-being.

Radisson watched the Iroquois build a sweat lodge of sticks and animal pelts, which they then heated with stones made blistering hot in a campfire. The men took turns in these lodges, "making a noise as if the devil were there." They were usually only able to endure the heat for an hour or so, before rushing out and throwing each other into the lake. The fun ended when someone thought they heard gunshots. Radisson's new friends loaded him into a canoe and paddled away so quietly that he fell asleep. When he woke up the next morning, he was in a field of bulrushes that stretched to the horizon.

For days they travelled south on Lake Champlain and the lakes that connect to it, fearful of being chased by an Algonkian war party. They eventually unloaded the canoes and headed inland, toward the heart of the Mohawk country. All of this was new to Radisson. He was also learning a great deal about the Iroquois. One fact he picked up frightened him a bit: while the Iroquois did adopt Huron and Algonkian prisoners, they believed the French to be weak, ugly, unintelligent, and unable to cope with physical hardship or to assimilate. The Iroquois also understood the connection between Europeans visits and the spread of terrible diseases.[14] The teenager was heading to Iroquois country with the deck stacked against him.

IN THE LAND OF THE MOHAWKS

The Iroquois country was a place of vast fields of corn, walled towns so strong they were described by the English as castles, and wide trails linking those towns to other Iroquois communities spread out over two hundred miles. This had been a settled country for many hundreds of years, probably as long as England and France. The land of the Five Nations of the Iroquois was very much a country, ruled by a league council that met at the town of Onondaga, and by councils in each of the nations—the Mohawk, Oneida, Onondaga, Cayuga, and Seneca (the Tuscarora, or "Hemp Gatherers," who lived farther south, would join in 1722). The league was necessarily a loose, federal state, given how much value its society put on the liberty and autonomy of its people. Each member nation could separately make war and peace with nations outside the Confederacy. The Confederacy council's job was to maintain the unity of the country. They did this partly by suppressing the family and clan feuds that might ensue from violence between Iroquois people. Civil chiefs were chosen by powerful women called clan mothers, while war chiefs won their positions by becoming famous leaders of raiding parties and by proving themselves in hand-to-hand combat with their enemies. These two groups of leaders were often at odds, and when there was a political stalemate, the clan mothers met to settle any disputes.

Iroquoian society was complex, each village being made up of at least one giant, extended family—a clan—whose members had to adhere to rigid social rules. Clans took direct responsibility for their members, even collecting the "presents" needed to keep the peace when someone was killed or wounded.[15] Within those clans were matriarchal lineages, family linkages based on a complex system of kinship than ran through the mother's maternal family line. The lineages and clans could form moieties, alliances within the community that roughly resembled a club or formal clique. These kinship structures owned the longhouses and kept a treasury of most of the community's wealth—wampum belts and beads, beaver robes, exotic pipes, and other pieces of artwork. This wealth was redistributed through the community in feasts and rituals. Nothing like this existed in Europe, where ancestry was traced through the father's line, property belonged to the individual, and, when they paid taxes, the king owned the money and could use it for the common good or spend it on himself.

Someone flying over the Iroquois country in 1652 would have seen huge clearings in the forest, tens of thousands of acres planted with corn and beans. There would have been thousands more acres of grasslands and weed-filled tracts of exhausted Iroquois farm fields, hundreds of acres of trees stripped of their bark to kill them in order that Iroquois men could clear land for new fields, and cabins at the edges of the cornfields where men and women stayed while planting, harvesting, and logging.

An aerial view of the time would have revealed these big clearings and smatterings of small villages and some very large towns with rows of bark longhouses surrounded by strong wooden walls that were part fence, part woven palisade. Some would have been surmounted by hawthorn branches that were as effective as barbed wire at keeping out people and animals. Trails, wide enough to be called roads, linked the five major Iroquois towns and the scattered hamlets that were built from time to time as temporary lodgings closer to corn fields and fishing sites. People travelling across any part of the St. Lawrence Valley and the fertile land south of the Canadian Shield could expect to see similar vast cornfields to the ones in the Iroquois country. (Champlain once called the Huron country a "land of meadows.") Travellers' stories from this time are full of accounts of various people, towns, and camps in this "wilderness." It was not, in other words, *terra nullius*, the legal term for empty land, but rather settled country where people jealously protected their hunting territories and farmland from squatters and invaders.

The people living in the Iroquoian cultural region—confederacies and nations like the Susquehanna, Huron, Erie, Neutral, Petun, and the Five, and later Six Nations Confederacy of the Iroquois—understood the value of law as a way of keeping the peace. They had developed a set of rules regarding property and personal injury, and had also created an effective mediation system to deal with disputes. Their codes were old and complex, and Radisson made it his job, with the help of his sponsors in the community, to quickly learn them.

The property laws of the agricultural nations on the Great Lakes intrigued many European visitors. No Iroquois paid rent to anyone, yet each had a strong understanding of the value of farmland and hunting territory. The Iroquois had a system of mixed communal and private ownership (as did the French and the English prior to aristocrats seizing most common land at the end of the Middle Ages). Iroquois farmland was owned by the individual or by extended family who worked the fields, and the land was held in trust for the rest of the community while it grew crops. There were large swaths of land near Iroquoian villages that were cleared by men and women working together, then divided among the people who farmed it.[16] The Iroquois also had large, communal fields worked by groups of women and managed by an elected matron. A person who chose not to work in the community fields was not entitled to share in the clan's or village's store of corn, unless they found themselves unexpectedly in dire straits.[17]

While the men did most of the work to remove trees and brush—tough work in old-growth forests using stone axes, and, later, the soft wrought-iron axes bought from European traders—the land itself was owned by the women, who did all the rest of the farm labour.[18] Wealth and status did not accrue from owning land, but from the creation of surpluses that could be traded or ritually given away in a society that placed a very high value on public generosity and that despised miserliness. The Recollet missionary Pierre Sagard noted: "Every man taxes himself freely with what he can pay and without any compulsion gives of his means according to his convenience and goodwill."[19] Women needed to own their own fields and produce a surplus for the gift-giving that increased their family's social status, but they were also under pressure to work the community fields for the direct benefit of all.[20] As a man, Radisson was never expected to set foot in these fields, since the Iroquois had inflexible social rules about the genderedness of work. Men who did women's work were bullied and mocked. The very sight of a man carrying firewood was enough to bring ridicule from Iroquois men.

Because land was scarce, the Iroquois had to get as much as they could from their farmland. Before European contact, small farming communities, probably made up of one or two extended families, were spread between Georgian Bay, the Niagara Escarpment, the Canadian Shield, and the Finger Lakes. In the early fifteenth century, these small hamlets began to consolidate into larger, stronger villages that were farther away from each other. By the beginning of the seventeenth century, the Huron had moved from the Toronto, Rice Lake, and Lake Simcoe areas to the Penetanguishene Peninsula on Georgian Bay, a home territory of just 340 square miles.[21] About 20,000 to 30,000 people lived on this peninsula.[22] Their diet relied almost exclusively on corn, which they supplemented with small amounts of fish and game.[23] The Huron also cultivated corn to trade with the nomadic people of the Canadian Shield, and with Iroquoian neighbours when their crops failed from time to time.[24]

The Iroquois looked for similar farmland, and found sandy patches of land in the Mohawk Valley and near the Finger Lakes. Both the Huron and the Iroquois needed 50,000 to 70,000 acres of land in active cultivation to grow enough corn just to feed themselves. It had to be well-drained, sandy soil that they could cultivate with hoes, as they had no metal plows and no draft animals. "Rather than being underpopulated, it is much more likely that the area was approaching a population maximum," historical geographer Conrad Heidenreich has said about the Huron.[25] For example, the Attingneenoungnahac, a Huron nation, had a tribal area of 10,400 acres, of which 9,976 was sandy loam. The Jesuits estimated the Huron population to be 3,800 people, requiring a minimum of 7,776 acres of farmland, or 78 percent of their total land resources.[26] The Iroquois faced similar challenges. In a supposed wilderness, Indigenous farmers were short of prime land. Late in the 1600s, the Iroquois solved the problem by starting livestock and orchard farms in their own homeland and by opening farms on the north side of Lake Ontario, but in Radisson's time, farm-field exhaustion was one of the many crises that the Iroquois struggled with.

Then there were the hunting lands, where Radisson found himself when he reached Lake Champlain. Anthropologist Anthony Wallace, who researched hunting-territory ownership in the Great Lakes region, found no hunting territories deliberately shared with other First Nations.[27] In fact, Wallace examined the written historical record and interviewed Indigenous historians and could find no land in the modern northeast US and eastern Canada that wasn't owned by an Indigenous group as either a settled area or hunting territory. First Nations, he found, were quite careful about delineating the boundaries of the land they claimed. "Hunting grounds were as definitely a part of tribal territory as village areas," he noted.[28] One Cayuga (Iroquois) chief, speaking at a land cession council in 1789, said: "Our ancestors had certain Marks, each Tribe had a certain Boundary or Line they called their own, of the Land the Great Spirit gave them."[29] One chief described his people's hunting territory in Ohio in 1785: "It begins at the Little Miami and runs from thence across to the Great Miami. Further than this our line does not extend."[30] Indigenous people left markers and signs on trees and rocks, like the ones posted by European traders and explorers, who claimed the land on behalf of their respective governments. And so when Radisson wrote of the Iroquois "country," such a place truly existed.

In this country, the Iroquois developed a complicated society that was very much a meritocracy, where a person could show their worth and rise from prisoner to a member of the League council in a very short time; or, just as quickly, be tagged a failure and killed. This was the game that a teen-aged Radisson was drawn into. The Iroquois were spiritual people with an innate and well-developed understanding of human psychology. They were also enthusiastic joiners of secret societies (so much so that, in the 1700s, many, including Mohawk leader Joseph Brant, became Freemasons). Structured, formal societies and fraternities evolved to help cure the sick, bury the dead, and fight wars. Members were obligated to work hard to learn their society's rituals and teachings. In return, the societies gave individuals a chance to show their intelligence and dedication to the community. The system was a stark contrast to that in Europe, where men like Radisson would be denied the opportunity to reach their full potential, the rigid class system there an impenetrable ceiling to even the most brilliant, dedicated, or ruthless man.

The Iroquois were also a wealthy people. In the 1600s, Europeans regularly marvelled at how every Iroquois had a home, more than enough meat and fish to eat, as much land as they needed or could use, warm winter clothes, and access to rich artwork in the form of wooden and stone tools, beadwork, sculpted smoking pipes, masks, and musical instruments. By contrast, almost every European family at this time slept in a single bed in a sparsely furnished hut or small cottage, often shared with livestock, on land rented from an aristocrat who, in turn, relied on the patronage of a king, or, much more rarely, a reigning queen. Poor people lived on the roads, begging and stealing whatever they could get before succumbing to diseases like tuberculosis. No one begged or starved in the Iroquois country.

European peasants and townspeople typically ate black bread or gruel; unlike the Iroquois, they rarely saw fresh meat (unless they were among the fortunate few). The Iroquois had leisure time to travel, trade, fish, and hunt. In Europe, only aristocrats were allowed to take animals from the forests. European peasants were tied to the land and rarely, if ever, left their farms to do anything but buy and sell at the local market. If they were particularly unlucky, the men might be obliged to follow their landlords to war.

The Iroquois stored their wealth in wampum, porcelain-like shell beads that were made into large, impressive belts and jewellery. Wampum belts recorded the important political decisions of the nation, and the individual beads were, one seventeenth-century writer said, the money that brought the furs from the forest. Wampum was so highly valued in eastern North America that, until the 1780s, Harvard University accepted it as payment for tuition. Most people in Radisson's France had no such wealth, but rather struggled to hang on to whatever little bit of cash they had in the hope that their savings would get them through the famines that hit parts of Europe with grim regularity. Wealth was in the hands of the aristocracy. The typical European of Radisson's class would rarely even see a gold coin.

So, for an ambitious young Frenchman with very little to lose, being captured by the Iroquois offered opportunity as well as terror. Radisson seized the opportunity.

Orhima

Radisson arrived in a country in terrific flux: its people flush with victory over the Hurons; its culture disrupted by the arrival of things taken in war and in trade; its villages filled with adoptees, refugees, and slaves; its people haunted by the memory of countless friends and family members lost in wars or who had died of strange new diseases.

No one knew when the next epidemic would hit, and the Iroquois were desperate to rebuild their population. Every war, even the most successful, took the lives of young Iroquois men. Leaders were becoming so scarce that clan mothers couldn't fill some of the vacant chief seats. It took years for the men, women, and children taken in the Iroquois Confederacy's "mourning wars" against the other Great Lakes nations to find their place in Iroquois communities. Many of the Huron who were brought to the Iroquois country at the end of the Iroquois-Huron war, just two years before Radisson was snatched, struggled through their days, terrified of displeasing their captors. Radisson's own fate was to become a young Iroquois aristocrat. First, though, he had to get to the Iroquois country alive and in good health to face the quick judgment that awaited him.

Eventually, Radisson's party started walking inland from Lake Champlain toward the Mohawk country on the eastern end of the Confederacy territory, moving between the foothills of the Adirondacks that broke the horizon to the north and the limestone flatlands and rolling hills of the Mohawk Valley. On their second day on the trail, Radisson's captors came across a couple of men whom the Mohawk warriors seemed to know. They talked for a very long time; then, about twenty women appeared on the trail carrying dried fish and corn, which they cooked for the warriors before loading themselves with the men's baggage. All then walked on a well-beaten trail until, at dusk, they came across a small fishing village where more Mohawks welcomed them.

It soon became apparent that Radisson was to be part of the night's entertainment. A young man in the camp began to stroke Radisson as a challenge to fight. Radisson turned toward him, and the young Mohawk grabbed the French boy's hair and began to pull. The other Mohawks each chose a side in the fight, half of them backing Radisson, the others cheering on their own. (The Iroquois were eager gamblers and would bet on just about anything.) There doesn't seem to have been much punching. The boys clawed at each other with hands and fingernails, and, when they got the chance, attacked with their teeth. Radisson seemed to be winning the fight when his opponent kicked him. Radisson, who was still wearing his hard French shoes—probably wood-soled clogs, which his captors had given back early in the trip—answered with a kick of his own; the Mohawk boy went down, and Radisson stayed on top of him until older men broke up the fight. The older warriors gave the boys fish to eat before cleaning them with water, then greasing their bodies and fixing their hair. For the next two days, Radisson had free run of the fishing camp.

In the same longhouse where Radisson won his wrestling match-cum-catfight, Mohawk doctors were busy removing birdshot from the man

Iroquoian longhouse reconstructed near London, Ontario. (Photo courtesy of Ontario Museum of Archaeology)

Radisson had wounded on the day he was captured. Radisson says during the journey back from New France, the wounded man showed Radisson "as much charity as a Christian might have given," and gallantly gave him a box of red paint, the colour of freedom.

Since leaving Lake Champlain, the Mohawk warriors and their captives had travelled south into the Hudson Valley, then across to the Mohawk River Valley. When they left the collection of bark houses at the fishing camp and started moving inland again, Radisson was given a twelve-pound bundle of tobacco to carry. Imitating the Mohawks, he hoisted the bundle on his head. The war party travelled through forests of oak, beech, hickory, maple, and walnut on wide trails shaded by the canopies of the giant trees. From time to time, they would walk into second-growth forests and open land. The land north of the Mohawk Valley is beautiful, rolling countryside cut by deep ravines carved by tributaries of the Hudson, the Mohawk, and East Canada Creek. The travellers met more people along the trail, mostly hunters and fishers. Now the war party began to increase as they came across other Mohawk returning from raids with newly captured Hurons.[31] Late one evening, they arrived at the main Mohawk town, Tionnontoguen, near the modern-day city of Schenectady, New York, but decided to camp outside the town, rather than enter it in the dark.

There was a reason for the delay, one that Radisson had been dreading. At dawn, the people of the town came out its main gate and formed a gauntlet that extended a quarter mile down a trail leading through corn-fields to the town. Townspeople, carrying clubs, burning sticks, branches full of thorns, and other weapons, formed parallel lines that the captives were made to run through. The gauntlet was meant to be an unpleasant welcome to the village. For those who were to be tortured to death, it marked the gateway to hours or days of constant pain.

Much has been written about Iroquoian tortures and whether Europeans exaggerated them. Much of that scholarship is made up of agenda-pushing claims by people who see Iroquoian societies as brutal. Still others claim the violence didn't happen at all. In fact, it did, but careful reading of the European records shows the number of those who actively participated in ritual torture, compared to the overall population, was actually quite small. As well, most captives were not put through ritual torture. Entire Huron communities voluntarily joined the Iroquois without any violence or even much social stigma after their country collapsed in 1650. Women and children were rarely harmed after their capture. Even among men, the chances of adoption and integration, especially for those who willingly set out to join an Iroquoian community, were very high.

Iroquoian torture rites served several purposes. They maintained the state of terror that gripped the entire Great Lakes region for decades as the Iroquois expended their dominance. They also gave captured warriors—especially those disabled by their wounds and injuries—a chance to die with honour. The torture rites also had a religious connotation that might have extended far over distance and time. Historian Bruce Trigger saw strong similarities with the sacrifice practices of pre-conquest Meso-America: the ritual's culmination was often the removal of the warrior's heart in full view of the sun. More recent scholars, such as Adam Stueck,[32] see the rites as closely connected to Iroquoian ideas of death, mourning, and rebirth. Certainly, those who survived the ritual saw themselves as reborn and remade members of the Five Nations. Radisson was one of those survivors.

But did this torture really happen? In Radisson's time, no First Nation got such bad press as the Iroquois. Champlain never said a single good thing about them after he started the French-Iroquois War. The Jesuits, who wrote many volumes about their missions in the Great Lakes region, consistently painted them as the enemy, believing them to be Satan's frontline warriors. French Canada's historians tend to paint them as an existential threat to the French in North America. (In French-Canadian narratives, Iroquois villains conveniently shuffle off the stage in the mid-1700s, to be replaced by English ones.) Mohawk historian Scott M. Stevens has eloquently shown how the torture rite became the core of seventeenth- and eighteenth-century anti-Iroquois propaganda, and documented his people's struggle to resist having it define their culture and politics in both the past and present.[33]

So let's get a few things out of the way. While it's true that Iroquoian society was far less violent than European novelists and non-fiction writers have depicted it, episodes of ritual torture are documented in the archaeological record and in the writings of dozens of eyewitnesses from the time of first contact until the War of 1812. That torture has been used as a means of both denigrating and defining Indigenous people. Novelists from James Fenimore Cooper, in *The Last of the Mohicans* (1826), to Franklin Davy McDowell, in his unreadable and probably now-unpublishable Governor General's Award-winning *The Champlain Road* (1939), to Brian Moore's *Black Robe* (1985), to Joseph Boyden's *The Orenda* (2013) have all mined this vein. Set at the collapse of the Hurons just before Radisson arrived at Trois-Rivières, *The Orenda* was criticized by scholars like Hayden King for focusing too much on ritual and military violence (and the triumph of colonialism).[34] Relying on novels that use one of Indigenous Canada's greatest calamities as a backdrop and judge First Nations people on the details of torture adapted from the historical record is akin to reading Rudolf Höss's autobiography of his years as Auschwitz commandant to get a grasp of how mid-twentieth-century Europeans lived and felt.

Still, despite the claims of a few writers, torture narratives were just not Jesuit fantasies.[35] All the agricultural people of the Great Lakes tortured some of their prisoners to death. These were almost always young warriors who posed existential threats to their captors (as Radisson did). A society with no jails, an abhorrence of bullying, humiliation, and corporal punishment, as well as a powerful warrior code, had evolved in how it dealt with one of warfare's most vexing problems. Warfare became much more lethal and genocidal with the disruptions caused by epidemics, the introduction of guns, and the struggle for furs. It was the Iroquois' misfortune to win this struggle and be tagged as monsters by enemies who wrote its history.[36]

Europeans of that period also used torture, primarily to extract confessions and to punish. The penalties for treason in England—burning alive for women; slow strangulation, castration, disembowelling and dismembering for men—were commonly meted out in public, especially in London. Europeans were probably far less shocked by descriptions of Indigenous torture than we are now. It's why the Jesuits turned their torture stories into martyrdom myths that reached back to the supposed Roman torments of early Christians for their faith, and why they insisted that all Christians tortured by Indigenous people maintained their faith in God. The Jesuits believed the missionary fields to be soaked in the blood of martyrs. It made for great fundraising, and, eventually, saint-making.

I'm going to break the fourth wall here: I was attracted to Radisson's story partly because he saw so much of the world, but also because, like me, he admired the Iroquois (in my case, all the Iroquoians, as I spent much of my life in the Wendat [Huron] homeland on Georgian Bay). Radisson is the only writer of his time who openly did so. And while some of his storytelling might be dubious, the accuracy of his captivity account has never been seriously challenged. Radisson had no philosophical problem with Iroquoian torture and may well have participated in some of it. Condemning

Indigenous people for the treatment of prisoners they believed impossible to assimilate is a grotesque unfairness. And to be smug about the latter is to ignore (or be ignorant of) Canadian soldiers' reputation in the two world wars for not taking prisoners. We can ignore the German murder of Soviet POWs in the Second World War, and Soviet atrocities against German POWs and female civilians after the war. And we can try to forget about modern-day tortures like waterboarding and long-term solitary confinement, both of which attack the sanity of their victims. In fact, an argument could be made that the modern media has made us more tolerant of torture and murder, and that Western society's insistence that its hands are clean, based on supposed faithful adherence to the Geneva Convention, is quickly becoming a myth.

Radisson's fate would at least be decided quickly. The boy would not be left to rot in some jail or worked to death in a camp.

Radisson's war party stripped him naked, and Radisson's captor, who had come to like the boy, gave him a sign to run as fast as he could between the rows of men, women, and children. As he moved toward the gauntlet, Radisson could see the scalps of his two hunting comrades laid out on the ground.

One teenager went at Radisson with a hatchet trying to brain him or inflict the kind of ugly, scarring wounds that would make Radisson unfit for adoption, but someone blocked the Mohawk boy. Radisson says it was an "old" woman. (Since the woman had teenage children, she's likely to have only been in her late thirties or early forties, which might seem old to a teenager.) The woman led Radisson around the gauntlet, through the village gate to her longhouse, and gave him something to eat. The Huron prisoners did not fare nearly as well, and had to make the run, though the gauntlet was not meant to be lethal. People filed into the longhouse to look at Radisson. He wasn't sure why, and he worried that he was about to face the full horror of the Iroquoian torture ceremony. In fact, the "old woman" and the visitors to her longhouse were discretely negotiating to save his life.

For the first time, Radisson was under the wing of an older woman. During his time in North America, women, usually motherly or grandmotherly figures, were often his protector and saviour, strongly suggesting that Radisson had an appealing vulnerability and attractiveness. Since the Mohawks only adopted people who were good looking and had pleasing personalities—and rarely adopted young men, who could be dangerous—Radisson must have had considerable charisma. It's unlikely that Radisson's female protector was at the warrior camp by accident, and it doesn't seem like much of a stretch to suggest that the warrior credited with Radisson's capture, or another member of the raiding party who was related to her, had sent word into the town the night before, knowing the woman wanted a son and was powerful enough to get Radisson.

The negotiations continued for some time. A group of old men came into the longhouse and sat around Radisson, smoking their beautiful clay pipes. After they finished smoking, they led Radisson into another longhouse, where there were even more men smoking. Radisson was made to sit by the fire, which conjured up fears that he was about to be burned alive. But the woman who had protected him against the gauntlet again showed her face. Clearly, she was a person of considerable power. She spoke to the men, who answered her with an approving "Ho!"

The woman left the longhouse with Radisson and took him back to her home, where she tied a beaded sash around his naked waist and began to sing and dance in front of him. Then she took a comb from a box, gave it to a young woman, and watched as the latter greased and combed Radisson's hair. He had been painted before he ran the gauntlet, and the women quickly got rid of those pigments, which marked him out for torture. The three of them then roasted some ears of fresh corn in the longhouse hearth—Radisson burned himself slightly when he pulled his share from the fire—and, after they ate, the older woman gave Radisson Dutch-made blue stockings, shoes and a cape, and cloth to make a loincloth-style underwear. Then she checked Radisson for lice, picking off the insects and squeezing them between her teeth.

Radisson, with his spectacular gift for languages, soon learned that this woman, who was now his adoptive mother, was born a Huron but had been taken as a child and adopted. Eventually she was given the name and power of a clan mother. She married a war chief and had borne nine children, but she held power in her own right, not from the success of her husband. Two of her daughters died young and three of her sons had been killed in the war, likely sent on raids she helped plan. Orhima, one of her sons, was killed leading a raid of thirteen warriors against the Fire Nation at the south end of Lake Michigan. The raid occurred three years before Radisson's capture, and she still felt the pain of Orhima's loss. This remarkable woman, whom Radisson often praises in his writings but never names, took a big risk adopting a Frenchman. Maybe, as a "foreigner" herself, she was more open-minded than the rest of the clan mothers.

Radisson liked her and his adoptive father. He quickly became attached to the Iroquois, displaying, at times, the zeal of a convert. "I did what I could to get familiarity with them," Radisson would write years later. "Yet I suffered no wrong at their hands, taking all freedom, which the old woman enticed me to do. But still they altered my face wherever I went and [gave me] a new dish to satisfy nature."[37]

Within a few days, Radisson was living the life of an honoured guest, or so it seemed. He didn't have to do the mundane farm chores that would be expected of a French peasant boy. He was no longer a member of France's lowest class, expected to defer to any priest, aristocrat, or well-connected rich man who crossed his path. Nor, it seems, was he made to do the hard work of clearing land, building longhouses, and hauling logs to keep the town's walls strong. Radisson was being tested, but he saw his time in the Iroquois country as a kind of vacation. His adoptive mother gave him a little gun that he used to hunt grouse and squirrels. When he wasn't picking off small game, he was playing with a group of young companions. But, perhaps because he was smaller than the Iroquois boys, Radisson's adoptive mother wanted Radisson to spend more time with her two daughters, who liked to grease and comb his hair every morning. Still, he did go out on some hunting trips, and any time Radisson shot some game or was given gifts, he passed these along to "my purse-keeper and refuge, the good old woman." Once, Radisson realized he hadn't thought about life back in New France for five weeks, strongly suggesting that whatever he'd left behind wasn't nearly as fun as living among the Iroquois.

Within six seeks, he had learned a lot about Iroquois manners. Radisson became Orhima, the woman's lost son. Once, the old woman asked Radisson whether he was Asserony, the Mohawk word for a Frenchman. He answered he was a Panugaga, one of her people. On that day, Radisson's family threw an adoption feast.

The woman's husband had little say about the adoption. He was a wealthy man, able to afford to host a feast for three hundred men to announce Radisson's adoption. He was also one of the Mohawk's most important war chiefs. Still, he did not have the political clout of clan mothers like his wife, who met in secret councils of their own and had the power to make or break chiefs. Through the years, he had scarred his right thigh nineteen times to record the men he had killed with his own hands. He'd been wounded by seven arrows and six gunshots. As a war leader, he had led many raids against the Mohawks' enemies and earned a reputation as a brave, generous leader who handed over many of his captives to younger men to let them share in the glory. By 1652, he was sixty years old, but lean, strong, and still capable of leading men into battle. Radisson was, even years later, proud of his "parents." Historians have, with some reason, called Radisson a man of few loyalties, but his writings show some real affection for the couple who adopted him, the "brothers" who became his friends, and the sisters who so lovingly looked after his clothes, hair, and body paint.

While living in the Iroquois country, Radisson saw things that would appall people now: the killing of prisoners, the enslavement of captives (many of whom would likely later be freed), but he also saw a very strong community of clan and family that worked hard to ensure everyone had food, clothes, shelter, and a share of the profits from trade. Iroquois society placed a huge value on the inherent worth of every individual person, which gave each of them tremendous power over their own lives. Respect for elders and leaders was expected and there were subtle differences in class, but Radisson saw a civilization that did not have the brutal class differences and the humiliating obligations piled on the peasantry under France's Bourbon monarchs. There were no priests in the Iroquois country trying to audit the inner sanctum of his soul to ferret out heresy. There were no criminals being humiliated, no children beaten, no beggars being whipped out of town.

In all of Radisson's surviving writings—a full-sized book manuscript, plus many letters—he never mentions his biological parents. We only know of his sisters, and that's because one married Groseilliers. Never once does Radisson compare his life before his capture with his experience as part of a Mohawk family. Nor does he speculate about the worries of whatever family he left behind or mention their relief when, years later, he turned up alive. Sometimes silence speaks volumes. So Radisson was a willing adoptee. Before the feast to initiate him as an Iroquois, his "sisters" cleaned him and styled his hair, tying both his locks with wampum-covered thongs. His new mother gave him another expensive suit of clothes, tied with valuable wampum belts. His relatives gave him bead bracelets and a fabulous ceremonial wampum belt that rested around his shoulders and reached down to his heels.[38]

At the adoption feast, Radisson's new father made a speech in which he talked about his many exploits in war, then used a hatchet to smash a cooking pot filled with sagamité, the corn-gruel staple of the Iroquoian diet. The real party food, roasted moose meat, was carried to the guests by young men, who piled it onto wooden trays and walked around the jammed longhouse, filling the bowl of anyone who wanted to eat.

A less astute man than Radisson might have decided he was out of danger, but the adoption of prisoners was not permanent until they had proved capable of filling the place of the person mourned by the family. Radisson, at least in the early months, never seems to have taken the patronage of his adoptive parents for granted. He worked hard to master their language, although he found the Huron dialect, which he heard from adoptees and slaves in the village, to be somewhat easier to learn. Fortunately, he had a spectacular talent for languages. He would, through his life, become fluent in three European tongues and at least six Indigenous languages.

Despite his new speaking skills, there was still much for him to get used to. The Mohawks, like other Iroquoians, lived in crowded towns and villages surrounded by strong palisade walls. Mohawk longhouses could stretch for two hundred feet. Shaped like a long Quonset hut with rolled ends, the longhouse was divided into sleeping and living quarters. Each house sheltered members of the same clan. There were nine clans among the Iroquois, with memberships cutting across the various members of the league, but just three clans among the Mohawks themselves. People new to living in such tight, crowded homes in a complex, ritualistic society had to learn local manners, customs, and taboos very quickly if they were to succeed in pleasing their hosts.[39]

The longhouse family sections were not completely closed off, and people living in them could expect no privacy because a walkway extended along the middle of the entire house. Longhouses were made of a wooden frame covered with bark, with holes cut into the peak of the roof to let out the smoke. Even burning dry wood, the Iroquois had to put up with smoke that stung the eyes and often led to blindness among the elders. This may seem like a tough way to live, but the average French peasant had the same problems with smoky little houses, and typical European families also expected no privacy when so many, even members of the nobility, crowded into shared beds.

The 1600s were part of a great worldwide age of gruel, and anyone passing judgment on Iroquoian cuisine needs to know that the farmers of the Great Lakes country had a similar, though better, diet than most other people in the world.[40] The basic food of the Iroquois was sagamité, boiled cornmeal seasoned with fish, meat, nuts, sunflower seeds, ground beans, or whatever else was available, or eaten straight. The Iroquoians didn't use much salt in their food, nor did they flavour sagamité with herbs. Eaten without anything to spice it up, it, sagamité must have been very bland, and Radisson, raised on wheat, had trouble digesting it in the first days after his capture.

But the Iroquois' meaty diet was a treat for a French peasant boy. Before the fur trade, the Iroquois mainly hunted deer. By the time Radisson arrived, venison was still very important, but the Iroquois also ate the fur-bearing animals that they trapped for their trade with the Dutch. They killed bears and captured their cubs, which they raised in large pens. Bears, being omnivorous, could eat anything the Iroquois threw out. They are smart, adaptable, and grow to adult size in four years. While the meat is dry and somewhat gamey, the Iroquois seemed to like it. At least one European visitor to the Iroquois country saw tame adult bears wandering through the towns, begging for food scraps.[41] At the same time, the Iroquois killed and ate raccoons, which were serious cornfield pests (raccoons love to vandalize cornfields by picking cobs, taking a few bites, and throwing the ears away), woodchucks, which dug up the cornfields and are somewhat easily caught and killed by dogs, and the dogs themselves. Bears and dogs were killed and eaten at important ceremonies, usually by warriors before they left on raids, a practice that continued among the Iroquois for a century after Radisson's time. As the decades went by and Iroquois men spent more time away from their villages working in the fur trade, the Iroquois ate more small animals. Women and children hunted the animals that lived around villages, using bows and arrows and small guns like the one given to Radisson.

Fishing is not particularly good in the Mohawk Valley. The falls along the river and on the Hudson, where the two rivers merge, prevent large runs of spawning fish, so the local catch was limited to catfish, suckers, and perhaps bass and perch. Smaller streams were likely emptied of brook trout soon after a town was built within easy walking distance. The four Iroquois nations to the west had much easier access to the big spawning runs of Atlantic salmon from Lake Ontario and traded these fish to the Mohawks.[42] All the Iroquois shared the big eel fishery of the St. Lawrence River, which they fought the Algonquins to control.

Iroquois men respected women. No European, no matter how hostile, ever accused them of abuse or rape. The Jesuits said the young Huron and Iroquois women were promiscuous. Ethnologists and historians, writing in the mid- to late-twentieth century in the wake of anthropologist Margaret Mead's idyllic description of free sex among the Samoans, have adapted Mead's fantasy to the Great Lakes wilderness. If, as some authors have written, teenagers spent much of their free time making love in the woods, Radisson doesn't seem to have shared in this activity, since he never mentions it in his writings. Whatever the young Iroquois might have been doing in the woods, as a community they valued stable marriages, and if a couple—especially one with children—seemed on the verge of breaking up, friends and family tried to help them work through their problems.

Unlike Christians, the Iroquois did not seek religious conformity, and, unless Radisson left it out of his writings—which is doubtful—did not try to instruct him or convert him to their religion. Still, he would have seen their spiritual beliefs all around him: the curing ceremonies, the ritual sacrifice of prisoners, dogs, bears, and their "eat all" feasts. The Iroquois religion was pantheistic, combining the idea of gods who had sway in peoples' lives with a belief in the natural spirituality of the land, water, sky, and living things. There would be time for Radisson to learn the Indigenous story of the creation, when water creatures piled mud on the back of a great turtle to form the world.

The Mohawk village was full of sights and sounds that were exciting and alien to Radisson. He was rich, with his little gun, his fine cloth clothes, and his access to the wealth of his parents. He also had those remarkable social skills, along with an insatiable curiosity. Unknown to his "parents," he was also very ambitious, with little understanding of consequences. Living the life of a rich Mohawk teenager suited Radisson well, at least for a time. But Radisson's ever-shifting loyalties—if he ever had any in the first place—were about to change again.

Escape

One fall day in 1651, Radisson met three of his Mohawk friends in a cornfield outside the town. The Mohawks wanted to go on a hunting and camping trip in the Lake Champlain region and they hoped Radisson would come with them. Radisson wavered, saying he would rather stay in the village to get to know his mother better. The other young men pestered him until Radisson agreed that all of them should visit his family's longhouse and talk it over with his mother. Radisson was surprised when his mother gave permission for him to go. She also gave him a sack of cornmeal and three pairs of shoes because moccasins wore out on long trips. Radisson's two sisters carried his pack into the forest, then took their leave and headed back toward the village.

The hunting party pushed through the bush until they came to a lake. Radisson was already tired and wasn't pleased with the sparse food that the hunting party had packed. The burden of lugging all their supplies eased up on the third day, when they built a small boat of branches and elm bark in less than two hours and used it to float through a chain of lakes and rivers. Finally, they came across deer tracks. Radisson and one of his Mohawk friends stayed in camp while the other two men followed a buck. Five hours later, after dark, they were back at camp with the stag's meat, two dead bears (obviously small ones), and a beaver. The men fired up their copper kettle, boiled and ate some of the meat, and fell asleep exhausted.

Now that their food problem was solved, three members of the hunting party got to work on what was likely their real job, trapping beavers to trade with the Dutch in the Hudson Valley. They set traps and came back to their camp after a few hours. Along the way, the Mohawks and Radisson heard a man singing. They took cover in the bush until they could see the stranger was a local Algonquin man. When they confronted him, the man said he had been tracking a bear for hours. In truth, the stranger was very, very bad news.

The hunters took him to their camp, and while some of the Mohawks were cooking supper, the stranger began whispering to Radisson. He wanted news of Trois-Rivières and Quebec, saying he desperately wanted to return to New France, where his family lived. Radisson said he wanted the same thing, though he claimed years later that he didn't mean it.

"Do you love the Algonquins?" Radisson asked the stranger.

"Do you love the French?" the Algonquin replied. "Brother, cheer up, let us escape, the Three Rivers are not far off."

Radisson replied, "My three comrades won't let me, and they promised my mother they'd bring me back again."

"So would you rather live like the Huron, who are slaves?" the Algonquin asked, "or be free and back among the French, where there is good bread to be eaten? Don't worry, we can kill them all with their own hatchets tonight when they are asleep."[43]

Radisson agreed. He later wrote that he believed the Iroquois to be mortal enemies of the French, who "had cut the throats of so many of my relations, burned and murdered them."[44]

The young Iroquois men asked the Algonquin what he was whispering to Radisson about. The stranger made up some lies, and all five men, weary from the day's long walk and engorged with meat, quickly fell asleep. Or seemed to. The Algonquin stayed awake for a few hours, then gave Radisson a nudge.

The Algonquin got up and sat near the fire, looked over at the sleeping Iroquois and gently slipped their guns and hatchets away from them. He handed one axe to Radisson just before he killed his first victim. Radisson did his share of killing, but was not enthusiastic as, "to tell the truth I was loathsome to do them mischief that had never done me any." Still, Radisson drove the hatchet deep into the skull of one of the sleeping men as his victim lay on his stomach on the cabin floor. The young Iroquois rose up for a moment, then slumped back to the ground with a loud moan that almost woke up the third victim. The Algonquin used his hatchet on that man, too, while Radisson finished him with a gunshot.

"I was sorry to have been in such an encounter, but [it's] too late to repent," Radisson wrote years later.

The Algonquin cut off the heads of the three men to take back with him to his own people and dropped the bodies into the river. The killers took three of the four guns in the camp, all the gunpowder and shot, two swords, the hatchets, all the wampum, much of the cornmeal and some of the meat. They travelled by night along the river and hid in the woods under their canoe during daylight. They travelled that way for two weeks and were terrified whenever they heard other people. Finally, they arrived at Lake St. Pierre on the St. Lawrence River above Trois-Rivières, within striking distance of home.

They paddled all day and arrived late in the afternoon at a beach, just west of the three mouths of the Nicolet River. Trois-Rivières was a relatively short trip across the Nicolet delta and downstream on the St. Lawrence for a few miles. They could almost see the town, but they were still in the woods. The shores of the lake—a widening of the St. Lawrence River—were a marshland of bulrushes and tall grass (now part of the Lake St. Pierre world biosphere reserve). Rather than drag their canoe into the woods behind the swamp, they hid it among the cattails and walked two hundred paces into the woods to light a fire to cook their meal of meat and corn flour. They were exhausted, so they slept until sunrise, when the Algonquin woke Radisson and suggested the two of them make a dash to the village. Radisson knew the Iroquois kept a constant vigil over Trois-Rivières. He didn't want to be careless, but his companion was insistent. "Let us be gone, we are past all fear. Let us shake off the yoke of a company of whelps that killed so many French and black-coats (Jesuit priests), and so many of my nation. Nay, Brother, if you do not come, I will leave you. I will go through the woods until I am among the French houses, and I will light a fire as a sign that they should help me. I will tell the Governor that you stayed behind. Take courage, man!" Then he picked up his gun and the pack that held the rest of his things, including the heads of Radisson's Iroquois friends.

Radisson weighed the options. He could go, and possibly end up captured within sight of the town, as he had been before. But if he stayed, there was a very good chance of being labelled a coward by his own people, especially if the Algonquin told the governor that Radisson was afraid to come near the town. Then there was a more practical problem. If he decided to use the canoe to make the last part of the trip, he would have trouble handling the boat by himself, especially if there was a headwind.

So, again, against his better judgment, he went with the Algonquin. After two weeks of travelling in the dark, they would make the last leg of the trip by canoe in daylight. That morning, it was sunny and clear, the water calm. They could see for miles. At the edge of their range of sight were dark spots that the Algonquin insisted were geese. But they weren't geese. It was a full-scale Iroquois war party. By the time the two fugitives realized their mistake, warriors were paddling furiously toward them. Radisson and his companion struggled to get back into the marshes, and by the time they reached the reeds, the Iroquois were only about a mile away, in plain sight. Soon, the warriors were within musket range of the two murderers. The fugitives tried to lighten their load and conceal their crime by dropping the heads of their three victims into Lake St. Pierre, but the heads bobbed to the surface near the canoes of their pursuers, inspiring the Iroquois to paddle even harder. Looking down, Radisson could see the lake bottom, but the water was still too deep to jump into and wade. Musket balls started hitting their canoe. At least two struck Radisson's companion, who sprawled, dead and bleeding, across the canoe with a bullet through his chin and throat and a second, massive wound to the shoulder. By then, Radisson was surrounded. He fired a couple of musket shots toward his pursuers, but had no chance to reload. As his canoe sank, some of the Iroquois pulled him from the water, while others tossed the body of his companion into a canoe. Radisson knew he was in an awful lot of trouble. For months, the Iroquois had allowed him to decide whether he wanted to be one of them, and he had betrayed their trust by murdering three innocent men. In any other country, Radisson would have been a dead man.

Soon, all the canoes were pulled up on a beach. There was some disappointment among the warriors that only one of the fugitives had survived. The Iroquois built a big fire, carved the heart out of Radisson's erstwhile companion, and cut off his head, which they jammed onto a stick and carried to one of their canoes.[45] They threw the rest of his body into the fire as some of the other warriors dealt with Radisson. The Iroquois stripped him naked, trussed his arms behind his back, tied a rope around his waist to show he was a prisoner, then led him to the canoes, where they started interrogating him. Radisson couldn't, or wouldn't, answer their questions, so the warriors punched him and pulled out one of his fingernails.

Radisson quickly became depressed. He was so close to the French settlement, and now he was about to be dragged back to the Iroquois country to be killed. He really didn't see any other possible outcome. Escape was impossible: there were 150 men in this war party. They had already captured, in the Quebec City area, seventeen Hurons, two French men, one French woman, and carried the heads of twelve Algonquins (counting the man who had escaped the Mohawk country with Radisson). As they paddled upstream, the prisoners sang their mournful death songs, a ritual captured warriors tried to continue until the moment of their deaths. The Iroquois would not let the prisoners talk with each other and moved them from canoe to canoe to keep them from plotting.

An old Iroquois man in Radisson's boat interrogated the teenaged Frenchman. Radisson, of course, blamed the dead Algonquin. Radisson talked about his adopted family and gave away the details of the hunting-trip murders. The Algonquin, Radisson said, had come into the camp while the four young men were cooking. He had eaten with them, then said his goodbyes and gone back into the woods. That night, while Radisson and the three Mohawks were sleeping, the Algonquin crept back into the camp and killed Radisson's companions. For some reason, he had spared Radisson and forced him to travel with him to Quebec. The old man believed most of the story, but he couldn't protect Radisson from his captors. This was a far larger and much less intimate group than had captured Radisson the year before. No one saw him as an innocent boy taken in an ambush. He was the obvious accomplice of a murderer, if not a killer himself, and the three Iroquois heads tossed from the fugitives' canoe on Lake St. Pierre proved it.

On the first night, the war party camped on a sand beach. The prisoners were tied spread-eagle to posts buried in the sand. Stakes were driven on both sides of each prisoner's neck, and, when the prisoners were staked to the ground, a cord was tied between the posts so they couldn't move their heads. Similar trap-like structures held their legs, so the prisoners were completely immobile. At dusk, the mosquitoes and other biting insects swarmed by the thousands. All night, the prisoners tried to blow the insects from their faces, but there was nothing they could do to protect their bodies. Radisson recounted, "having no use of our hands, we are cruelly tormented. Our voyage was laborious and most miserable, suffering every night the like misery."

This routine—tied up in a canoe by day, pinned down under the stars, rain, and mosquitoes at night—lasted as the flotilla made its way up the Richelieu River to Lake Champlain, across the height of land into the Hudson and Mohawk valleys, and across the Saratoga Plain. In that hunting territory, the war party came across several bands of Iroquois who gave the Mohawks wampum to reward those who most eagerly tortured the prisoners. One man had a finger cut off, others had nails torn out, and it was common for the warriors to shove prisoners' fingertips into the bowls of burning tobacco pipes. Almost all of them had the backs of their hands whipped until they were numb. None of these tortures was life threatening, however. Attacks on the vital parts of the prisoners' bodies occurred only after the Iroquois decided whether they were good candidates for adoption, or if they should die.

Soon, Radisson found himself back at his home village. This time, he would not escape the gauntlet. Certain he would be killed for the murder of the men in his hunting party, Radisson said his "fear of death [took] away the fear of blows." Nineteen prisoners were brought to the gauntlet, while two were left behind with the trophy heads of the Algonquins. "Who would not shake at the sight of so many men, women, and children armed with all sorts of instruments: staves, hand Irons, eel skins wherein they put half a score of bullets? Others had brands, rods of thorn, and all such like that the cruelty could invent to put their prisoners to greater torments."

All prisoners were on their own. There would be no help for Radisson this time. All had their hands tied so they couldn't deflect the blows. Those who seemed the most afraid or who tried to delay the start of their run were singled out for the most violence. The people along the gauntlet began to call out for the prisoners to run. Mohawks who didn't want to be part of the gauntlet stood nearby in groups, watching it. The whole thing, Radisson wrote years later, was "the image of Hell." Captured Huron warriors sang their death songs, women and children prisoners screamed and cried, and the people along the gauntlet cheered and laughed.[46]

A warrior led each captive on a leash. He had control over the prisoner's speed and, if he wanted to, he could trip the captive or simply yank them to a stop. Radisson believed most of the people along the gauntlet were friends and family of members of the war party. But among them, close to the village, were Radisson's mother and father and their two daughters. His mother grabbed him by the hair, yanked him from the gauntlet, shoved him into the hands of her husband, and the family led him to their longhouse.

This was not enough to save Radisson. He had broken the pact he'd made with the community at his adoption feast. He had also committed murder. Breaking with the community meant his family and his clan no longer protected him. As for the murders, Iroquoian law placed his entire clan in debt to the extended families of the murdered men; a debt that could only be settled by a vast transfer of wealth between clans. An Iroquois murderer would not be punished personally, but would be subjected to the humiliation of seeing his extended family lose much of their property and status. In Radisson's case, those who wanted to kill him could argue he had not only failed his family, he had shown himself to be a duplicitous, murderous adoptee, unworthy of protection by Iroquois law.

As was so often the case, the young Frenchman had little understanding of the forces that were shaping his life. Later, his failure to understand the ways of England's power elite would prove his ultimate undoing. This time, he underestimated the power of his mother and the strength of Iroquois law. Over the next few days, his family paid condolence presents to the families of the murder victims. The killer's fate, however, still hadn't been settled. The community would get to vent their anger at Radisson over the next few days, but though they had every right to be, the three dead men's relatives weren't among his torturers. Possibly, they had accepted the settlement offered by Radisson's family and clan.[47]

After his arrival back at the longhouse, Radisson's father pushed the teenager—whose arms were still tied behind his back—to the ground. "You have no sense. You were my son. You made yourself my enemy. You did not love your mother, nor me, who gave you life. You would still kill me."

Radisson's father told his sisters to give him something to eat. Radisson was trembling and had no appetite, but he thought he could show the old warrior some courage by eating the food that was given to him. He was aware how much the Iroquois valued courage, strength, and generosity. He told him of his trip with the Algonquin, although it's not clear in his writings whether he told the old man the truth, or the fictional version he'd tried to pawn off on his captors. The family listened carefully, hoping to hear facts that might prove Radisson wasn't a murderous ingrate. A group of armed men burst into the longhouse and found Radisson sitting by the fire. One spoke loudly to Radisson's father, who made Radisson get up and go with the men. His mother and sisters began to scream and cry as Radisson was led away to what he expected to be his execution in an open area near the centre of the town.

There, he was reunited with the rest of the war party's prisoners. Most were bloody, burned, and bruised. One Frenchman had been so badly beaten that he was almost dead, so his captors cut off his head and threw it into the fire. Radisson was made to climb a scaffold where five other captives were tied at various heights. The men still sang their death songs as the sky, which had been sunny all morning, clouded over. Rain soon began to fall in sheets, driving all but the most determined of the torturers—most, apparently, young boys—back into their homes.

When the rain let up, more people arrived back at the scaffold, some carrying dry wood that they used to light fires under the prisoners. The boys shot little arrows at the victims and climbed up to pull out any facial and body hair that they could find on the men. Radisson had four of his fingernails yanked out and his torturers made him sing. When he was too weak to talk or sing, they gave him a warm tea to revive him. Then, as night fell, he was taken to a longhouse, where he was tied, still naked, to a post. He was alone for an hour, until a woman came into the cabin with her four-year-old son. The mother gave the boy a piece of flint and told him to cut off one of Radisson's fingers, but the child wasn't strong enough to hack through the bone or to separate a joint. He did give Radisson a deep cut and sucked some of the blood from the wound.

The next morning, Radisson was taken back to the scaffold and told to sing his death song. When Radisson's mother arrived, she told him to stop singing. Giving him some meat, she told him to be cheerful, that he would not die. But Radisson couldn't be sure. At that point, an old man shuffled over and plunged the Frenchman's thumb into the red-hot bowl of a pewter tobacco pipe. The man silently refilled and smoked the pipe three times, burning Radisson with each bowlful, leaving his thumb swollen and black. When the man finally walked away, Radisson's mother dressed the burned thumb in cloth and styled the young man's hair. Then she left. A warrior heated a sword in the fire until it was red hot and ran it through one of Radisson's feet. Another warrior tied one of his own bare legs to Radisson's and dropped a hot coal between them to show he was braver than the captive. Radisson insisted later that it was the Iroquois who flinched first, that the man had to be rescued by his friends, who cut the bindings. Someone else crushed the tip of one of Radisson's index fingers between two stones, leaving him with a lifelong disfigurement. When Radisson's family came back to the scaffold, they chased away an old man who was trying to gnaw off one of Radisson's thumbs.

While Radisson was suffering these nasty but non-lethal tortures, many of the other captives were dying, after being burned alive. This was as much a contest between killers and victim as it was a slow execution. The Iroquois' goal was to break the prisoners and make them beg for death. If they could endure all these tortures while retaining their dignity and self-control, the prisoners would win renown and respect. There may have been an element of psychological and sexual sadism involved, but this was, for the most part, a horrific game and ritual with strong religious and political overtones.

At midday, Radisson was taken from the scaffold to a longhouse, where sixty old men, the civil leaders, or "old stones," met in a council. Radisson sat among them for a half hour while they silently smoked their pipes. Then, inside the crowd, Radisson saw one of his brothers, whom he had not seen since he was brought back to the village. His brother was dressed sumptuously, wearing belts and a necklace of wampum. In one hand he held a hatchet, in the other an expensive, red stone pipe. On his back hung a medicine bag full of healing herbs, tobacco, and hunting charms made of wolves' bones, as well as other mystical, personal items.

Radisson's father took his place among the village leaders and lit his pipe. Seven female and two male prisoners, along with ten children ranging from three to twelve years old, were brought into the house. Radisson was the only prisoner who was still tied. One of the chiefs rose to his feet and made a long speech, raising his hands to the heavens; then, gesturing toward the earth and the fire, he spoke, working himself into a sweat as he did so. Other chiefs followed, making similar speeches. Most of the prisoners were then set free into the village with new, adoptive families. Radisson was the only prisoner left in the longhouse, still naked and tied up.

Radisson's trial began. His adopted father, wearing only a breechcloth and hat, rose and spoke for an hour, denouncing the Algonquins over and over, until Radisson's mother arrived. Wearing two wampum necklaces around her arms and an expensive beaded belt around her waist, she began to sing and dance, moving through the chiefs and dropping the wampum among them. Radisson's brother then rose and sang a military song. But the young captive did not think his family was winning the chiefs over. At most, he thought, they might let his brother give him a quick death with the hatchet. Eventually, both son and father left the longhouse.

The chiefs debated for a very long time. Every now and then, they threw an offering of tobacco into the fire. The longhouse was opened, and Radisson could see there were about two hundred people waiting outside. About twenty of the chiefs left for a while. No one took their places. The other forty stayed, and, after more hours had passed, Radisson's family returned, and everyone sat down to smoke some more. Radisson's father rose up, sang a song, dropped a wampum belt at the feet of an old man, then cut the cords that bound Radisson's arms.

"The joy that I received at that time was incomparable, for suddenly all my pains and griefs ceased," Radisson recalled. "He bids me be merry, makes me sing, to which I consented with all my heart. Whilst I did sing they hooped and hollowed on all sides. The old man bid me 'ever be cheerful, my son!'… [My] mother, sisters, and the rest of their friends sang and danced." His father took him by the arm and led him to the family's longhouse. As he limped toward his home, Radisson could hear people cheering from the council longhouse.

Radisson hadn't eaten all day. Now he was ravenous. He gorged himself while his mother tended to his wounds, cleaning them with water and herbs, and scraping ash out of his thumb. His father left the cabin and returned with healing roots, which were chewed by Radisson's sisters before being applied to his wounds. The medicine worked. The next day, Radisson's swellings had gone down. It took another two weeks for most of the burns and cuts to heal, but the hole in his foot needed an entire month to close, so Radisson stayed in the longhouse, ate when he wanted, and, as he wrote years later, was always among happy, kind friends and family.

So how was Radisson saved? Radisson's parents had compensated and consoled the families of the murdered men for their loss, possibly even before Radisson was recaptured. Incredibly, considering the Iroquois didn't adopt French prisoners, his family was able to win him another chance. Radisson still had to face enough torture to prove he was worthy of saving, however. In the end, Radisson embraced those who had tortured and spared him, and became one of them once more.

Radisson's capture, torture, and rescue was, for him, a kind of death and rebirth. As his father reminded him, the Mohawk family had given him life. Radisson was now utterly grateful and completely devoted to them. Living in Tionnontoguen before his escape, he had only half-heartedly pretended to be Orhima for the sake of his adoptive parents. Now he would *become* Orhima. Radisson decided he wanted to be a great Mohawk like his father. He would succeed where Orhima had lost his life, fighting the Fire Nation.

DODCON

The summer of 1652 was over, and once he could walk again, Radisson spent the late fall and early winter hunting near his village. Every month, someone in Radisson's family, usually his brother, made the two-day walk to the Dutch trading post of Fort Orange on the Hudson River to trade for a new white cloth shirt for him. The young Frenchman was never allowed to make the trip himself. His sisters and mother kept him at home, where they made sure his hair was fashionably styled and his body paint fresh and unsmudged.

There were feasts in the village throughout the fall as the war chiefs, on the instructions of clan mothers, recruited men for raids on the Algonquins, the French, and the people living to the west and south of the Iroquois that were to take place the following spring. It was during these years that the Iroquois empire pushed its power deep into the Great Lakes-St. Lawrence lowlands and the Ohio Valley, and even farther west, as the Iroquois prepared to raid the Sioux.

Radisson's father started planning for an attack on the French and Algonquins of the St. Lawrence Valley, collecting a group of warriors early in the autumn and tutoring them through the winter. Every night, the young men came to see the old war chief to learn how to fight like Iroquois and hear about the wrongs done to them by the Algonquins. Radisson, enamoured with his father, wanted to go with the war party, knowing his family would be impressed if he took up his hatchet against the Fire Nation as his namesake had done four years earlier. But he suspected his father worried that he might try to make another break for it.

Radisson's father told him war was the fastest and best way for the teenaged Frenchman to win the respect of the Iroquois, and with it, real citizenship. "I venture to ask him what I was. He presently answers that I was an Iroquois as himself. 'Let me revenge,' said I, 'my kinsmen. I love my brother. Let me die with him. I would die with you, but you will not let me because you go against the French. Let me again go with my brother.

The prisoners and the heads that I shall bring, to the joy of my mother and sisters, will make me undertake at my return to take up the hatchet against those of Quebec, of the Three Rivers, and Montreal in declaring them my name, and that it's I that kills them, and by that you shall know I am your son, worthy to bear that title that you gave me when you adopted me.'"

The old war chief replied, "have great courage, son Orhima, your brother died in the wars, not in a house. He was of a courage not of a woman. I go to avenge his death. If I die, avenge you mine."

The attacks on New France the following spring would be the worst in the colony's history, a true siege that came very close to extinguishing the colony and all its inhabitants. Many of the Huron refugees, driven from their homeland just two years before and huddled in longhouses outside the walls of the French towns, made peace with and joined the Iroquois. As for the French at Trois-Rivières, they were prisoners inside their own fort through the summer and fall, and were picked off one by one by the Iroquois. As one chief later said, "the French could not step outside the door to piss without being killed." Radisson's half-sister Marguérite's first husband was one of the casualties, leaving her a widow with two small children, and open to the wooing of Médard Chouart, the self-styled Sieur des Groseilliers (Lord of the Gooseberries).

Radisson worked all winter to get his mother's permission to go on the Fire Nation raid. But she worried Radisson would get lost in the woods, and believed he needed another year in the village, learning Iroquois culture and language, before heading off to war. Radisson was now sixteen or seventeen, probably not quite as big or as strong as the rest of the warriors,[48] and likely still a novice when it came to wilderness survival.

Radisson admits to using flattery and dissembling to win her over. It helped that his father also believed Radisson was ready to go; when it came to war, his decision carried weight. When spring came early, Radisson and the rest of the war party, which included his adoptive brother, celebrated their departure at a feast hosted by his father. The old chief said he wished he was already fighting in the St. Lawrence Valley, but he was proud to be home to celebrate the departure of his two sons to avenge the family's losses.

A few days after the feast, as Radisson was out fishing with one of his sisters, the twenty-year-old leader of the expedition, probably Radisson's mother's nephew though one of her sisters, came to the longhouse and told Radisson's parents that he loved Radisson as much as any other member of the war party. He would fight beside him to the end, if it came to that. Soon afterwards, the raid's leader threw his own feast to celebrate the expedition's departure. The ten men leaving for the west were the guests of honour, where, Radisson says, "we all did sing and make good cheer of a fat bear." When they set out, unassimilated female Huron captives carried the warriors' packs as they travelled west through the Iroquois country.[49] Symbolically, they were moving through the great longhouse of the Iroquois League, from its eastern door, the land of the Mohawks, through the lands of the Oneida, Onondaga, Cayuga, before exiting through the western door, guarded by the Seneca on the Genesee River. There was still thick ice on the lakes and rivers and plenty of snow in the bush as they walked across the country. After a week's hike, they came to Nojottga, the main town of the Oneida, where they stayed for a couple of days and added another warrior to their expedition. Soon afterwards, they reached Nontageya, the main town of the Onondaga. This was the heart of the league, the place where the council fire was kept and its most important meetings and ceremonies held.

Everywhere they went, the Iroquois stuffed the young men with food, so much so that the warriors didn't even bother to look inside the packs that had been made for them back home. When Radisson finally opened his, he found six pounds of gunpowder and fifteen pounds of shot, two shirts, a cap, eight pairs of shoes, material to make a pair of breeches, a blanket, a cape, one thousand black and white wampum beads, and a collar threaded with nettles for tying prisoners. Radisson was already carrying a gun, a hatchet, and a dagger.

They kept walking through the Five Nations, visiting the Cayuga and the Seneca. In the westernmost Iroquoian towns, people marvelled to see a Frenchman willingly, eagerly travelling with Mohawk warriors. The raiders were now near the far end of the Iroquois homeland. The warriors sent their baggage porters home and trudged through the woods on snowshoes. In open country, most of the snow had melted as spring took hold, so they changed into their moccasins to make better time. Radisson was relieved because he wasn't as fast on snowshoes as his companions. They kept walking for another ten days, hunting deer and wild turkey on the flatlands behind the Niagara Escarpment. Eventually, they reached the Niagara River somewhere above the falls, where the warriors stayed nearly two weeks to build four walnut-bark canoes.[50] They paddled upstream, dodging chunks of ice, and found the snow on shore deepening the closer they got to Lake Erie.

The raiders fought the Niagara River's strong current for four days, until they reached the shore of Lake Erie (at modern Buffalo, New York) and saw it was jammed with ice pushed to the end of the lake by the prevailing southwest winds. Thick snow that lingered on the ground and the ice jam on the lake kept them stuck for another two weeks. The Mohawk warriors marvelled that the seasons seemed to be going backward as they left the Seneca country's spring behind and entered winter on the Lake Erie snowbelt, one of the snowiest places in North America. Finally, the wind switched south, clearing the shore of ice and bringing with it some warmth. Streams along that stretch of the Lake Erie shore cut deep ravines through the soft shale of the flat shoreline, causing these creeks to rage like rivers in the spring flood. The warriors dodged them by paddling over Lake Erie, which Radisson called "the sweet sea." The weather improved, putting the men in good spirits. After the misery of being locked in by ice, they were happy to paddle for six days and sleep on shore every night.

The weather grew warmer every day and the lake stayed calm enough for the little brigade to keep moving southwest. The canoe trip saved them from walking across the wetlands, including the big Waterford marshes behind the lakeshore in what's now northern Pennsylvania and Ohio. Behind them, on the south shore of the lake near its outlet to the Niagara, lay the lands of the Erie, a small nation with a language and culture similar to the people of the Iroquois League, and with whom the Iroquois were at peace, for now. To the northwest lay the lands that had belonged to the Neutral Confederacy until the Iroquois destroyed some of their villages in 1651 and convinced them, and hundreds of Huron refugees living among them, to move to the Iroquois country.

The warriors passed the Cleveland cliffs and the Bass Islands, then turned inland when they reached the Maumee River, which empties into Lake Erie at what's now Toledo, Ohio. The river, which flowed through the now-drained Great Black Swamp, was in those days an important highway. They paddled that river for half a day before their first portage, then had to pull their canoes from the river and carry them around rapids.

Days later, after travelling a hundred miles inland, they came to a small lake somewhere southeast of Lake Michigan, where they hid their canoes in the forest, then walked for days more, crossing several fairly large streams by building rafts. Radisson found the region, now part of Indiana, to be desolate, sometimes without enough wood to make a fire, other times with forests so dense and rivers so choked with fallen trees that he and his party couldn't use their canoes. One day, the war party came across a strip of mysteriously flattened forest that intrigued Radisson. It had probably been flattened and chewed up by a tornado, which are common in that part of North America.

The 1641 Taunton Map, made in Quebec and now kept in a British archive, shows the route to the Fire Nation quite clearly. It was drawn by a French surveyor, who used information gathered by the Jesuits from both the Huron and the Iroquois. The Maumee is marked as the canoe route to the southwest, while the Fire Nation is shown living in the land that is now southern Michigan and northern Indiana. The map marks the Fire Nation as an important people, equal to the Iroquois in size. Radisson's war party was coming at the Fire Nation from the south, with the Ohio Valley as their escape route.

The group split up when they reached the edge of Fire Nation territory, with Radisson and the youngest member of the war party being sent to scout along a small river. The other eight lurked around a Fire Nation village, which, like Iroquois towns, was a collection of bark longhouses surrounded by a wooden wall. Radisson and his comrade had a small canoe that they either built or found, and they used it to get to a small lake. The day-long trip was brutal as they had to pull the canoe through shallow water and around dead trees that had fallen into the river. Finally, they arrived at a four-mile-long lake surrounded by thin forests and bushes. Radisson and his companion hid their canoe and began walking along the shore, carrying only their weapons. Halfway along the lake, they saw two women on the far shore. Radisson's young comrade climbed a tree to see if there were more people.

They weren't sure what to do. Radisson argued that the women were likely travelling with men. They could easily take the women, but if men showed up, they would be forced to shoot, and there was no way of knowing how many people might hear their shots and come to help. They could flee, but Radisson's companion reminded him that they couldn't possibly get back down the river before nightfall. So they hid, and when rain came that night, they tried to sleep and ignore their empty stomachs. The next morning, they left the lakeshore and headed back the way they came.

The rain raised the level of the small river, reducing the number of places where the two warriors had to push or pull their boat. As they paddled along, Radisson spotted a strange animal, a giant salamander called a hellbender that measured:

> ...four feet, her head very big, like a Turtle, the nose very small at the end...
> the neck of 5 thumbs wide, the body about 2 feet, and the tail of a foot

& a half, of a blackish color, with great eyes, her teeth very white but not long.[51] That beast was asleep upon one of the trees under which we were to go; neither of us ever seeing such a creature were astonished. We could not tell what to do. It was impossible to carry our boat, for the thickness of the wood; to shoot at her we would at least be discovered, besides it would trouble our Company. At last we were resolved to go through at what cost so ever, and as we were under that hellish beast, she started as she awaked, and with that fell down into our boat, there were herbs that served to secure us from that dreadful animal. We durst not venture to kill her, for fear of breaking our boat. There is the question who was most fearful?

They decided to leave the creature alone. It seemed to be happy enough to sit still in the boat, and they thought they could dump it out the next time they portaged. At first, Radisson was terrified of the thing, but he and his friend soon became used to it, and the Iroquois boy even came up with a name for it. They decided to take it with them to the camp and show it to the rest of the war party. Then things became more comical. The giant salamander was soon joined by a squirrel, which tumbled into the canoe from an overhanging log and ran from end to end for a quarter of an hour, trying to escape but unwilling to swim. The salamander hissed and put two of its legs near the edge of the boat. Radisson used a paddle to flick it into the river, and it swam away. When they got close to the shore, the squirrel made a leap for it.

Back at the camp, no one else in the war party had seen anything in a day and night of scouting, so they felt safe enough to light a big fire to cook dinner and dry off. The next day, the entire group set out on foot toward the place where Radisson and the young warrior had found the two women. Before they got to the lake, they came across fresh tracks, which they followed until they saw a woman carrying wood. This convinced them there was a house or even a village not far away. The leading warrior scouted the area until he saw five men and four women fishing. The war party came up from behind and killed them, then found their cabin and took the embroidered deerskin clothing the Fire Nation people had left behind. The young Iroquois dumped the bodies into the river, then snuck through the woods until they came across a wide trail leading to a village. The warriors moved toward the village only by night. Daylight hours were spent on their stomachs in a vast cornfield, eating stolen fish. Very late on the second night, one of the warriors crept into the village to get water, since they were all thirsty. When he rejoined the party, they made plans for an ambush the next day.

They waited in the bush, fighting off bugs, until mid-afternoon. About twenty people walked through the area, but none was close enough to snatch. The raiders considered going deeper into the woods to emerge at the edge of a cornfield where many of the villagers were working, but ultimately decided that wouldn't work, either. At dusk, four men and three women, on their way to fetch wood, spotted the war party. The Iroquois were forced out to fight. They killed two of the men in hand-to-hand fighting, shot two who tried to escape, and ran off with the three women, along with another who was unlucky enough to be on the trail. By now, the whole countryside was aroused and dozens of Fire Nation warriors were looking for the Iroquois. High on adrenalin and the thrill of danger, the raiders reached a river and crossed it in a stolen canoe.

Their second day on the run, the Iroquois tried to interrogate their prisoners but couldn't understand them, even though the Fire Nation language sounded vaguely Huron, which Radisson and most of the other Mohawks knew. The war party marched through cleared land, around large fields and through the woods, and came across an area forty-five miles long and thirty miles wide where the forest had burned and many of the dead trees had been knocked down by the wind. In the middle of those burnt lands, they set up a camp and made the prisoners sing their death song.

The war party stayed in that desolate country for two weeks, living off cornmeal and boiled turkey until their food ran out. Day after day, they did everything they could to feed themselves and their prisoners. They even gathered deer dung to boil with whatever meat they could get. Disgusting as that sounds (it also made everything bitter), Radisson later wrote that hungry stomachs "make good favour." Knowing they couldn't last much longer without food, the warriors killed two women and made broth from their body parts. Radisson had no qualms about sharing in this macabre meal.

The next day, they arrived near another village, where some of the warriors killed a woman and her child who were outside the walls. Afraid of pursuers from this new town, for the next three days they hurried to return to the first village they had come across. En route, they were discovered by twenty-five or thirty men and women. But despite their better numbers, the Fire Nation people were frightened off by the Iroquois' guns, which were "a terror to them." The women fled first. The men, who were likely covering their escape, were hit with Iroquois arrows and bullets. Two men were left dead at the scene of the fight and five more were taken prisoner. The youngest Iroquois warrior, the boy who had gone on the scouting mission with Radisson and who had marvelled at the hellbender salamander, was wounded by two Fire Nation arrows and a vicious club wound to the head. His colleagues "burned him with all speed, so that he might not languish long," which was the traditional way of giving a mortally wounded warrior a hero's death.

The war party—always described by Radisson as "we"—killed two more of their prisoners and ran for two days without sleeping or eating to get to the place where they had hidden their canoes. When they reached the landing site, they went through their loot: two bags of corn, some deerskins, pipes, red and green stones, a bit of powdered tobacco, a few small loaves of corn bread, some girdles and garters made with what Radisson thought was goat's hair but was likely bison fur, some well-made bows, arrows, and clubs, and headgear made of bear paws and snakeskin. After searching their prisoners' baggage, the warriors split up to hunt for food and then get a few hours' sleep. At midnight, they began paddling downstream. When daylight came, they sent a warrior to climb a tree to see if they were being chased or were headed into trouble. The scout reported that the river they were on emptied into a small lake about twenty-five miles across. Radisson wrote that they found another river nearby thick with spawning salmon and sturgeon, which were easily caught. This gave the warriors the food they needed to get themselves and their prisoners back to the Iroquois country. The war party felt safe enough to spend three days hunting at the lake. While there, they came across two Fire Nation women who had escaped from the Iroquois country and were trying to get back to their own people. The warriors tied up and brought to the camp to join the three surviving male prisoners.

The war party reached the Ohio River and paddled northeastward. They passed the Falls of the Ohio, circled south of the Erie nation and, at what's now Pittsburgh, turned left onto the Allegheny River, whose headwaters are just inland from the Seneca homeland.

As they pushed upstream and left the main branch of the river, the members of the war party realized they had too many people and too much loot to carry in their small canoes. Rather than risk being swamped, they portaged their boats and walked for nine days through high country, using their boats only to cross creeks and small rivers. Finally, they came to a large lake with many islands, where they began work on new boats. They also divided up the booty. Radisson and his brother got two of the six prisoners (a man and a women), along with four scalps, strongly suggesting they had a large role in the prisoners' capture.

For the warriors, the lake was a summer paradise, with plenty of bears and deer to hunt. The lake led to a straight river (likely back to the Allegheny) requiring many portages. The war party killed two hundred beavers as they travelled, collecting enough fur to cover the cost of their guns. In this river valley, which was part of the Iroquois hunting grounds, they met many Iroquois who gave them news from home. After paddling several more days, they crossed the height of land between the Ohio Valley and the Great Lakes to reach the western door of the Iroquois country, where many women, including Radisson's sisters, were waiting for them.

Betrayal (Again)

Radisson received bear, moose, and deer grease, along with twenty beaver skins and several deerskins as his share of the raid's profits. He gave his sisters his two scalps to display and six deer hides to make into coats. The woman prisoner he gave to his mother "as a slave." Radisson made the Fire Nation woman carry his loot eastward through the Iroquois country. At each village, the war party was met with feasts and celebrations. Radisson's sisters pampered him, undressing him for bed every night, greasing and styling his hair, painting his face and hand-feeding him meat as he lay between them, covered with a fur robe. Finally, after days of walking, Radisson was back at Tionnontoguen. He had come to the town twice as a prisoner, but now he walked through the gate a hero. A crowd of people cheered the war party and called Radisson "Dodcon," which he interpreted as "devil," a name the Iroquois gave to warriors who were especially ferocious.

This time, the gauntlet began about a third of a mile from the village. Again, Radisson's mother showed up, singing and leaping with joy. Radisson turned his prisoner over to her, and, again, Radisson's mother showed her compassion and her power by rescuing the Fire Nation woman from the gauntlet and torture, telling the villagers not to meddle with her. The rest of the prisoners, including the man who had been given to Radisson's brother, were soundly beaten by the people lined up along the trail into the village. The Fire Nation man died later the same day.

The male prisoner was tied to a post by his hands, with his backs to his tormentors, next to a small fire of bark and dry wood. The fire was used to heat iron and steel weapons like swords and axes. For hours, the Mohawks burned the hands and arms of the victim. Then they attacked the vital organs, castrating the man, broiling pieces of his flesh, and breaking his teeth with clubs.

Throughout the night, the prisoner was given water and a little rest if he seemed about to lapse into unconsciousness or shock. When it was clear he was dying, the torturers attacked the major organs, ending the victim's suffering by braining him with an axe.

Radisson stayed away from the torture sessions. His own narrow escape seems to have left him with no taste for it. His mangled index finger and his scarred foot would be ugly reminders throughout his life of his two horrible nights on the scaffold. He was more interested in military glory and the physical rewards that came with it. Being Radisson, he took stock of the gifts given to him by the community: wampum necklaces and collars, lots of beads, pendants, and embroidered girdles that were worth a fortune. These gifts were bestowed at special feasts, where talk once again turned to war, this time against the Dutch. The Mohawks, the Iroquois nation closest to Fort Orange, had always been frustrated by what they thought were high prices charged by the Dutch for guns, hatchets, blankets, and wampum (which the Dutch bought from the people who made it, at Long Island, and then brought up the Hudson). The Iroquois wanted to do something to bring those prices down. The idea of war against the Dutch was controversial: if the Dutch fled the Hudson Valley and never came back, the Iroquois had no other easy way to acquire these items. Their potential English trading partners were still hemmed in on the Atlantic coast by the other, often hostile Indigenous groups around them, and the Iroquois would have to cross the Appalachians and a lot of enemy territory to reach them. The Iroquois could make peace with the French, but they would still have to travel for days to exchange their furs and would be competing directly with their Indigenous enemies to the north. Making things worse, the French would not trade guns to non-Christians (a policy that contributed to the destruction of their allies, the Huron), while the Dutch were willing to sell firearms to anyone who could afford them. So, instead of destroying their farms and towns, the Iroquois decided to contain the violence to simply bullying and humiliating the Dutch traders and settlers. For the first time, the war party allowed Radisson to come with them to the Dutch fort and interact with other Europeans.

Radisson and his friends, carrying the beaver pelts they had collected in the Allegheny Valley, set out on a two-day walk to the Dutch colony around Fort Orange (now Albany, New York). Arriving at a farming hamlet, they took over the place, stealing meat out of the settlers' pots, going through their cupboards, and drinking their wine. According to Radisson, "those beer-bellies,"[52] the Dutch farmers, did not have the courage to take on the gang of young toughs. Once they were drunk, the Iroquois duelled with swords, but Radisson, who drank his wine more slowly and was used to alcohol, just watched from the side.

On their fourth day out from the Iroquois village, they arrived at Fort Orange, the Dutch colony's major trading centre and administrative seat. If word of their abuse of the Dutch settlers had reached town, it didn't seem to matter. The traders courted the Iroquois, giving them prunes, raisins, and tobacco. The Iroquois went from house to house, looking for the best deals for their furs, then walked into the main trading fort with the leftover pelts.

Through all this, none of the settlers realized Radisson was French until he was exposed in the fort by a French soldier employed by the Dutch, who said to him, in Mohawk, "You're a stranger. Are you French?"

Radisson thought he was safe in his Iroquois clothes and his paint and grease. So he lied, telling the soldier that he was, indeed, Mohawk. Maybe his accent gave him away, because the soldier switched to French, and demanded to know how Radisson had fallen into the hands of the Iroquois. Radisson was amazed. He'd thought the soldier was Dutch, and quickly answered in his own language. The soldier was ecstatic, so much so that Radisson thought the man was losing his mind. The Dutch traders crowded around him. Radisson wrote that he was blushing as they thrusted bottles of beer and wine at him. They offered to hide Radisson, but the teenager said no. Some of the women in the little fort dragged him into their homes, giving him tobacco, bread, meat, and wine. The Iroquois followed him "in a great squadron through the streets" and the Dutch people looked at him "as if I had been a monster," until he came to the governor's residence, where he met Johanis Dyjckman. The governor and Radisson talked in French for a few hours. Dyjckman wanted to hear all about Radisson's life among the Iroquois and admired the young man's ability to adapt and survive. He offered to ransom Radisson from the Iroquois, but Radisson turned him down.

After so many months living as an Iroquois, Radisson suddenly found himself torn once again between his adoptive parents and his family back in

Trois-Rivières, between his Iroquois persona, with all its status and privilege, and the life of a French peasant boy who had almost no chance of rising above his low social station. Radisson adored his new family, admitting, "For then I began to love my new parents that were so good & so favorable to me." They certainly seem to have cared more for him than his father and stepmother, who had shipped him off to the Canadian wilderness. Possibly he thought the Dutch couldn't afford to pay enough to bribe his wealthy parents, or that his mother would never let him go at any price. He also may have realized that the offer itself would be a sign to his family that he should be kept away from Fort Orange, although Radisson said later that he didn't accept the offer because he didn't want to be beholden to the Dutch.

But there may also have been a more practical reason for Radisson's refusal. The Dutch in the Hudson Valley did not trade with the French in New France. Whatever the state of peace and war between the two nations, the monopolies and charters granted by the governments of the trading companies that owned New Netherlands and New France prevented legal trade with anyone but licensed merchants in the home country. Nor were people allowed to just visit, though some bootleg traders likely did break the law. Even if he was able to make the relatively short trip back home, he would be going through Iroquois lands to the still-besieged New France. To get back to Trois-Rivières, Radisson would have to be protected by the Dutch as he travelled down the Hudson to Manhattan. Then, penniless,

Manhattan (New Amsterdam) in the early 1660s, at about the same time Radisson was a refugee in the village.

he would need to make the two- or three-month trip across the ocean to Holland, before getting back to France (if there were no war between the two countries, and he could get a passport, that is). But, of course, no one in France wanted him and, as a seventeen-year-old with no land and no skills, he had no way to support himself except through work as a day labourer. Radisson decided, if he wanted to return to Trois-Rivières, he would have to wait until he had the chance to make a break for New France directly from the Mohawk country.

The French-speaking soldier tried to talk Radisson into staying, and tears came to the eyes of both men as the soldier told him he was in the "company of wolves." Then he said something that ate away at Radisson for weeks. Someday, he said, the French might send troops against the Iroquois, leaving Radisson exposed to anger from his adoptive family and a charge of treason from the French, and all the ghastly punishments that came with it.[53] The threat of the Iroquois turning on Radisson was lame and Radisson knew it, but the idea of vengeance from his own people seemed very real. (Thirteen years later, an expedition under Alexandre de Prouville de Tracy did, temporarily, crush the Mohawks and lay waste to their farms and towns.) Radisson had already promised his Iroquois relatives that he would be willing to wage war against his own people, but now he was starting to understand the real implications of fighting the French.

For now, Radisson chose his Mohawk family, and he and his friends, loaded down with the things they bought from the Dutch, made the two-day walk home. Back at their town, the Mohawks seemed satisfied with the trading mission, the last of the year. They were expecting to "pass that winter with our wives"[54] and "eat with them our sagamité in peace." Radisson's plan was to wait for his adoptive father to return home from his own raid on Quebec and see what the future might hold.

Still, something profound happened to Radisson that day in Fort Orange, and it's surprising his Mohawk family didn't notice the change. Radisson had been reborn through torture when he was re-captured in the summer of 1652. He had lived for more than two years as a member of a real family, with parents guiding his growth into adulthood, doting sisters, a brother with whom he had bonded as a comrade in war, and a community that lavished greater and greater wealth and status upon him. He was proud to be a Mohawk. His people were conquering an area the size of France, unlike the French settlers, who huddled in a few precarious communities alongside broken, defeated Huron and Algonquin refugees.

But the visit to Fort Orange had left Radisson feeling European again, or at least European enough that he was again agonizing over whether to escape. Radisson believed he had found his destiny, "to discover many wild nations." He now realized he was a sort of hybrid, a Frenchman with a set of language and wilderness skills that might be very valuable to the French side of the fur trade, if sold to the right people.

"I remitted myself to the fortune and adventure of time, as a thing ordained by God for his great glory," Radisson rather pompously wrote years later. It was his first mention of God, and it seems an utterly insincere reference, since Radisson never once credits God with saving him from his many close calls. Nor did he show anything but contempt for the captive Christian Huron women who were at the bottom of the Mohawk social order, and who were only fit to be "slaves," lugging his baggage and war loot. He never, as a fellow Christian, did anything to help them or to convert anyone.

For two weeks, Radisson mulled his options, finally deciding to defect to the Dutch. He worried that the fuss that had been made over him at Fort Orange might have caused the Mohawks to mistrust him and question his loyalty, so Radisson decided to make his disappearance look like an accident. In a remarkable moment of self-awareness, he thought the Mohawks believed him to be so vain (and, perhaps, greedy) that he would never leave them without his fine clothes and wampum collars, so he went out of the town with nothing but his hunting gear.

Radisson covered his tracks by asking his brother if he wanted to come along on the hunt. The brother was busy courting a blonde Mohawk who was the daughter of a Dutch settler, and who belonged to one of the Mohawks' best families, so he took a pass.[55] Radisson left his longhouse on the morning of October 28, 1653, carrying just a hatchet and a few other weapons, and headed east toward the Dutch colony, staying away from the main trails as he travelled. To any Iroquois who came looking for him, it would appear that Radisson had become lost in the woods. Then he ran for the Dutch settlements as fast as he could.[56]

By the second morning, Radisson was exhausted and very hungry. The weather was fair, and the sunshine (along with fear of capture and death) gave Radisson a second wind. He ran until about four in the afternoon, when he came across a farm at the edge of the Dutch settlement. Radisson crept around the edge of the clearing until he saw a man cutting wood. Going nearer, he called to the farmer. The man nervously approached, believing Radisson to be a Mohawk warrior. Radisson did nothing to dissuade the man, and offered to trade beaver pelts in the farmer's home, if there were no other Iroquois there.[57] The farmer led Radisson to his cabin, sat him down at the table and laid out some food. Radisson claimed to be an Iroquois who had learned some French after living in Quebec. Saying he had something important to convey to the governor, he asked for a pen, some ink, and some paper. The farmer was amazed to see this young Mohawk, covered in body paint, sitting at his table writing a letter. The man promised to deliver it to the fort, which was two miles away, and pledged not to tell anyone he met along the way about the strange visitor in his home.

The man left Radisson alone with his wife, who seemed to like him a little too much. The farmer's wife asked Radisson if Mohawk women liked sex as much as Dutch women, and offered to let him decide. Radisson was tempted, but he was too overwhelmed with fear of the Iroquois to take the woman up on her offer. That night, he and the friendly farmer's wife heard Iroquois men singing nearby, which likely put a damper on any second thoughts Radisson might have had. So instead of hauling Radisson into her bed, the farmer's wife hid him behind sacks of corn. He stayed in that cramped space for an hour until four Dutch men and the French soldier arrived, carrying a suit of clothes.

They scrubbed away the superficial signs of Radisson's Iroquois identity, the body paint, and the hair grease.[58] Radisson left the farm when night fell, sad that he had nothing to give the Dutch couple for their courage and hospitality. At Fort Orange, Radisson went straight to the governor's house, where he spent the night after talking with Dyjckman for a few hours. The next day, the governor gave Radisson another suit of clothes and introduced him to Joseph Noncet, a Jesuit priest who had also recently escaped the Iroquois. Noncet, who seems to have quickly bonded with Radisson, collected enough money from the merchants of Fort Orange to send Radisson to France, via Amsterdam.

Iroquois warriors searched the fort as the Dutch and French in Fort Orange readied Radisson for his escape from the upper Hudson Valley. On the second day, Radisson's mother and sisters walked through the Dutch settlement crying loudly, calling out for Radisson by his Mohawk name and begging people to help find him.

On the third day after his defection, Radisson was spirited out of the fort and put on a boat. After a couple of days on the Hudson, he was in Manhattan, which he called "a town fair enough for a new country." Less generous writers have described it as a miserable little company town whose "inhabitants were considered less citizens than employees, [with] no real legal system."[59] Lower Manhattan's reputation hasn't changed much. In the 1650s, it was considered a bad place where the locals drank too much and were obsessed with easy money. Still, for a teenager just out of the upstate bush, the sights, sounds, booze, and sensual delights of Manhattan must have been fantastic. He stayed in the little Dutch settlement for three weeks, eating the finest local Dutch cuisine, absorbing more of their language, and living within the wall built across the southern part of the island by Peter Stuyvesant.

Radisson walked through the town, re-familiarizing himself with life in a European community. Fort Manhattan was in the southwest corner, inland from Battery Park and away from the marshes along the East River. Dense rows of houses filled some of the space between the fort and the wall. The Dutch had made themselves feel at home by digging a canal along what's now Broad and Beaver streets, between the wall and the sea. Bridge Street was named for one of the crossings over that canal. The lower part of Manhattan Island was much narrower in 1653 than it is today. The southern part of the island was roughly triangular. Below the rolling, rocky landscape of what's now Central Park, the island narrowed sharply, and the higher ground gave way to swamp, especially on the Lower East Side. Most of the land west of Trinity Place and east of Church Street was under seawater. Radisson wandered around all of it, talking to people, going into the shops, killing time until he could catch a boat to Europe.

Radisson arrived in Amsterdam on January 4, 1654. He didn't stay in the cultured milieu of Rembrandt's Amsterdam for long, however, and he couldn't afford to be a tourist. He quickly became sick of Holland's cold, damp weather, which followed him as he sailed to France. Somehow, through all of this, he was able to pay for his food and passage. Perhaps, thanks to Fr. Noncet's intervention, Radisson was travelling on Jesuit guilders and francs as he made his way in a great circle back toward New France. The Jesuits were an international corporation with the means to pay for all his travel and the clout to get the teenager across borders. In the spring, Radisson arrived at La Rochelle, the main port for commerce with New France, where he found a transport that would carry him back to the colony. The trip would keep him cooped up on a small, crowded sailing ship for three or four months.

Meanwhile, only a month after Radisson defected to the Dutch, the Iroquois and the French made peace.

Book Two:
Back to the Iroquois (1654–1658)

In the summer of 1653, the Mohawk war chief Canaqueese, whose father was Dutch, arrived very unexpectedly at Quebec, dressed head-to-toe in wampum-covered clothes and adorned with belts of the precious beads. Canaqueese, whom the French called "The Flemish Bastard," was no friend of theirs. But, as the Mohawk and Dutch go-between, he succumbed to European geopolitics and pressure from his trading partners at Fort Orange. Being at war with Cromwell's England and needing as many friends as they could find, anywhere they could find them, the Dutch wanted peace with the French, both in Europe and North America. At the same time, the four western members of the Iroquois League wanted peace, at least temporarily, so they could crush the Erie nation. Canaqueese despised the idea of peace with the French, who were so badly beaten that they seriously considered abandoning Quebec, but he bent to the pressures placed on him, at least temporarily.

The Iroquois dictated tough peace terms. The treaty was with the French, not their Algonquin allies. To make peace, the French had to abandon the Indigenous people who had been their comrades-in-arms for more than forty years. The Jesuits were fine with this, knowing peace would give them the chance to reconnect with hundreds of Huron Christian captives who had been assimilating into Iroquois society. They also thought peace might allow them to establish an Iroquois mission like Ste.-Marie among the Hurons, their town on Georgian Bay, and become power brokers, as they had in the Huron country. Meanwhile, the French traders—and Quebec was a company colony—saw peace at any price as their only hope of staying in business, even if they had to stand by and watch the Iroquois hijack some of the Algonquin fur brigades. It was a gross betrayal, but it was simply business.

In May 1654, Radisson was on a small fishing boat headed out of La Rochelle. He arrived in the Gulf of St. Lawrence that summer, after months cooped up and tossed around the Atlantic. Radisson made landfall at Percé Rock, with its two gigantic holes weathered through four-hundred-million-year-old Devonian-period limestone.[60] He left the fishermen behind and found some Indigenous people to take him upstream to Quebec. A rare northeast wind helped the party make it there in just five days, despite the river currents and tides being against them.

Radisson finally closed the circle with his arrival at Trois-Rivières. To his relatives, he must have appeared to have risen from the dead. He had certainly been luckier than his brother-in-law, who had been killed by the Iroquois a few months after Radisson was taken. His half-sister, Marguérite, was now a widow in a colony on the verge of collapse, with no family to support her and nothing to live on but the proceeds from her small store and her tiny farm. She was, most likely, supporting Radisson's two full-blood sisters, too.

Marguérite solved her financial problems by marrying Médard Chouart des Groseilliers,[61] whom Radisson probably knew from his earliest months in Trois-Rivières. Born Médard Chouart—he named himself Sieur des Groseilliers (Lord of Gooseberries) after his family's small gooseberry farm in Picardy—he would later take on a much larger role in Radisson's life. Marguérite already had three children and would bear Groseilliers five more before he abandoned her (and Canada) to try to make his fortune in England. Groseilliers initially seemed like a good catch, since he had a farm across from the village on the St. Maurice River. He had also social-climbed his way into the merchant class, making deals with Montreal traders for stock to use in the fur trade.[62]

Groseilliers was nearly forty years old when he met Radisson, who was still in his late teens or, at most, his early twenties. Born in the Champagne region of France, Groseilliers arrived in Canada in about 1641, when he was twenty-five years old. Groseilliers—who would always have a strange relationship with the Jesuits—was hired as a labourer by the priests and travelled with them up the Ottawa River-Lake Nipissing-French River canoe route to Georgian Bay and the Huron country. He was one of the people who helped build the fortified mission of Ste.-Marie among the Hurons, near what's now Midland, Ontario. The large stone mission house, and the fort around it, was hundreds of miles from the nearest French settlement and was a self-sufficient headquarters to which Jesuit priests withdrew after months of living in Huron villages. At Ste.-Marie, they could live as Europeans on a sort of French manor farm, with people like Groseilliers doing the heavy work. By 1647, Groseilliers was back in Quebec City, where he married for the first time. His wife, who would die at the end of the decade, bore him a son, whom he named Médard. By the early 1650s, he was looking for a wife among the women of New France, but there weren't many single women in the colony. Radisson's widowed half-sister, with her small business and her farm, was a good catch, despite the large number of dependants who came with her to the marriage. By 1654, Groseilliers and Marguérite had had their first child, Jean-Baptiste. Médard accused Marguérite's two sons by her first husband of being juvenile delinquents and unloaded them on foster families. Gossip spread through the colony that the charges against the boys were trumped up, Groseilliers' way of abandoning the children. This thuggish behaviour seemed in character for Groseilliers, who had recently settled an argument with another trader by beating the man with the blunt end of his sword.

The Jesuits had come to hate the old trader since Groseilliers' days in Huronia. Paul Ragueneau, head of the Huron mission, even wrote to Louis XIV's chief minister Jean-Baptiste Colbert in 1664 to warn him of "a man named Des Groseilliers, a fugitive from Quebec, who abandoned his wife and children there and is now with the English in New England... [He is] capable of anything, audacious, tireless and headstrong in his enterprises, who has travelled the country and been everywhere among the Huron and Ottawa, and has shown some animosity toward the French."[63] Ragueneau, a man with powerful connections at the very highest levels of the French nobility, would shadow Groseilliers for two decades. He was convinced Groseilliers had whipped up the Iroquois in 1664 to try to destroy New France, and that he enjoyed eating human flesh, both of which may well have been true.[64]

The nun Marie de l'Incarnation, who knew Groseilliers well, described him in 1665 as having "a spirit of contradiction and bad humour." She blamed him for the English capture of the Dutch colony in present-day New York State and northern New Jersey, writing that he gave such glowing reports of the place to his friends in Boston that the English became determined to take it, and that he then gave the English advice on how to do so.[65] At the time, the French were making serious overtures to buy the Dutch colony, which opens up some very intriguing historical "what ifs."

Groseilliers was stubborn, greedy, ruthless, sneaky, and treacherous. He had no known loyalties. He also had no social skills or political instincts. Unlike Radisson, he didn't seem to care much about the Indigenous people or what they thought of him. Radisson, knowing the Indigenous people of the Great Lakes thought beards were disgusting, made sure he had no facial hair. (He may have shaved or, like Iroquoian men, plucked out hairs as they grew.) Groseilliers, by contrast, travelled the wilderness with a full beard, which, at least once, put both traders under suspicion. He was also capable of spectacular lapses of judgment and outright, outrageous treason, so it was easy for his critics and enemies to believe all the gossip that dogged him everywhere he went. In England, it would be Groseilliers, not Radisson, who would be the focus of foreign spies who tried to turn him, and who was the centre of spectacular fantasies by enemies who believed he wanted to create a Colonel Kurtz-style personal empire in the American wilderness. In the end, at the height of English anti-Catholic paranoia, it would be Groseilliers who showed up at the court of Charles II with a French Jesuit, a move that cast a long shadow over Radisson.

When Radisson arrived back in New France in 1654, Groseilliers was preparing for an expedition to the west in a final attempt to get rich and, almost as an afterthought, to get the French fur trade running again after the disaster in Huronia. Just as Radisson was reuniting with his sister, Groseilliers left with what the Jesuits describe as "a young man." Radisson later told the Royal Society and two kings of England that he was Groseilliers' companion on this trip, but the historical record, along with Radisson's own vague and inaccurate accounts of the voyage,[66] suggest otherwise. Radisson may have written his way into Groseilliers' story to impress his English patrons, who loved adventure tales. It's more likely Radisson stayed around Quebec and Trois-Rivières for three years, working off his debt to the Jesuits. He left few footprints from this time in his life, just a single signed legal document in Quebec City dated 1655.

These are Radisson's "lost years." Despite his claim to have travelled to Lake Michigan and into the Mississippi Valley with Groseilliers in 1654, we have no idea where he really went and what he did. He was likely one of the handful of men hired to protect Jesuits Gabriel Druillettes and Léonard Garreau when they tried to use the Ottawa River canoe route to get to the upper Great Lakes and establish a mission among the Odawa. The Iroquois ambushed the canoe brigade at Lake of Two Mountains, just upstream from the junction of the Ottawa and St. Lawrence Rivers. Garreau was killed and Druillettes fled back to Quebec City, while the Odawa, who were supposed to be guiding the priests and laymen, manoeuvred around the Iroquois and went west, up the Ottawa. If Radisson did go with them to the settlement of Michilimackinac, at the junction of Lake Michigan and Lake Huron, he would have learned a great deal about the geography of central North America—knowledge that would be useful to him later; but we can't be sure he got this far.

There may be other reasons why Radisson deliberately cast a layer of fog over these years. In his many writings, he's open about murder, cannibalism, treason, and quite a few other details, except sex, considered off-limits to writers of his day. There may have been some method in this. Radisson did most of his writing about his adventures while cooling his heels in London in the late 1660s, when he was also on the prowl for an advantageous marriage. He may also have been trying to keep a secret: his own bigamy. Radisson did write about a plan to spend the winter of 1653–1654 in the Mohawk country with his "wives." In the later 1650s, when he was in the west, he was constantly trying to work himself into the extended families and clans of the Algonquins, Cree, and Sioux of the Upper Lakes.[67] We know he managed to have himself adopted again, this time into an Algonquin family. Marriage was an easy way to ingratiate himself with his Indigenous trading partners, and the Indigenous people expected those marriages. People claiming to be Radisson's descendants lived in the Michilimackinac region of what's now Michigan until after the War of 1812, when most of them immigrated to Canada. At least one large, prominent family of Great Lakes mixed-race people, the Longlades, claim to be Radisson's descendants.[68]

But whatever he did in the "lost years," Radisson did not go west to the Great Plains with his brother-in-law. This "voyage," and his claim to have personally visited the Mississippi River and Hudson Bay, are the most problematic aspects of Radisson's writings. They are sometimes used to discredit all his narratives. At the very least, Radisson has left some confusion, with a few writers believing he made all of those trips but was sloppy with dates and others (like me) believing he stole the story of the "unnamed traveller" who went with Groseilliers in 1654 and added some details from his own later trip to give some colour to his account. In 1654, Groseilliers was leaving for Lake Superior at the same time that Radisson was returning to Trois-Rivières from France, and the documentary record—Radisson's distinctive signature on a deed in Quebec in November 1655—makes it clear he was in the St. Lawrence Valley at a time he claimed to be almost a thousand miles away in the Upper Lakes region. Radisson claims, likely with considerable truth, that he "stayed not long in a place."

Radisson probably spent most of the "lost years" helping his family, gathering information from Indigenous and French traders by escorting missionaries up the Ottawa River, and doing some fur trapping. An account of one of Radisson's expeditions includes a graphic description of an ambush at the Long Sault in which Radisson and a few Indigenous friends managed to surprise some Iroquois and take prisoners whom they then killed and ate.[69] The trouble on the Ottawa River strained the shaky peace between the French and the Iroquois, but, for the most part, the truce held. Both sides could always blame the Algonquins, who were not party to the deal, for any problems.

Meanwhile, Groseilliers' 1654–1656 trip to the upper Great Lakes would give new hope to New France. Not only did he and his companion (whoever he was) make new trading partners among the Ojibwe, Odawa, and the Huron-Petun (Wendat or Wyandot) refugees living along the northwest coast of Lake Michigan and the southern shore of Lake Superior, they also became familiar with the geography of southern Lake Michigan and met people who not only knew of the Mississippi River, but had travelled to the Gulf of Mexico and had seen Spanish ships. This opened the way for French claims to the Mississippi and for settlements like St. Louis, and New Orleans. (Many early and mid-twentieth-century writers claimed Groseilliers, or more likely his partner, crossed the height of land into the Mississippi Valley. On this trip, though, it's doubtful, since Radisson says the Sioux, who lived there, had never met a European until 1658.) Groseilliers and his partner made one very important connection on their trip, however: with the woodland Cree, who lived in the vast forest between Lake Superior and the beaver-rich Hudson Bay lowlands. For all his personal faults, Groseilliers' bold expeditions gave him information that he used to synthesize French knowledge of the geography between the eastern edge of the Great Plains and the Atlantic, and between the Ohio Valley and Hudson Bay.

Groseilliers knew he should be careful with this information. The Jesuits, who often acted as much as scientists and geographers as priests, were piecing together the canoe routes to the north and west. Groseilliers— and, later, Radisson—knew these routes were valuable intellectual property. So did the Indigenous people, who realized, like any smart entrepreneur, that there were many competitors, Indigenous and European, who would love to steal their businesses. But it was the fifty fur-filled canoes paddled by Algonquins and Petun that returned with Groseilliers that really caught the attention of the people of New France. After almost a decade of being on the losing side of a war that had made the western canoe routes too dangerous for anyone to use, the trading company that owned the colony had considered walking away from the operation. Now, the colony was financially secure, at least for a few years.

Groseilliers' trip happened at a time when terms of peace with the Iroquois were still being cobbled together. For the first time since Champlain had started the war with the Five Nations in 1609[70], the French and Iroquois leaderships seemed to be forging some real diplomatic relations, though neither side trusted the other. Missionaries, believing God was at work, were more optimistic. Having abandoned their fortified mission at Ste.-Marie among the Hurons just six years before, the Jesuits finally received permission from the Iroquois Confederacy council for a new mission in the Iroquois country. Being Jesuits, they decided to make their headquarters at the political capital of the Confederacy, at the main village of the Onondaga.

To make this new deal with the Onondaga, the French were willing to throw away the Huron, who had settled as refugees at Quebec in 1650. That the government of France had done nothing to help the Huron should come as no surprise, given that European governments did almost nothing to help their own people in hard times. The Jesuits—who were constantly short of money despite their aggressive fundraising among the rich women of Paris—picked up the cost of feeding and looking after the Huron when they were sick. This endeavour was financially crippling, and took much of the money and manpower that could have gone into more viable missions. (The Jesuits recouped some of their costs by trading food for any furs the Huron wore or could trap.) The French could justify the betrayal of the Huron because there were so many Christian Huron living as adoptees and captives among the Iroquois. In a game whose score was the number of souls "saved," the future lay with the Iroquois, not with a small band of Huron refugees. To the Jesuits, the Huron, even the Christian ones in Quebec, were people of the past, and the Jesuits were willing to betray them for the greater glory of God.

If the Jesuits got everything they wanted—trade, the chance to convert the Onondagas, a solid, permanent toehold in the Five Nations—then the Iroquois would become spiritually and economically dependant. They might even hand their country over to the Jesuits, the way the Huron had in their darkest hour in 1649. The Jesuits had used the same strategy in

China and Paraguay. In China's Imperial court, the Jesuits were scientists and political advisors to the emperor. In Paraguay, they had created *reducciones*, where Indigenous people lived clustered around Jesuit missions. These people were converted to Christianity and put to work as peasants by the missionaries, who lived as their feudal masters for more than a century.[71] The Huron mission, which had come so close to creating a Jesuit-run state along the lines of the *reducciones*, had been a false start. The Jesuits were desperate to try again.

Huron leaders in the settlement near Quebec weren't fooled about the nature of the peace and their miserable place in it. Aaoueate, a Huron war chief, scoffed at the Onondaga leaders' claims to have "dropped the war song." Aaoueate told them:

> You are faithless rogues, your hearts are full of venom, and your minds of knavishness; if you talk of peace, it is only to employ a treachery more baleful for both us and the French. I know your wiles only too well. Content yourselves with the eating of the heads of the Huron, but know that you do not hold the other members. My people still have feet and hands, legs and arms... burn me... do not spare your tortures—all the more I am a dead man. My body has already become insensible, and neither your fires nor your cruelties will shock my courage. I would rather die today than be indebted to you for a life you give me only with the intention of depriving me of it by some treachery.[72]

MASSACRE ON THE ST. LAWRENCE

Once the peace treaty was made between the French and the Iroquois, the Jesuits and the civil administration of New France stood by and watched the Five Nations pick away at the Huron refugees who'd settled on Île d'Orléans within sight of Quebec City. The Onondaga were the most aggressive. They made secret missions to the island to pressure the Huron headmen into moving their people to the Onondaga country. At the same time, the Iroquois, especially the Onondaga and the Mohawk, tantalized the Jesuits with invitations to build missions all over their countries. Once the Confederacy Council gave permission for a fortified Jesuit mission, the Huron were expendable, and everyone knew it. On May 18, 1655, Mohawk warriors landed on Île d'Orléans, hid between the Jesuit mission church and the small fort that guarded the settlement, and waited for the Huron to finish Mass. The French stood by while seventy people, most of them women, were killed or taken prisoner. One was Jacques Oachonk, who the Jesuits claimed was the most fervent Christian among the Huron refugees. The Mohawks herded the prisoners into forty canoes and paddled in front of Quebec's Lower Town, forcing the Huron to sing their death song loud enough for the settlers on shore to hear it. At Trois-Rivières, the Mohawks camped at the town's riverfront. They let Jesuits console their prisoners, but the priests did nothing to save them.

The cynical behaviour of the priests and the colony's administrators scandalized the farmers and traders of New France. The Huron knew they couldn't stay on the Île d'Orléans, but the colony's governor would not give them a place to farm on the mainland. It was obvious to everyone that the Huron had been sold out. One nation of Huron, the Attignawattans, who had lived along Nottawasaga Bay on southern Georgian Bay, decided to join the Mohawks. Their former neighbours in Huronia, the Arendarhonon, went to the Onondaga. Some French settlers, disgusted by the cruelty of their own leaders, collected money to set up farms on the north shore of the St. Lawrence for the few Huron who survived as an independent group.

At the same time, the nations of the Iroquois League were fighting among themselves for dominance over the humbled French and their allies and for any new trade that might come from these negotiations; if, by some fluke, the peace lasted, that is. In July 1654, a Mohawk chief brought two French prisoners back to Quebec and bitterly complained that the French, rather than the Onondaga, should have negotiated the peace deal with the Mohawks. The Mohawks being guardians of the eastern door of the Five Nations Confederacy, the Mohawk leader asked the French, "ought not one to enter a house by the door, and not by the chimney or the roof of the cabin, unless he be a thief, and wish to take the inmates by surprise? We, the Five Iroquois Nations, compose but just one cabin, we maintain but just one fire, and we have, from time immemorial, dwelt under one roof… Well, then, will you not enter that cabin by the door, which is at the ground floor of the house?"[73] It was clear the Five Nations were not as united as they had seemed.

In 1657, with the new Onondaga mission of Ste.-Marie de Gannentaha already built, a French contingent was organizing a trip to the Jesuit outpost. Two Jesuits, Paul Ragueneau and François Duperon, both veterans of the Huron mission disaster, and a group of French soldiers and lay workers, including Radisson, were to join the new project just outside the Onondaga's main town near modern Syracuse, New York.

It was a strange decision for Radisson, who had fled the Mohawks just a few years before. They were unlikely to risk breaking the peace by capturing and harming him, but there was a strong likelihood of a confrontation between the young Frenchman and his adoptive family. Maybe he wanted to go back, on his own terms, and as a Frenchman. Perhaps he missed them. Or possibly he was still conflicted about who he was. His writings reflect this shifting identity: he writes as a Mohawk on the Ohio Valley raid, his descriptions of places, events, and comrades being the words of a dedicated, active participant. "They" becomes "we." By the time Radisson returns—and this is just a couple of years after the Ohio raid—the Iroquois are "they" again, but just barely. "Friends, I must confess I loved those poor people entirely well," he wrote years later.

So, for whatever reason, Radisson offered his services to the Jesuits, and they accepted. The Iroquois sent word they would go to Montreal to meet the Jesuits, their employees, and some Huron who were planning to settle in the Iroquois country.

The Onondaga had a special hatred for the Huron. After the Huron Confederacy collapsed and Christian Huron had settled with the French on Gahoendoe,[74] the French quickly built a stone fort, complete with a small cannon, and had tried to establish a Jesuit-run community. After a disastrous winter of famine, the Jesuits and most Hurons left for Quebec in early spring, while the leaders of the few hundred Huron who stayed behind pretended to negotiate with the Onondaga. Invited by the Huron, a delegation of Onondaga chiefs came to the fort in the summer of 1650 to arrange for the refugees to join them. Instead, the Huron murdered the Onondaga leaders, then fled to Quebec. It's likely some of the people involved were among the Huron who'd settled on Île d'Orléans just seven years before. The Onondaga hadn't forgotten.

The peace with the French and the Huron was an illusion. Huron refugees living among the Erie had incited them to raid the Seneca. Though at first the Eries' chances of winning looked good, the Five Nations being on the verge of coming apart due to infighting among members, the decision was ultimately a disastrous and fatal one. The Erie were a strong people, and the Iroquois Confederacy needed all its men for the war on its western flank. Strategically, the Iroquois had no choice but to trim its enemies list, at least temporarily, and it needed to block the French from selling guns to the Erie.[75] At the same time, the Onondaga worried about the growing strength of the Mohawks who, according to Iroquois law, were masters of the trade route to the Dutch, and decided who among the other Five Nations got to trade for guns and other metal items. The Mohawks treated the Onondaga traders badly whenever the latter were caught trying to sneak through their territory to deal directly with the Dutch.

As brokers of this new peace, the Onondaga became masters of the trade route with the French. Now, they hoped, French guns would start flowing into their country. Almost as important, the French had the fine tools and expertise to fix broken guns. Since most of the guns sold by the English, French, and Dutch were almost certainly old war-surplus weapons, gun repair was becoming as important as gun sales. The most optimistic of the Onondaga hoped they could craft a real, lasting military and political relationship. They also hoped the French would build and garrison a fort like Ste.-Marie among the Hurons, which many recalled was strong enough to stop invaders in their tracks during their Georgian Bay campaigns five years previously.[76] The fort had been too strong for the Iroquois to attack, and had thus blocked them from raiding into the densely populated northwestern part of Huronia. A similar fort might one day protect the Onondaga.

Despite protests in New France that the expensive new mission left the colony stripped of soldiers and men at a time when the St. Lawrence fur-trade project was on the verge of financial collapse, the French leaders had little choice but to give in to the Onondaga's peace overtures. The wars had cut off trade through the Ottawa Valley-St. Lawrence canoe route. The Iroquois seemed to be winning everywhere.

For two weeks early in the summer of 1657, the French and Huron waited at Montreal for an Iroquois delegation to arrive and escort them up the St. Lawrence and across Lake Ontario to the Genesee Valley. The Huron leaders who supported surrender made speeches, saying it was better to die in the Iroquois country among so many of their own people, who had already joined the Five Nations, than it was to live on the sufferance of strangers in Quebec or to be murdered in their own country.[77]

The Iroquois arrived at Montreal in an ugly state of mind. Some of their men had recklessly decided to run the Lachine Rapids, and seven had drowned when one of their canoes broke up on the rocks. Now they wanted revenge for the loss of their friends and for other past wrongs. The Iroquois would not attack the French passengers, who already had a strong fort in their country; instead, they would take out their rage on the Huron, reminding themselves of treacheries and slights by an age-old enemy that was reduced to just a band of refugees.

At the French settlement of Ville-Marie, the little fort at Montreal, the Iroquois leaders spoke of their heartfelt friendship with both the French and the Huron. All sides gave presents, with the Huron adding several more to console the Iroquois for the loss of their companions. For the next eight days, the Huron, French, and Iroquois bought or made canoes and small boats that were light enough to carry around the rapids on the St. Lawrence. When they left Montreal, there were some eighty Iroquois, one hundred Huron women, about a dozen Huron men, and twenty French, including two Jesuits, and Radisson. After the first day, about thirty of the Iroquois left the flotilla and went inland to raid the Algonquins. On the second day out, the Iroquois claimed the canoes were dangerously over-loaded for the trip across the Lake of Two Mountains and Lake St. Louis, at the upstream end of the Island of Montreal, demanded the Jesuits and the rest of the French reduce their baggage. The priests complied, leaving about seven French men on shore to guard the French property and hunt up more boats to ferry the supplies upriver. Instead of doing that work, however, the soldiers just walked back to Montreal and stayed there.

Each group—Iroquois, French, Huron—in the rest of the party crossed Lake St. Louis, then portaged the rapids above it using their own separate canoes.[78] Radisson rightly describes the region as "a delightful and beautiful country." They could see deer and moose on shore, plenty of ducks and geese, and the river's water was so clean they could watch the fish swimming below their canoes. As they paddled, they trolled for fish and speared them in the shallows. If the weather wasn't too humid, they could see the Adirondack Mountains breaking up the horizon to the south and the west. From the St. Lawrence, the mountains look like big, rolling grey hills. Radisson was sure these mountains were the source of the water that made the St. Lawrence's rapids roar so frighteningly.[79]

The late summer warmth hung over the river in a blue-grey haze. It made the shoreline appear ghostly and the islands look like scenes in a watercolour painting. Idyllic as this country was, the Huron felt anxious: they suspected the Iroquois, who were constantly whispering among themselves, were about to turn on them. Sure that something was up, two Huron men and three women cut out from the rest of the pack of canoes, sang a goodbye song, and headed downstream, back toward Montreal. The Iroquois did nothing to stop them. Instead, they pushed upstream until they reached the archipelago of small islands below what's now called Cornwall Island, and made camp on one of them, possibly Thompson or Stanley Island at the southwest end of Lake St. Francis.[80] Before setting out that morning for the day's paddling, the Iroquois split up the French in the Iroquois canoes. Radisson found himself in a boat with three Iroquois and one Huron man. When they came in sight of the island where they were supposed to make camp, one of the Iroquois loaded his gun. Both Radisson and the Huron noticed, but neither suspected what was to happen next.

As the canoes got close to the shore, one Iroquois swung at the Huron with a hatchet. At the same time, the man with the gun fired point-blank, putting a bullet in the Huron's head. The Huron fell, spurting blood and brains, at Radisson's heels. "My feet soon swam in the miserable Huron's blood," Radisson wrote years later. The man quivered as the Iroquois finished him off with knives. At the same time, the Iroquois told Radisson, in their language, to have courage, "for they would not hurt me; but as for him that was killed, he was a dog, good for nothing." The Huron in the other canoes panicked as they watched the Huron's corpse tumble from Radisson's canoe. The rest of the Huron landed on the island, where one of the Iroquois leaders reassured them they were safe. The women huddled together while eight of the Huron men reached for their weapons. None of the Iroquois stopped them. In fact, one Iroquois war chief, speaking on their behalf, menaced those among his warriors who tried to hurt the Huron.

The Huron seemed to believe the war chief. So did Radisson and the French, and they all went inland to some high ground to begin setting up camp. As they worked, a large group of warriors painted for battle sprang from the woods and began killing the Huron. While the men were being massacred, the Onondaga leader sat by the leader of the Huron, a famous war chief, and promised he would "not be killed by dogs." Unwilling to sit and watch his people being slaughtered around him, the old Huron war chief took out his hatchet and struck down an Iroquois. A moment later, the Huron leader was dead, along with the rest of his warriors. Only Jalaka, an old Huron man who had spared the lives of captured Iroquois during the previous decade's war, was allowed to live. The Jesuits blamed this man, a former Christian, for much of the trouble that was to follow.[81]

The Onondaga brought the Huron women together as the men's corpses were tossed into the St. Lawrence. The women stood silently for two hours, until late in the afternoon, when the Iroquois took Fr. Ragueneau to their camp and explained the slaughter was revenge for the men who had drowned at Lachine.[82] When the priest returned to the French camp, he found Radisson and the rest of the French—except for a boy and a "good looking" lay brother—armed and ready to fight. Instead, Ragueneau took them back to the Iroquois camp, where the warriors promised, again, that the French weren't in danger. The senior Jesuit borrowed some wampum from the Iroquois commander and offered three gifts. Throwing down one string of beads, he said the gift showed his desire for peace and friendship. The second gift was given in exchange for the lives of the Huron women, and for their safe conduct to the Iroquois country. The third was to encourage the Iroquois to help the French and their belongings arrive safely in the land of the Onondaga. The Iroquois promised to do all three, but said they were free to do what they liked with the women, since the French had betrayed them, and they had no protectors. Ragueneau didn't wince at this true accusation. Instead, he simply asked the Onondaga chiefs to make sure the masters of the canoes took bundles of French belongings into their care, rather than just dump them on the shore. Later, out of sight of the Onondaga, the Jesuits would write that the Huron brought the troubles down on themselves by agreeing to join the Iroquois. Since the French were not willing to lift a finger to protect them, it's hard to see how the Huron had any choice.

FEAR IN THE THOUSAND ISLANDS

That night, the Iroquois, French, and the Huron survivors finished making their camps and went to sleep, if sleep was possible. The next morning—the eighth day travelling upriver from Montreal—they headed inland. Radisson was left behind with a handful of Iroquois travelling in two canoes.

As they dragged their big elm canoes alongside the miles of rapids, through the islands near modern Ogdensburg, New York, and Brockville, Ontario, Radisson was stuck with unpleasant company. One was a large man, slightly younger than Radisson, who was nasty, dull, immature, and lazy, while a second canoe that shadowed them through this part of the river carried an Iroquois and his wife, a couple who obviously hated each other and rarely spoke. Radisson tried to break up the monotony by conversing with his canoeing partner in the young man's language, but the Onondaga paddler could not be charmed. When they were among Iroquois, the warriors in the other boats noticed the hostility and entertained themselves by making sure this unhappy team was never broken up. As the flotilla headed from the flat-lands at the upper edge of the St. Lawrence Lowlands toward the Thousand Islands, the hostility turned to passive-aggressive behaviour, then to low-level violence erupting in short fights on shore. The Iroquois stepped in whenever Radisson or his canoe partner reached for a knife or gun, but otherwise sat back and enjoyed the show. "When we were in the boat we could not fight but with our tongues, flying water at one another." This, to the Iroquois, was ridiculous, unmanly, and rather pathetic behaviour.

Despite the lousy company, Radisson enjoyed most of the trip. There were so many deer in the upper St. Lawrence Valley that the travellers could take all the meat they wanted. Still, they kept killing them, "more for sport than for need. We, finding them sometimes in islands, made them go into the water and after we killed about a score, we clipped the ears of the rest and hung a bell to them, and then let them loose. What a sport to see the rest fly from that that had the bell!" They also saw lots of bears travelling together at night, far more than any of the Iroquois had ever seen, or had heard of from their elders.

Then, in the Thousand Islands, just as they were about to leave the big river for Lake Ontario, things started getting even stranger. On the river-side, the travellers came across a clearing. Trees had been cut to make one of the small, temporary forts built by war parties in that part of the world; but one tree, stripped of its bark, had been left standing in the middle of the clearing. There were drawings on it:

> ...painted with a coal, six men hanged, with their heads at their feet, cut off. They were so well drawn, that ... [clearly] one of them was Father [Ragueneau] by the shortness of his hair, which let us know that the French [who] were [travelling] before us were executed. A little further another [picture] was painted of two boats, one of three men, another of two, whereof one was standing with a hatchet in his hands striking on the head. At another were represented seven boats, pursuing three bears, a man drawn as if he were on land with his gun shooting a stag.[83]

In fact, Ragueneau was still alive, but Radisson couldn't be sure of that until he caught up with the Jesuits.

Radisson, who had been very anxious since the island massacre, was ter-rified. He felt alone and vulnerable, full of guilt and regret for not travelling with the main party of Frenchmen. The Iroquois told him he was safe, that even if the rest of the French were killed, Radisson would be spared. Having seen what happened to the Huron men, Radisson was now quite skeptical of his guides' assurances.

The weather was hot and the air so humid that it hung like a wet blanket over the river. The wind was still, and the canoes moved slowly because some of the Onondaga were sick. Then, when things had seemingly settled into a routine, Radisson's canoe partner, the man who sniped at him all day in the boat and often fought him at night, loaded his gun. Radisson picked up his musket, expecting to have a shootout in a bark canoe, but the Iroquois motioned to Radisson to be quiet. Up ahead, in a tree at the shore, Radisson suddenly saw the bald eagle that was the real target, so he "stooped down like a monkey," ready to shoot his antagonist if the young Iroquois was lying. A moment later, the eagle was dead and in the boat.

When Radisson's canoe landed at that night's campsite, Iroquois warriors searched his baggage and took his gun. They asked for his powder and his shot, then opened a bundle of Radisson's belongings and took out his comb and other personal things. Dejected, Radisson sat by the campfire. The woman tending it gave Radisson a strange look, one that made him mistrust the Iroquois even more. A sick Iroquois man called Radisson over and asked him to take off his clothes and get into his canoe. Radisson wanted his gun and made it clear he wouldn't go into the boat without it, so the Iroquois gave it back. The Iroquois man then climbed in, made a few paddle strokes, and ordered Radisson to climb out of the boat, into the river. They argued for some time. Radisson was sure the older man was going to drown him, but calmed down after he realized the canoe was over a sandbar and that the water was just a little over knee-deep. The lake bottom was covered with freshwater mussels, which was what the man wanted. Radisson gathered about a half a bushel of mussels while peering through the darkness to make sure the sick man wasn't paddling away.

Back on shore, Radisson was handed a dish of meat and broth. He ate for a while, but the menace returned when a man came up to Radisson and made him hand over his shirt, leaving him "with nothing but my drawers to cover my nakedness." He then took out a knife and cut the string of a medal that Radisson wore on his throat. "He was a great while searching me and feeling if I was fat… I thought [with] every foot he was [going] to cut my throat. I could not bear it. I had rather die at once than being so tormented."

Radisson moved away from the man and sat near the fire-tending woman, but she, too, became frightening. She put her hands on his head and began combing his hair with her fingers, saying Radisson should be cheerful, that her husband was the man who had taken his shirt and medal and pawed over his body. "He loves me and knows that I love you, and have a mind to have you to our dwelling." Then she got up, took the shirt from her husband, added one of her blankets, and said to Radisson, "Sleep."

Radisson was exhausted. He decided he would rather be brained in his sleep than see the blow coming while he was awake. So he found a sheltered spot and quickly fell asleep, certain he would never wake up.

The psychological games continued the next day. The weather was still hot and muggy, making a day on the water much more appealing than a day on land. The Iroquois gave Radisson all his things back that morning and filled a bag with food, but they also laughed at him for being afraid the night before. A few even said they'd hoped for better entertainment. Later in the day, Radisson's canoe ran into a rock, making a hole big enough to put two fists through. The current yanked the canoe around, and Radisson's unpleasant companion had to jump into the river to save the paddles. Radisson noticed the Iroquois swam using a sort of dog paddle, rather than with an overhand motion. The two men dragged the canoe to shore, where they traded insults while repairing it with bark and pine gum. Sometimes Radisson wasn't sure what the insults meant because he only understood what he called "low Iroquois," or Mohawk, and not the language of the Onondaga. But when Radisson's companion tried to put the blame on the Frenchman and told the other Iroquois Radisson had deliberately tried to wreck the boat, the two canoe-mates started brawling again, punching and cuffing each other until they were too tired to fight anymore.

While Radisson is always the hero of his own stories, this strange pairing suggests the young Frenchman—now about twenty or twenty-one—was something of a novelty to the Iroquois and, perhaps, a bit of a lightweight who wasn't taken seriously by the older warriors on the trip. The Iroquois saw this kind of bickering as effeminate and comical. Savignon, a Huron who travelled to France with Champlain in 1610, was appalled by the sight of men bickering in the streets and ridiculed Parisian men when they argued without killing one another or at least coming to blows. Iroquoian men did not interrupt each other, nor did they engage in public verbal quarrels unless they were willing to take the dispute to a violent conclusion. Arguments in front of other people, therefore, were very rare.[84]

Between the fighting and the boat repair, Radisson was now at least two days behind his companions and nearly a week away from the main flotilla of

Huron women, Iroquois, and Frenchmen. He was alone with his nemesis for three unpleasant nights before finally reaching the main camp, where some of the Iroquois men were cutting up a bear that they had killed. Days later, they were near the upper reaches of the St. Lawrence, watching eagles and ospreys taking fish from the river. Whatever sadness Radisson felt for the murdered Huron men seems to have passed as the canoeists moved from the flatlands of the lower river through the islands of the Canadian Shield. When they reached the large islands near the outlet of Lake Ontario, the landscape changed back to flat limestone plains. Big silver Atlantic salmon were spawning on the gravel banks, so the Iroquois could take as many as they wanted, along with enormous brown-and-yellow sturgeon that lurked in deeper, calmer channels and were easy to kill with spears. Some of these fish were more than six feet long, two hundred years old and, according to Radisson, tasted somewhat like lobster.

The Iroquois camped at a basin shaped "like a half moon" (possibly Big Sandy Bay on Wolfe Island), a place where the water teemed with fish and eels that could be clearly seen in thirty feet of clean water. The travellers came across nine Mohawks living in bark cabins who were on their way back from a raid against the Eries, bringing with them two captive women, a six-year-old child, and a twenty-five-year-old man. Some of these Mohawks knew Radisson and seemed to have no hard feelings over his escape. They gave him a garland of wampum and a girdle made of what Radisson thought was goat's hair, but was probably bison. The Mohawks wondered when he would be coming back to visit.

"I promised to come there as soon as I could arrive at the upper village (of the Onondaga). I gave them my hatchet to give to my father, and two dozen brass rings and two shooting-knives for my sisters, promising to bring a cover for my mother." They wondered why Radisson left and how he got away. Rather than admit that the Dutch traders at Fort Orange had helped him, Radisson claimed to have travelled twelve days back to the French town of Trois-Rivières.

The Mohawks were impressed. They were also reassuring: the warriors said the pictograph on the tree at the St. Lawrence shore was not a threat to murder the French, but a commemoration of a raiding party against the Algonquins. Seven canoes returning from an expedition into the shield country had come across two Huron canoes carrying eight men who were heading downstream to live among the French. The Huron and Iroquois (despite being officially at peace) had fought until three Iroquois and six Huron were killed, another Huron was taken prisoner, and the last man escaped.

The Mohawk and Onondaga, along with Radisson, feasted that night while members of the war party casually pulled out the fingernails and burned the hands of their adult prisoners, making them sing as entertainment. The next morning, they parted company. Radisson was still in a group of Onondaga that lagged behind the main party ferrying the Huron women and the Jesuits. He knew they were getting close because he could see French shoe prints in the sand. The Iroquois had cached ten casks of corn for the stragglers, food that Radisson's party badly needed, deer hunting having become very poor, the last of their bear meat eaten, and there being no time to fish.

Leaving Wolfe Island as the summer's heat wave continued, the voyageurs found the water of Lake Ontario to be calm. They headed south, to what's now the New York side of the lake and, when a breeze picked up, rigged a crude sail that carried their canoe far offshore. Iroquoians did not like to travel miles from land, their boats not being built to handle the stress of large waves. Indeed, the afternoon ended, as so many hot Great Lakes summer days do, with a thunderstorm preceded by a wind squall that made Radisson and his whiny canoe companion, the same man who had nagged him through the Thousand Islands, paddle for their lives. The squall hit hard, with a wall of rain that piled into the boat from the wind-whipped waves. Radisson was sure he was about to drown. And to add to his misery, his companion began to expound on religion, a topic that never seemed to interest Radisson unless there was some chance of a profit.

See your God that you say is above? Will you make me believe now that he is good, as the black-coats [Jesuits] say? They do lie, and you see the contrary; for first you see that the sun burns us often, the rain wets us, the wind makes us have shipwreck, the thundering, the lightnings burns and kills, and all come from above, and you say that it's good to be there.

For my part I will not go there. Contrary they say that the reprobates and guilty go down and burn. They are mistaken; all is good here. Do not you see the earth that nourishes all living creatures, the water, the fishes, and corn and all other seasonable fruits for our food, which things are not so contrary to us as that from above?

He raised his gun and hatchet. "I will not be above; here will I stay on earth, where all my friends are, and not with the French, that are to be burned above with torments."

The two men finally focused on the problem at hand and made a sort of storm anchor. They took a bag of corn, tied it to a rope and dropped it so that it hung twenty-four feet below the bow of the canoe. Then they moved toward the stern. The canoe swung its bow into the wind, and the weight at the stern raised the prow that faced the waves. This helped reduce the chance of the canoe being swamped completely. Like most Lake Ontario squalls, this one passed quickly, although, to the two canoeists, it probably seemed to last a very, very long time. Once it passed, they made for the shore, reaching land somewhere near the mouth of the Black River.

The summer heat wave broke while Radisson and his unhappy travelling partner were canoeing along the east shore of Lake Ontario. They set up a camp on Stony Island, the last island en route to the Iroquois country, then set out the next day across open water toward the mouth of the Oswego River, a hazardous trip if the winds shifted to the south or the southwest. Those winds, travelling across so much open water, pushed big waves onto shore. As they paddled in the darkness somewhere along the coast, they saw lights from the campfires of the expedition's advance party and made for shore just as a strong westerly wind picked up. The waves were so big that for two weeks the entire expedition was pinned on a strip of coast with dangerous rocks and high bluffs. Several of the canoes were torn apart on the beach. When the weather finally lifted, they paddled the rest of the way to the Oswego "where," Radisson wrote, "for delightfulness was what man's heart could wish. There were woods, forests, meadows." The flotilla broke up, and again, Radisson travelled with the Iroquois instead of the French. They had been on this trip for more than a month, and Radisson desperately wanted it to be over.

While they were in this little paradise just inland from Lake Ontario, one of the women on the expedition gave birth. Radisson had seen the woman lying nearby, a "fair, comely lass." They had shared some corn earlier that night, and Radisson had killed a toad that frightened her. Later the same night, she went into labour and very quickly delivered the baby, whose cries woke up Radisson and the rest of the camp. Radisson watched as she dried the baby boy at the fireside, then began feeding him before quietly lying down with the child. But before the expedition left the camp, the baby became seriously ill. Radisson gave some thought to baptizing him, then decided not to, fearful of being blamed for the baby's death, which happened soon afterwards.

They were now about ninety miles from the French fort. When three Frenchmen from the mission met Radisson's group to escort them inland, one of the priests scolded Radisson for "being so timid in not daring to fling water on the head of that poor innocent to make him happy." Huron labourers carried the packs of the French and Iroquois until they reached the mission, which was on a small lake. The French had built strong fortifications surrounded by wheat fields that stretched out a mile and a half from the settlement. There were also large fields of Indian corn, plots of turnip, and pens filled with fat hogs.[85] The woods were filled with nut trees, and passenger-pigeon flocks were so thick that the birds could be caught in nets by the hundreds when they passed by on their migrations. The French priests and their forty soldiers and labourers were free to come and go, to visit the Onondaga and fish in their streams. Radisson and the rest of the newcomers wanted to see the country, but they were hit with a month-long fever that they attributed to the change in climate. When they finally got away from their French-style house and explored the Onondaga country, Radisson fell in love with it.

RUNNING FROM ONONDAGA COUNTRY

Lake Onondaga is small and surrounded by low hills. Although it is in the region of the Finger Lakes, it is not one of them. Some of the springs that feed it carry salts from ancient marine deposits deep underground. Salt springs are rare in eastern North America, and they drew thousands of birds and mammals that could then be easily caught. This made the area a magnet for hunters for thousands of years and, when people started growing corn, beans, and squash hundreds of years before, the countryside around the lake had the right soil for Onondaga farms.[86]

While their fort was being built on Lake Onondaga, the Jesuits fanned out across the country. The Jesuits were popular with Christian Huron adoptees, who hadn't seen a priest in seven years. The Huron introduced them to members of their Iroquois families. The people of the Onondaga villages listened politely to what the Jesuits had to say, their lack of argumentativeness often wrongly convincing the Jesuits they were making progress toward converting the whole country.[87]

Iroquois leaders and the country's brightest thinkers also listened to the Jesuits. The priests were well-educated in science, law, and philosophy, which meant they were interesting guests, if the Iroquois could get them to stop talking about Jesus. Some Iroquois were intrigued by the French knowledge of astronomy. One of the Jesuits' better "tricks" was their ability to predict lunar eclipses, a feat that had been used, at least once, to frighten the people of the Huron country into believing the Jesuits were spiritually powerful and would make very dangerous enemies. For their part, the

Jesuits worked hard to learn the various Iroquois dialects. Jesuit Fr. Pierre Chaumonot, who would spend eighty years in the North American missions, put together a French-Iroquois dictionary within a few months of his arrival in the Onondaga country.

Radisson was visiting the main Onondaga town, trading for corn, when he heard that the old Huron, Jalaka, who had been spared from the massacre on the St. Lawrence, was now travelling through the Iroquois homeland agitating against the French and the Jesuits for what he saw as their lying and treachery. He had an eager audience among non-Christian Huron adoptees, who blamed the Jesuits for weakening the Huron Confederacy by sowing religious and social divisions among its peoples, and who rightly claimed the French had betrayed the Huron refugees. The old man warned the Iroquois they faced the same fate as the Huron—epidemics, division, dependence, and defeat—if they did not drive out the French. In this, he was backed up by former Huron, who said the Jesuits wanted Iroquois souls to torture in hell,[88] and the Mohawks, especially Canaqueese, the half-Dutch-half-Mohawk chief who had reluctantly negotiated the peace. The Iroquois Confederacy should never have let the French build a fort and plant crops, Canaqueese said, but it was not too late to fix the problem.

The Jesuits had succeeded in places like China because they had always been able to quickly learn the etiquette and politics of their hosts' governments. This skill failed them in the Iroquois country. The Jesuits made the mistake of believing the Onondaga's main town was the capital of the League, and that all Iroquois were governed by the League council. Winning over the Iroquois would take more than just impressing the country's civil chiefs. And, by sidestepping the Mohawks, they had insulted the leaders of the League's largest nation.

This was made clear in the League council when Canaqueese spoke against the Jesuits using a metaphor that he had already spread among the Mohawk: "We of the Five Iroquois Nations compose but one cabin. We maintain but one fire. And we have, from time immemorial, dwelt under one and the same roof." The French, he said, had not come in through the door, they had climbed onto the roof and dropped through a smoke vent. They had come as bandits, not as friends.

Suddenly, the mission and the priests themselves seemed to be in great danger. The French made the mistake of believing they had made peace with the entire Iroquois Confederacy forever, and that the League council, which met in Onondaga, could make agreements that bound the entire country. In fact, the

Five Nations was a very loose federation. The individual nations could not wage war on each other, nor could individuals and Iroquois clans engage in blood feuds against other Iroquois, though each nation could make its own foreign policy, and individuals—in a country that placed so much value on the dignity and autonomy of its own citizens—could start their own feuds against foreigners that, invariably, led to all-out war. Canaqueese made all this very clear.

The French were at Onondaga on sufferance, and, unlike the Huron when they lived in their old homeland, the Five Nations were not dependant on the French for trade. The value of the French lay in their use by the Iroquois, who employed the threat of competition to force the Dutch to keep prices down, but the Mohawks had already started using the English in Massachusetts to do the same thing. In addition, the war against the Erie was almost over, a victory that gave the Iroquois complete control over the fur-rich upper Ohio Valley. The French were becoming redundant. Warnings of pestilence and witchcraft spread throughout the Iroquois country by the old Huron warrior Jalaka, made sense to many who heard them. By mid-fall, the Mohawks were trying to raise an army of five hundred men to drive the French out, even if it meant breaking with the Onondaga and risking the stability, and possibly the existence, of the Confederacy itself. The Mohawks hoped to get around this problem by enlisting what Radisson called "Aniot" warriors, people whose nation was not a member of the Confederacy, and who were willing to take the blame for breaching the peace.

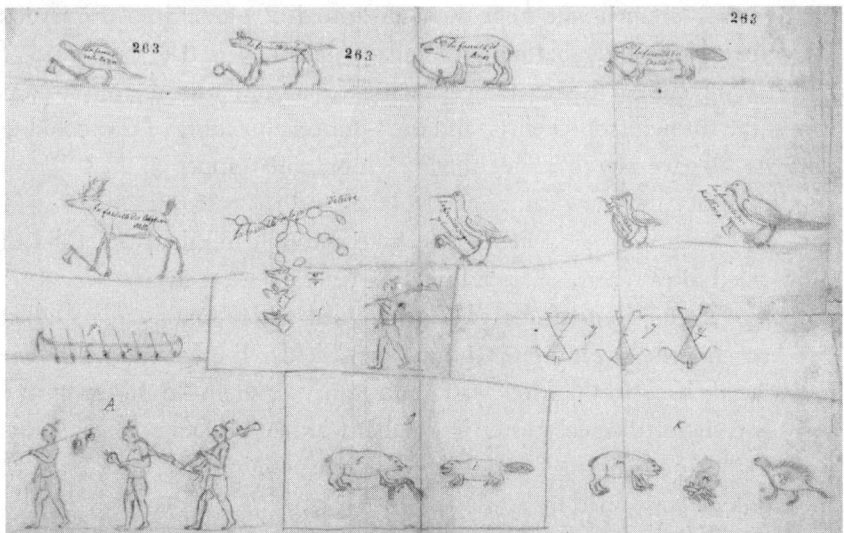

Iroquois clan symbols. (Report on the nine Iroquois families, with totems, 1666. Library and Archives Canada.)

The very presence of the French amplified the factionalism in the League council and its lack of consensus on foreign affairs. On July 24, 1656, the League council had asked Fr. Chaumonot to chair a meeting to try to work out a solution between the Mohawks, who wanted the French out, and the Seneca, who were the most pro-French Iroquois nation. Chaumonot was able to speak his hosts' language well enough to recite the laws of the nation. He also knew how to recite the names of the country's great founders. Having performed the proper ceremonies, he watched as the council leaders debated for hours. In the end, they couldn't reach a consensus, and the clan mothers, who met secretly, couldn't come up with a solution either.

There could be no guarantee of protection for the French, but the Onondaga insisted they were welcome to stay in their little fort. The presence of the French priests was tearing the Iroquois apart, just as the earlier Jesuit mission had split the Huron and left them vulnerable. Time for the Jesuits was running out, despite the Onondaga promises.[89] Canaqueese tried to recruit warriors by saying the French were easy prey, hogs that had grown far too fat on the land of the Iroquois, the not-so-subtle suggestion being that they could be eaten the same way.[90] In fact, the French soldiers would have been a tough enemy for the Iroquois, especially inside their fort, but, with ten-to-one odds in their favour and the home country advantage, the Iroquois would have prevailed eventually.

The Jesuits, no slackers when it came to politics, responded with diplomacy of their own. They had at least one friend among the chiefs on the Confederacy council who kept them informed of plots. Still, the Jesuits knew they were vulnerable and unpopular. Almost every day, they heard of new conspiracies, of feasts held by war chiefs to attract more recruits, of war songs, the throwing of hatchets, and the symbolic breaking of clay cooking pots. As fall gave way to winter, the French became trapped in the Iroquois country. Once the snow came and the lakes and rivers froze, the only way back to Montreal was an impossible hike through hundreds of miles of snow-filled forests, across high hills and large, dangerous rivers.

Far away in Montreal, hostilities increased when Aniot raiders killed two French farmers who were working their fields. The Aniot brought the men's heads back to the Mohawk country and set them up on stakes as a sort of crude recruitment poster. Now that war had broken out, the Jesuits realized they needed to get out of the Onondaga country before the rest of the Confederacy joined in.

The French went to work cutting boards to make flat-bottomed boats like those used on the rivers in France, boats strong enough to make it across the windward end of Lake Ontario and down the St. Lawrence, but with a shallow enough draft that they could still be guided downstream in the rapids of the big river.

Jalack, the former Christian Huron who hated the French, got wind of the boat building while pretending to deliver some corn, and decided the Jesuits were building an ark. This is not as absurd as it sounds. The Jesuits had passed themselves off in the Huron country as sorcerers who could make the moon disappear (by using an almanac to predict a lunar eclipse) and make it rain to put an end to droughts (having successfully prayed for rain during several long, dry spells). They spoke of the power of their God and the terrible punishments unleashed in the days of the Old Testament. The Jesuits also spoke of Jesus's miracles, the wonders of heaven, and the terrible punishments of hell, which resembled an eternal version of an Iroquoian ritual torture. The Huron knew the Jesuits had brought disease with them that killed more than half their people. The priests had converted entire villages to Christianity, then forbade the rituals that were an important part of the people's social life. The Huron had become politically unstable, Christian chiefs having offered political control of entire nations to the Jesuits, while followers of the traditional religion and culture wanted the French to leave their country. The split allowed the Iroquois to swoop in, carry off vast numbers of people, and send the rest scattering across the Great Lakes and the St. Lawrence Valley. Looking at the situation from the point of view of a man who saw these calamities as the fruits of sorcery, the idea of ark-building, and of the calling down of a Biblical-scale flood, does not seem illogical. Jalack, quite frightened by his discovery, went into the Onondaga town to spread the news, which soon became the talk of the community.

The Onondaga elders gathered in council and decided to visit the fort to see if Jalaka's story was true. The Jesuit mission would be searched, and the priests interrogated to determine if, in fact, sorcery was going on. The Jesuits' own spies tipped them off about the raid, giving the French a little time to hide the partially built boats under a false floor that they quickly built in the fort's main hall. The Onondaga leaders missed the boats when they searched the place, and left believing the Jesuits had only the twelve bark canoes that were in plain sight. Still, tensions increased throughout the winter, with false alarms on both sides. Once, a French soldier was almost pulled from the doorway of the fort. He wounded his attacker and shouted to his comrades that the fort was about to be stormed, but the danger passed and the blood feud that would have been created by the wounding seems to have been

The Aionwá:tha (Hiawatha) belt. Made of blue and white "wampum," this belt symbolizes the unity of the Five Nations.

appeased in the usual Iroquoian way, with some gift-giving. Meanwhile, the French kept working on their boats and packing their belongings as they waited for the ice on the lakes and rivers to break up.

As spring approached, the French started making serious plans to abandon their fort quickly and quietly. There were several serious road-blocks, though. The Iroquois had always insisted some of the French should live in their villages. The missionaries countered with an invita-tion to all the French and their Iroquois hosts to come to the fort for a late-winter feast. The Iroquois, whose manners required them to agree, and who enjoyed feasting, were curious about the way the French lived and quickly accepted. As the guests arrived, their hosts greeted by them with trumpets, drums, and waving flags. The French sang songs in their own language. But while one of the Jesuits was still under escort by the Iroquois, he fell and pretended his arm was broken. This was serious busi-ness: the Onondaga had promised to protect the French, and, under their law, the French had the right to demand compensation. If the damages weren't paid, the priest's people could launch a blood feud against the people who were supposed to watch over the Jesuit.[91] Rather than come into the Jesuit fort, the Iroquois left the priest with the French and went back to their town to wait for news.

Every day, the Onondaga elders sent messengers to the French fort to ask how the priest was faring. The French, who were counting the days until spring, said the Jesuit was on the mend, but making a slow recovery. Radisson, who knew the Iroquois better than anyone in the fort, came up with a solution that would not only persuade the Iroquois that the French were still their friends, but would give them a chance to get away from the Mohawk army that was supposedly on its way. They would hold a feast where everyone could celebrate their friendship and show their desire for the priest to return to good health. The priest would be there, his arm in a sling, while the French entertained the Iroquois with food and music.

The feast was to be an "eat-all," a type of celebration common among the Huron, Iroquois, Algonquin, and Naskapi of Labrador. It was an old tradition, from the days, hundreds of years previously, when the Iroquois depended on feast-or-famine hunting. When the guests arrived, each of them carrying a dish and spoon, they were given vast amounts of food, all of which they were expected to consume. The French spent days cooking and getting the outdoor feast site, which wasn't far from the fort, ready for the party. Even the Jesuit faking a broken arm was busy in the kitchen. They refused to let the curious Iroquois observe the preparations, and kept them out of the fort until everything was ready. This piqued the Iroquois' curiosity even more, so when the food was brought out, the men in the Onondaga town were eager to see it. Meanwhile, the French were doing the last of their packing, burying anything they couldn't carry with them.

The meal was sumptuous. The French had put nearly everything they had into their pots and oven, including all but one of the hogs. They took all their wheat flour and made it into bread and biscuits. The smell of baking pork and bread must have wafted from the fort and done as much to summon the two hundred Iroquois men and women as the trumpets the French blew to announce the beginning of the feast. The French rolled out a dozen big copper pots filled with corn mash and mincemeat and the feast began, with speeches from the Iroquois praising the French for being such generous hosts. Then came dishes of broiled and salted waterfowl, cooked turtles, fish, and eels. All of this was served up while the French sang and a young man, likely Radisson, played guitar and acted as master of ceremonies.[92]

The Jesuits, whose account of the last days of the mission is, for the most part, a ham-fisted piece of propaganda that tries to explain away the failure of their colony, described Radisson's role in the deception:

> He who presided at the ceremony played his part with such skill and suc-
> cess that each one was bent on contributing to the public joy. They [the
> Onondaga] vied with one another in uttering piercing yells, now of war,
> now of glee; while, out of complaisance, the wild men sang and danced in
> the French manner, and the French in that of the wild men. To encourage

them more and more in this fine game, presents were distributed to those who best played their parts...[93]

As the hours wore on, the party became an ordeal. The Iroquois, as good guests, were supposed to eat and stay awake as long as their hosts were willing to entertain them. Out came big pots of bear and venison broth thickened with corn or wheat to make a sort of gravy. When an Iroquois started to nod off, the French chided him to stay awake and gave him drums to beat and whistles to blow. Before dawn, the Iroquois cried out, "*skenon*" (enough), and said they couldn't eat anymore. The hosts agreed the feast was over, and said they, too, needed rest. The French let them fall asleep at the feast site, then crept back to the fort, broke out their boats from under the floorboards, and fled the Onondaga country. The fort was closed up as though the French were still in it. The remaining hog was left on sentry duty to wander around the inside of the building and make noise as though there were still people inside.

Some of the French—at least one historian says Radisson was one of them, though the records of the time don't point fingers at him—wanted to murder their guests, then go into the town and kill the handful of warriors and the rest of the people who had not been invited to the feast: six hundred women and elders and one thousand children. This, the would-be murderers said, would put an end to the Iroquois threat forever. But smarter people, led by the Jesuits, prevailed. A mass murder of the Onondaga, organized around treachery committed at a sacred feast, would not intimidate the rest of the Iroquois, it would have engendered a war of extermination against the French, a war that the Iroquois would have won very quickly. The Five Nations, even without the Onondaga, still vastly outnumbered the French settlers in Quebec and were as well armed as any of Louis XIV's soldiers. Radisson, of all people, knew this, as did old Huronia hands like the Jesuits Ragueneau and Duperon.

Centuries later, the question remains: were the French in any real danger? All the perceived menace rose from the talk carried to the Jesuits by Christian spies among the Iroquois, but there was no sign of a break between the French and the Onondaga. And there's little historical evidence the Mohawks were prepared to attack inside the Onondaga homeland, a breach of the French-Onondaga peace that would have humiliated the elders who kept the council fire of the Five Nations and created a diplomatic incident that could have split the Confederacy apart. The French may well have whipped themselves into a state of panic based on a few bits of bad information and gossip that had, perhaps, been carefully planted by the Mohawk leadership.

Even after the Aniot raid near Montreal, Mohawk emissaries had tried to make amends to the French; until, that is, French soldiers grabbed some Mohawks and clapped them in irons to send to the Mediterranean as galley slaves.[94] Later, the new governor, Viscount d'Argenson, angry at the waste of money and time spent on building and staffing the mission, criticized the Jesuits and their garrison for fleeing the Onondaga country, suggesting they were cowards. He may well have been right. Nine of the soldiers escaped well ahead of the main contingent and raced to Montreal as quickly as they could. Sixteen more followed fast behind. As far as the Jesuits were concerned, the Devil had conspired with the Iroquois to run them out of the country.

The last of the French used oars to break the ice of the lakes and rivers to make passages for their boats. Back at the fort, the Onondaga left the French settlement alone for a week, giving their hosts a chance to catch up on their sleep, and providing even more evidence that they were not planning a massacre. The French, however, were well up Lake Ontario's eastern shore before the Iroquois noticed they were gone.

The French had taken a huge risk by leaving at the first thaw. Real spring was still weeks away, and they had yet to cross the eastern Lake Ontario snowbelt. The winter of 1657–1658 was milder than usual, but the prevailing north and southwest winds were likely to jam the ice into the shore along the

The Iroquois tribal council. Though somewhat stylized, the illustration shows the gravitas of the meetings. The wampum belt along the bottom of the picture shows their importance in record-keeping and ritual. (Joseph-François Lafitau, *Moeurs de sauvages*, 1724)

French escape route. The many cliffs along the shore east of the Oswego River gave the French an even thinner margin for error and bad luck.

The weather was miserable: "In our journey we had bad weather, high winds, snow, and every day rain on our backs... the navigation proved worse and worse because we came into a colder country and into the most dangerous precipices," Radisson wrote. The St. Lawrence River, he added, was full of chunks of ice, which, with the high water, made it even more dangerous. Then the French became lost. Familiar landmarks having become invisible in the snow, they were gripped with the kind of panic that makes even experienced wilderness travellers and sailors make stupid mistakes. When one of their boats was swamped in the current, three men, trying to swim to shore, were drowned in the bitterly cold river. The boat drifted to shore with a fourth man, who could not swim, but remained alive as he hung onto it. In some places, the river was frozen over, but the ice was so thin that the French had to keep testing its strength by hacking at it with hatchets. Some men fell through it into water up to their necks. Radisson's description of the trip makes it clear that it was an "every man for himself" affair, a humiliating, anxiety-filled retreat from enemies who, in the minds of the French, could be lurking anywhere.

This fear was exacerbated when Radisson reached what he called Murder Island, the place where the Onondaga had killed the Huron men during Radisson's upriver expedition the previous summer. The French had

Modern reconstruction of the French settlement at Ste.-Marie among the Iroquois, which is now an Indigenous-themed historic site.

brought with them a Huron woman who had seen the massacre and hidden on the island until French travellers to the Onondaga country found her later that summer. Because she was a Christian, the Jesuits had asked her to leave the Onondaga and come with them. Recognizing the place, she wanted to get away from it as quickly as possible.

It took six weeks to reach Montreal. The flotilla arrived the day after the river broke up. No one in the town seems to have known they were coming, and the people of the tiny village presumed the flotilla was an Iroquois war party.

Ragueneau, the senior Jesuit, wrote:

All the French settlements regarded us as persons come from the other world and could not sufficiently marvel at the goodness of God who had, on the one hand, miraculously delivered us from such evident peril, and, on the other, freed from uneasiness all the French of Montreal, Three Rivers, and Quebec. The latter were feeling almost obliged to bear, at the hands of the Iroquois, things that were unbearable, and had to restrain themselves from checking their excesses of insolence, for fear lest retaliation should fall upon us who were a prey to, and at the mercy of, the common enemy.

And, indeed, we reached our journey's end betimes; for we learned at Montreal that two hundred Agnieronnons [Mohawks], who had come with hostile intent, were near there; and even on the way we had perceived traces of them, and seen the fires of several scattered bands, who would have given us a rough reception, had we not hastened our progress.

Some other hostile parties also appeared at Three Rivers, taking prisoner three young men who had just left the place to go to their work; nor could any attempt at rescuing them be made, though the Iroquois dragged them off in plain sight of all the people of the village. At Quebec, the same enemy made his appearance in the neighboring fields, killing people almost at our very doors. He pounced upon poor Algonquin women, taking them by surprise in broad noonday, killing some of them on the spot, and leading the rest away captive—who, however, were afterward recovered. Our Frenchmen, the Hurons, and the Algonquins pursued the enemy, and intercepted him; but the murderers made their escape, disappearing as soon as they had shown themselves and had perceived their inferior strength.

Still, the Jesuits saw some success from the mission. The priests kept a grim score of the souls they "saved": some four hundred Iroquois had been baptized, mostly dying infants and old people, so the mission had some worth. The rest of the Iroquois were given the opportunity to be saved. On Judgment Day, God could do what he wanted with them.

In fact, the Onondaga were impressed, if not bewildered by the French escape. They hadn't believed the French were strong enough, or skilled enough, to make a trip to Montreal, at least the way mortal people might do it. Jalack, the Huron, wasn't the only person in the Iroquois country who was convinced the Jesuits were sorcerers with fantastic powers. In the week between the eat-all feast and the first Onondaga visit to the fort, snow fell and the river had frozen over, hiding evidence of the French departure and leaving open the possibility they had used magic to get away.

According to the Jesuits, some of the Onondaga gave in to their curiosity and

> ...climbed into the house to see in what state our people were amid this fearful silence. Here their wonder was changed to alarm and perturbation. They opened the door; the chiefs entered, and went all over the house, ascending to the loft and going down into the cellar; but not a Frenchman appeared, alive or dead. They looked at one another, were seized with fear, and believed that [their disappearance] had to do with demons. Not a boat had they seen, and even if they had, they did not imagine our Frenchmen so rash as to consign themselves to currents and breakers, to rocks and frightful dangers, amid which they themselves, though very dexterous in shooting these rapids and cascades, often lose their lives. They persuaded themselves that their visitors had either walked off on the waters, or flown away through the air, or, as seemed to them more likely, had hidden in the woods. They made search for them, but without success, and then decided, almost as a certainty, that they had made themselves invisible, and that they would come and pounce upon their villages just as suddenly as they had disappeared.[95]

After a couple of weeks of rest in the tiny settlement of Ville-Marie, Radisson went inland, back to Trois-Rivières, where his brother-in-law, Groseilliers, was getting ready for another trip west. This time, Radisson would go with him, and the trading team of Radisson and Groseilliers was born.

Book Three:
Pierre and Médard Go West (1658–1660)

WHAT WAS A beaver hat?

It's a simple question, but understanding what a beaver hat was, and what it meant, is important for the rest of this story. Clothes made the man in the 1600s, as they had for hundreds of years, and the beaver hat was the height of fashion in Radisson's time. It wasn't just a simple head covering. It was a means of communication, and it was often the most expensive thing a man possessed. If manners maketh man, the beaver hat made a man a gentleman.

For nearly two hundred years, men's fashion had been as unchanging and drab as it was during the time of the Puritans. The early Victorians invented the modern business suit, with its jacket, tie, plain cotton shirt, and pants that reach the ankle. There have been variations, of course, but they're slight: double-breasted and single-breasted jackets, vest or no vest, pleats or no pleats. Wide ties get replaced with narrow ties until the cycle swings around and wide ties come back. The well-turned-out man also wears the best watch he can afford. The business suit is complete when the wearer steps into a good pair of clean, shiny leather shoes.

For today's man, class signalling isn't done through the display of gold and jewels, but with the quality of the suit, shirt, timepiece, and shoes. The streets of contemporary society are full of men turned out in off-the-rack wool, cotton, polyester blend, and silk suits, cheap ties, and ill-fitting but passable shoes good enough for the workplace. Wealthier men, and those who know how style can help with upward mobility, wear tailored suits that fit well, shirts with sharp collars, fashionable ties, and expensive shoes. All suits look pretty much alike until you see a man in a bespoke silk suit next to one wearing a suit that costs a day's pay.

In the 1600s, social and economic signalling through clothing wasn't subtle. No one had to check the labels on outfits. By the end of the 1500s,

17th-century French illustration showing beavers at work near Niagara Falls.

men's fashion had gone through a revolution. The ruffed collar and rather drab, dark clothes of Elizabeth I's time were fashions that came from Spain. In the early part of that century, wealthy men dressed to look more dashing, wearing colourful, well-tailored jackets and breeches with high boots, topping the look off with a large, black felt hat.

This was an age when class was everything, and the rich spent money to separate themselves from the great mass of poorer people and dressed to audition for promotion to a higher class. It was a society that, at least in Western Europe, was no longer completely feudal, and where social mobility and success in business depended on making friends higher up the ladder who became patrons and sponsors. (Radisson was able to do this in England, but never pulled it off in France.) In most places, clothing was still regulated by sumptuary laws, which prevented upstarts from scraping up enough money to buy a good suit of clothes which would send out the wrong class signal. Some cloth, like silk, was off-limits to non-aristocrats, as were some colours.

But the beaver hat could be bought by anyone with enough money. Paired with a well-made suit, it helped create the sharp-dressed man. People in those days, including peasants, spent all they could to have at least one fabulous suit of clothes for special occasions.[96] The nobility and the very wealthy—who were often not the same people—were willing to spend whatever it took to set themselves apart from those who ranked below them. Samuel Pepys, a man who was notoriously tight with a shilling, was still willing to pay about $1,000 in today's money for a beaver hat for every-day use.[97] Now, even though beaver pelt prices have dropped to almost nothing due to fur being out of style, a beaver felt hat like those worn in the mid-1600s, made partly by machines, would still cost about $600.[98]

In some ways, a well-off man in the 1600s saw a beaver hat similarly to how we see shoes: he'd be no more likely to leave his house without his hat than a man today would leave barefoot. That said, the average male, especially in a fleeting moment, is unlikely to pay close attention to another man's footwear (women, on the other hand, do). A better analogy might be the car, which can say a lot about a man, even with just a quick glimpse: wealth, occupation (imagine a pick-up truck with a company name on the side), frugality, concern for the environment, connection with the outdoors, age, taste, sexual availability (sometimes rather dishonestly), domesticity (think minivan with family doodle cartoons in the back windows), economic class, and even politics. Now we are closer to understanding what a beaver hat represented to those in the seventeenth and eighteenth centuries. The beaver hat was not an article of clothing, it was a big, flashing sign that described the owner, or at least projected how he wanted to be known. The hat changed enough from year to year that men who followed fashion needed to make frequent upgrades. And to make sure poorer men never came close to catching up, some governments brought in strict rules about the sale of used hats, supposedly to prevent the spread of lice.

There were complex rules of etiquette surrounding the use of beaver hats. The hat could be worn inside, but not in a church or in the presence of the sovereign. When it was removed, the hat was to be held in a way that prevented people from seeing inside it. It had to be tipped to ladies and to social superiors. Radicals like the Quaker sect, whose members believed in social equality, caused scandals by refusing to follow these rules, but they still wore beaver hats.

Like any other fashionable but unnecessary status symbol, the beaver hat had a backstory: the owners knew the hat's material came from the wilderness of America, home of strange animals and exotic people. People couldn't read enough about America in the 1600s. The Jesuit Relations (the journals published by the Jesuits in the early years of their missions) and books published by other "explorers" were bestsellers among the aristocracy and the middle class. Priests raised a fortune from the rich ladies of Paris to pay for the missions, gifts that were rewarded with exciting letters from the wilderness. Kings sat for hours listening to people like Radisson and Champlain recounting their wilderness exploits.[99] The hardship and adventure of the fur trade meant high costs to the industry, but it was a great story for marketers: dashing explorers risking their lives to get furs so the man-about-town could look like a man of action, just like the Three Musketeers. When people figured out how to make just-as-good felt from rabbits, the flamboyant fur-felt hat almost immediately went out of style, replaced first by plain, simple hats, then by the silk top hat made from cloth from the exotic Orient.

The beaver hat fashion and European penetration into the Great Lakes region are inseparable. New York State was founded on the fur trade, and Europeans would never have gone to the American Midwest, the "Old Northwest" of Minnesota, northern Michigan, and Wisconsin, or almost any part of Canada in Radisson's time if they hadn't been after furs. Colonization for farming began around some of the fur-trade forts in the seventeenth century, but as an idea it really belonged to the next century.

The Thirty Years' War, the most devastating war in Europe prior to the twentieth century, led to the first permanent settlements in Canada and much of the American northeast. That's because the war made the beaver hat so fashionable that everyone just had to have one. In 1600, Europe had all the fur it needed. Russian and Scandinavian trappers sold their furs to traders who took them west to the rich cities of Germany, France, and the Low Countries. Fur wasn't that important to the garment trade, which relied on wool (England's big export), linen made from flax, and silks traded overland, and, increasingly, by sea from China. Until about 1550, wealthy Europeans wore hats made of fine cloth that looked much like berets, but that were trimmed with cloth of gold, jewels, and, sometimes, a bit of fur. Poorer men wore wool-felt hats that were either cone-shaped or like Robin Hood-style caps. Wool felt, however, doesn't hold up in rain, and it doesn't keep its shape. It also couldn't be made into a hat with a wide brim.

Felt-making was invented by nomads in central Asia thousands of years ago. It was known to the ancient Greeks and Romans, who set up small factories to make felt from old cloth and fur lint. Felt was, and still is, an industry that uses the waste of other manufacturing: worn-out or rejected clothes, scraps of other textiles, bits of fur. Reduced to lint, pressed onto screens—like lint in a clothes-dryer filter—then consolidated into a stiff, unwoven cloth, thick felt was cheap. Offering reasonably effective protection against arrows, it was frequently used to line the inside of armour to keep soldiers warm. Like so many other technologies, felt-making became a lost art in the West when, at the end of the fifth century, Rome fell to Germanic invaders, who likely had no use for felt: Europe, for all its wars, invasions, and empires, was still a continent of forests with clearings of farmed land, and in the north and east, in the vast marshlands of Poland and western Russia, furs were still easy to get. Felt-making survived in the Byzantine Empire, Greco-Roman civilization's eastern hold-out, but the felt was used mostly for making cheap clothes and hats. In the 1300s, the sultan of the Ottoman Turks (who had not yet snuffed out the remnants of Byzantium) made white felt caps required headgear for his ordinary subjects.

Meanwhile, trouble in Russia would eventually spell trouble for the North American beaver. In 1240, Tatar invaders rampaged through Russia and into the Ukraine, sacking Kiev. Skilled tradesmen, including hatters, fled west into Poland and Germany. By the late 1300s, they had discovered the wonderful properties of the beaver pelt's inner fur, which made felt lint strong enough to hold a wide hat brim. The felt-hat industry had taken centuries to evolve, and its epicentre was now in Eastern Europe, where there were still plenty of beavers.

Empires come and go, and in the first half of the 1600s, the Swedish Empire came and went. During the Thirty Years' War, Swedish troops were all over Central Europe, making their fabulous hats the envy of friends and foes alike. These big-brimmed black hats show up in Rembrandt's *Night Watch* and in paintings of King Charles I of England and his Royalist generals, like Prince Rupert of the Rhine. The officer in armour, with his steel doublet and helmet, morphed into the dashingly clad, caped, and booted swashbuckler of the early gunpowder age.[100]

Once the wide-brimmed beaver hat came into style, it didn't take long for European and Siberian beavers to be driven to the edge of extinction. Hatters from Russia to Ireland needed beaver pelts. That's why trading companies began sending scouts to parts of North America where

The gentleman and his beaver hat: in Hendrik van der Burch's *The Card Players* (1660), a Dutch gentleman wears a beaver hat that was essential to the costume of middle and upper-class men. The young servant is a reminder that other colonial trade was much more grim than the North American fur trade.

beavers flourished.[101] These were the "explorers" written up in high-school history books, brave adventurers who ingratiated themselves with the Indigenous people and relied on them to show the way into the continent.

Beavers had always been hunted by Indigenous people. Their fur is warm, their meat palatable, although a bit stringy (it's a red meat that tastes like beef or moose if slow-cooked into a stew). The teeth made good wood-working tools. Beavers are extremely easy to hunt in the winter, when their fur is at its best. Like their smaller cousins, the muskrat (which are also quite tasty and have a fine pelt, although without the thick undercoat used by felt-makers), beavers spend the winter inside the dome-shaped lodges that they build in the ponds that form behind their dams. Beavers could be trapped, but it was easier to walk across the frozen ponds, tear open the lodges, and haul the animals out. Women and men both did this work.[102] Even under the hunting pressure of the Iroquois, Huron, Neutral, and other people of the region, beaver were still common in the early 1600s, when French traders began asking their Indigenous partners for as many beaver pelts as they could provide. Very quickly, beaver became a currency among the First Nations. Big expenses such as compensation for serious crimes—given by the families of the guilty to victims and/or their families, the way Radisson's Iroquois family had paid for the killing of his hunting partners—were calculated, at least among the Huron, in beaver robes.

A French wrought-iron axe traded in the Georgian Bay area before 1650. Thousands of axes and tons of other iron and steel trade goods were carried up the St. Lawrence and Ottawa Rivers in the 200 years that it was a major canoe route.

These days, we have a skewed idea of the fur trade. Americans visualize fur traders as half-mad mountain men capable of killing grizzlies in hand-to-paw combat. Canadians' views are a little more accurate, but not much. In the northern part of the continent, our image is of hardy voyageurs paddling gigantic birchbark canoes across the open waters of the Great Lakes and up into the Canadian Shield. In fact, in the seventeenth century it was the Indigenous people who did almost all the work: hunting or trading to get the furs, cleaning and tanning the hides, transporting those furs hundreds, and sometimes thousands of miles to towns in the St. Lawrence or Hudson Valleys. After selling the furs, they had to make the return trip loaded with bulky, heavy trade goods like iron axes, copper pots, knives, swords, and other metal tools and weapons, through the portages and strong currents of the Ottawa and Mattawa Rivers, over the height of land and along Lake Nipissing, to the French River and northern Georgian Bay, where they then could go south to Huronia or west to the Algonquin-speaking heartlands.

The French trader was not a trapper or a labourer (except when carrying his share on a canoe trip, something expected by Indigenous people). He was a broker whose skill lay in quickly learning the Indigenous languages. (Most Iroquoians, and probably many other people living in the Great Lakes region believed anyone who did not learn their language was, to be blunt, stupid.) Huron was the lingua franca of the early fur trade. People who spoke the dialects of the Five Nations could understand it, but it was a struggle for Algonquins, whose language is very different. French traders, sent as young men to live with the Indigenous people—just as Radisson did with the Iroquois—were paid very well for their services, but if they couldn't quickly learn Huron or one of the Algonquin languages, they were demoted and pulled out of the field.

The French fur trade didn't need a lot of Frenchmen. It just needed smart, brave ones. Even without raiders and hijackers lurking along the canoe routes, it was a somewhat risky and complicated venture: ships sank, First Nations allies were sometimes blocked by their enemies from reaching trading posts, and the price of beaver pelts fluctuated in the European market. The pelts then had to be sent on a dangerous final trip to Russia, because the Russians knew the secret of extracting beaver "wool." But the profits could be enormous, and the Indigenous people would pay almost anything, at first, for European hardware. The French (and Dutch, and, later, the English) trade goods were often shoddy, with axe heads made of soft metal that blunted easily and peeled apart on seams, glass beads so poorly made that they were sometimes flat on one side, and copper cooking pots so thin that they could be punctured in the slightest of accidents, but they were an improvement over stone tools and clay pots that required hundreds of hours of work to make. The fur business made those who invested in the French trading companies wealthy and, for a time, improved the lives of First Nations people. Yet this was a trade that was easy to hijack, disrupt and, if necessary, destroy. It altered the power balances that existed in pre-contact North America. Worst of all, it led, in the interior nations, to the unleashing of plague waves of European childhood and zoonotic viruses when the French, in an effort to make Quebec and the Huron country feel more like home, brought over very young children, cattle, horses, pigs, and chickens.

Radisson wasn't part of the kind of fur trade that exists today. He wasn't trying to gather furs to make coats for old ladies. He was, rather, a key part of a big-money urban fashion industry backed by wealthy, well-connected investors with contacts and partnerships throughout Christendom. The stories of wilderness adventures in new worlds added more romance to the beaver hat, but the entire enterprise was really all about the money.

MASTERS OF THE ROUTE

When Groseilliers returned from his first western adventure, the Jesuits wanted to know who and what he had seen. Radisson believed the Jesuits wanted to make themselves masters of trade in the north, or at least make sure it stayed in the hands of French Catholics and not Dutch or English Protestants. During the years that Groseilliers and Radisson were scouting the upper and western Great Lakes, Jesuits were trying to make sense of Canadian geography. They knew the general shape of Lake Ontario and Lake Erie, but weren't yet sure about how the smaller Great Lakes connected to Lake Huron. They also knew of Lake Superior, and realized it was huge. The shape and size of Lake Huron and Lake Michigan were mysteries to them, but they had a good understanding of the geography of Georgian Bay, Lake Simcoe, and the Kawarthas. The priests knew of the Ohio River, but did not understand it connected to the Mississippi. Radisson and Groseilliers had probably figured that out. They also knew, from Indigenous friends, that the Mississippi was a gigantic "forked river," with one branch, the Missouri, coming from the west and the other, according to Radisson, flowing toward Mexico. Radisson, however, did not have a good grasp of North America's vast size; he believed, for instance, that both the Gulf of Mexico and the Pacific Ocean weren't far from what is now Missouri, Illinois, Iowa, and Minnesota.

On their doomed 1610 trip to Hudson Bay, Henry Hudson and his crew had enough sailing experience to have a decent idea of where they were. Other explorers added to that knowledge, so that every map of Canada made in the early to mid-1600s had the rough image of Hudson and James bays looming over the Great Lakes. Radisson and Groseilliers didn't discover Hudson Bay, but they were the first Europeans aware they were tapping into furs that came from the swampy lowlands surrounding it. In 1660, Jérôme Lalemant, head of the Jesuit mission in Canada, wrote of four known or suspected canoe routes from Quebec to Hudson Bay. Even though the Jesuits had never travelled on any of them, at least two of the routes—pried from Indigenous people—are accurate. It appears the Jesuits and Radisson simultaneously realized that a sea route to Hudson Bay would provide an end run around the Iroquois and all the troubled nations of the Great Lakes. Once the Jesuits learned Radisson and his brother-in-law had come to the same conclusion, they found themselves up against the traders in a very high-stakes game.

Radisson and Groseilliers left New France in the late summer of 1658.[103] They had planned the trip through the previous winter and thus bought or borrowed all their stock-in-trade, probably in Montreal. The Jesuits got wind of the expedition and wanted to send priests with the two traders. Groseilliers seems to have been open to the idea, but Radisson convinced him the priests would just slow them down and contribute nothing. The traders found two Huron refugees living in Quebec who would be their guides. These Huron wanted to go to Lake Michigan's Green Bay to find their wives, who were living in a refugee village. The two French traders also claimed to have been granted a business license from the colony's governor. At Montreal, they ran into the corruption that would always hamper enterprise in New France: the governor of that town wanted Radisson and Groseilliers to take two of his men, neither of whom had experience in the bush, and give these men most of the profits. Years later, Radisson would harangue the Montreal leadership as cowards and thieves who didn't have the courage to take risks on their own, but who were always ready to skim off any profits.

Obviously, Radisson and Groseilliers had a problem they needed to fix before heading up the Ottawa River canoe route to the west. Radisson told the French officials, "We knew what we were, discoverers before governors.

We are masters as well as servants." If the Indigenous trappers came to Montreal to trade, Radisson and Groseilliers would be happy to have the governor around to give some weight to the proceedings, they would even cut him in on the profits for his efforts, but otherwise he wasn't needed, nor were his men. This, of course, was not what the governor wanted to hear.

"The Governor was much displeased at this, and commanded us not to go without his leave," Radisson later remembered. So the two traders turned to the Jesuits, who started pushing again for a free ride for their missionaries. For weeks, Radisson, Groseilliers, and a trader who is never named in Radisson's writings (but may have been one of the Le Moyne brothers of Montreal) wandered the St. Lawrence trying to round up enough government and/or Jesuit support to get past the bureaucratic bottleneck.

Finally, a group of Odawa and Ojibwe traders showed up at Trois-Rivières, having used the St. Maurice River canoe route that looped through central Quebec, rather than the Ottawa-St. Lawrence route along the edge of the Iroquois country, to bring some Jesuit priests back from the interior. They were willing to take Radisson, Groseilliers, the third Frenchman[104] and, presumably, the two lonely Huron back west with them, license or not. The legality of the whole thing was, at best, unclear. In one passage of his writings, Radisson says the governor of Trois-Rivières understood the value of the expedition and gave permission for the traders to leave, but Radisson also says they left under cover of darkness. Despite Radisson's many complaints about government corruption and greedy bureaucrats, the entire expedition was probably illegal.[105]

But not according to Odawa, Huron, or Ojibwe law. Indigenous traders owned the canoe routes.[106] People who opened a trade route and made alliances with new foreign partners were called "masters of the route," rights they had never handed over to the French. The Indigenous traders took those rights very seriously: traders like Étienne Brûlé, who learned the routes and tried to freelance his own trade, were killed off. With the passing of the Huron Confederacy, the Odawa and Ojibwe now owned these routes, and French traders were their guests.[107]

There were choke points in the canoe routes that First Nations often exploited.[108] The Kitchissippirini, an Algonquin band, lived on Morrison Island in the Ottawa River, near the present-day community of Pembroke, and operated a tolling station at the top of a set of rapids. This type of tolling was common on the rivers of Europe, especially in Germany, where it paid for many castles on the Rhine. But, by and large, the routes could be travelled fairly freely with the permission of their owners.

The canoe routes, especially the route up the Ottawa and Mattawa Rivers to Lake Nipissing, then down the French River to Georgian Bay, were the great highways to the west, and were vital to the trade with Europeans that so radically changed the lives of the Indigenous people of the Great Lakes country. The Iroquoians—the Great Lakes farming people who included the Iroquois League, the Huron Confederacy, and smaller corn-growing nations—along with their Indigenous customers, received tons of wrought-iron axes from the French that were used inland as money, weapons, and, most importantly, tools for clearing farmland. The European traders also dealt in knives, fish hooks, iron arrowheads, and spearheads. The traders and inland trappers' wives received tons of hardware and cloth that made their hardest work much easier. Eventually, the French, Dutch, and English would also trade livestock (especially to the Iroquois). The women were just as eager as their brothers and husbands for the fur trade to grow, even though it fell on them to do the work of preparing hides and growing corn to trade for furs. In summer, they lived apart from the men; husbands and brothers left their villages with big baskets of dry corn to trade with the hunting people who lived on the Canadian Shield, carried bundles of furs through the Great Lakes country down to Montreal, and lugged heavy metal objects along the gruelling portages as they paddled back up the rivers.

Radisson and Groseilliers' goal for this trip was very simple, and kept secret from everyone, including the Indigenous people: find a way to cut out the middlemen. They wanted to do away with the current system, where furs might change hands two or three times on the route between the trappers' camps and the warehouses in Quebec. Each person who touched and moved the furs expected to be paid in "gifts." The Indigenous people, like the aristocrats of France, did not see themselves as merchants or wage earners, but they didn't tolerate stinginess, either. Groseilliers, who had already been west, probably came up with the idea of dealing directly with the fur hunters, who turned out to be Cree and Sioux. The Ojibwe and Odawa middlemen, who were to be cut out of the trade, were sophisticated business people who knew the interior far better than the French. It would take lies and deceit to make this work, so it was a good thing Groseilliers was coming along.

First, they had to ditch the governor's men by sneaking off without them. Radisson's Indigenous partners weren't interested in chauffeuring and feeding them, either. So it was settled: Radisson, Groseilliers, and their third partner would meet their travelling companions in the reeds of Lake St. Pierre, some eighteen miles above Trois-Rivières, the same place Radisson had been caught when he escaped from the Mohawks six years earlier. When the trio slipped out of town at midnight, a sentry called out to them, but when Groseilliers, who'd been a sort of mayor of the place, answered back, the sentry supposedly hollered, "God give you a good journey." By six in the morning, Radisson, Groseilliers, and their unnamed partner were in the field of reeds, but they couldn't find their Odawa guides. Thinking they'd somehow been cheated, the three French traders hurried upstream and caught up with the canoe brigade near the mouth of the Richelieu River, at the modern-day town of Sorel.

The trading party, which was led by a blind chief from Lake Superior's south shore, sorted out their canoes so they had three full boats. Most of the travellers were Odawa and Ojibwe, except for a man and his wife who were from a people the French called the Sorcerers.[109] This couple knew the French, and had travelled to the Huron country with the Jesuits a decade or so earlier. They wanted to go west to visit Fire Nation friends who were now refugees at the rapids on the St. Mary's River between Lake Superior and Lake Huron.

The Indigenous traders knew the canoe routes intimately. The men were powerfully built and covered with tattoos of sacred signs and clan symbols. While they were tough and strong, there weren't enough of them to fend off a large Iroquois war party, a danger that followed them until they reached the upper lakes, Michigan or Superior.

To complicate matters, one night at a camp on the St. Lawrence River between Trois-Rivières and Montreal, the French trader who'd accompanied Radisson and Groseilliers leapt out of his sleeping blankets and began screaming and shaking, waking everyone up: he'd dreamed they were all prisoners of the Iroquois. The Huron, Ojibwe, and Odawa, firm believers in the accuracy of dreams, were mortified, as was the French trader whose dream it was. Judging from his actions afterwards, he may have suffered a panic attack or maybe even a psychotic break. He decided to flee back to Trois-Rivières, and the Huron and some of the western traders went with him. Now there was just Radisson and Groseilliers, which suited them just fine. A three-way split of the profits was now reduced to two.

The dream, however, seemed accurate: the next day, after they had left Radisson and Groseilliers, the French trader and his companions saw a canoe carrying Iroquois warriors. The trader and the people with him quickly made it to shore, hid their canoe and ran off in different directions. The Frenchman stayed close to the riverbank so he wouldn't get lost in the woods, but the Huron and Odawa went deep into the forest. As night fell, the French trader fell asleep on the riverbank, hidden in high grass near the concealed canoe. His companions, believing the dream came true, found their canoe at first light but didn't see the sleeping man, so they hurried off. Left alone in the woods, the trader woke up without guides or a boat, twenty miles from Montreal.

After a couple of days on the water, the canoe arrived at Trois-Rivières without this man. Everyone, French and Indigenous, believed the trader was dead. Two weeks later, some moose hunters found the man half-starved on the riverbank, clutching his gun. He had lived on wild grapes, which was not enough food to keep him alive but did delay his death. His troubles weren't over yet. Once he had enough food in him to make the trip to Trois-Rivières, the governor had him thrown into jail. The local people, seeing how terrified this man was, and how hungry and miserable he'd been since he was marooned, convinced the governor to let the poor man go. He was one of many people who would have terrible luck doing business with Radisson and Groseilliers.

Back on the Ottawa River, the two traders, now utterly dependant on their Indigenous hosts, bonded tightly. They swore they were brothers, ready to live and die with each other. Not only would they be one family and business entity, they would rewrite the past to make Radisson an important part of everything Groseilliers had ever done—whether Radisson had been there or not. Their bond was to last a very long time. Radisson and his brother-in-law, despite their very different personalities, would be one single, symbiotic entity as they travelled the Atlantic world, and they would enter history together as Radisson and Groseilliers.

Three days after the French trader panicked and fled, Radisson and Groseilliers came across a campsite where the embers still glowed in the firepit. There were tracks on the shore where seven canoes had been pulled from the water. The campers had left hieroglyphs on the trees showing they were Odawa, not Iroquois. Radisson and Groseilliers' brigade paddled hard until they caught up with them. The two French traders were welcome, as were other allied people heading west up the Ottawa River. Now there were fourteen canoes in the flotilla. This was probably for the best, since, the day after the last Odawa joined the flotilla, its vanguard arrived at the Long Sault portage and came across some Iroquois who had seen the traders as they'd gone down the river toward Montreal and patiently waited for them to come back. The Iroquois had built a small fort, but this time the Odawa saw them first.

Radisson, hoping to ingratiate himself with his new Odawa friends, volunteered to go with another man to scout the Iroquois fortifications. The Odawa knew they had to get past the Iroquois. It was too late in the season—probably it was September by the time Radisson and Groseilliers made it to the Long Sault—to try to find another canoe route around the Iroquois. Radisson saw the fort was built on solid rock and was not much more than a circle of logs lying on top and against each other. There was no way to launch a night attack and breach the wall from underneath, the way the Iroquois had broken into so many Huron towns. The strategists among the Odawa—although Radisson claimed this was his idea—decided to cut down a tree that would fall on the Iroquois' log wall, and then rush through the breach. This was one time when guns would be almost useless. After getting one shot off, there would be no time to reload, and the killing would have to be done with hatchets and arrows.

But Radisson had another idea. It was almost night, and he approached the fort, offering peace that would be sealed with gifts of wampum. The Iroquois could see the size of the Odawa trading party and knew they had a poor chance of getting out of their fort alive, so they exchanged pleasantries with Radisson. Hours later, after dark, the Iroquois slipped away, and the trading party seemed now, at least temporarily, safe on the river. The Odawa party cautiously left their camp at daybreak. Two faster canoes that scouted for the main Odawa party came across an Iroquois hunter as he was setting up a cooking pot over a campfire near the foot of a portage. The Iroquois ran off to warn his friends, leaving a bundle of beaver furs behind. The Odawa scouts were also terrified. As they hurried back along the portage to the main part of their flotilla, they came across Groseilliers, who dropped his backpack and ran back to the Odawa camp. There, he implored Radisson to give one of his encouraging speeches.

Radisson's talk worked. Rather than head back down the river to the safety of Montreal, the Odawa would try to outmanoeuvre the Iroquois, and fight them if necessary. For hours, everyone near the portage—Iroquois and Odawa—snuck through the woods, trying to avoid each other, both sides afraid of the other, and neither wanting to fight. Eventually, a few men on either side fired some bullets and arrows at each other and the fight was on. The Iroquois tried to swim across the river and some might have drowned, but Radisson also says there were Iroquois in canoes helping their men get across to an old fort on the other side of the Ottawa.

The Odawa decided to keep up the attack. They tied the bundle of beaver skins taken from the first Iroquois's campsite to the front of their lead canoe and used it as a shield. Guns of this period were more like shotguns than rifles. Their slow-moving bullets caused massive tissue damage at close range but couldn't penetrate a bundle of furs at a distance. Still, the Iroquois were able to kill an Odawa man with a lucky shot, then they ran back into their fort, with the rest of the Odawa close behind. Radisson and the Odawa made a bomb from a keg of gunpowder and set it off at the base of the fort's palisade. The wall survived the blast, but three Odawa bombers did not. This didn't stop Radisson from making a sort of grenade from three pounds of gunpowder wrapped up in bark, which he tossed over the wall. This bomb blew a hole in the palisade and the Odawa entered the Iroquois stronghold just as darkness and sheets of rain began to fall. In the darkness, many of the Iroquois escaped from the hand-to-hand fighting inside their fort and ran away into the woods. When the brawl was over, the Odawa counted the bodies of eleven Iroquois and two more of their own dead. The Odawa also had four Iroquois prisoners.

That night, Radisson and some of the Odawa broiled and stewed the flesh of some of the slain Iroquois, then, after filling their bellies, built the cooking fire much higher and burned the bodies of the dead Odawa, giving them an honour reserved for the best warriors. The campsite, with its carved-up corpses, blood, gore, and burnt bodies, must have been a sickening place. Even so, Radisson, writing years later to King Charles II and the Royal Society of London, would be utterly blasé about the horrors of Indigenous warfare: "At the break of day we cooked what could accommodate us [it's not clear whether he means Iroquois flesh], and flung the rest away. The greatest mark of our victory was that we had ten heads & four prisoners, whom we embarked in hopes to bring them into our country, and there to burn them at our own leisure…"

Since the Ottawa River was the superhighway of central North America in the 1600s, there were bound to be more Iroquois travelling on it, and, two days after the Long Sault fight, the Odawa brigade came across yet another raiding party. This one had seven big canoes carrying ten to twelve men each, enough men to wreck Radisson and Groseilliers' expedition. The Odawa were able to bluff the Iroquois into believing the up-bound brigade was far bigger than it really was. Some Iroquois immediately went to shore and built a log stockade. The Odawa, pretending to be unworried, did not. Instead, they quietly killed the four Iroquois prisoners, and, after night fell, dodged the Iroquois' scouts and hurried upriver. They pushed their canoes through rapids, their feet and legs cut up by the rocks, and paddled without a break for four days on the calmer water.

They finally let up on this gruelling pace by resting at the confluence of the Gatineau, Rideau, and Ottawa Rivers, and camped near Lake Leamy on the north shore across from the cliffs where the home of Canada's prime minister now looms over a large pool of deep, black water. The waterfalls just to the west were given the name "Rideau," French for "curtain," because the river, from the south, falls straight over a forty-foot cliff of hard limestone into the Ottawa River. The falls, in the middle of what's now official Ottawa, still look like curtains, and in the 1600s people could get behind the wall of water and walk the full length of them. Samuel de Champlain probably walked behind the falls, and so did Radisson. "The water runs over the heads with such impetuosity and violence that it's incredible," he wrote years later.

The trip wasn't all sightseeing, however. After their hard paddling from the Long Sault, the men were hungry. Some started fishing, others hunted. In the distance, they could hear the pounding of the Chaudière (French for "kettle") Falls, the beginning of a set of long portages. These falls, just a few hundred yards from Canada's parliament buildings, were shaped like a giant bowl in which the entire Ottawa River plunged and churned and could be heard for miles. They were a sacred site for people who lived in the area and the many travellers who used the Ottawa as a great highway to the West.

Champlain, who had visited the Chaudière on his way upriver almost half a century before, described the Ottawa-area riverscape: "Here are many small islands which are nothing more than rough, steep rocks[110] . . . At one place the water falls with such force upon a rock that with the lapse of time it has hollowed out a wide, deep basin. Herein the water whirls around to such an extent, and in the middle sends up such big swirls, that the Indians call it *Asticou*, which means 'boiler.' This waterfall makes such a noise in this basin that it can be heard for more than two leagues away." The people who passed by this spot performed a ceremony using tobacco placed on a dish, which was dropped into the churning pool of water at the foot of the falls for the use of the spirits that lived within the waters.[111]

The beginning of the portage at the foot of the Chaudière Falls marked the end of the canoe route's easiest part. Above the Chaudière lay miles of rapids, long portages, and dreary stretches of the river where the men had to walk along the shore and drag their canoes through the rapids. There was also Tessouat's tolling operation on Morrison Island near the modern town of Pembroke. After that, the landscape changed from swampy plains to the rugged country of the Canadian Shield, where the rather ordinary landscape of the lower river becomes spectacular as the Ottawa flows through the hills. There, the river comes straight from the north, making it a highway to the Great Lakes and the subarctic that was used for centuries by tens of thousands of people right up until the early 1800s. This was no easy trip: Radisson, Groseilliers, and their Indigenous companions weren't just carrying canoes along the many portages. They lugged packs holding their food, guns, ammunition, blankets, clothes, and the extra shoes that were vital for long walks over rough paths, and they carried thousands of pounds of iron axes, swords, knives, copper, and iron cooking pots, tools, gunpowder, lead shot, beads, bells, and other things. Imagine going on a canoe trip and taking a good part of your local hardware store with you.

On the upper Ottawa River, they met people living in camps and villages on the shores of the river. They were fishers and traders who grew a bit of corn but mainly lived off hunting. This part of the Canadian Shield was a mystical place where, on cliffs along the waters' edge, people painted religious and historic images in red ochre. Some of these rock paintings are still there. Fear, however, kept the travellers from enjoying this part of the trip. The Iroquois' determination to close this route made every portage a potential ambush site, so the Odawa fur brigade moved as fast as it could.

19th-century watercolour of the Chaudière Falls, near what's now downtown Ottawa, Ontario. The falls, which are sacred, are now almost unrecognizable because of industrial and condominium development.

The travellers slept on the floors of their birchbark canoes, and everyone, including Radisson and Groseilliers, was exhausted.

Once they reached northern Georgian Bay, they headed west along the channels between the Canadian Shield and the northern shore of Manitoulin Island. The travellers often found themselves out of food because the hunting was poor, but from time to time they received the hospitality of the people who lived along the Lake Huron coast. The Odawa travellers, whom the French traders had known for just over a month, always shared whatever fish and game they caught with Radisson and Groseilliers. By the time the Odawa canoes reached the Serpent River on the north shore of Lake Huron, the travellers felt safe enough to camp on land for the first time in three weeks, but they still kept a night watch for Iroquois raiders

Radisson was always impressed by his guides' ability to find food and the lengths they would go to get something to eat when food was scarce. Somewhere on the north shore of Lake Huron, one of the Odawa canoe men saw a beaver poke its head from the water. Rather than fire a shot that would likely have been wasted, the man threw himself over the gunnel of the canoe, swam deep into the water, and returned a moment later carrying the very-much-alive beaver "in his arms as a child, not fearing to be bitten. By this we see that hunger can do much."

Soon afterwards, they were in the chain of islands between the north end of Manitoulin Island and the outlet of the St. Mary's River, paddling along the flat shorelines that were home to the Ojibwe then, and now. This was one of the busiest places on the Great Lakes. To the south are the straits leading to Lake Michigan. To the northwest is the gateway to Lake Superior, and, even more important to the local people, the whitefish spawning beds in the rapids of the St. Mary's that supported the entire settlement of the Saulteaux, or Ojibwe,

17th-century painting of an Ojibwe warrior. (Library and Archives Canada)

people. Once they reached the Saulteaux village, Radisson and his travelling companions finally had all the food they could eat. They set up camp and gorged themselves for days on whitefish, or *assickmack* in the Odawa language. This fish has a skin so strong that it can be skewered and roasted slowly over a fire in a wrapping as tough as tinfoil, and come off the stick as a mild, moist white fish that is somewhat like haddock.

All the while, even while they were with the Saulteaux at the St. Mary's Rapids (Sault Ste. Marie in French), Radisson and the Odawa were afraid of an Iroquois attack. Five Nations raiders had already hit the Ojibwe several times, though plans were in motion among the Ojibwe that would decisively end the Iroquois threat.[112] Fear of staying too long, along with the realization that it was late in the travelling season, with days getting shorter and nighttime temperatures slipping below freezing, forced the canoe brigade to leave this town and keep moving west.

LAKE SUPERIOR COUNTRY

Despite Radisson's fear of the Iroquois, there was a very large part of their worldview and culture that stuck with him, even years after he had left their country. He was well-aware of Indigenous manners and the expectations placed on him by his hosts. He, along with the Odawa, recognized the bounty of the land was not free. Radisson and the Odawa had not needed "to put hand to the purse" while feasting with the Ojibwe at their fishing ground on the St. Mary's. They did, however, have to make tobacco offerings to the land the way they had at the Chaudière Falls: "we must pay out of civility: the one that gives thanks to the woods, the other to the river, the third to the earth, the other to the rocks that stays the fish." The canoe brigade had arrived at the beautiful, bountiful St. Mary's River half-starved, and all of them, Radisson included, were grateful for what it gave them.

And the land kept giving. It was fall, but Lake Superior was calm and the air was clear. Fruit and nut trees along the south shore and on the islands were loaded with food, which filled Radisson's cooking pot every night. But the land offered more than food. On a river the Odawa called the Pauabickkomsibs, an Odawa took Radisson a few hundred yards inland from the shore of Lake Superior and showed him nodules of copper littering the stream bed. The Great Lakes people had used this copper for at least five thousand years, trading it, and some native silver, across North

America. Native copper tools and weapons show up in graves and burial mounds in thousands of places in eastern North America. The copper was so pure that it could be heated and pounded into knives, spearheads, arrowheads, fish hooks, gaff hooks for hauling large fish into canoes, and many other tools and ornaments.

Indigenous copper mining on Lake Superior started at about the same time, or even earlier, than the Bronze Age in the Middle East, and more than one thousand years before the people of Europe began using metals. So why hadn't the First Nations had the same progression of copper, bronze, and iron technology? The answer lies in geology. There's no tin in eastern North America, and bronze can't be made without it. The ancient Egyptians, the classical Greeks, and the people of Western Europe could get tin from Cyprus and Cornwall in southeast England. Bronze is easy to make, if you have the copper and tin, and it's an alloy that is much stronger than pure copper. Even without tin, Indigenous people mined hundreds of tons of copper from the Lake Superior country and traded it from the Arctic to the Gulf of Mexico. Big decorated shells from the Gulf of Mexico, volcanic glass from Yellowstone that made spectacular spearheads and knives, as well as exotic foods and other valuable items were traded back into the mining country.

Radisson wanted to load up with copper, but his friends told him there was a lot more along the route. In some places, Radisson says, he saw nod-

ules weighing more than a hundred pounds, a believable boast if you look at the amount and purity of the copper mined from the region two centuries later.[113] It says something about the easy money of the fur trade that Europeans didn't try to exploit this spectacular resource until the beaver hat fell out of fashion.

In some places, the sand dunes on the windward coast of Lake Superior stretched so far that they reminded Radisson of what he'd heard about the deserts of North Africa. Some dunes behind the

Ojibwe fisherman, one wearing traditional clothes, the other with a French hat. (*Codex Canadensis*)

shore were so high that the Odawa climbed them to get a panoramic view over the treetops and far out onto the lake. Radisson liked watching the wind whip up little dust devils and spent much of his time on shore looking out over the lake at the big waves and the islands along the sculpted shore. He was always open to new sights and enjoyed each day of the trip as the shoreline changed: sometimes there were rock walls, other times miles of golden-sand beaches framed by trees at the height of their brilliant fall colours. Radisson was always fussy about his food when he could afford to be, but, unlike the Jesuits, Champlain, and so many others who travelled the canoe routes, he did not constantly whine about the bugs, the weather, or the hard work of canoeing or portaging, nor did he feel superior to his Indigenous travelling companions. On Lake Superior, he finally felt safe from the Iroquois, so when he saw canoes in the distance, his blood was no longer chilled with dread. In his writings, Radisson rarely mentioned Groseilliers, who, though equally or perhaps even better skilled as a woodsman, saw travelling as a profitless part of the money-making process, a sort of expense, rather than as an adventure to be enjoyed.

Eventually, Radisson's brigade overtook canoes belonging to a small hunting band that lived to the south. These people were amazed the Odawa had made a safe trip all the way to New France and back and were impressed with the trade goods they'd brought up the Ottawa River canoe route. After a night of partying in their hosts' camp, Radisson and his friends gave the local people gifts of French trade goods and were rewarded with presents of fresh moose meat and bear grease. There was so much that they preserved what they couldn't eat right away.

The Odawa canoe brigade, with wide-eyed Radisson and grumpy old Groseilliers, continued along the Lake Superior shore toward the homeland of the Dakota Sioux at the lake's western end. Radisson was always satisfied with the scenery and could have written a brochure for the tourism outfitters of Michigan's Upper Peninsula. The coasts, he wrote, "are most delightful and wondrous, for it's nature that made it so pleasant to the eye, the spirit and the belly."

Soon they came to a place the Odawa called Nanitoucksinagoit, a rock in the lake that was a sort of sandstone Rorschach test: the local people believed it resembled a Manitou spirit while the French saw the devil. The Odawa gave it presents of tobacco and shot arrows at it. Huge waves broke along the coastline cliffs, making a roaring noise so loud that the travellers could hardly hear each other talk. The rock walls were thick with seagulls, which made Radisson wrongly think he was close to the sea itself. They were, in fact, at the Pictured Rocks and the Doric Rocks, which are now protected by the United States' National Park Service. This stretch of the Lake Superior shore near Munising, Michigan, is still a spectacular wilderness of geological marvels set in cold, topaz-coloured water. The caves carved by the pounding water pushed by the prevailing north and west winds thrilled Radisson. One was like "a great Portal, by reason of the beating of the waves. The lower part of that opening is as big as a tower, and grows bigger in the going up. There is, I believe, six acres of land. Above it a ship of 500 tons could pass by, so big is the arch. I gave it the name of the portal of St. Peter, because my name is so called, and that I was the first Christian that ever saw it. There is in that place caves very deep, caused by the same violence." Radisson wasn't exaggerating. Such an arch did exist, but Radisson's name didn't stick to it. The structure was called Grand Portal Arch, and small ships carrying tourists could, indeed, sail into it in the 1800s, but it collapsed in a spectacular rock fall in 1900. In 1999, most of what was left of the arch tumbled into Lake Superior.[114]

As Radisson travelled through this country, he thought of crowded Europe and the vast spaces around him that seemed like wasted land: "the country was so pleasant, so beautiful and fruitful that it grieved me to see that the world could not discover such enticing countries to live in. This I say because that the Europeans fight for a rock in the sea against one another, or for a sterile land and horrid country... Contrarywise those

Grand Portal Arch, Lake Superior.

kingdoms are so delicious under so temperate a climate, plentiful of all things, the earth bringing forth its fruit twice a year, the people live long and lusty and wise in their way. What conquest would that be at little or no cost; what labyrinth of pleasure should millions of people have, instead that millions complain of miserable poverty!" This was one of the few times he advocated colonizing the interior, and he happily saw a time when the First Nations people who had treated him so well would be shunted aside.

Radisson, enthralled as he was by Lake Superior and natural artistry of its shore, knew he and his travelling companions had to be careful. This stretch of coast is a challenge to even the most skilled canoeist. The water may be beautiful, but it's icy cold year-round and will kill a person who falls into it within minutes. Changes in the wind remake sandbars almost instantly. There are no good landing places for fifteen or twenty miles at a stretch, and the waves blast into shoreline-cliff crevasses, making explosive sounds, "most like the shooting of great guns," Radisson said. They reached the three Huron Islands, midway along the south coast of Lake Superior.[115] Radisson named these Trinity Islands, a rather unimaginative label that didn't stick. A mighty river, the Huron, empties into a very deep bay near these islands.

Bad weather trapped the canoe brigade near the river's mouth, so the men went hunting and killed some moose that were easy to spot in the flat, open country inland from the lake. Moving on, Radisson and his friends broke down beaver dams, letting the water behind them rush out, exposing vast beds of brown muskeg and pastures of moss two-feet thick. For sixty miles, the beavers had turned the countryside into treeless muskeg swamps that often blocked the canoeists' way when they were forced ashore by bad weather. These wetlands became a bigger problem when the Odawa brigade moved inland toward the height of land. Sometimes Radisson had to crawl on all fours on the moss, dragging his canoe behind him. When they pulled down beaver dams, the land shook as the moss and muskeg recoiled from the weight of the water. The ground was so soft that a man could easily end up in muck up to his shoulders if he trusted the moss and grass and tried to walk upright on it. The Odawa warned Radisson that, once he started sinking into the quicksand-like muskeg, he needed to fling his body sideways into the water and spread his weight, holding onto clumps of moss, "and go so like a frog."

Once they reached higher land, they found it criss-crossed with trails made by other travellers. They were now at the Keweenaw Peninsula, and the local people saved eight days of paddling by portaging across the base of that long point of land. This was the heart of the copper-mining country.[116] Radisson heard there was an entire island of copper offshore. If this was an exaggeration, it wasn't much of one. After commercial mining began in the 1840s—often in pits dug out by Indigenous people and littered with the stone mallets they used to mine the copper—some 18 billion pounds of almost pure copper was extracted from the Lake Superior shore area before mining stopped in the 1960s.[117] The copper veins were in strips several miles wide, and tons more had been pried by out of the bedrock by the glaciers and dumped on the land. This "drift copper" was what Radisson had seen among the rocks in streams earlier in the trip. The Odawa also told Radisson of the copper mines farther up the Keweenaw, but his companions, faced with short paddling days and the closing in of winter, didn't have the time or inclination to give him a tour.

They came across a group of Cree people that Groseilliers knew from a previous trip. The Cree came from north of Lake Superior and moved between the upper edges of the Great Lakes and Hudson Bay, where many of them spent the summer. The great disruptions of the epidemics, the Iroquois wars, and the fur trade forced nations to rewrite their borders. Like the Ojibwe, who were the first people in the region to tap into a steady supply of guns, axes, and knives, the Cree had been expanding their territory. At first, the Cree and the Ojibwe had fought, but quickly made peace when the Cree made it clear they would make way for the Ojibwe and shift their attentions westward. (They would eventually become a major force on the Plains, once they got horses.) The Ojibwe, in turn, spread out from their traditional homeland at the junction of the Upper Lakes and would own much of the land between Lake Ontario and Lake of the Woods. The Cree made most of their gains at the expense of the Sioux, who lived along the western edge of the Great Lakes. The borderlands between the two groups were relatively empty and the Cree-Sioux fighting had been almost bloodless until now. Radisson and Groseilliers wanted to mediate to restore peace and make trade deals. The Cree and the Sioux, on the other hand, wanted guns, and were willing to keep a sham peace until they could get them. At the same time, the Odawa moved northward from their old country on the Bruce Peninsula. Hundreds of Huron-Petun refugees from southern Georgian Bay were also trying to find a safe place to live, one that was far away from the Iroquois raiders who followed wherever they went. These people, now calling themselves by the Huron name Wendat (which was morphing into Wyandot), had been the best traders and most powerful people north of Lake Ontario just a decade before. Now they were fugitives on the verge of starvation.

If the politics seem overly complicated today, it was even more confusing in Radisson's time, when small groups like the Menominee and Potawatomi, the Winnebago, and Algonquin refugees were also travelling the Lake Huron-Michigan-Superior junction area, trying to find some secure place to settle and make a living.

Groseilliers' old Cree friends on western Lake Superior were happy to see him, since they were short of knives, hatchets, and cooking pots.[118] Radisson and Groseilliers lavished gifts on these trading partners. This made some of the Cree suspicious and jealous of each other, something Radisson didn't expect to see, and he tried to use charm and gifts of his own to heal the rifts that the traders caused in the local community.[119]

Finally, the brigade reached Chequamegon Bay, at the southwest end of Lake Superior in what's now the extreme northern part of Wisconsin. Radisson and Groseilliers kept going for a few days to a spot where the lake teemed with big sturgeon, some of which were seven feet long, and with pike that grew well over forty pounds. The Indigenous people were just five days from the end of their journey, when they would return to their individual band wintering grounds. The Odawa, along with Radisson and Groseilliers, gave thanks to their various divinities and spirits before the group broke up. Radisson decided the location would be a great place to build a trading post. Rather than try to keep up with the Odawa as they went overland, and loaded up with metal trade goods that would have made the hike into a tortuous endurance test, the two French traders told the Odawa they would stay close to the wonderful (but migratory) fish for a couple of weeks.

The Ojibwe, who had made the trip with the French and the Odawa, weren't sure where their wives were camped, or whether they had been forced away from their usual winter camps by their enemies, the Sioux. They went off to look for their families, and said they would be back with their wives, once they found them. If the families were dead, Radisson and Groseilliers promised to help the Ojibwe wage a war of revenge.

Alone now, Radisson and Groseilliers went to work building a log cabin surrounded by a palisade strong enough to keep out "murderers" from the many nations that surrounded them. The entrance was at the waterside, the cabin was in the middle, and the land side had a triangular bastion that gave the two men a good field of fire against anyone who tried to rush the place. Radisson and Groseilliers tied little bells on the branches of the trees around the tiny fort as an alarm system, but this proved a bad idea in a country with so many tree-dwelling squirrels, birds, and other small animals. Radisson worked on their cabin for a few days then went off to fish and to shoot birds. Geese in that part of the world seemed to have no fear of a man with a gun, and some tried to chase Radisson away. Three of them were shot down in Radisson's first blast. Other birds, curious to see what happened, flew into range, and goose was on the menu for the two traders for the next five days.

Radisson and Groseilliers worked alone on the fort but were visited from time to time by local people who came to see how the French built things. Groseilliers shooed them away because he didn't want them to see their weapons stash: five muskets, two rifles, three fowling pieces that fired birdshot, three pairs of big pistols and two pocket ones, along with swords and daggers, "so that we might say that a coward was not well enough armed." Radisson believed mistrust "is the mother of safety, and the occasion makes the thief." Foxes stole a bag holding some of the birds that Radisson shot, and squirrels got into the food caches. Radisson thought local people or raiders had stolen the food, and the two Frenchmen began ratcheting up their fear of attack until they found the bag and birds in a hole in a tree about a mile from the little trading post. Moose were plentiful in the area, but the young Frenchman, always fussy about what he ate, preferred birds and rarely went anywhere without a shotgun loaded with birdshot.

Food, like everything else that was not connected to the actual building of the fort, became Radisson's problem. He solved it by massacring far more animals than the two men could possibly eat. Groseilliers had probably learned some building skills at Ste.-Marie, in the Huron country, which had triangular bastions on its corners that the old man mimicked in his new fort. He always worked alone, grumpily beavering away and shooing off everyone who came by. Twelve days after Radisson and Groseilliers started the project, some of the Ojibwe river men arrived back with dozens more young men carrying food and expecting to find the two Frenchmen starving. They had underestimated Radisson and Groseilliers, who had both become experienced woodsmen. Radisson had sixty ducks and geese stashed away in the fort, along with many sticks of drying moose meat. The Ojibwe offered to help them move inland and carry the traders' merchandise.

The arrival of Groseilliers into Radisson's life marked the beginning of Radisson's often cynical and dishonest treatment of his hosts during wilderness business dealings. For example, the Frenchmen cooked up a plan to tell their closest Indigenous friends they had taken all the rest of their metal merchandise out into the lake and dumped it, to be protected by what Radisson called his "devil," his word for the Indigenous spirit called the Manitou. This spirit would not let the axes, knives, and other valuable things turn to rust or be found by other people. (In fact, they buried it all.)

Radisson did treat the Odawa and Saulteaux to a feast of game birds. The party lasted for three days, likely without making a serious dent in Radisson's hoard of waterfowl. The two Quebec traders broke up all their boats and used the birchbark to strengthen the little fort. They spread this extremely flammable bark—birchbark will burn in a pelting rain—around the building and let the local people know they would set it on fire if the post was attacked. With this little piece of real estate and the cynical, often ugly influence of Groseilliers, Radisson temporarily developed an arrogance that detracted from the eager, open-minded boy who'd fallen in love with the Mohawks and the other Indigenous people he'd met on his adventures: "We were Caesars, being nobody to contradict us," he wrote ten years later about having all his baggage carried inland by Indigenous women. "We went away free from any burden, whilst those poor miserable [people] thought themselves happy to carry our Equipage, for the hope that they had that we should give them a brass ring, or an awl, or a needle."

Radisson's attitude continued to get worse. About four hundred of the wild-rice-harvesting Menominee people of Lake Superior's south shore came to meet the French traders, and Radisson would later compare them with "the fools of Paris" who had crowded the streets to cheer Louis XIV when he brought his bride, the Infanta of Spain, to Paris after their marriage in 1660 (an event that Radisson did not see). He saw them as suckers who would pay any price for his friendship.

The Menominee convinced the traders there was money to be made if they settled in their town, so Radisson and Groseilliers gathered some of their trade goods and went with them. Four days after leaving the shore of Lake Superior, they arrived at a large town on Lac Courte Oreilles. There were more than one hundred longhouses and cabins, with no palisade for protection. People turned out to give the traders an ecstatic reception. Since the destruction of the Huron eight years before, trade into the northern Great Lakes had dried up, and people, especially women, needed the hardware that the French sold. Radisson and Groseilliers gave three sets of presents to the men, women, and children of the town, telling them to remember their journey and preserve it in their oral histories so that they would be talking about Radisson and Groseilliers a century later. The first present was a copper cooking pot, two hatchets, and six knives, along with a blade for a sword. There, they got word that a great Feast of the Dead was being planned by the nations of the region, who described it as a "kettle," or cooking pot. Radisson explained it to his English readers: "The kettle was to call all nations that were their friends to the feast which is made for the remembrance of the death; that is, they make it once in seven years; it's a renewing of friendship." Radisson heard this very important feast was to be held the following spring. "The hatchets were to encourage the young people to strengthen themselves in all places, to preserve their wives, and show themselves men by knocking the heads of their enemies with the said hatchets. The knives were to show that the French were great and mighty, and their confederates and friends. The sword was to signify that we [the French] would be masters both of peace and wars, being willing to help and relieve them, and to destroy our Enemies with our arms."

While France was the greatest military power on the mainland of Europe, the last statement was very much an idle boast, as the Hurons in the crowd had learned a decade ago at their great cost. France could barely protect its toehold on the St. Lawrence, let alone the First Nations of the interior. The days of one or two Frenchmen scaring away an Iroquois war party by firing off a few guns was long gone. Since many possessed their own, the Great Lakes people knew what a gun could and could not do, and understood its limitations, especially the slowness of reloading. Radisson was smart enough to know that the pledge was utterly reckless. It was a promise he would never have made a year or two earlier, and one he could not possibly have expected to keep.

The second gift was directed at the women:

"The second gift was of 2 and 20 awls, 50 needles, 2 graters of castors [hide scrapers], 2 ivory combs and 2 wooden ones, with red paint, 6 looking-glasses of tin. The awls signify to take good courage, that we should keep their lives, and that they with their husbands should come down to the French when time and season should permit. The needles … to make them robes of castor, because the French loved them. The two graters were to dress the skins; the combs, the paint, to make themselves beautiful; the looking-glasses to admire themselves."

To the children, the traders gave brass rings, little bells, and "rasades [glass] of diverse colors." Radisson asked a man to gather the children together and then had them scramble for little prizes that the traders threw high in the air. The traders made another empty promise that the French would protect these children from their people's enemies, the toys giving "them wherewithal to make them merry and remember us when they should be men."

Once the presents had been handed out to the adults and tossed into the crowd of kids, the Odawa, Menominee, and Ojibwe leaders called Radisson and Groseilliers to a council and feast of friendship. After the meal, the feasters had a mourning ceremony for the recently dead, including the men lost on the trip from Quebec. This involved the ritual giving of gifts to help ease the grief of friends and relatives of the lost men. Then came what Radisson called the "dancing of the heads," when dancers used scalps and skinned heads to celebrate victories, including the recent skirmishes along the Ottawa River. The feasting and gift giving rituals lasted three days. When they were over, the two French traders believed they had ingratiated themselves with their hosts.

Next, Radisson went to work learning the family and clan structures of his hosts. The Huron and Petun refugees on Lake Superior belonged to Iroquoian clans that Radisson would have known from his time in the Iroquois country. The local people, the Odawa and Ojibwe, had *duodems*, their own kind of giant extended families, along with fraternal and mystical secret societies. One of the senior chiefs, the blind man who'd made the return trip to Quebec, was the traders' host for the first couple of days, but Radisson and Groseilliers abandoned him for the home of "an ancient, witty man" whose wife was "old, nevertheless handsome," and a very large family. Radisson thought he and his partner could get away with snubbing the blind chief because "we were demigods." He was aware enough to make sure the old couple adopted him "for my father and the woman for my mother, so the children consequently brothers and sisters. They adopted me. I gave everyone a gift, and they to me."

This was fortunate for Radisson. The Ojibwe made a strong distinction between *Inawemaagen* (relatives) and *meyaagizid* (foreigners and, usually, enemies). The former were entitled to share in everything their family and clan had. A person was not part of Ojibwe society unless born or adopted into one of the dozens of duodena, the clans that were the main social organizations in the community. Radisson later identified himself as a member of the marten clan. The duodena were more than just extended families. They had property rights over trade routes, decided how resources would be shared, where villages would be set up, and had an important say in larger questions of war and peace. Radisson had seen a similar social construct in the Iroquois clan system and understood it well. Most Europeans, however, could not fathom it. They were always looking for leaders—the equivalent of kings and aristocrats—who could speak on behalf of entire nations and command their "subjects" to live up to any deals they made with the French. Radisson, unlike Groseilliers, the Jesuits, and later French traders, knew exactly how to engage with this very complex social and political system, and he had the added advantage of his fantastic gift for languages.[120]

It is unclear if Radisson and Groseilliers married Indigenous women on the trip. Marriage would have been a very quick way to establish an unbreakable family tie with their hosts. The traders were far from home, and Groseilliers' marriage was something he put little time and energy into. The Indigenous leaders of the Upper Lakes wanted these family ties, and the literature of the fur trade abounds with stories of First Nations leaders arranging marriages between their daughters and traders. In fact, Ojibwe leaders would, in the eighteenth and nineteenth century, demand marriages between white fur traders and Ojibwe women before they would even begin to discuss trade, and there's no good reason to believe this policy began after Radisson and Groseilliers lived among them. No one in the interior, including Radisson and Groseilliers, thought this was a one-off trip, that the Frenchmen would leave the Upper Great Lakes and never return to their wives and any children who stayed behind. At the time, the Frenchmen planned to become masters of the Ottawa River route. Groseilliers even began calling himself "Admiral of the Ottawa." Radisson and Groseilliers publicly promised to be allies, protectors, and suppliers to the Ojibwe. Their pledges seemed believable: the Ojibwe could see the tons of furs that had been collected from the Sioux, the Cree, and the Menominee, which they knew would make the Frenchmen rich and eager to come back.[121]

So it's a safe bet that they were paired off with Indigenous women during this trip. The silence in Radisson's writings about sexual relations with First Nations women probably isn't just prudery. The stories were written when Radisson was in England, waiting to ship out to Hudson Bay in the service of the king and the city merchants, and he had many good reasons to portray himself as an honest bachelor. A good marriage in England might have cemented relations with the city's merchant class. And, since Groseilliers had already developed a bad reputation in the 1660s as a man who had abandoned his wife and children in New France in order to turn traitor, it made no sense to add bigamy to his list of sins, especially with his brother-in-law looking on. (Radisson and Groseilliers would not be the last traders to trample over Indigenous women and leave them stuck with children. Fur traders continued doing this well into the 1800s.)

Certainly, the two Frenchmen needed some of the comforts that came with village life. The Indigenous and French traders had arrived in town just as winter was setting in. This part of what's now the Upper Peninsula of Michigan and northwestern Wisconsin is in the Lake Superior snowbelt. Until the lake freezes in late January, bitterly cold winds crossing Superior from the north and west pick up steaming moisture from the lake and dump it on the land until the snow is more than three-feet deep. Once the lake, or at least most of it, freezes over, prairie and Arctic winds arrive as drier, bitterly cold air, and temperatures plunge down to about forty below zero. (At this temperature, -40 is the same in Fahrenheit and Celsius.)

The arrival of winter caused the people in the Menominee town to break into small bands and head into the deep woods in search of game. The town was too big to have enough animals nearby to support everyone through the winter, even with the corn and wild rice from that fall's harvest, so people split up into family and clan groups and headed to winter hunting and ice-fishing grounds. Suddenly the self-described "Caesars of the wilderness," these "demigods," were on their own, stuck in a near-empty village, left with about sixty people to fend for themselves in a land where winters are so hard that few Americans choose to live there even now. The only date left on the traders' social calendar was the Feast of the Dead in five months, when the hunters and trappers would leave their winter camps and come back to the town. It would be a very, very long winter for Radisson and Groseilliers.

THE HUNGER WINTER

"Now we must live on what God sends, and war against the bears in the meantime, for we could aim at nothing else, which was the cause that we had no great cheer," Radisson realized. At first, he and Groseilliers were lucky to be attached to a group of hunters and their families who, in the first two months of winter, found and killed dozens of hibernating bears that they ate or rendered for their fat. Hunting for deer, moose, caribou, and what Radisson calls "wild cows" but were likely American bison, was also fairly good in those milder autumn months. At least one cougar also went into the cooking pot. As the snow piled up, the people made snowshoes, which put the two Frenchmen at a disadvantage. They had used them before, but not well enough to keep up with their hosts.

It quickly became much colder. Moisture blown inland from the giant lake stuck to trees as hoar frost that made the woods look like a Christmas card scene. But within weeks, there was so much snow on the pines and cedars that it blocked the sun when it made one of its rare appearances through the snow clouds. This, and the short late-fall and early winter days, made the landscape depressingly dark and bleak to those struggling on the ground. The snow was so deep and fluffy that the hunters had to remake their snowshoes, crafting six-foot long "rackets," as Radisson called them. Radisson and Groseilliers constantly tumbled into the snow, and their hosts had to stop what they were doing to help them back onto their feet. The snow got so deep that even the local people could barely move around; and when they did, they made so much noise that the animals they hunted were given clear warnings. For two months, Radisson, Groseilliers, and their hosts had had an easy time stalking game. Now hunger stalked them.

Then news came of more trouble. The Huron-Petun refugees and Odawa at Michilimackinac, on the straits joining Lake Michigan to Lake Huron, had started fighting with each other. In the summer and fall, they were close to waging war. Now all of them, several hundred people, were in the northern wilderness, starving along with Odawa, Menominee, and Ojibwe. The Huron-Petun refugees, former corn farmers with just a few years of hunting experience in this northern wilderness, were having the worst time of it. Radisson had little sympathy for them, believing their trouble with the Odawa was caused by greed and their desire to resume their role as middlemen in the fur trade between the French settlements on the St. Lawrence and the western Indigenous people. By mid-winter, as snow piled higher than normal and the temperature plunged, almost everyone on Michigan's Upper Peninsula and the country at the southwest end of Lake Superior was starving. "Everyone cries out for hunger; the women become barren, and dry like wood. You men must eat the cord, being you have no more strength to make use of the bow. Children, you must die," Radisson wrote a decade later. He even mocked his own arrogance. "French, you called yourselves Gods of the earth, that you should be feared, for your interest; notwithstanding you shall taste of the bitterness, and be too happy if you escape."

People who had given feasts for Radisson and Groseilliers just a few months before came back to the town starving, their eyes sunken, cheekbones protruding, yellow skin stretched like parchment, unable to even collect a bit of wood to make a fire. By now, Lake Superior was frozen, the snow squalls had stopped, and the temperature was likely in the -40s or even colder. Families, sleeping in huts made in holes in the snow, woke each day and counted their dead. The groans of the dying and the mourning cries of the living deeply disturbed Radisson. The arrogance and contempt for the Indigenous people that had attached to him when he began travelling with Groseilliers disappeared and was replaced with empathy for the people of the Upper Lakes. "Good God, have mercy on so many poor innocent people, and of us that acknowledge thee, that having offended thee punishes us. But we are not free of that cruel Executioner. Those that have any life seek out for roots, which could not be done without great difficulty, the earth being frozen two or three feet, and the snow five or six above it."

They cut the bark of vines that grew on some of the trees, boiled and dried it, crushed it into a kind of flour, and made soup from it. They got some nourishment from this nasty broth, but the mixture left them drymouthed and feeling like they'd eaten nothing but wood. They'd eaten their dogs long ago, so they struggled to work their way back to the places where they'd butchered animals in the late fall, hoping scavenging animals had left something behind. They found and boiled some of these bones, along with a few of the crows that had helped pick them clean. And when they'd drank this broth, they boiled the bones again. And again. They boiled leather intended for clothes and shoes. They took leather tents apart and boiled them. They boiled the beaver pelts that were, for Radisson and Groseilliers, the purpose of the trip. They boiled the skins that mothers used as diapers.

Through all of this, the Indigenous people looked suspiciously at Groseilliers. "Seeing my brother always in the same condition, they said that some Devil brought him wherewithal to eat, but if they had seen his body they should be of another opinion. The beard that covered his face made as if he had not altered his face. For me that had no beard, they said I loved them, because I lived as well as they."[122] As usual, Groseilliers' insensitivity to local customs and feelings brought suspicion and trouble down on both men. This would happen several times, in various countries, for almost thirty years. Radisson, too, was sometimes suspect. Some of the

Lake Superior people called him "The Iroquois" and wondered where his loyalties really lay.

Yet, unlike the starving Hurons trapped on Gahoendoe in 1649, who, with horror, ate the bodies of their dead relatives, or Radisson's hungry Iroquois war party that cooked and ate a prisoner in the Fire Nation seven years before, the people at this camp preferred to starve than to eat human flesh. Radisson, who never showed any qualms about cannibalism, had to respect this taboo.

Opportunity showed itself when two half-starved Sioux men arrived in the camp with their emaciated dog. Radisson offered to buy the pet, but they would not sell. There was no way to put pressure on them: the rest of the people in the camp, hungry as they were, would not steal from these men. This didn't stop Radisson. Late one night, he pretended to go behind the Sioux men's lodge to relieve himself, and quietly called for the dog to come out. Then he lured it away from its sleeping owners, pulled out a dagger, and stabbed the dog to death. Radisson carried the animal's body to his own cabin, where the dog was, Radisson writes, "broiled like a pig, cut in pieces, guts and all, so every one of the family had his share." Whether to cover up this act of canicide or to make the most of the windfall, one of the people in Radisson's cabin went back to the killing spot, gathered the bloody snow, and brought it back to be boiled into soup.

The Feast of the Dead

Nasty as this crime was, Radisson believed it was the food he and his "family" needed to get the strength to keep going. He probably got away with it, since, a few weeks later, eight leaders of the Sioux (whom the Huron among the refugees called Nadoneseronons, the Nation of the Beef) arrived in the camp. They carried corn and a grain that was probably wild rice, and the hungry Menominee and the Odawa, Saulteaux and Wendat refugees gladly accepted it as a gift. The Sioux women greased Radisson's feet and legs. Radisson and his family painted the Sioux women red. Then the Sioux women stripped Radisson naked and clothed him in leather and white beaver fur. The women wept on Radisson's head for him and members of his family, before the Sioux elders and chiefs offered tobacco to the fire and shared peace pipes. The next day, the interpreters summoned Radisson, who understood the languages of the people he had wintered with, but knew no Sioux, to meet with the Sioux leaders again. This time, they took out a treasured red stone pipe, its bowl as big as a fist and its stem several feet long. Eagle tail-feathers were tied in a fan shape over the stem of this fabulous pipe. Radisson and the leaders of the camp took the eagle's tail and hung twelve iron arrowheads on the pipe, planted hatchets, knives, and armour into the earth, and made a kind of rack from these metal things to set the pipe upon. This symbolized the alliance being created between the Sioux and the two men who claimed to be able to speak for all French people everywhere.

Everyone smoked their pipes in silence, then Radisson and Groseilliers spoke to the Sioux chiefs through an interpreter: "Brethren, we have accepted of your gifts. Ye are called here to know our will and pleasure that is such: first, we take you for our brethren by taking you into our protection, and for to shew you, we, instead of the eagles' tail, have put some of our armors, to the end that no enemy shall approach it to break the affinity that we make now with you." Then they took the twelve iron arrowheads from the pipe, held them up, and said those points would pass over the whole world "to destroy your enemies, who are ours." The arrowheads were reattached to the pipe stem. Next, Radisson took the sword and told the Sioux to have courage, since it would be used to vanquish their enemies. Then the hatchet was pulled out of the ground and waved around, with the French saying the axe would be used to kill the Sioux's enemies and to build a fort to protect them when they came for the Feast of the Dead. The ceremony ended with Radisson or Groseilliers throwing a handful of gunpower into the fire, causing a small blast and filling the lodge with so much smoke that the people inside had to leave. The Sioux had never seen a gunpowder explosion and they didn't like it. It took some persuasion by the camp leaders, through the interpreter, to convince the Sioux that this was not some kind of sorcery, or an insult, and that they should come back into the lodge for the rest of the ceremony.

18th-century illustration of the Feast of the Dead. This illustration shows the Feast of the Dead witnessed by Jean de Brébeuf in 1636. The feast held by the First Nations of the southern Lake Superior region used the same ritualistic elements.

Despite all their big talk, the Sioux were not impressed by Radisson, Groseilliers, and what they saw around them. The camp was a miserable place where people suffered every day, even after they started eating the food brought by the Sioux. Scurvy set in, and Radisson and Groseilliers' gums started to bleed. The people in the camps were so weak that they hadn't dragged the dead out of the lodges and buried them in the snow. People kept dying in that miserable village before the new warmth of spring and its rain arrived to clear the snow and restore the balance between the hunters and their game. The first break came after a late-winter thaw, when the snow thickened, then re-froze. Men could easily walk on the icy snow-pack, deer could not. The hunters chased them down and cut their throats with knives. Even this change of luck didn't end the pain that came from months of hunger, though. Famine had wrecked the victims' stomachs and guts, and many of the people became sick when they ate the fresh meat.

After about three weeks, the survivors of the famine had revived enough to travel to the Feast of the Dead. The rendezvous was between a small lake and a meadow. When Radisson and Groseilliers' host band arrived, people from eighteen nations had already set up camp. There were about five hundred people gathered in the new settlement, living in longhouses holding extended families of twenty people or more. The men, now healthy enough to work, built a very large palisade that protected both the new village and a small stream that provided the people with water. This wooden wall was set up in a couple of days, just before thirty young Sioux men arrived carrying deer hunting equipment. These men, with their heavily painted faces, were the vanguard of a larger group. There was still some snow in the camp, so some of the host people cleared out a large circle in the centre of the lodges, where soft boughs were laid on the ground and fires were set up for a feast. Big kettles full of meat were hung to boil over these fires, where the Sioux sat silently for five hours. The leaders of the new community made speeches to them, which carried on for some time. When the Sioux finally spoke, they said the elders of their band would arrive the next day to renew their friendship with the local people and make a new alliance with the French. This had not been an automatic thing: many of the young Sioux wanted to wage war against the French and the Christian Indigenous people who had arrived uninvited in their country.

The elders, dressed in gorgeous clothes adorned with painted feathers, arrived the next day with great pomp. Before them came young people carrying bows and holding small shields on their shoulders painted with images of the sun, the moon, and animals. Their faces were painted in various colours and patterns. Their hair, which had been cut evenly by using fire, was styled upwards. They left a long tuft at the top and tied it with leather straps decorated with freshwater mussel pearls, what Radisson called "Turkey stones," along with bits of swan down. Their robes were held together by belts of snakeskin hung with bear paws. Grease sprinkled with red earth or ochre covered their bodies. The men's ears were pierced in five places with holes large enough to put a finger through. Some wore stars or half-moons made of shiny copper. Their capes, of buffalo or moose skins, were embroidered with freshwater pearls and coloured porcupine quills, and they wore boots made of buffalo skins. Each man carried long knives or swords, war axes with stone heads, or carved, round-headed wooden war clubs. Some wore the scalps of enemies on their arms.

The chiefs, who arrived next, wore full-length leather coats that touched the ground. Each one carried a valuable, beautifully made pipe and a small sack holding his best possessions. They hadn't painted their faces, but they wore elaborate hairstyles and headdresses. Last came the women with so much baggage that they could barely be seen under their loads. The women unloaded their bundles, which held the skins used for their tents, and set up them up in less than half an hour.

The most important Sioux chiefs and elders went into the biggest lodge in the village, where fires were kindled, to hear the leaders of the Odawa, Ojibwe, and the refugees from the Iroquois war make long, eloquent speeches. The Sioux offered gifts to the French, along with plenty of flattery, to entice them into a trade and military alliance. The Sioux then promised to take Radisson and Groseilliers to the heart of their country to show the bounty that was the traders' for the taking. The mountains were lowered, the valleys rose, the way would be very smooth for the French, the Sioux said. Branches on the trails had been cleared away and bridges were built over rivers so the French traders' feet would always be dry. The doors of their villages, the homes of their wives and daughters were always open to them. Since the French weapons that the Sioux had received in trade through Odawa middlemen had given the Sioux the power to defeat their enemies, the French had given them life.

A second set of gifts was given to the people of the village, to show they were still allies of the Sioux and under their protection and that the Sioux were happy to be invited to the Feast of the Dead. A third gift was given to ask the Odawa and Ojibwe to keep their fort doors open to the Sioux if the Sioux were attacked again, and to fight to save the Sioux if they and their families were threatened. The Sioux also gave the gift of bison hides as a way of asking the French to sell them more guns.

The two traders, probably at Groseilliers' insistence, put on the kind of show that was common in any early encounter between Europeans armed with gunpowder weapons and Indigenous people who were not. It wasn't something Radisson would have done on his own, since he'd always profited by fitting in with the Indigenous people and effectively becoming one of them, not by trying to dominate and intimidate them. Radisson and Groseilliers were given wooden bowls for a feast. Rather than just sit with the Sioux and the refugees, they grabbed two small boys and had them walk ahead of them, carrying the bowls and spoons. Then they found four men to carry their guns in front of them in a sort of parade, while Radisson and Groseilliers each carried a pair of pistols, a dagger, and a sword. Radisson and Groseilliers wore hats—more like crowns—embroidered with painted porcupine quills. Their hosts assigned four beautiful young women to lay bearskins on the floor for them in a place of honour.

Four elders arrived in the lodge with their red stone pipes in their hands. One old man said he thanked the sun, that he had never seen a day that made him so happy. He took off his robe and placed it over the shoulders of the French. Then one of the young women brought a hot coal for the old man to light his pipe. The host people rose, and one of them started to sing. One of the Frenchmen told the Sioux through an interpreter that the French would protect them and take them into their families. Then the French, who had loaded all their muskets with gunpowder but no bullets, signalled for the Menominee or Odawa men carrying their guns to fire them. In all, a dozen guns went off. Radisson and Groseilliers pulled out their swords and waved them around, then threw a handful of gunpowder into the fire.

After this show, the feasters went to work on their food. The women served a meal of wild rice gathered by canoeists from the small lakes of the region. After this first course, the women filled, lit, and brought the pipes back to the men before the meat courses began.

The next day, it was the turn of the Ojibwe, Odawa, Menominee, Huron-Petun refugees, and their French allies to give gifts to the Sioux, both to show their friendship and to acknowledge they were visitors on Sioux land. Radisson told the Sioux he and his people had come "from the other side of the great salted lake, not to kill them but to make them live." He said the Sioux were both the "brethren and the children" of the French, a claim that must have left the Sioux somewhat perplexed. This fantastic claim of French dominance and sovereignty was backed up with the mediocre gift of a copper cooking pot. The second gift symbolized the empty promise of a military alliance in which the French, as "masters in peace and war," claimed to be able to protect the Sioux. The French, Radisson claimed, had the power to subdue anyone and everyone in the world, including whatever enemies the Sioux might have. The Cree, whom the Sioux were so suspicious of (and whom some warriors among them desperately wanted to fight), were good friends of the French, the traders lied, and Radisson, on behalf of that great power, France, would make sure the peace was maintained. This worthless promise was sealed with a gift of six hatchets.

Radisson and his brother-in-law tried to set themselves up as peacemakers between the Cree and the Sioux. If, they told their hosts, the Sioux should break the peace, the French would become their enemies and "would reduce them to powder with our heavenly fire." The same would happen to the Cree if they attacked the Sioux. Instead, everyone should go wage war against the peoples of the west, whom Radisson and Groseilliers didn't know, and didn't care who they were or what happened to them. These threats and incitements were backed with the gift of six hatchets. Now came a third present, for the Sioux to lead the dance at the Feast of the Dead, and a fourth, for allowing the French safe passage through this country. The gift for the Feast of the Dead dance was two dozen knives, while safe passage in the country was rewarded with six graters, two dozen awls, two dozen needles, thirty-six little tin mirrors, six combs, a dozen small bells, and some vermilion. One elder who had been especially helpful to the traders got an axe, several others were given sword blades, and the beautiful women who waited on the people at the feast were given two necklaces and some bracelets, which came with the requirement that all the women "should love us" and feed the two traders when they came to their lodges. When the gift-giving was over, those who had received presents chanted "Ho! Ho! Ho!" in thanks.

It was all bluster and lies, of course. Radisson and Groseilliers weren't even trading within the letter of French or Indigenous law, and they certainly didn't have any standing as French ambassadors. None of the pledges of national alliance or even friendship was worth anything more than the word of these two con men. They couldn't get the Sioux any more guns than the ones they had with them, and they most certainly could not bind the administration of New France, which was still in the hands of a private company, or the government of France, in any kind of alliance or trade deal with anyone. But they still carried on, these self-styled Caesars of the wilderness, in this Kiplingesque farce.

Fifty men, including Radisson, were dispatched from the camp to find the Cree and tell them they were now safe. After walking for days though the bush, Radisson found the Cree back at the place where hunters had stockpiled meat and animal grease for the Feast of the Dead. Radisson, despite his constant search for a good meal, had a miserable time at this camp because he'd become snow-blind from the strong spring sunlight reflecting off a still-frozen lake that he crossed on the last day of the hike. He could barely see for seven or eight days and worried that his eyesight might never recover.

Now the Cree, with half-blind Radisson in tow, went to the main Feast of the Dead camp. The people from nineteen nations, now decently fed and temporarily at peace, played sports like lacrosse, gambled, sang, and danced. Some of the younger men tried to climb poles slathered in bear and moose grease, and those who succeeded received prizes. The highlight of the opening day was an eat-all feast like the one the Jesuits and their men had used as a weapon against the Onondaga. Men and women were invited to this party. To entertain their guests, the hosts put on war pantomimes: young men acting as though they were stalking their enemies, fighting, and capturing them, cutting off their heads. Drumbeats, women singing harmonies, and older men playing rattles accompanied this performance, along with the feasters, who called out the kinds of scenes they wanted in a sort of improvised show. One of the actors pretended to pull an arrow out of his body, another played the role of a sentry and caught one of the "enemy" creeping around the camp. With the promises of peace made at the feast's opening—as dubious as those promises may have been—people who had, just weeks before, been lethal enemies, now settled for play-fights.

The Feast of the Dead was a Huron tradition that had recently spread to the hunting peoples to the north and west, who adapted it to fit their way of life. A Huron village moved about every fifteen or twenty years as the fields around it became exhausted and infertile from growing corn. During the time the village existed, the Huron placed the bodies of their dead onto platforms built in the trees or on frames. The Huron believed the body had two souls: one that stayed in the cemetery while the body decayed, then flew away in mourning doves, and another that remained with the bones themselves. From time to time, the souls of the dead were reincarnated into babies, which explained why some people bore a striking resemblance to a lost relative. The dead had to be revered. Their names could not be said aloud unless the name was a title (like the Roman "Caesar" or the Kitchisspirini's "Tessouat") or had been given to an adoptee, the way Radisson had inherited Orhima. To insult the name of a dead relative was the worst thing a Huron could do to another, and the community expected such an insult to be met with deadly force.

Even the Feast of the Dead was arranged in a sort of code. Jean de Brébeuf, who watched the planning of a large one at Ossossane, near modern-day Midland, Ontario in 1636, said the leading chiefs of the town spoke of it as "the kettle," while preparing for the feast was described as "lighting the fire for the kettle." If it was postponed—and these feasts were so politically charged that they sometimes got delayed if there were divisions in the community or spats with the leaders of surrounding towns—the chiefs talked of "overturning the kettle."

Once it was clear the feast was to be held, the Huron and those who adopted the Feast of the Dead went to work exhuming the dead. There seems to have been a special religious society, or at least a group of volunteers, who did most of the unpleasant work of cleaning the bones. Usually the older ones had almost no flesh, just a leathery shell of parchment-like skin. Newer tree tombs contained bodies that were only partially decayed. The families of the dead watched and mourned as whatever was left on the bones of their relatives was stripped away and thrown into a fire. Those who had recently died were simply taken down and rewrapped, to be reinterred whole.

Young men volunteered to dig a pit about twenty feet across and line it with furs and grave presents. Then they built a scaffold to hold the bones until the Master of the Feast dumped each bundle into the pit. The sheer brilliance of the Feast of the Dead, this reburial, lay in the idea that the bones—the souls—of individual people were very deliberately mixed together in a symbolic kettle. Here was the community, in death, becoming one great spiritual entity forever. It was important to invite every ally to be a part of this great spiritual unification. Friends and relatives from other villages and foreign nations cemented their friendship and kinship with the feasters by bringing some of their dead, too: the same kind of external bonds created by marriage were made in a funeral rite. All of this was a huge community project. The collection and cleaning of bones, the making of the pit, the giving of the furs, the games, the gathering of food, especially meat, and cooking for days of feasting, all required people to work together. Feasts of the Dead were shows of wealth and generosity. Everyone brought the most expensive gifts they could afford. Radisson and Groseilliers handed out presents every day for two weeks at ceremonies to renew alliances, marriages, and, most important, for the dead themselves.

In return for Radisson's little metal presents made during his speeches, he received three hundred beaver robes, each one an elegant piece of clothing made from several beaver skins. These fantastic presents, even when they were taken apart and destroyed to make felt hats, were worth a fortune. In fact, the gifts to Radisson from this single Feast of the Dead were enough to save the colony of New France at a time when Paris and the fur trade's financial backers were seriously considering giving up their besieged toehold on the St. Lawrence.

This was one of the very few Feasts of the Dead held in the Upper Great Lakes.[123] People in the region—the Ojibwe probably being early adopters—had held their first Feast of the Dead just a generation before, and, within a couple of decades, French missionaries would snuff the ritual out, just as the Canadian government would later try to crush the potlatch, a West Coast gift-giving celebration in the Pacific Northwest, and ban traditional dances on the Prairies.

The big Upper Peninsula feast of 1659 brought some peace to this troubled part of the world, and Radisson and Groseilliers quickly took advantage of it. First, they went southwest to visit the Sioux. The journey took more than a week, the two traders arriving at a place where the Sioux had built solid houses covered with skins and mats. There were about seven thousand men in the town and many had more than one wife: Radisson claimed one man had fourteen. This was Radisson's kind of place. There was corn to eat, but the Sioux made most of their living from hunting. The men were skilled buffalo hunters, who harvested on the flatlands south of the Canadian Shield, and expert trappers, who went north to take beavers that Radisson thought were the best furs in the world. They also, Radisson wrote, controlled copper, lead, and silver mines along Lake Superior.

Radisson went along with the Sioux on hunts on the prairie and may even have reached the Mississippi.[124] The "Buff," he learned, was "a furious animal" capable of killing a man. Every year, these great beasts gored or trampled Sioux hunters, who did not yet have horses and hunted bison on foot, with dogs. In the summer, when Radisson hunted with the Sioux, they went after the animals on the plains and in meadows, but it was easier to kill them in the winter, when the buffalo that lived in the borderlands of the grass plains and in forested country herded among stream-valley trees for shelter and stomped out "yards" in the snow. (Deer also do this.) Radisson was impressed by the size of these great animals, but was even more enthralled by their horns, which were not as long as those of a European ox but were thicker. Some, Radisson later wrote, were so big that a man could barely lift them. The Sioux used these horns for meals because they could hold three quarts of food or water. They relied on these animals for everything, from tent skins to hair oil, and hunted them from the south shore of Lake Michigan to Lake Superior, as well as in the Mississippi Valley.

Radisson and Groseilliers stayed with the Sioux for six weeks, enjoying their hospitality and trading for beaver furs, before heading east to the Ojibwe. It took them nearly two weeks to get back to the main Ojibwe community, and they arrived just at the height of the summer moose-hunting season. Radisson, Groseilliers, and an Ojibwe friend killed so many moose that they needed to rely on the kindness of strangers to help them get the meat back to the main camp, which now had about twenty longhouses and lodges. There, they spent the winter with enough food to see them through, and the people of the region were spared the starvation that had taken so many in the months before the Feast of the Dead.

Through the summer, while Radisson travelled, Groseilliers had traded for furs with the Cree, Ojibwe, and other people on the peninsula. He was determined not to starve again, so he also bought and stashed enough dried corn to carry him and Radisson through the winter. Being Groseilliers, he hid his corn dealings from his neighbours in case they had another hard winter and expected him to share—just as they had shared with him so many times. In fact, he bought and hid enough to feed all the people on the canoe brigade he was organizing for spring. The traders had so many furs that they would need hundreds of people to carry them to Quebec.

Groseilliers did come down with something Radisson calls "falling sickness" (likely some kind of vertigo caused by an ear infection), but Radisson nursed him back to health. Radisson spent much of the long, cold winter piecing together the geography that he would use later to travel to Hudson Bay, and trying to figure out a way to convince the Cree to show it to him.

STRICTLY BUSINESS

Once their second winter in the Upper Lakes started to loosen its grip, it was time for Radisson and Groseilliers to slip away to retrieve the hatchets, knives, and other hardware from the hiding spots near the ruins of their little fort on Lake Superior and set up their new trading post nearby. They soon found out, however, that their plan wasn't going to be easy to execute. An Indigenous group, who Radisson calls the "Octanaks," had built a fort very close by, and he was afraid they would find his stash. The north winds had blown ice into the bay, but Radisson was willing to risk his life crossing it. The sun was blazing as he and Groseilliers struggled across, each pulling sledges piled high with furs. Groseilliers stumbled and cursed as he tried to drag his, so Radisson offered to trade. This arrangement didn't last long. One of Radisson's legs went through the ice into the frigid water, leaving him with an ugly cut and a sprained knee. They tried to press on. "To leave our booty would be to undo us," he wrote a decade later, but Radisson couldn't stand upright or go any farther. Groseilliers stripped Radisson, wrapped him in a beaver robe, and left him on a sled piled high with furs while he kept going until he reached his fort. Groseilliers was too weak to go back for Radisson, so he went to the Octanaks for help. A couple of the young men were willing to rescue Radisson, but they expected gifts, which Groseilliers grudgingly gave them.

It took Radisson more than a week to recover. The pain in his knee kept him awake night and day. Groseilliers put Radisson's injured leg into some sort of traction and rubbed it with warm bear oil, and it healed, at least enough to walk on. At the same time, Groseilliers kept working on the new trading post. People were showing up to barter furs, and some Ojibwe wanted Radisson to leave the new post and travel with them to collect more beavers. Radisson, always more eager than Groseilliers to see the country, made the mistake of agreeing, and on the third day of the trip his wound reopened and his knee gave out. His travelling companions left him in the woods to look after himself and catch up. Radisson struggled on in pain, navigating by the sun and never being sure of where he was. He had about ten pounds of food and, with some irony, later remembered he had no hatchet or gun. He kept going for five days, doing most of his travelling in the morning when the pain was less intense, until he came to an abandoned lodge. He stayed there for days, his clothes in rags, with almost no food left.

The Odawa were looking for him, and one of the searchers found him just as he ran out of food and firewood. The man carried twenty pounds of food, which Radisson devoured after the two men had shared a pipe of tobacco. The man reassured Radisson that a village of Huron refugees, mostly Christians, was close by. Two clans had created this village, which seems to have been a satellite of the larger centre of Michilimackinac, the long-settled strategic meeting place between Lake Huron and Lake Michigan. Once his leg was better, Radisson and his companions paddled southwest along the shore of upper Lake Michigan, heading toward Green Bay, and took whatever ducks and fish they needed. They visited more Sioux villages, where some people kept bison in pens.

Meanwhile, Groseilliers had left the trading post and was back in the Cree village, pestering his hosts and their guests about religion. He seems to have thought of himself as more than a trader and wilderness emperor. He also had ambitions to be a missionary, either in the belief he could redirect the souls of the Cree from hell to heaven, or to impress the Jesuits back home. He had lugged some religious pictures all the way up the canoe route and through the winter snow and took these out when he got the chance. Some Sioux traders came into town to see Radisson and Groseilliers, but rather than make speeches and exchange gifts, Groseilliers took out a small picture of Mary, Joseph, and the baby Jesus fleeing from King Herod and showed it to the Cree and Sioux visitors. The lifelike image of a woman seemed to disturb one of the Cree, who wept, pulled at his hair, and tumbled toward the lodge's hearth. When the man regained his composure, he told the two French traders that members of a Sioux band had stolen his wife. To him, the Virgin Mary represented his lost wife, the donkey she rode on symbolized the bison, and Joseph was an image of the Cree man, in a long robe, searching for his wife. To some of the other people in the lodge, the image was a piece of sorcery. This was not a great way to win Christian converts, and might well have sown suspicion among the Cree that the two Frenchmen were not what they seemed.

Groseilliers made far too many of these faux pas, so it's probably a good thing that he stayed in a village where people knew him while Radisson did most of the networking with strangers. That spring and summer, Radisson worked his way through the jumble of people with different languages and customs sheltering on the Upper Peninsula and along the frontier between the Cree and the Sioux, where the shaky peace held through those warm months. He gathered more furs and set up new trade relationships that he expected to exploit when he returned to the Upper Lakes with his next load of guns, axes, pots, and other hardware.

The Sioux, like most Indigenous people, grew fond of Radisson. It helped that he promised the French would build ships and come to see them, give them guns, and fight alongside them. In return, Radisson developed respect for the Sioux, brave hunters and warriors who lived in a land of plenty and killed only what they needed. Unlike many other people in the region, the Sioux had no trouble making a living and feeding picky French guests: Radisson saw bison everywhere. The Sioux wanted to become wealthier by opening trade routes and strategically blocking the Cree from becoming the main hunter-trader allies of the French. Both the Cree and the Sioux accused the other First Nation of treachery, with each side engaging in the kind of slander and duplicity that Radisson says reminded him of the sleazy dealings among courtiers at a European monarch's court.

Neither the Cree nor the Sioux were about to hand themselves over to be ruled by the French, nor did they want to be just labourers and customers, so they were careful not to spill too many of their secrets about regional geography. Radisson and Groseilliers were not explorers. The countryside might be new to them and to Europeans back home, but a typical Sioux, Cree, Huron, Odawa, Ojibwe, or Algonquin trader, or Mohawk warrior, knew eastern North America better than do most people who live there today. They saw the country close-up from their canoes and trails as they travelled across it. They took the time to find the land's spiritual places, admire its beauty, taste its rivers, and sleep under its sky. It's likely not an exaggeration to say that the people who traded with Radisson were familiar with most of the continent, from the Great Plains to the Atlantic, and from Hudson Bay to the Gulf of Mexico, and with the people who lived there. If they hadn't seen these places and people themselves, they knew people who had. It was not in their interest to hand this knowledge over to the French. They knew it was valuable intellectual property that, along with their labour, gave them bargaining power they could not afford to lose.

That's why the Cree told Radisson it was a bad time to head from the Lake Michigan-Lake Superior region to the "northern sea," the name given to Hudson Bay by the French. Radisson wanted to be the first Frenchman to make the overland trip to Hudson Bay and he may have already come up with the idea of a direct sea-based fur trade with the Cree. He had a fairly good idea of where Hudson Bay was, but he didn't know the canoe route from Lake Superior and needed Cree labour and political support to make the trip happen. The Jesuits had already pried the details of the Ottawa River-Temagami-Moose River route from the Nipissings of what's now Central Ontario, or at least had a general idea of it, but none of the French knew the geography of the vast lakelands and swamps between Lake Superior and Hudson Bay, an area the size of France. They didn't know of big rivers like the Albany that were natural, easily travelled highways, and the Cree did not want them to know. So the Cree said it was duck season. Maybe they could go later, in rabbit season or moose season.

To keep Radisson happy, they drew a crude map that helped confirm Radisson's sense of geography, but which would have been rather useless to a stranger in the vast half-water, half-land landscape north of Superior. The Cree also tried to scare Radisson off by telling him of big, bottomless lakes and rivers in the north, places where the ice never melted and where vicious birds with beaks as sharp as swords waged war against the local people. Radisson wasn't sure these stories were true, but he got the point. So, for now, he had to settle for adding to the furs that he got during the Feast of the Dead and his trip to the Sioux, and filling his cooking pot with the ducks that fattened themselves on the wild rice that grew along the shores of the shallow inland lakes. There were so many ducks and geese that hunters could sometimes kill three with a single arrow shot. It was not unusual to see six hundred swans in a migrating flock. The summer sun was so strong that Radisson could cook duck eggs by leaving them for half an hour on the hot sands of a Lake Michigan beach. As fall approached, the band kept moving, taking more birds, snaring hundreds of moose,[125] and catching and drying fish taken from spawning grounds in a vast, rich land where the only real danger came from other people.

Radisson's Cree hosts were wary of strangers, though generous with friends. The Cree kept only one wife, which, Radisson believed, left the men much happier than the Sioux, who had so many. In the summer, they wore deerskin clothing, but, when the weather was right, preferred to wear little or nothing. In the winter, they dressed in very warm clothes made of beaver pelts. The Cree were great hunters, probably the best Radisson ever met, but they were also careful with nature. When they hunted beavers, they left the immature ones in their dens and came back for them in a later hunting season. Radisson says the women worked at least as hard as the men, and everyone in the community tried to dress well and wear jewellery, some of it made from turquoise from the far southwest, some from a green stone found along the Lake Michigan bay that now carries the name Green Bay.

The Cree did not adopt prisoners. They didn't grow many crops that needed foreign women's labour, and their winter bands were too small to handle the disruption of the adoption process. Nor did they torture male captives, believing that ritual to be cruel. The Cree told Radisson it was much more humane to dispatch them with a knock on the head.[126] The

Cree seemed like kind, generous people who weren't likely to run out of furs, and they liked Radisson, so he travelled with them between the north end of Lake Michigan to western Lake Superior. Heading north, Radisson hoped, would give him the chance to tap into a supply of even cheaper furs. The Sioux sent messengers to keep in touch with Radisson, but, despite all the courting, they didn't have many beaver furs. The Feast of the Dead and the next summer's trade with Radisson had wiped them out.

Radisson may never have realized the startling honesty of the Cree, Sioux, Menominee, and the rest of the people of that region. Here was one Frenchman wandering the countryside lugging and dragging a fortune in beaver skins and expensive trade goods. "Accidents" could easily have happened. He could have "drowned," "fallen off a cliff," "fallen through the ice," or just disappeared. Itinerant peddlers who were licensed, or who, like Radisson and Groseilliers, traded illegally, were rare but not unknown in the Upper Lakes, and the presence—or absence—of these two men would have little impact on relations between the Indigenous people and the French. Yet here was a country where robbery and theft were so uncommon that Radisson and Groseilliers could trudge around, freeloading food, shelter, labour, and, likely, sex, from the locals without any obvious fear of being quickly and discreetly put out of business. It's unlikely they would have been able to move hundreds of miles through Europe carrying a fortune in easily disposed of merchandise for very long without some bandit or greedy lord taking it illegally or legally. The Cree, Ojibwe, Sioux, and the rest of the Indigenous people Radisson and Groseilliers met along the way somehow managed to maintain a safe country without relying on the crushing power of absolute monarchies, police forces, jails, or corporal and capital punishment. It would be interesting to see how far two peddlers openly carrying about a million dollars' worth of stuff down back roads would get in these parts of Michigan today.

One of the great questions of history is whether Radisson made a trip to Hudson Bay in the spring of 1660. Some historians think it's possible, that there was enough time between the end of that winter and his mid-summer departure from Lake Superior for Montreal for Radisson to reach the Northern Sea. A careful reading of the people involved and the geography makes this unlikely. Radisson and the Cree—the only people who knew the routes, which belonged to them—would have had to gather supplies, paddle to the north shore of Lake Superior, head up the Nipigon or one of the other rivers flowing from the north, cross the height of land and travel hundreds of miles down the huge rivers of the Hudson Bay basin, which were frozen well into May, then do the whole trip in reverse. We know the Cree did not want to show him the route, and there was no good reason for them to make the trip in a time of year when their families needed them to hunt. We also know Radisson was supposedly back on Lake Superior in time for the beginning of the summer fishing season and left for Montreal a few weeks afterwards. That gave him at best between ten and twelve weeks to make the Hudson Bay trip.

It's clear the Cree wanted to trade with Radisson and his local partners on Lake Superior, and had absolutely no need to make a rushed trip at their own expense to the northern edge of their country to satisfy the whims of a tourist. The Cree had brought everything they might need to Lake Superior, including their families, and were settled in for the summer. In his writings about the Lake Superior trip, he spends much more time describing Cree women than he does on the Hudson Bay journey:

"It was a pleasure to see that embarking, for all the young women went in stark naked, their hairs hanging down," Radisson wrote ten years later. "I thought it their shame, but contrary they think it excellent and old custom good. They sing aloud and sweetly. They stood in their boats, and remained in that posture half a day, to encourage us to come and lodge with them again. Therefore, they are not altogether ashamed to shew us all, to entice us, and animate the men to defend themselves valiantly and come and enjoy them." Likely, they needn't have done this much work to seduce Radisson, if, in fact, that's what they were trying to do.[127]

Some history books say Radisson and Groseilliers did so well on this trip because they explored new, untapped sources of furs at the edge of the subarctic. Radisson is clear that it was the Cree who came south *en masse*, with more furs to add to his haul from the Feast of the Dead. Some four hundred Cree arrived at Lake Superior through the summer to join three hundred of their friends and relatives who were already at the camp. By mid-summer, Radisson and Groseilliers had seventy tons of beaver pelts, making the trip to Hudson Bay unnecessary.

Radisson skips over all the details of this supposed trip in his writing, probably because he didn't know anything about the geography. Had he seen the flat-topped hills along the north shore of Lake Superior, these cuestas and mesas from an ancient desert, he would have mentioned them. Nor does he write about the giant rivers and vast marshlands of the Hudson Bay lowlands. He grossly underestimates the northern sea's distance from Lake

Superior, gives no details of the timing of the trip: comparing the extremely detailed description of his journey from Montreal to the Onondaga country to this barebones story of "exploration" shows how very empty it is. In claiming to be the first European to make this trip, Radisson pulled off another con job, just as he had when he wrote an entire story about travelling with Groseilliers to the Mississippi years before.

In his writings, he briefly mentions finding a stone house on the shore of Hudson Bay or James Bay that he says was built by poor Henry Hudson and his men after mutineers had marooned them almost fifty years previously. It takes a huge leap of imagination to believe Radisson found, or was taken to, the exact place on that gigantic body of water where Hudson came ashore (if, in fact, Hudson even made it to the coast). Then, almost by magic, Radisson's back on the southwest shore of Lake Superior with no more furs than when he set out.

So why lie? There are several possible answers. The first is that it makes a better story, though Radisson only wrote a few dozen words about the supposed trip. The second may lie in Radisson's ideas about law. In Indigenous law, such a voyage would have made Radisson master and owner of the trade between the Europeans and the Cree of Hudson Bay. This was no small thing. It would give him the right to trade, and to decide who would pay a royalty to use the route. Strikingly, however, Radisson never seems to have made this claim publicly among people who followed Indigenous law. His "discovery" would also hold some weight in European law, which had no concept of "master of the route," but it did strengthen Radisson's case that he had some sort of right to go back to Hudson Bay and trade. When he claimed in writing to have made the Hudson Bay journey, he was pitching the idea of a subarctic fur trade to people whom he needed to impress with his credibility as an explorer and who might have simply opened the Hudson Bay fur trade without him.

Anyway, in July 1660, Radisson started pushing east along the south shore of Lake Superior, with this Ojibwe and Ottawa friends helping to lug all those tons of furs. After a two-day trip, they arrived at one of the many "sturgeon rivers" in the Great Lakes region. This one is probably just east of the base of the Keweenaw Peninsula. The Cree killed more than one thousand of those big fish in the two weeks they were there, drying or smoking much of the meat. (Smoked sturgeon tastes remarkably like bacon.) Soon, there was the threat of violence in the air: some women found an Ojibwe man, dead from a gunshot, near the camp. A few days later, near the base of the Keweenaw Peninsula, seven Iroquois men were spotted camped on a beach, near their canoes. The local people were sure these warriors had spent the winter near the shore of Lake Huron, then gone northwest to Lake Superior.

"I cannot say that they were the first that came there," Radisson wrote. "God grant that they may be the last." The Iroquois ran into the bush when they realized they'd been spotted and the Cree had to settle for a captured gun, some axes, and a copper pot. The presence of Iroquois in their country convinced the Cree and the Ojibwe that a trip down the Ottawa River canoe route that summer was a very bad idea. This left Radisson and Groseilliers stranded in the Upper Lakes. They thought they might be able to find enough locals to ferry them home, but they needed hundreds of people to lug their furs over the portages. Radisson was heartbroken. He had hoped to arrive at Quebec with a small army of Cree and his many tons of fur. This overwhelming show of success would take care of the serious charges they faced back in the colony for their illegal trip and make them the most successful traders in New France. They would be saviours. Now, Radisson fretted, a chance like this wouldn't come along for another decade. As the days went by, more rumours of war with the Iroquois swept through the south shore of Lake Superior,[128] but they didn't stop Radisson and Groseilliers, who knew they had to leave by July of 1660 if they were to get back home by fall.

Radisson and Groseilliers convinced the local leaders to convene a council, with hundreds of people in attendance. The chiefs made it clear they believed the expedition would be wiped out. "Brethren," one said, "why are you such enemies to yourselves to put yourselves in the hands of those that wait for you? They will destroy you and carry away captives. Will you have your brethren destroyed that loves you, being slain?" Then he made a pitch to Groseilliers, who had been pestering the local people with talk of missionaries. "Who will then come up and baptize our children? Stay until the next year, and then you shall have the number of six hundred men in company with you. Then you can freely go without intermission. You shall take the church [congregation] along with you and the fathers and mothers will send their children to be taught in the truth of the Lord."

Groseilliers, who was sitting with the elders in the middle of the crowd, asked for silence and began to speak. He tried to make his hosts feel like cowards and ingrates. He told them the way to protect themselves from the Iroquois, and anyone else who was better armed, lay in accompanying

Groseilliers and Radisson to Quebec to open a trade in weapons. If they didn't, they would be overwhelmed in their own homeland.

"You will see if the enemy will set upon you that you will be a-trapped like the beavers in a trap. How will you defend yourselves like men? It is not courageous to let yourselves be caught like beasts. How will you defend your villages? With beaver skins? How will you defend your wives and children from the enemy's hands?"

Then Groseilliers motioned for Radisson to stand and speak. As Radisson got up, Groseilliers said, "Show them the way to make war if this is their choice."

Radisson took a beaver robe from the ground and hit Groseilliers on the shoulder.

"Does this make me a warrior?" Radisson asked.

It's weapons that kill, not your robes. What will your enemy say when you perish without defending yourselves? Do you not know the French way? We are used to fighting with arms and not with robes. You say the Iroquois waits for you because some of your men were killed? It is only because you have no weapons that they can dispatch you with ease. Do you think the French will come up here when the greatest part of you is slain through your own fault? You know they cannot come up here without you. Shall they come up here and baptize your dead? Shall your children learn to be slaves among the Iroquois for their fathers' cowardice?

You call me Iroquois. Have you not seen me risking my life with you? Who has given you your life, if not the French? Now you will not venture because many of your confederates have come to visit you and will venture their lives with you. If you deceive them, you must not think they will come another time for shy words nor desire. You have spoken of it first. Do what you want. For my own part, I will venture to choose to die like a man than live like a beggar. Not having the wherewithal to defend myself, I say farewell. I have my sack of corn ready. Take all my beaver pelts. I shall live without you.

Then he walked away.

The Cree decided to stay put, but the Ojibwe and probably some Odawa finally gave in. A brigade of several hundred canoes, some four hundred people in all, set out from the area just east of the Keweenaw Peninsula and headed toward the big rapids on the St. Mary's River. Along the way, they saw evidence of Iroquois raiding parties, but no warriors. Once past the Sault, they kept to the north shore of Lake Huron and went into the white quartzite hills at the lake's northwest corner, then south through the archipelago created by Georgian Bay's drowning of the Canadian Shield until they reached the mouth of the French River. With hard work, they paddled and portaged their way to Lake Nipissing—"the Lake of the Beavers"—and portaged over a few hills to reach the Ottawa River valley, lugging all those tons of furs. They did it all at the height of mosquito season, when the bugs were so bad that they made sleep almost impossible. Some men could only get a good night's rest by burying themselves in shallow pits in the sand. The big portages, like the one at Tessouat's old tolling grounds at Morrison Island, left them sweating in the brutal humidity that lies like a hot, wet blanket over the Ottawa Valley every summer. By early August, they were back at the Chaudière Falls and the Rideau River, where they could make good time on many miles of slow, deep water.

FINDING ADAM DOLLARD

At the end of this stretch of the Ottawa River, they came across a scene of horror. Above the Long Sault Rapids, about forty miles upstream from Montreal, they saw the grizzly sight of the mangled bodies of Adam Dollard and his men hanging from trees along the riverbank. Dollard, and sixteen other young Frenchmen, about sixty Huron and four Algonquins, had gone up the river at the first sign of spring to ambush Iroquois returning from the north. This raid, Radisson says, was a fight to save the struggling colony of New France, which needed the Iroquois' furs. As well, it was supposed to be proof to all the people of the region that the French could impose their will on any nation, even the Iroquois. Dollard and his men portaged around the rapids and had just reached the calmer water upstream when they saw the Iroquois fur brigade.[129] An advance party of the French expedition found the Iroquois' leading canoes, and a fight on shore left both sides bloodied and falling back on their main force. Dollard's Algonquins, who were likely members of the bands that lived along that part of the river, knew of a new fort nearby. It was a small stockade, barely able to hold twenty men, but at least it offered some defense for the French, who took it over and shut their Indian allies outside. This proved to be the first of several serious mistakes.

The Iroquois set up their own base nearby. Some were adopted Huron, and they visited the camp to persuade their former countrymen to give up. Many did leave. Still, the French and the allies who stayed had a good chance of surviving a siege by the two hundred Iroquois in the fur brigade, but another Iroquois army, probably headed toward Montreal down the St. Lawrence River, now swung north and reached the Ottawa River by paddling the sluggish creeks that wander through the flatlands northwest of Montreal. Dollard and his men were doomed. Even if they could get a message to Montreal, there weren't enough men in the town to save them.

For whatever it was worth, the French antagonized the Iroquois by cutting off the heads of men killed in the first skirmish and sticking them on poles above the little French fort. After two days of siege by the men of the Iroquois fur brigade, Dollard and his men looked out from the fort and saw another six hundred warriors camping and preparing for battle. That convinced most of the rest of the Huron to make whatever peace they could. They had little bargaining power, and they were tied up and put to preliminary tortures, as though they had been taken by force. Annaotaha, the most famous Huron war chief, did negotiate with the Iroquois, who were quite willing to adopt them all, but the French fired on the Iroquois before terms were settled.

Early 20th-century painting of Adam Dollard at the Battle of Long Sault. Dollard was considerably younger than the man shown in this picture, but the battle did end with Dollard trying—and failing—to toss a keg of gunpowder over the stockade wall.

Annaotaha went back into the fort and was one of the few Huron who stayed through the whole battle. In all, the siege lasted about a week. The Iroquois fired at the fort day and night to keep the defenders from getting any sleep. The men inside had no water. They dug a pit, hoping to make a well, but the fort was on high ground. Finally, during one of the Iroquois charges against the fort, Dollard, in a desperate attempt to kill enough Iroquois to shock the rest into abandoning the siege, lit a fuse on a barrel of gunpower and tried to toss it over the wall into a crowd of warriors. The barrel hit the inside of the wall and bounced back. The explosion killed most of the men inside the fort—the lucky ones—and blew a hole in its walls. The Iroquois stormed inside and killed all but one of the French, who, after he was captured, pulled out a pistol and killed the man who had taken him. This prisoner quickly went to the torture stake. Some of the Huron were also burned, but almost all were adopted and a few managed to escape and bring news of the battle to Montreal.

Radisson and his fur brigade arrived at the battle site about two months later, while the body parts of Dollard and his men still hung in the trees. He could see the Iroquois and French forts and the trees around them shot full of bullet holes. The sight was enough to frighten many of the men in his brigade, especially after a rumour swept through the camp that Montreal had been destroyed, and it took more promises from Radisson to keep the fur brigade moving. The travellers were too afraid to portage around the Long Sault, fearing they would come across Iroquois raiders, so they shot three sets of rapids and made a two-day run into Montreal. The village was still there, and French-Canadian historians like Abbé Lionel Groulx would later claim Dollard's heroism had saved the town. That may be true. The big Iroquois army to the south of the Long Sault was close to Montreal and might have been heading for that tiny settlement. This was French Canada's Alamo. Years later, Dollard's story changed from one of a failed robbery to a heroic martyrdom and became part of the survival narrative of the French in Canada in the face of the brutal hostility of the Iroquois, and later, the British.

Still, it was a stinging defeat for the French, which demoralized the colonial community until Radisson and Groseilliers showed up a few months later with their fantastic load of furs and convinced many of the settlers and merchants that trade with the west was possible after all.

After a few days in the little trading post at Montreal, Radisson, Groseilliers, and the Odawa and Ojibwe paddlers headed downstream to Trois-Rivières, where they received a hero's welcome. Soon after, the brigade set out for Quebec City, just a few days ahead of a Mohawk war party that was travelling the same route. The arrival of the brigade in Quebec, even to critics like the nun Marie de l'Incarnation, proved the value of Radisson and Groseilliers, since they had finally made Canada a paying proposition.

The Taxman

What happened next will always be open to conjecture. There are several accounts of the supposed bureaucratic hell inflicted on Radisson and Groseilliers when they arrived at Quebec. Probably none of them are true. This doesn't mean the various people who told the story are liars. They're litigants. And, in the heat of legal battles, cognitive dissonance and selective hearing take over.

This is Radisson's version of what happened, recounted years later in a way that stressed his victimhood at the hands of corrupt French authorities for an audience of English nobles who enjoyed stories of French sleaze. Radisson claims Groseilliers was tossed into jail for trading with an expired license. This is very unlikely, though the story shows up in many high-school texts. But we do know that the colony, which was still a private business operation without direct financial support from the government of France, was broke. The previous year, the export of furs brought in by the six other French traders who had gone inland earned less money than the colony cost the shareholders. The forts were in bad shape, settlers were scared to come

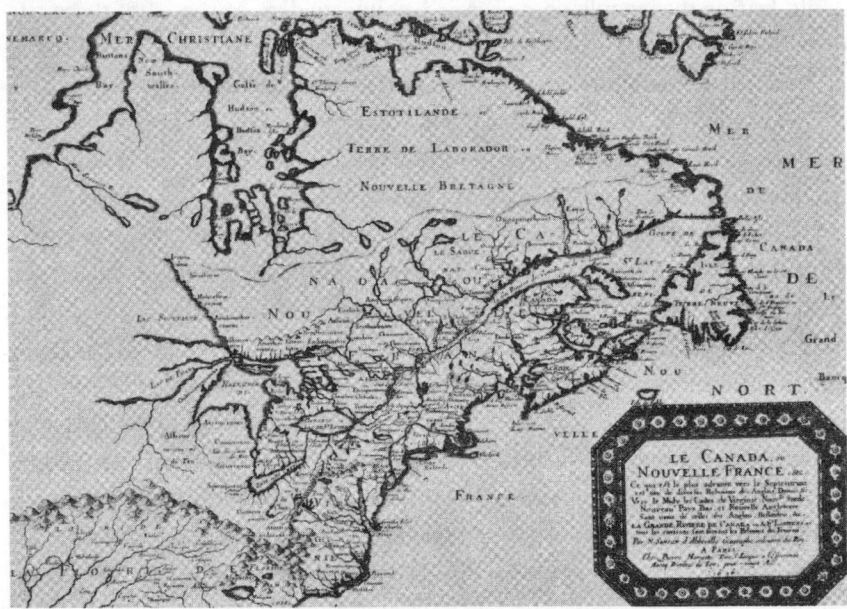

How the French saw Hudson Bay. This 1656 map, by Sanson, may have inspired Radisson to try to reach Cree fur traders by sea. Sanson made the mistake of placing James Bay very close to Lake Superior. Radisson repeated the same error in his fictitious claim that he visited Hudson Bay in 1660.

from France, and many of the best young men of New France—some ten percent of Montreal's population—had died with Dollard. Montreal was left cut off from its trade and so short of supplies that even basic food had to be shipped upriver from Quebec City. There was no sign that the situation would improve anytime soon. New France's governor, Pierre de Voyer d'Argenson, Vicomte de Mouzay, was about to leave Canada with very little personal profit and not much to show for his years in the colony.

To truly understand the situation, it's important to know how much money was at stake. Radisson brought back 140,000 pounds of beaver pelts worth 70,000 livres, according to Marie de l'Incarnation, the astute nun who recorded the colony's affairs. At this time, the livre, or French pound, was worth about one-tenth of an English pound, but the amount was still a fortune, worth nearly two thousand ounces of gold. This bonanza, according to Radisson, was met with greed by the governor, while its owners got nothing but ingratitude. "[T]he Blighter licked his chops with it," Radisson later wrote.

The governor whacked the two French traders with 10,000 livres in fines. Part of this money was to pay for a new fort at Trois-Rivières. The rest, Radisson claims, was pocketed by the governor. Then there were the trading taxes: another 14,000 livres. This left Radisson and Groseilliers with about 45,000 livres, or £4,500—about $900,000 US dollars in today's money—to divide,[130] though we don't know whether it was an even split. Still, if the two brothers-in-law carved up the money somewhat evenly after they'd paid their suppliers, they should have been able to set themselves up with land in France to rent to peasants or invest in anything they wanted. Instead, they blew it all with breathtaking speed.

First, Groseilliers headed to France to appeal the fines and taxes. Despite Radisson's later whining, Groseilliers received a rather warm welcome at the

Marie de l'Incarnation. One of the most prominent clerics of New France, she praised Radisson's and Groseilliers' fur-trading skills but believed them to be little more than criminals.

Paul Ragueneau, head of the Jesuit mission in New France and arch-enemy of Médard Chouart des Groseilliers.

court of young Louis XIV and got much of the fine money back. Then he almost immediately lost it in a failed business deal—and, as usual for Groseilliers, an expensive court case—in La Rochelle. Now calling himself the Admiral of the Ottawa River, Groseilliers surrounded himself with servants and paid flunkies. He brought at least six of them back to New France, including a badly needed gunsmith who was supposed to work for Groseilliers at Trois-Rivières. It's clear that Groseilliers, at least, planned to stay in the colony, and not defect to the English.

So what happened to drive them out of Quebec? Almost everything written about Radisson and Groseilliers claims the two men decided to betray France because French bureaucrats stole their profits and refused to listen to their plans for trading expeditions to Hudson Bay. Events say otherwise. Groseilliers' success at the French court and his hiring of so many people show he planned to make more inland trips, based out of his home near Trois-Rivières, and that Radisson was likely to be a key part of that trading business. That grandiose title of Admiral of the Ottawa River confirms this.

So it wasn't Governor d'Argenson's corruption that sent Radisson and Groseilliers to the English. In fact, it was the Iroquois. In 1661, after the Dollard disaster, the Iroquois blockaded every trade route inland from Montreal, and kept their foot on the throat of Quebec City. At the same time, the French fur-trade monopolists were fighting with each other about the right to trade, or even store furs in Montreal.[131] There was simply no way for Radisson and Groseilliers to get back on the Ottawa River and return to the west. They needed a new way to get to the Cree and their furs. And the situation was made worse by a temporary collapse in fur prices on the French market that year. Hudson Bay was the answer for two impatient, greedy men who wanted to take over the inland trade and do it as cheaply as possible.

First, Radisson and Groseilliers set out on a small boat from Quebec to secretly meet the same ship that brought Groseilliers back from France. The brothers-in-law came up with a plan to take the ship to Hudson Bay. This time, they would be trading without any kind of license—in effect, they'd be smuggling. They reached their rendezvous point, Percé Rock, a favourite place of Radisson. This northern expedition was thwarted by a Jesuit who was waiting at Percé to tell them that the Order had their own scheme for exploiting Hudson Bay for the good of New France and the missions. The plan involved sending Jesuit-employed traders up the St. Maurice River and overland to James Bay.[132] The Jesuits did not have much success as missionaries, but they certainly knew how to gather information from settlers and Indigenous people about Radisson and Groseilliers, whom they saw as threats to their own missions and plans for a northern fur trade that would pay for them. The Jesuits, with their effective intelligence network and their clout with French authorities, had made sure Radisson and Groseilliers' ship would not be coming.

This priest had more words of warning for Radisson. He said Radisson and Groseilliers should stop their treason—going against the official trading monopolies—and that Radisson should free himself from Groseilliers' malignant influences. The Jesuits kept a long list of Groseilliers' sins, which the priest quoted at length. The traders, now ship-less, were stuck with all the trade goods they had bought in Quebec for their subarctic expedition and now needed a place to trade them.

They rowed or sailed a small boat to Acadia, where they thought they had a few friends in the fur trade. There, they received an ugly reception. French settlers and traders in what's now New Brunswick and Cape Breton Island didn't want them around. Radisson and Groseilliers walked southwest until they reached Port Royal, Nova Scotia, which, though settled by the French, was under English control. It was there, rather than when the governor of New France supposedly ill-used them, they decided to turn traitor. Going over to the English would give them a chance to show everyone that their Hudson Bay plan worked, and would get them back into the beaver trade. However, England's rigid class system and its vicious hatred of foreigners, especially Roman Catholics, would ensure the plan didn't make them rich.

Book Four:
Radisson in London and Moosonee (1660–1675)

There was no great mystery about Hudson Bay in the mid-1650s. It was out of sight and out of most people's minds, but anyone who wanted to know about it just needed a good map. In 1610, Henry Hudson had sailed from England looking for a northwest passage from the Atlantic to the Pacific. Passing south of Iceland, Greenland, and Baffin Island, he went through Hudson Strait into what he assumed was the Pacific Ocean. Several more weeks of sailing led Hudson to a dead end, and he and his crew were forced to put in a miserable winter on the bay. When Hudson proposed spending a second season there, his men mutinied, and set him, along with his son and seven loyal crew members, adrift in a small boat. They were never seen again.

In 1612, Sir Thomas Button went into the bay with two ships, hoping to find Hudson and his men. Button sailed along the west coast of the bay until he reached the Nelson River, where he built a house and spent the winter. (If Radisson did reach Hudson Bay in 1660, as he claimed, and saw a house, it was almost certainly this one.) Button and his crew barely survived the winter and returned to England on one of their ships. Ice crushed the other one.

Five years later, Jens Munk, a Dane, arrived in the bay with sixty-four men and two ships. After a winter of cold and scurvy, only Munk and two of his men were still alive. They managed to find the strength to sail back to Denmark, more than 3,500 miles away, an astounding accomplishment. (Capt. William Bligh of HMS *Bounty* is remembered for his spectacular seamanship, having made a trip of the same length across the South Pacific before his crew set him and his supporters adrift in a small boat in 1793. But Bligh had eighteen strong men to row and a much more forgiving climate.) Thomas James and Luke Foxe sailed around the bay from 1631–32, charted much of its featureless coast, and proved it was not the Northwest Passage.

James had, in his bestselling book about the trip, mentioned the bay's potential as a source of furs, but, since it was now obvious Hudson Bay was not the road to China, exploration of the area stopped. The Jesuits in Quebec, who likely read James' book, soon realized they could reach the bay by land and pay for the North American missions with the profits of a Church-run fur trade while collecting Cree souls at the same time.[133]

Radisson, a collector of maps, friend of the northern Cree and a devoted student of geography, knew Hudson Bay was the boreal forest's northern boundary. He'd also been told by the Cree that it was the best area for beaver trapping. Not only were there plenty of animals, but they grew very thick undercoats to handle the minus-50-degree winters, so each fur was worth more than a beaver trapped in milder places like the Iroquois country.

Radisson and Groseilliers set out from Nova Scotia for Boston, the main English port in America, to try to find a captain who would sail an end-run around the French, Iroquois, and Odawa and take them to Hudson Bay to trade. They quickly made the acquaintance of the Gillams, a family of ship owners and captains. After more than a year of planning and gathering things to trade, Gillam took Radisson north to Labrador, but he could not, or would not, go farther into the Arctic after seeing the pack ice south of Baffin Island. They returned to Boston in 1663 with furs they'd collected along the Labrador and Newfoundland coast, but they all lost money on the trip.

17th-century engraving of Percé Rock. In Radisson's day, this rock, at the end of the Gaspé Peninsula, had two natural piercings.

The Hudson Bay trip seemed to be at a dead-end, and the brothers-in-law found themselves stuck in New England. But then Radisson's luck changed. In 1664, English commissioners arrived in Boston to see if New Netherlands, the Hudson Valley and Manhattan colony that had just surrendered to the English, was worth keeping or should be returned to the Dutch in treaty negotiations. (The French were also kicking New Netherlands's tires.) The commissioners were ordered to examine Dutch possessions in present-day New York and New Jersey and, if the assets were any good, begin the work of transferring them to English sovereignty.[134] Among them was Col. George Cartwright, a friend and business agent for George Carteret, then chief bureaucrat in the Royal Navy, and a man named Sir Robert Carr. The New Englanders might overlook suspicions that Cartwright was a Catholic, but they could not turn a blind eye to Carr's womanizing. (He supposedly kept a "naughty woman" with him in Boston.) This made the two commissioners social outcasts in puritanical Boston, so they had time to meet new friends. Radisson and Groseilliers proved to be interesting companions. It was because of Groseilliers' friendship with the two commissioners that the Jesuit mission leader Ragueneau later accused Groseilliers of helping the English snatch New York from the Dutch.[135]

Cartwright, through his mentor Carteret, had strong ties to the English Royal family. Along with his navy work, Carteret had the near-impossible job of handling Charles II's money. The king did not receive a salary in the usual sense of the term. Rather, he had to pry annual taxes out of Parliament and rent from his tenants. From that money he carried the cost of most of the government, the navy, his giant court, and his extended family of mistresses and their children. Carteret, who was quick to see the possibilities of the Hudson Bay fur trade, was the man who made the rest of Radisson's project happen. Born on the Channel Island of Jersey, he was more comfortable speaking French than English. Prior to the recent civil war between Charles I's Royalists and Puritan-dominated Parliament, he'd been a Royal Navy captain and comptroller until the fleet defected to Parliament. Carteret went back to Jersey to sit out the war, and when Parliament won, he seized control of his home island and offered it as a sanctuary to the Stuarts. They didn't take him up on the offer, but they did remember his loyalty. When Cromwell's fleet finally took Jersey, Carteret was welcomed to the Stuarts' court-in-exile in France.

Carteret was fifty years old when Charles II was restored. He was offered the job of navy treasurer, with diarist Samuel Pepys working in his office and, unknown to Carteret, documenting his life. Carteret saw the economic opportunities of North America very clearly. He was an investor in the Province of Carolina. Cartwright was in Boston partly to oversee the transfer of much of New Jersey from Dutch control to Carteret's personal absentee ownership. Carteret was at the height of his powers when his right-hand man met Radisson and Groseilliers and realized the two fur traders had a very good plan. It was Cartwright who convinced them to give up on Boston and go to London.

The *Charles* left Nantucket in the spring of 1665 under the command of Benjamin Gillam of Boston, along with Radisson, Groseilliers, Cartwright, and a cargo of 547 beaver skins, 154 otter skins, ten fox pelts, and some Brazilian sugar. The cargo was worth £540 and seven shillings.[136] They may have sailed to New York City and picked up the cargo before heading northeast. With the prevailing westerlies behind her, the *Charles* made fairly good time, even though her captain had somehow missed the Gulf Stream. Somewhere off the coast of Spain, Dutch privateers aboard the *Caper* attacked the *Charles*. Gillam fought them for two hours, but his ship was no match for theirs. Still, the fight gave the passengers time to throw all official, incriminating papers from the New York transfer overboard. The papers held vital secrets that would have been very valuable to the Dutch government. Had they been found and turned over to people who understood what they meant, the papers would have scuttled British plans for keeping the Dutch colony. They would have also revealed Cartwright to be an important man on official English business, and who would thus fetch a good ransom.

Dutch pirates were notoriously cold-blooded. Even their great admiral, De Ruijter, was accused, in his pirate days, of making people walk the plank, or, more precisely, of tying English civilians together and throwing them into the sea without bothering with the trouble of running out a board.[137] Radisson, Groseilliers, Cartwright, Gillam, and the crew of the *Charles* must have been terrified until they learned they had been captured by a less vicious breed of pirate who kept the ship and its cargo but landed his captives on a forlorn stretch of Spanish coastline. The Dutch sailed away with the *Charles* and the furs, but Radisson had more valuable cargo: knowledge of the rich fur rivers of south Hudson and James Bay. It took the *Charles*'s passengers until December to find passage to London. But deep in this misfortune lay a very large nugget of luck: if the *Charles* hadn't been taken by the Dutch, Radisson would have arrived in London at the height of the Great Plague. Still, he got to see the tail end of it, and the enormous social and political upheavals that resulted.

Once they got to England, Cartwright turned Radisson and Groseilliers over to Carteret, who wrote to Charles's foreign minister, Lord Arlington, on December 14, 1665:

> Hearing also some Frenchmen discourse in New England of a Passage from the West Sea to the South Sea, and of a great trade of beaver in that passage, and afterwards meeting there with sufficient proof of the truth of what they had said concerning the Beaver trade, conceiving great probability of truth of the passage, and knowing what great endeavors have been made for the finding out of a northwest passage, I thought them the best present I could possibly make to His Most Sacred Majesty, whereupon I persuaded them to come to England.[138]

This bragging would spread through the English court and across the country; and, within a few weeks, news of the arrival of the two Frenchmen and the English plan for a northern fur trade would spread to the Continent. Even in the mid-1600s, business news was highly valued information, and stories of Radisson and Groseilliers' pitch to the English king quickly set spies in motion in both France and Holland.

DIRTY OLD LONDON

"We arrived in England in a very bad time for ye Plague and ye wars," Radisson wrote a few months after arriving in London.[139] The London that Radisson and Groseilliers first saw from the dirty Thames was a medieval city: a walled town of about two square miles anchored on the east by the Tower of London, and on the west by the filth-filled River Fleet (which now flows into the Thames through a sewer), Baynard's Castle, the Temple Bar and, farther along, the sprawling mess of Whitehall, with Westminster Palace and its surrounding buildings as a separate community upstream. Slums spread northward from the old Roman walls toward St. Albans, east past the Tower, and grew in the much less populated industrialized city on the river's south bank, Southwark. This was where the very lowest people lived, where Shakespeare and his friends had played in the Globe theatre, competing against the handful of bear-baiting theatres nearby for entertainment pennies from working people and the middle-class.

Only one bridge linked the city with the south shore, but the river was alive with boatmen whose water taxis and private boats ferried people across, as well as up and down, the filthy river.

The built-up area of London was home to 300,000 people, making it the third-largest city in Europe. (Only Paris and Constantinople were larger.) London, like all the major cities of the time, consumed people. Until the nineteenth century, a steady flow of migrants from the country replenished the many thousands who died of plagues, sweating sickness, influenza, cholera, smallpox, and other diseases that spread through the crowded, dirty streets. The city's birthrate was minimal and infant mortality high. People stewed in their own sewage and rotting garbage, which lay in the narrow streets to be picked through by human and animal scavengers. The government saw no need to pay for a sewage system, so wealthier people used outhouses while the poor simply threw their filth into the streets. There was no concept of zoning: houses were crammed together with factories, slaughterhouses, and warehouses. Hat-makers, dyers, tanners, and anyone else using chemicals for their job set up workshops cheek-to-jowl with crowded tenements.

Animals were still brought into the city and butchered at Smithsfields, also traditionally the place where heretics were burned at the stake, so that the smell of rotting offal hung over that part of the city. London was also full of fish markets, stables, swine pens, and poultry coops, which added to the stench and fostered diseases like influenza. In contrast, the city also had hundreds of high-end jewellers and tailors who sold their work to the wealthy, especially members of the court.

Along with the stink of animals and people, there was the noise. The sounds of cities have utterly changed since about 1900, when the first cars and trucks went onto the roads and the hum of rubber tires on asphalt became the predominant background noise of the modern city. Seventeenth-century London would have sounded like a vast barnyard of horses, dogs, pigs, poultry, milk cows, and goats, kept as personal livestock. Steel-clad wheels rolled over cobblestones, ungreased axles on carts made an awful racket, and everywhere there were people hollering about their goods for sale and the services they would perform. And there was constant noise from people talking, swearing, and even making music. Nights would have been fairly quiet and much darker than those in our electrified cities, but the dawn would have brought a cacophony of crowing roosters, barking dogs, and the sounds of thousands of other animals.

It was also a colder city than it is today. Radisson lived during the Little Ice Age, when the Thames froze with ice strong enough to hold fairs and carnivals once a decade on average.[140] Radisson was in the city for at least one Thames ice fair, in 1667. (The last would be held in 1814.) The cold would have frozen the city's filth and helped keep down the stink, but the thaws that followed left great puddles of sewage, wash-water, and household garbage in the streets. All of this made a fine home for the black rat, the small, rather gentle carrier of plague-borne fleas.

A time traveller would certainly notice the churches: spires rose everywhere, and Londoners lived in parishes that provided what little social welfare could be had in the city. Elizabeth I had dealt with poverty by outlawing it through punitive Poor Laws. Parishes gave out bread and clothes to the old, the sick, and the very young, and ran houses of correction where the rest of the poor were expected to keep busy spinning and weaving wool. (Those who were deemed to be just lazy were beaten and thrown out of the parish.) With no professional police, the city was a resort for criminals: petty thieves, burglars, pickpockets, armed robbers, thugs, rapists, and murderers. It was also struggling with terrorism. Radisson arrived in London just six years after the Restoration of the monarchy. The English Civil War—between evangelical Puritans and their allies in more extremist Christian sects—led to the public beheading of Charles I in 1649, and the establishment of a short-lived parliamentary republic, which morphed into a military dictatorship under Oliver Cromwell.

The Restoration of the Stuarts in 1660 brought a veneer of normalcy back to the government, but there were still many fringe players who never accepted the settlement. Fifth Monarchy adherents, millenarians who believed 1666 would bring a settling of accounts with tyrants, and Papists all plotted in city homes and taverns. In June 1661, fifty rebels had tried to whip up an insurrection against the newly restored monarchy in the futile hope of reviving Cromwell's republic. Led by Thomas Venner, a radical preacher, they fought a hopeless battle in the streets against government troops. Twenty of the rebels were killed in the fighting and another dozen were hanged, drawn, and quartered for treason. The next year, government spies exposed a plot involving royal guards who had agreed to allow assassins into Whitehall Palace to kill the king. In 1663, plotters planned yet another rebellion, this time in the countryside, with a secret contingent in London ready to kill the king. Thirty of those conspirators went to the quartering block at Tyburn. Plotters relying on astrology and public nostalgia for Oliver Cromwell cooked up a plan in

1665 to break into the Tower of London, steal the weapons there, and inspire a general uprising through the city that would (yet again) culminate with the king's murder. Eight old Cromwellian soldiers were caught and executed for the plot, and hundreds more were jammed into the Tower and the city's prisons. The government ordered the veterans of Parliament's New Model Army to leave the city and the new Royalist regime pushed through the Five Mile Act, which kept dissenter ministers away from any town, unless they had the government's permission to enter.[141]

For Radisson, London offered a lot to see and do. Theatres re-opened after Charles II was restored, and they flourished. Everyone went, from the king to the poorest of his subjects. Actresses were a huge draw: several of England's ducal families started from the king's liaisons with various famous actresses. Prince Rupert, the king's eccentric cousin, fathered at least one child with a thespian renowned for her looks. The king was also a source of entertainment: well-dressed people could wander into the palace and simply loiter about, hoping he would show some interest in them. On Sundays, Wednesdays, and Fridays, anyone could watch the king eat dinner with his family and friends, and people were allowed so close to the table that the fast-fingered could grab from it. They weren't likely to get stabbed with a fork, since the latter were just coming into vogue.

The poor, and those among the upper classes with a taste for violence, were more likely to go to spectacles involving cruelty to people or animals. Bull- and bear-baiting, which involved the pairing of vicious dogs and big, potentially violent animals, were popular. So were hangings, brandings, pillorying, and the ducking of scolds. Some of these punishments were as cruel as anything the Iroquois did to prisoners. Brutality was a common part of life, so much so that Iroquoian visitors to Europe were appalled at the violence they saw in the streets, especially the beating of women and children and the humiliation of criminals, something that was not done in Indigenous societies.

In 1610, a Huron teenager named Savignon went to France with Champlain and was disgusted by urban French life. He despised the public violence, the sight of men bickering in the streets, and the grotesque economic inequality. This, he believed, showed Europeans were weak and ungenerous. He commented on the abuse of women and children by husbands and fathers, the exploitation of young people, and what he saw as the lack of a real community. He embarrassed his hosts by returning to the Huron country and reporting on the social failures of France. It's only been in the last couple of generations that mainstream Western Europe and North America have come to agree with Savignon about family violence, or at least pay it lip service.[142]

YE PLAGUE

The Great Plague simply added to the miseries of the city. Its first fatality was recorded in the second week of April 1665, in the parish of St. Paul's, Covent Garden. Radisson was still in Boston, and likely never heard of the epidemic until he arrived in England. It seemed mild in those early months. By the end of April just three people were dead, all of them in the poorer neighbourhoods in the west end of the old walled city. Nine people died in May, still hardly enough to cause much alarm. It wasn't until June, when nearly three hundred died, that people began panicking and leaving the city. In London, the death rate from plague rose to about 20,000 per 100,000. (At least 70,000 out of the 350,000 who lived in the city died of plague in less than a year. The real toll could have been as high as 100,000.) The peak was 7,165 plague deaths in the week ending September 19, 1665, although even that figure may be low. The government ordered the killing of London's pets, and the campaign was effective: Pepys recorded in his diary that about 40,000 dogs and 200,000 cats were killed. Unfortunately, these animals were the only real defense the city had against black rats, the plague's real carriers.

By the early summer, the entire court at Whitehall, along with its belongings, was on the move. The king, the Duke of York, Prince Rupert, and their hundreds of hangers-on moved to Hampton Court, Henry VIII's palace on the edge of the city; then, as the plague spread, it moved again, to Salisbury. The court eventually settled in Oxford, Charles I's headquarters against Parliament years before, while a handful of public-spirited civil servants and bureaucrats stayed in the city to organize a mass burial of the dead. The king was living in the university town when Radisson arrived in London. "To see a person sick of the sores," Pepys wrote:

> ...carried close to me by Grace-Church in a hackney coach. My finding the
> Angel Tavern, at the lower end of Tower Hill, shut up, and more than that,
> that the person was then dying of the plague when I was last there, a little
> while ago, at night... To hear that poor Payne, my waterman, hath buried
> a child and is dying himself. To hear that a labourer I sent but the other

day to Dagenhams to know how they did there is dead of the plague, and that one of my own watermen who carried me daily, fell sick as soon as he landed me on Friday morning last… is now dead of the plague… doth put into me great apprehensions of melancholy, and with good reason.[143]

This was about the time Radisson would have arrived in the city if the *Charles* hadn't been captured. Still, in September, when Radisson and Groseilliers passed through the city, the diarist John Evelyn wrote how he saw "all along the City and suburbs… a dismal passage and dangerous… so many coffins exposed in the streets and the streets thin of people, the shops shut up and all in mournful silence, as not knowing whose turn might be next."[144] Corpses kept piling up in the streets through the fall. By then, plague had spread through all of England, wiping out towns and leaving parts of the countryside so stricken that crops rotted in the fields for lack of people to harvest them. The spread of the plague was slowed by that year's cold winter, which began just a few weeks after Radisson arrived. Spring brought a renewed onslaught, but nothing as severe as the previous summer. By August 1666, after a year of death, there were just thirty fatal plague cases in London.

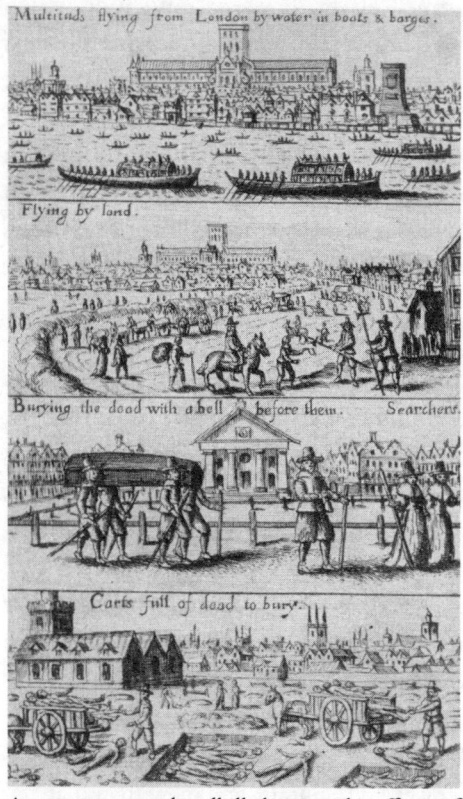

A contemporary handbill showing the effects of the Great Plague of 1665. The rich fled London, while the poor, and those who tried to help them, died by the thousands.

The short stay in plague-stricken London must have been a letdown for Radisson, who had childhood memories of Paris and had seen Amsterdam in 1653 on his return from the Iroquois country, when the Dutch city was one of Europe's most dynamic centres for art. The two Frenchmen likely landed from their ocean vessel somewhere on the main docks in the city centre and were then ferried on a smaller boat by watermen past the rafts and scows where so many Londoners were living to avoid the plague. They passed under London Bridge, which was still covered with buildings and adorned with spears skewering the heads of the King's enemies, and were taken upriver past Whitehall and Westminster, Richmond, Kingston, and back into the countryside to Oxford, a fifty-mile trip. We know Radisson was at the King's court by the end of the year because the secretary of the Royal Society, who had stayed in London and taken his chances, wrote to scientist Robert Boyle:

> Surely I need not tell you from hence, that it is said here with great joy of the discovery of a North-west passage... lately represented by him to his majesty at Oxford, and answered a royal grant on a vessel, to sail into Hudson Bay, and thence into the South-Sea, those men affirming, as I have here, yet with a boat they went out of a Lake in Canada, into a river, which they discharged itself North-west into the South-Sea, unto which they went, and returned North-East into Hudson Bay. I hope, if this be truth, I shall receive the favour of your Confirmation.[145]

This news caused a sensation among the brightest minds in London. In those days, upper-class men were expected to be intellectuals with a sense of adventure. Indeed, for many of that generation, adventure—through civil war and revolution—had thrust itself upon them. They dressed like swashbucklers, invested in risky trade ventures in exciting places, and loved to hear first-hand stories of exotic locales and dangerous exploits. Now they had the chance to learn from Radisson, who had spent so much time in the North American wilderness among its fiercest and most interesting peoples. (Groseilliers, who was not one for words, seems to have tagged along. In any description of the pair, Radisson's name always came first, even though he was the younger man.)

Radisson quickly received the patronage of George Monck, the first Duke of Albemarle, the most powerful lord in England. He was, quite literally, a kingmaker. Monck had a good political barometer and no known scruples. As a young man, he'd been a mercenary in Europe, then returned to join the English forces fighting to put down various rebellions in Ireland. Early in the Civil War, he'd shown loyalty to Charles I and was given command of Royalist troops brought over from Ireland. But as with so many successful people of his time, Monck's loyalties were fluid. When he was captured by Parliament's army, Monck quickly changed sides and rose through the ranks to become one of Cromwell's better commanders and one of his best friends. He was a powerful force during the Commonwealth years when Radisson was travelling through the Great Lakes country. Monck was given command of Parliament's army in Scotland, and spent years there running the place as a local dictator. When Cromwell died in 1658, Monck knew the English "republic" was dead, too: it had crumbled in Cromwell's last years, when the Lord Protector was king in all but name. Cromwell's quiet son Richard inherited his father's power, leaving the public baffled by the nature of the regime that governed them. Was it a monarchy or republic? If royal, why was the rightful king not on the throne? If republican, who had elected this new dictator?

Richard Cromwell—Tumbledown Dick to Londoners—was nowhere as vicious as his father (or, for that matter, his sisters) and refused to use the violence needed to pull the Crown out of the gutter to create a new Cromwellian dynasty. Within months, it was clear that the only solution was a return of the Stuarts. Monck, with his own army behind him, watched without making a commitment as political factions in England brawled with each other, then he stepped in to put together a deal that pardoned all but a few of the hard-core republicans and those who had a direct hand in the show trial and execution of Charles I. The new king made Monck a duke, the highest rank in the British peerage, and he remained the most formidable warrior in England until his death in 1670. Monck was also a greedy man, though his critics said his wife was even more avaricious. Radisson was very, very lucky to have landed this patron. He would never win this kind of backing in France. Soon, he would add even more intriguing men, Charles II and Prince Rupert of the Rhine, to his list of powerful friends.

It was Carteret—the financial wizard who found ways to pay for the Royal Navy and the king's stable of lovers, illegitimate children, and whores—who was given the honour of introducing Radisson to the King. Radisson and Charles II were about the same age (Radisson was about thirty, the king was thirty-five.) Being men of action and adventure, they could talk easily together. In his spare time between wars and intrigues, Charles had accumulated a string of mistresses—when Radisson arrived, he had at least one teenage child.[146] The king, who had seen action on the battlefield as well as in the bedchamber, and who had spent so much of his time living on charity and dodging his murderous English republican enemies, was enthralled by this young Frenchman who had seen so many exotic people and places and lived through so many adventures.

Both men were accustomed to a grotesque amount of violence. Radisson had come close to death at the hands of the Iroquois and had seen the cruelty of American war. Charles had survived the English Civil War—barely. His father had been publicly beheaded in Whitehall when Charles was twenty. Two years later, Oliver Cromwell thrashed Charles II's army at the 1651 Battle of Worcester and massacred most of the survivors. The fugitive royal claimant hid in a tree, the "Royal Oak," before slipping through the country in disguise and making it back to France.[147] Charles was stuck in France during the civil strife known as the Fronde, which likely caused Radisson's emigration to Quebec and his wandering the Low Countries at times when he believed the French government would sell him out. (It was by no means certain that the Stuarts would be restored, and, within a few years of the execution of Charles I, the courts of Europe had effectively recognized Cromwell's regime as the government of Britain.)

Charles II, a man just as comfortable speaking French as English (he was, through his mother, a first cousin of Louis XIV), wanted to hear all about Radisson's adventures. And Radisson obliged, spinning out his stories and convinced the king that the trouble and expense of a North American enterprise would fit with a new British policy of self-sufficiency through imperial trade.

Stories of the exotic people of the New World, of their government, their wars, their spectacular country, were woven in with Radisson's tales of capture, freedom, adventure, and travel across unimaginably large forests, lakes that were incomprehensibly vast, and on rivers that made the Thames and the Seine seem like creeks. The king wanted all these stories written down.[148] So did the Royal Society, which Charles had founded. The society mimicked the laws of the Great Library of Alexandria by requiring sea captains and explorers to write about their travels so the Society could create a central repository of geographic knowledge, and it collected stories of adventurers like Radisson.

The king gave Radisson a painting of himself, along with a gold chain to wear around his neck, and the two French traders were set up for the winter in Windsor with generous allowances of twenty shillings a week. Whether they stayed in the castle or lodged in the town isn't clear, but we do know that the king's cousin Prince Rupert was living in the old fortress, surrounded by his books on navigation and his laboratory equipment.

Radisson got to work on the project and finished most of his autobiographies by 1669. They may have been written in French and translated, but more likely they were drafted by Radisson in English and edited by several people. Samuel Pepys almost certainly knew Radisson during his stay at court and engaged his hoarding instincts by snagging a copy of the original manuscript, which was, years later, barely saved from becoming wallpaper backing. In the 1880s, however, it was found and parts of it published. Radisson's book was written for the smallest of audiences, but they were the people with all the money.

RUPERT OF THE RHINE

In the months after Radisson's arrival, Carteret's star had faded. He took much of the blame for the failings of the English fleet in the ongoing war against the Dutch. By the time Radisson was writing his stories, Carteret was under attack in the House of Commons for suspected embezzlement. The king saved him from impeachment, but Carteret lost much his power. Prince Rupert of the Rhine took Carteret's place as Radisson's patron and organizer of the Hudson Bay trade experiment.

Rupert was a complex man. A great-grandson of Mary, Queen of Scots, and grandson of James I through James's daughter Elisabeth of the Palatinate, he was a refugee from the time he was a baby. Rupert's parents had been driven out of Prague Castle at the start of the Thirty Years' War and Rupert had almost been left behind. As a young man, he found work soldiering, then, in his early twenties, he cooked up a plan to set himself up as ruler of the island of Madagascar, where he'd be able to prey on shipping between the Cape of Good Hope and the East Indies. His idea was put aside when civil war broke out in England, and Rupert, just out of his teens, became the leading cavalry general to his uncle, Charles I. A ferocious foe to Cromwell and the Parliamentary forces, Rupert was so tall that he was easily spotted by his enemies on the battlefield, where he could always be found in the middle of the fight. He could be merciless, and was always impulsive. Twice in major battles, he chased Parliamentary cavalry so far from the battlefields that his absence caused the Royalists who were left behind to lose. He killed many men in cold blood, but deeply mourned his standard poodle when it was shot on the battlefield at Marston Moor. Charles I forced Rupert out of England after he surrendered Bristol, the second-largest city in the country, to an overwhelming force of Roundheads in 1645. It was a loss that effectively ended the war.

During his years in exile, Rupert and his younger brother Maurice took up piracy after a brief and unpleasant stint in the French army. At the start of the English Civil War, the Royal Navy had defected to Parliament. When the war was almost over, much of it defected back to the Royalists. In the summer of 1648, Rupert, who had never travelled on a ship as anything but a passenger, was sent by his uncle Charles to the French coast to make the best of what was little more than a shabby mutiny by the unpaid crews of English warships. The sailors had elected their own officers, but these new captains couldn't control their men, nor could they pay them. Rupert was willing to turn these ships into privateers to raise money for the bankrupt Royalists and to plunder sufficiently to keep the sailors paid. Rupert and Maurice scoured the coasts of West Africa and the Spanish Main, attacking anything afloat. Unfortunately, Rupert wasn't a lucky buccaneer. His heart was in the right place, but few of the ships he took were worth much. Starting with a dozen English ships, Rupert's fleet dwindled to just four manned by surly sailors until they made the mistake of sailing into a four-day hurricane off Barbados in September 1652. Maurice, just thirty-one years old, was swept overboard from the *Honest Seaman* and a guilt-stricken Rupert, who arrived in France the next spring with just two ships full of sick men, gave up piracy.[149]

The young prince struggled on through Cromwell's regime, hiring himself out as a mercenary to European princes. At the same time, he began inventing things: better gunpowder, a revolver pistol, an early version of the self-propelled torpedo, bullet-proof glass, metal alloys, landmines, and a method for blowing up underwater rocks that menaced navigation. Not all his experiments involved killing people and making bigger explosions. He perfected a new method of mezzotint engraving that made cheap, mass-produced art prints possible. (Some of his own prints survive, and they're quite good.) Like many men of his age, he thought he might discover a way to change the very nature of the elements, including making gold from base metals.[150] Gentlemen of that age were expected to be courtiers, warriors, men of science and reason, both effete and ferocious. Rupert was all those things.

Rather unexpectedly, the Stuarts were restored to the English throne eight years after Maurice drowned, and Rupert now had the connections and patronage levers to finally make some money. By the time Radisson arrived, Rupert had profited from his investments in exotic and sometimes immoral trade. In 1664, he put money into "The Company of Royal

Adventurers of England trading into Africa," which did business with the chiefs of sub-Saharan Africa and tried to dominate the West African slave trade. The profits were potentially enormous: one of the company's ships, captured by the Dutch, held 1,420 ivory tusks, 1,000 copper kettles and bowls, and three tons of pepper.[151] The company, however, could not survive in the face of Dutch piracy and its own bad management, and it folded in 1670. That year, the Hudson's Bay Company, the product of Radisson and Groseilliers' scheming and Rupert's connections at court and in the City, was given its charter, with Rupert as its first governor.

This remarkable document, still in the possession of the Hudson's Bay Company, contained not only the company's articles of incorporation, but also a deed to a vast area of northern North America and a monopoly on trade into Hudson Bay. The buy-in was £300 from each of eighteen investors, though, with various side-deals and payments-in-kind, most shareholders paid less. For almost all the investors, the cost of Hudson's Bay Company shares was just entertainment money, like buying a high-end lottery ticket. The Earl of Shaftesbury was a fairly typical investor. He put £300 into the company—a huge amount for an English farmer or working person, and three years' salary for an army officer—and it hardly put a dent in his £23,000 annual income.[152]

This kind of investing, through a joint stock company, was something new. The modern corporation began in the Protestant countries in the early 1600s, and was usually financed by bankers no longer hamstrung by the Catholic Church's rules against charging interest on debts. Owning stock and organizing a company allowed "gentlemen" and nobles, socially barred from working, to tap into fabulous profits to the lopsided advantage of European countries.[153]

The whole thing could be fun, provided investors had a little money to lose. For a fairly small buy-in of a few hundred pounds, foreign-trade investors became shareholders in an adventure, co-owners of a dream, and part owners of great stories. They could go to the harbour and see their ships being fitted out. They could watch the sailors—men who stood a very good chance of dying a horrible death in some distant place—making ready. The investors could see the trade goods—shabby basic hardware and cloth—loaded aboard, and watch the ships sail away. Then they waited, like lottery-ticket holders, for their ships to come in in a year or two. If they did, the treasure, whether it was furs, tea, spices, exotic woods, American silver, or Chinese tea, was theirs to sell and divide the profits. If the ships didn't come back, there were always new opportunities.

This was what Radisson was peddling, and for men of adventure like Charles, Rupert, Monck, and so many other Civil War survivors who'd developed a taste for action and risk, it was alluring. They really were "gentlemen adventurers," men who were easily bored and who thirsted for the jolt of adrenalin that had sustained them when they were young warriors fighting for, or against, Cromwell. They got those thrills from political intrigues, gambling, mistresses, and duels, and now they could buy into adventures that might make them a lot of money.

Radisson's talk of an expedition to the fur lands of southern Hudson Bay and James Bay made solid sense to men who were looking for new, exotic opportunities. At first, the Hudson's Bay Company's organizers also dangled the prospect of discovering the fabled Northwest Passage. Prince Rupert and Monck were early investors, putting money into the company in 1667, as did other members of the court and some of the brightest lights in the Royal Society, who were excited about the possibility of finding the Passage. The expedition had to be a commercial, not political or military enterprise, as Charles, who was secretly taking money from his cousin Louis, did not want to openly clash with France over the fur trade.

Charles left Windsor at the end of January 1666 for Hampton Court and, after the plague tapered off, brought his enormous retinue of courtiers and government officials to the sprawling, palatial mess of Whitehall, centred around Inigo Jones' banqueting house where Charles I was beheaded (and the only part of the palace that survived a huge fire in 1698). Somewhere around the end of March, Radisson and his brother-in-law, who seems to have been a non-entity to those who met him, left Windsor for London to get ready for what they hoped would be their first Arctic adventure under Charles II's patronage. But war intervened again. The Dutch and British fought running sea battles all summer, making the Channel and the waters around England unsafe. As an admiral, Rupert was needed with the fleet, which also added to the problems and delays of the Hudson Bay expedition. Then London burned down, extinguishing the plague, along with millions of rats that had infested the place.

THE GREAT FIRE

General George Monck and Prince Rupert were out of town commanding the English fleet and Radisson was cooling his heels in Westminster when

London caught fire. People were aware of the apocalyptic date, 1666, and the country was awash with portents of various kinds of doom. Some eager patriots thought the trouble would befall England's enemies: Pope Alexander VII was believed by Protestant extremists and a few Catholics to be on his last legs, with the gates of hell beckoning.[154] In Warsaw, a hen laid an egg marked with a flaming cross, a sword, a rod, and a drawn bow (it must have been a very large egg), and a coffin supposedly floated in the sky above Vienna.[155] A string of comets, or possibly meteorites, had lit up the skies through 1664, 1665, and 1666. All these portents were recorded in almanacs printed around St. Paul's Cathedral and sold throughout the country.

England was locked in yet another war with the Dutch Republic and this time the French had taken the latter's side. English people living inland from the coast were in very little danger, certainly not as much as faced the Dutch political class in the dying years of their republic: six years later, Prime Minister de Witt would be killed and eaten by his constituents. This, however, was a naval war, and wasn't personal. It was also one of the few wars where the parties involved admitted they were fighting to improve the prospects of big national corporations. The Dutch, pioneers of modern capitalism and, now that their country was free of its old Spanish masters, had become eager colonialists and wanted dominance of the sea so they could expand their trading empire. The English wanted the same thing. The French wanted to divide and conquer: keeping both sides at each other's throats would leave France free to dominate Europe. Despite

Contemporary illustration of London before the Great Fire. The building in the centre-right is the old St. Paul's Cathedral, which was already in bad shape before it burned.

the English's deep-seated hatred of all foreigners—whether Dutch, French, Spanish, Scots, Irish, or anyone else—this wasn't a race war or even a fight over ideology. Until the English were humiliated in a string of big naval battles, there was very little real animosity between the various sides. It was, rather, strictly business: corporate warfare with real guns. In 1666, the Dutch were winning, and the sea lanes weren't safe for English ships.

This war left Radisson stuck in London while two of his most important patrons, Monck and Rupert, were at sea. A Dutch fleet menaced the English coast, ready to take Radisson's ships if he did try to leave. At least the king was back in London and the court had settled in at Whitehall, with Radisson living nearby with his brother-in-law, both of them enemy aliens in a land known for its xenophobia.

The Great Fire began in the early hours of Sunday, September 2, 1666, in one of London's filthy little narrow streets, Pudding Lane. Supposedly, it started in the workshop of the king's baker. The fire leapt up into the medieval city's thatched roofs and was carried by the wind until it grew big enough to draw in air and generate its own powerful convection currents. The approaches to London Bridge were just a few blocks away. Ancient buildings built into the London side of the bridge had burned just before the Civil War, but there were still multi-storey wooden buildings on the Southwark side. Londoners fleeing along the bridge's six-foot-wide road needed hours to get across the Thames. On the first day of the fire, part of the bridge would burn, too. By Sunday afternoon, the fire was throwing off enough heat to melt the big chains that held London's docks in place when the Thames' level rose and fell with the tides. Molten roofing lead flowed like silver lava through the streets of the city as churches burned. Night was as bright as day, smoke and embers blew across the rest of the city.

The fire burned for three days. London's ineffective Lord Mayor, who oversaw firefighting, had a breakdown on the first day. Bucket brigades and small pumps pulled on sleds were useless against the great masses of fire. The wind generated by the firestorm carried burning thatch and embers across the city which set alight other neighborhoods. On the second day, while Samuel Pepys was in his garden burying his money and a big wheel of Parmesan cheese, and praying that his home near the Tower would be spared, James, Duke of York, took charge by ordering that rows of houses be demolished to stop the spread of the fire. Old St. Paul's, packed with the stock of the book publishers of Paternoster Row, was supposed to be safe

Radisson was in Westminster when London burned. He was lucky to survive the violence unleashed on foreigners after the fire finally burned itself out. The fire started just left of London Bridge. Flames surround the ruins of old St. Paul's.

from fire, but went up like a torch. Charred paper from the blazing cathedral landed as far away as Oxford. By Wednesday, almost the entire old city within London's Roman and medieval walls was gone. Refugees picked through the rubble and camped in shantytowns that sprang up by the end of the week to the north and northwest of the city. Wealthier Londoners could afford to stay in Southwark, but the land south of London was relatively undeveloped compared to the great city that had burned. Almost every major building between Whitehall and the Tower was gone. Only the Guildhall had escaped complete destruction. Great houses like Baynard's Castle burned along with all their contents. The cultural loss, in secular and religious art as well as in historic architecture, was incalculable.

The day after the fire, Pepys awoke to a burned-out city core surrounded by slums that had not been in the fire's path. Only the Tower, Westminster, and Whitehall served as reminders of what had been one of the world's richest cities:

> But there I left this smoking and sultry heap, which mounted up in dismal clouds night and day, the poor inhabitants dispersed all about St. Georges, Moorefields, as far as Highgate and several miles in circle, some under tents, others under miserable huts and hovels, without a rag, or any necessary utensils, bed or board, who from delicateness, riches and easy

accommodations in stately and well-furnished houses, were now reduced to extremest [sic] misery and poverty. In this calamitous condition I returned with a sad heart to my house, blessing & adoring.

The next day, Pepys was in the king's private chambers, warning him that looters might strip the surviving buildings along the edge of the fire line. Two days later, he described how he "went this morning on foot from Whitehall as far as London Bridge, through the late Fleet Street, Ludgate Hill, by St. Paul's, Cheapside, Exchange, Bishopsgate, Aldersgate, and out to Moorefields, thence through Cornhill, etc. with extraordinary difficulty, clambering over mountains of yet-smoking rubbish, and frequently mistaking where I was, the ground under my feet so hot, as made me not only sweat, but even burned the soles of my shoes…." In the meantime, the king went from Whitehall to the Tower of London by boat and ordered the buildings around the old fortress walls to be torn down to prevent fire from reaching the army's big gunpowder-storage depot. If the gunpowder in the tower had exploded, what was left of the east end of the city would have been flattened in an explosion that would have been felt for miles.

This was not a good time to be a foreign visitor in the city. Almost everyone believed the French and the Dutch were behind the fire. Eyewitnesses claimed to have seen foreign soldiers marching upon the city and setting it alight in retaliation for the burning of West-Terschelling, a town in the Dutch province of Friesland that had been torched by the English. Mobs soon went after foreigners, beating and killing dozens of them.

Radisson was lucky enough to have rented, or perhaps bought, a house in Westminster, so he was in no personal danger from the fire itself. However, he was, despite his command of English, a foreigner, and mobs were lynching anyone who wasn't English. Near Radisson's residence, some Frenchmen were pulled out of their houses, strung up along with other French and Dutch people who fell into the hands of the thugs and vigilantes, and forced to confess to starting the fire. Westminster, close to the court and far from the places where refugees gathered, was probably the safest place for Radisson to be, but that didn't mean he was completely protected from the mobs. The king and his brother were so busy tearing down houses and organizing relief for the homeless that they had no time to look after one fringe player in a city where the law had utterly broken down.

It's not clear how Radisson survived when so many other Frenchmen were murdered. All his stories are about his adventures overseas. Presumably, his friends in England knew what happened to him in their country. Certainly, he was in danger: the mob was killing foreigners. Some, like French watchmaker Robert Hubert, were forced to confess before being judicially murdered. Under torture, Hubert admitted to setting fire to Radisson's neighbourhood in Westminster, but the trial judge had trouble with this, since Westminster hadn't burned. In addition, Hubert was unsure of where he set the fire or where it burned because he'd been out of London when it started. The authorities spent some more private time with the unfortunate prisoner, a map, and a torturer until Hubert could get his facts right. The judge and jury knew Hubert wasn't guilty, but he was convicted and hanged at Tyburn a little less than two months after the fire anyway. Medical school students were collecting Hubert's body for dissection when a mob rushed the scaffold, took the body from the students, and tore it apart.

Radisson and Groseilliers may have taken shelter in Whitehall Palace, where the king's guard admitted very few foreign refugees, but wherever they hid, they must have lain very low. Hubert's judicial murder was meant to satisfy the mob, but vigilantes hunted foreigners for weeks after the fire. For months, the authorities were too frightened to publicly declare the fire an accident, although the *London Gazette*, the country's official newspaper, tried to dampen down the violence. By the time it was safe for foreigners on the streets of the great construction site where old London had stood, Radisson and Groseilliers were being investigated, this time as spies.

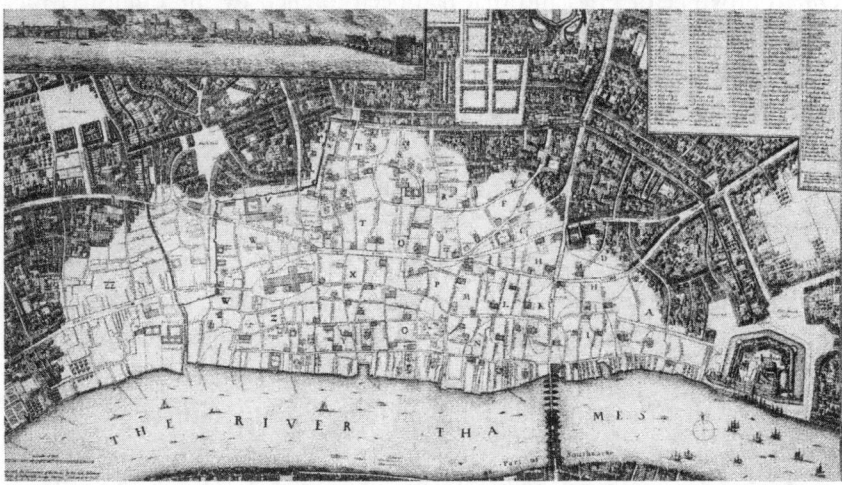

London after the Great Fire. Almost everything in the old city walls, and some suburbs west of the city, was destroyed. Gatehouses in the city walls were used to house the foreign scapegoats who survived the lynch mobs that patrolled the city in the days after the fire.

SPIES AND LIARS

Radisson, after a year of living through plague and fire, must have wondered why he'd defected to the English. Their country was in awful straits. The young king had been on the throne for just six years after a decade of revolutionary governments and it seemed like he had brought nothing but bad luck to his capital. England was losing wars against its neighbours. The ruling classes lived in fear of political and religious factionalism that could easily escalate to a new civil war. London was full of plague orphans and people left homeless by the Great Fire. Things wouldn't be as bad again until the Second World War.

At least Radisson could blame the Dutch, rather than his English friends or himself, for keeping him stuck in this wretched place. And, of course, the war had to end sometime. He would later wreak personal, if pyrrhic, vengeance upon the Hollanders a decade later while deep in the Caribbean. Still, for the first time since he was taken prisoner by the Mohawks, he found himself a victim of events very much beyond his control.

Not only did Radisson have every right to be depressed, he also had good reason to be paranoid. People really were out to get him. He and Groseilliers were the focus of espionage directed at the highest levels of government in France, Holland, and England.

The pirate captain of the *Caper* probably knew enough about Radisson and Groseilliers' plan for a northern fur trade to be able to brief the Dutch government, which meant the Dutch had been watching the two Frenchmen for a couple of years. The Dutch, like the French, also had moles in Charles II's court who tipped them off about Radisson's and his backers' plans for a big new trading company. The Dutch were also likely fed information by the French ambassador to The Hague, who was a friend of Paul Ragueneau, the former leader of the Jesuit missions to the Huron and the Iroquois. Ragueneau, now a friend of the powerful Prince de Condé, had been dogging Groseilliers for years, trying to thwart his plans. Ragueneau was sure Groseilliers was a traitor, a cannibal, and probably a heretic, and that Radisson was just as bad: an ingrate saved by the Society of Jesus who was now out to ruin Jesuit plans to trade on Hudson Bay to raise money for their missionary work. Whether or not the Jesuits were behind all the espionage, there seems to have been a solid connection between French and Dutch spymasters: the secret agent the Dutch dispatched to London was a French spy, Godefroy Touret, who worked for France for a decade in the town of Maestricht, and somehow knew Groseilliers.

The Dutch and their (temporary) French business allies seemed to have targeted Groseilliers as the less intelligent, most treacherous, and more gullible of the pair. Touret arrived in London a couple of months before the Great Fire. He rented a room near Westminster Abbey from a footman to the Duke of York and made friends with Groseilliers, who lived nearby with Radisson. The spy had chosen the right target. Touret pumped Groseilliers for information, then offered the Frenchman a Dutch passport and passage to the Netherlands as a guest of their effective ruler, Johan de Witt.[156] The English didn't appreciate Groseilliers, Touret said. The Dutch could give him a better deal, more ships, and the protection of their navy, which was still winning the war against England.

At the same time, Touret passed himself off to people living in London's ruins as Groseilliers' nephew, a fraud that Groseilliers discovered with some horror. Radisson, always more aware and suspicious than his reckless brother-in-law, could see Touret was living far beyond his income. Still, Groseilliers and Touret kept talking, though subsequent events cut their plans short. English government spies had noticed Touret, this curious foreigner who had arrived in town seemingly from nowhere and could afford to live for months without any sign of working or source of independent income. Near the end of the year, English agents picked up Touret and lodged him in one of London's unpleasant jails—an old city gate surrounded by rubble from the fire—but they couldn't get much out of him, at least not at first.

Touret's arrest put Groseilliers—"Captain Gooseberries" in some of the case records—in a bind. He got out of it in his usual way, by betraying Touret, claiming he had known all along Touret was a spy, and insisting he never seriously considered defecting to the Dutch. Groseilliers even managed to find a few witnesses to back up his story. But four months locked in the old Gatehouse jail on the ancient city wall convinced Touret that he needed a better strategy than trying to remain silent. London, both during and after the fire, was a tough place for any foreigner under the slightest suspicion of disloyalty to the English, which was why Groseilliers was working so hard to extricate himself from this mess. Touret decided to turn Crown witness, or, to be more precise, Crown perjurer.

Touret knew a lot about Groseilliers. Or at least he seemed to. Most of his story, however, was a fantasy that would have made Radisson—a great spinner of tales himself—blush. According to Touret, Groseilliers had a devious master plan to set up his own fur empire, start minting his own coins in the

New World, and use this weird money to buy furs from the Cree in Hudson Bay. (What use they would make of these coins was unexplained, and unexplainable.) Touret claimed to have extracted information from Groseilliers' servant—a man named Moreau who'd supposedly lived in Canada—that Groseilliers had told his wife he would soon return to her and that they'd spend the rest of their lives in great wealth. Had the various lords who ran the investigation and interrogated Groseilliers, Touret, Moreau, presumably Radisson, and the character witnesses scraped up by Groseilliers believed Touret's story

Diarist Samuel Pepys worked for Prince Rupert at the headquarters of the Royal Navy. Because Pepys, a renowned hoarder, took one of Radisson's manuscripts, the story of his adventures was preserved.

of business betrayal, Groseilliers would have ended up in jail, at least for a time. But then Touret came up with a story that could have sent Groseilliers to the gallows: the Frenchman, Touret said, had hidden a fugitive priest in London. This priest, on the lam from a convent in Lyon, was supposed to have fled France with fifty thousand stolen ecus (in those days a coin about the size of an old American silver dollar). Not only was the priest a rather skilled thief, he was also a counterfeiter, and it was this disreputable phantom clergyman who had the skills to create the coins that Groseilliers planned to use to build his independent fur empire. Touret had met the priest and heard the whole story from him personally. He accused Groseilliers of three capital crimes—counterfeiting, harbouring a fugitive, and sheltering a Catholic priest. Groseilliers must have been terrified.

Touret's stories were obvious nonsense and the English probably knew it. Or maybe, stripping away the parts about coins and priests, they weren't completely false. There's evidence that Radisson and Groseilliers were always on the make for the best possible deal—a bigger cut of profits, more ships, more status—and betrayal was the story of their lives. Archival evidence suggests Radisson and Groseilliers, separately or together, kept a back channel open to France, even when they were being supported and entertained

George Monck, 1st Duke of Albemarle. A man of fluid loyalties, the old Civil War general was always looking for a way to add to his fortune. He quickly realized the potential of Radisson's fur trade plans.

by some of the most powerful people in England, including its king.[157]

If Radisson knew of Touret, which was likely, he still managed to dodge all the scandal and accusations, and neither fur trader seems to have been tainted for long. But at the same time, strange things were happening in France, where an oddball imposter had also caught word of Radisson and Groseilliers' plans for a subarctic fur trade and pretended to beat them to it.

Touret, who eventually got out of jail and wandered out of history, had been a French spy in the pay of the Dutch. Laurens van Heemskerck, a Dutchman, was on France's payroll to spy on Radisson. Van Heemskerck was the great-nephew of Olivier van Noort, the first Dutch captain to sail around the world. In the vicious politics of the Dutch Republic, van Heemskerck, a captain himself, had thrown his lot in with Admiral Jacob van Wassenaer Obdam, so when Obdam was killed, in June 1665, at the Battle of Lowestoft, van Heemskerck found himself without a patron. Sidelined on land, van Heemskerck started spying for France at about the same time Radisson had been marooned in Spain by a Dutch pirate on his way to Europe from Boston. Either as a French mole or turncoat, van Heemskerck then went over to the English and fought the Dutch, with spectacular success. On August 8, 1666, he commanded a nine-ship squadron to the Dutch islands of Vlieland and Terschelling, where he landed nine hundred sailors and soldiers. The troops burned two big warships and nearly one hundred and fifty merchant ships. Monck and Rupert wrote to Charles II, saying the raid could not have succeeded without the skill of van Heemskerck.

No one knew it, but this was the single, great, glorious moment in van Heemskerck's life. He was, like Radisson, taken into Prince Rupert's circle.

The Dutch captain moved his wife and two small children to Dover. The Treaty of Breda, which briefly ended the war, left him unemployed, but van Heemskerck convinced Rupert and the king he could build a ship that could out-sail anything in the English fleet. Charles II was willing to pay a £20,000 bonus if van Heemskerck could pull it off. Rupert, with his love of inventions and gadgetry, was also a big supporter.

Now things got complicated for Radisson, not just because van Heemskerck had become intrigued with his Hudson Bay plan, but also because van Heemskerck called his ship *Nonsuch*, which was the name of a different ship that broke open the Hudson Bay fur trade for the English. Confusion between Radisson and Groseilliers' *Nonsuch* and van Heemskerck's ship not only bedevils the few modern historians who know this story, but also confused the courts at Versailles and the Vatican. Van Heemskerck's supposedly fast ship turned out to be a dud. First, he blamed the masts imported from the Baltic, saying they were too thin. So the English shipwrights replaced the masts with thicker, stronger ones from New England, but that didn't make the *Nonsuch* much faster. Charles and Rupert dropped van Heemskerck and paid him off with a couple of hundred pounds, which were quickly snatched by the Dutchman's landlord and other creditors.

Van Heemskerck did have one piece of luck, likely as a result of Radisson's big mouth. Radisson loved to tell stories of his adventures, and it's certain van Heemskerck heard them directly from the explorer. Within a few weeks, in the spring of 1670, van Heemskerck wrote to Jean-Baptiste Colbert, the brilliant minister running Louis XIV's government, telling him of his fabulous voyage to Hudson Bay on the *Nonsuch* and offering his services to the French crown.

Van Heemskerck created the fictional land of "North Florida." Supposedly located at the same latitude as Winnipeg, Manitoba, this was a tropical paradise of fertile

A contemporary engraving of Charles II as patron and founder of the Royal Society. A gentleman of the 17th century was expected to be a skilled scholar, a ferocious warrior, and a prolific lover. Charles tried to be all of those.

Prince Rupert spent most of his life waging war. Cousin of Charles II, he was an impoverished German noble who had no other career choice open to him. Rupert used his influence to launch Radisson's trading expeditions.

soils, open fields, placid locals (who happened to be white), rich fisheries, and many, many fur-bearing creatures. He said he made the trip with a companion "who had lived five or six years with the Iroquois and spoke their language well." North Floridians, who, fortuitously, spoke Iroquois, told the interpreter—who was almost certainly, in van Heemskerck's mind's eye, Radisson—"that there was a passage, though a distant one, by way of the California to the South Seas." So why hadn't the French known about this place sooner? Because, van Heemskerck said, his uncle, the great navigator van Noort, had found it and kept it secret, and Radisson had kept his mouth shut, too.

This fabulous place was, according to van Heemskerck, ready to be plucked. Not only was North Florida rich beyond the King of France's dreams, it was easy to get to, and its many great rivers made excellent harbours. The local people wouldn't put up a fight: they were "of mild features, docile, weak and without any courage." They had nothing but wooden bows for weapons and rarely made war because they lived with such abundance that greed and envy were unnecessary. The North Floridians were also dupes who would sell their furs cheaply. They were willing to convert to Christianity, which would make this both a commercial and a moral crusade. France had missed out on the loot from the Aztecs and Incas. Here was its big chance.

Bizarrely, and in the face of all the evidence from real explorers, including French expeditions launched overland from Quebec in the late 1650s and early 1660s, the French court bought van Heemskerck's story. The French government was exceptionally generous, much more so than Charles I. It gave in to van Heemskerck's demands for French citizenship, a house in Dunkirk, a large share in the company (something never offered to Radisson and Groseilliers), a twenty-year monopoly on trade, ships with crews, and fur-trade goods. Like the English (whether coincidentally or not), the French wanted Hudson Bay in their hands by the summer of 1670. The powerful Comte d'Estrades certainly knew of Radisson's plan and, in the summer of 1670, he put together a company of wealthy investors very similar in class and background to the rich merchants and court insiders who founded the Hudson's Bay Company.

But from that point on, van Heemskerck's expedition was a disaster. It left Dunkirk in mid-August, battling storms all the way. Two weeks later, it was barely off the southwest coast of Ireland. The little fleet stopped in Ireland to take on fresh water and repair one of the

If Prince Rupert had spent more time inventing and less on war, he might be known today for his many inventions. This is a mezzotint Rupert made of the execution of John the Baptist. Rupert invented the process, which made art prints affordable to working-class people.

ships. Only a month later, somewhere south of Iceland, a storm scattered the ships and two were lost. Van Heemskerck was captain of the surviving ship, which was now held together by ropes and cables. His crew didn't buy the captain's lie that Hudson Bay was just fifty-five miles away, so, faced with mutiny, the Dutchman turned back to France. There, he made his case for another expedition, and capped the campaign with a very public conversion to Roman Catholicism. Van Heemskerck's conversion got extremist Catholics in Paris fired up and won the support of the Vatican, which now wanted to send missionaries on the second voyage. In November 1670, the new expedition seemed to be taking shape. Then the French government backed out.[158] The investors went after van Heemskerck for their money, which, of course, he didn't have. At about the same time, Jesuit missionaries travelling overland from Quebec reached the shores of James Bay and found it to be lacking in pastureland, weak-willed white Indigenous people, and all the rest of the details from van Heemskerck's fictions. Van Heemskerck lived for another twenty years on meagre pay from French government jobs and stayed out of the hands of his creditors, all the while insisting he could find the Northwest Passage. In 1699, he died, unpunished, and was almost immediately forgotten.

Through the Touret scandal and the early machinations of van Heemskerck, Radisson cooled his heels in Westminster while Prince Rupert cobbled together the financial and political support for the Hudson Bay expedition. It required a heroic effort for the prince, whose migraines were severe and frequent that year. Twice he went under the knife and drill of the surgeon, who cut holes cut through his skull to relieve the pressure and let "a great deal of corrupt matter" flow from his brain. This eased his pain a bit.[159] He also lost two of his favourite dogs, which somehow got loose in the city. Still, he soldiered on, as much for his friends as himself. During this terrible time in his life, it's possible that Radisson, this odd Frenchman with his marvellous stories, was a great diversion for him.

With Rupert's help, Radisson's well-connected backers bought the ketch *Discovery* in the spring of 1667. The war was also finally ending. A Dutch fleet sailed up the Medway and into the Solent, seizing the best Royal Navy ships as prizes, and burning many of the rest. This last disaster left the English no choice but to sue for peace.

To the Bay

The Treaty of Breda, which put Holland's naval humiliation of the English down on paper, eventually opened an opportunity for the two semi-idle French "gentlemen adventurers" to finally get things moving. Radisson was still a young man, in his mid-thirties (although his contemporaries would have seen him as middle-aged), while Groseilliers, nearing fifty, was, by the standards of the time, an old man.

Radisson did find things to do while he waited for his next exploration to begin. He almost certainly went "clubbing," which was what people then called going out, evenings at pubs and private clubs where people drank ale, smoked tobacco, and sipped coffee. Living in Westminster, he was on the edge of the big court at Whitehall, with all its public and private parties, its debauched women, and over-the-top men. After fifteen years of control by the Puritans and their allies in Parliament and the army, the young, stylish people of London had a lot of energy to burn off. Everything that had been banned by the Cromwell regime, from theatres to booze to Christmas to dancing, was back with a vengeance.

So were bookstores. Their products were still censored, but with a lighter hand than in France. Radisson collected maps and charts and tried to piece

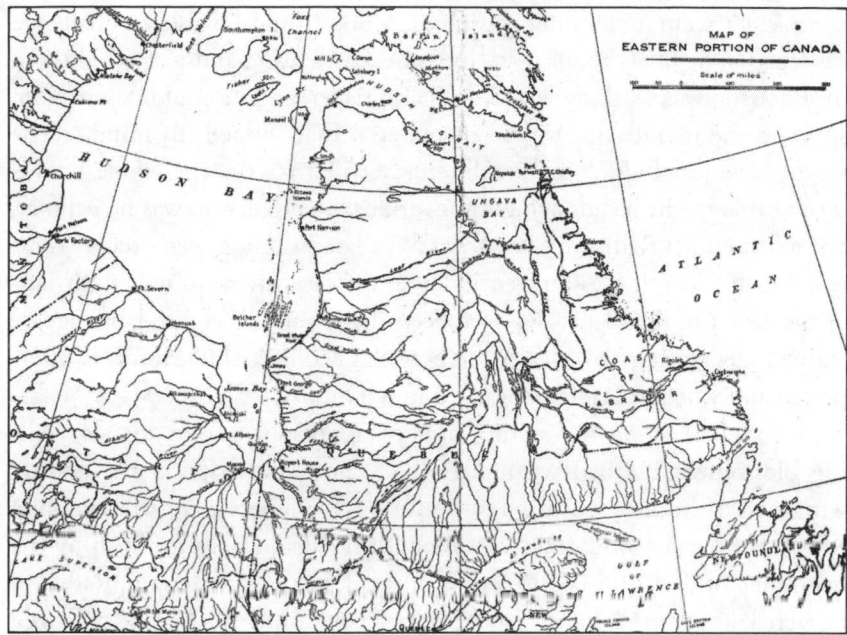

Early 20th-century map of the rivers of the Hudson Bay region. Many of them were vital waterways for Indigenous people.

together an accurate image of North America in his spare time. He was also in demand as a storyteller. Those less inclined to heavy reading were often happy to listen to men like Radisson spin yarns of strange places and interesting people.

Being a savant of languages—including French, Dutch, and half a dozen varied North American Indigenous languages—Radisson was able to tell his stories in detailed, colourful English. Europeans did, and still do, love stories of the Indigenous people of North America, and Radisson's tales of life with the Iroquois and in the Upper Great Lakes were exotic, thrilling, and, for the most part, true. So Radisson, partly to ingratiate himself with the king and with Rupert, and almost certainly to kill time, wrote down his story.[160]

Radisson's description of his voyages was never meant to be a permanent historical record. Surprisingly, despite brisk sales of other explorer's narratives, including the Jesuit *Relations*, Radisson didn't get his stories published. But, he probably didn't need to, given that he had the audience he wanted, the king, Prince Rupert, and even the new Royal Society, where such exotic tales were much in vogue. Radisson's stories are certainly directed to an audience of well-educated men. He didn't feel he needed a completely accurate chronology since no one would be able to challenge his facts, so he likely recalled stories as he was writing and just fitted them in. Radisson was working with a quill and paper, and he couldn't just open space in the manuscript to add in material that slipped his mind, so he might have just fudged the timeline rather that rewrite the whole manuscript. This might be annoying to historians, but Radisson was no scholar. For a first effort, Radisson's *Voyages* and his later writings were stellar work, more so because it was written in his most recently acquired, sixth language, English. (It might have even been the seventh or eighth language he learned, depending how the divide between Mohawk and Huron is interpreted and whether Radisson learned much Sioux.)

As he worked on his writing project, Radisson's genius for storytelling blossomed. He had written most of the manuscript in the ghastly winter after the fire and plague when most foreigners were still avoiding the post-inferno mobs, and likely thought he would have to finish by the beginning of the 1666 sailing season. Instead, because of the war, Radisson beavered away in Windsor and Westminster until he had a full-sized book manuscript. We know the original manuscript was transcribed and probably edited by someone hired by Hudson's Bay Company investors, but the story and words—betrayed sometimes by clumsy grammar—are Radisson's. Yes, there are elements that seem dubious, but Radisson, always a great self-promoter, is as reliable as the Jesuits in their heavily edited and extremely selective accounts of their missionary work in the Great Lakes-St. Lawrence region. And Radisson's manuscript is certainly much better than the outright fantasies and lies of van Heemskerck, who stole Radisson's story to try to beat the real explorer to the riches of Hudson Bay.

Radisson's writing project alleviated his boredom and frustration in the years when he was effectively trapped in the English capital. It also—along with the stories he told directly to Charles II—helped keep Royal attention on his next voyage to Hudson Bay and greased the wheels of state for Prince Rupert to pry a monopoly out of his cousin. The book was a promise of riches, a sort of treasure map for the king. While it's a fascinating read, Radisson's manuscript did more than just entertain the king—it gave Radisson credibility. Here, on paper, was the life of a man who survived and thrived over and over when most other men would not have. He had lived among the mysterious people of America. He could talk to them. He could beat them in battle. He had been to the edge of the known world. The Cree, with the bales of beaver furs that they brought to Lake Superior, had shown Radisson the great wealth of the Hudson Bay fur country. Perhaps more than any English king, Charles, who had seen war, fled for his life, lived in exile, and come out on top, could connect with Radisson's stories of adventure and survival.

Radisson was never a man of print. He could have made a lot of money from his book if he had taken a copy of the manuscript to Paternoster Row, near St. Paul's, and sold it to one of the publishers. Even after his book was written, Radisson continued to write long, exciting letters about his adventures on Hudson Bay, but never submitted

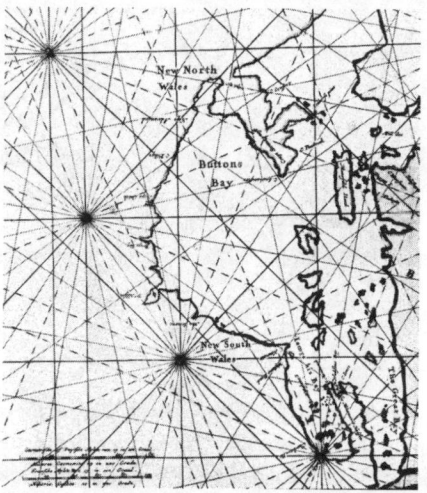

Official English navigation chart from 1660. The English had a good grasp of the geography of Hudson Bay before Radisson's defection, but had not realized its economic potential.

his stories to the news sheets or pamphlet-writers of the time (including his own father-in-law), nor was he interviewed by anyone. Why didn't Radisson take his books and stories to the press? Perhaps because he was brought up under the French Crown, which discouraged expression by people who were not clerics, aristocrats, or government propagandists. Or maybe he knew—like those Huron and Iroquois traders who had so jealously guarded their trade routes—that information was power, and that he would only share this power with people who might become his political and business patrons.

Whatever his reasons for writing the manuscript, it is a treasure. Without it, the Radisson story would have been lost. Along with the Hudson's Bay Company itself, it remains one of Radisson's two great legacies. As he wrote, he must have thought wistfully of his years as a kid in the North American wilderness, when he'd been a rich Iroquois warrior. Did he have enough self-awareness to realize he'd gone from being a successful independent trader to a pawn in the games of rich, powerful men who would never let him into their class? Did he realize he had fallen from entrepreneur to an employee who would be useful to his employers only until they knew how to find the woodland Cree of Hudson Bay and set up a fur trade with them?

In 1667, Charles II leased the small two-mast ship the *Eaglet* to Rupert and his fellow investors, while the dependable and ubiquitous

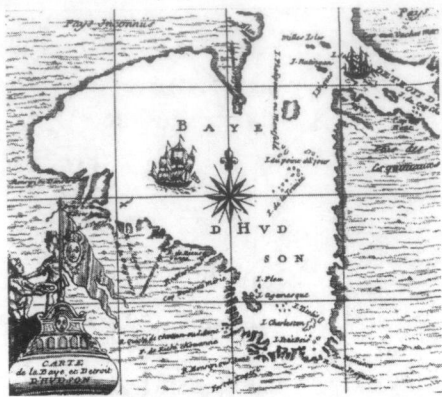

By the mid-1670s, the French had mapped southern Hudson Bay and had a much better idea of the geography of James Bay than did their English competitors.

Capt. Gillam of Boston was already outfitting the *Nonsuch*. Rupert issued orders to the captains of both ships, telling them of the importance of their mission and warning them to "use the said Mr. Gooseberry and Mr. Radisson with all manner of civility and to take care that all your company do bear a particular respect unto them, they being the persons upon whose credit we have undertaken this expedition."[161] The expedition was also given orders to look for a Northwest Passage to the Pacific Ocean, which, if found, would have made all of the investors spectacularly rich.

After a sumptuous dinner—one of many that lubricated negotiations for the financing of the expedition—the eighteen investors, who included the Duke of Albemarle, several earls, and some of the richest men in the city of London, headed to the wharf to catch a barge to Gravesend to see Radisson and the *Eaglet* off. The *Nonsuch* had already sailed and would make it to Hudson Bay carrying Groseilliers. But the *Eaglet* was no sea bird. Somewhere northeast of Ireland, she was caught in a wicked six-hour storm in waves so high that the men aboard were sure she was about to capsize. Even with all her sails down, the wind pushed so hard against the rigging that the *Eaglet* lay almost sideways in the grey, churning water. Fighting desperately to save her, the *Eaglet's* crew chopped down her main mast and pushed it overboard into the roiling, cold sea. With the main mast gone and the storm abating, the crew was able to regain control of the *Eaglet*, but she was in no shape to keep going westward, so they raised sails on the surviving small mast and limped back to Plymouth.

In a bit of disinformation, the *London Gazette* officially reported this in its August 13, 1668 edition: "Plymouth, Aug. 7. On Wednesday last (Aug. 5) came in the *Eagle* [sic]. Ketch, having in her way for Newfound-land been severely handled by storm, in which she spent her main Mast, and with some difficulty put back to refit." Once again, Radisson was stuck in England.[162]

Groseilliers and the tougher *Nonsuch* skirted the sea ice and arrived in August at the mouth of the Nelson River after a four-month journey through the bleak, grey waters of the North Atlantic and Hudson Bay. As they sailed south along the coastline, it became clear to the English sailors that Groseilliers, despite the stories he and Radisson told, had no idea about the geography of Hudson Bay. The navigators looked for the mouth of the river where the explorer Button had built a house in 1613, and somehow found the ruins at the outlet of the Nelson River. This was a big estuary surrounded by hills covered with scrubby pine forests that was dangerous to approach because of sandbars, strong tides that left miles of mudflats when low, but it was the seaport of one of the longest canoe routes to the west.

The Cree quickly found the ship and traded for the hardware and cloth that she carried. Groseilliers had also brought some wampum with him and used it to cement trading alliances with the Cree leadership. It was too late to return to England that year, so the crew of the *Nonsuch* built a fort, which they named after the king, and settled in for a very long, cold winter. Daytime high temperatures plunged below -20°F in December and stayed there for four months, while nighttime lows hovered at about -40°F.[163] And of course the winter nights would have been very long. At least there would have been plenty of opportunities to see the spectacular northern lights, given that the region has little cloud cover in winter. And the food was good: the traders found the country to be alive with rabbits and birds that they shot without much difficulty.

Capt. Gillam, who lived on the Atlantic and knew how to look after men trapped for the winter, had brought dried fruit to fend off scurvy. Because the captain kept them busy and well fed, surprisingly few men died that winter. In the spring, they were able to contact the Cree to let them know the *Nonsuch* was still in business. It took most of the next summer for ice to clear from the bay, so Groseilliers and his companions got in another trading season before finally getting past Hudson Strait and heading home in August 1669.

The trip was very profitable for the investors, and not just because of the payoff from the sale of furs. Charles II was so impressed when Rupert told him of the expedition's success that he very generously granted the investors a trading monopoly in Hudson Bay, along with half of what's now Canada and part of North and South Dakota: that is, all the land in the drainage basin of the rivers flowing into Hudson Bay.[164] None of this was his to give, of course, and at the time, no one saw the grant as anything more than a gentle legal warning against French intrusion in the new English trade. Charles II and his first cousin Louis

XIV had a strange, rather passive-aggressive relationship: Charles was secretly financing his palaces and stable of mistresses with bribes from the French king, while Louis was hoping Charles would finally come out as a Roman Catholic and purge England and Scotland of their Protestant heresy. Charles probably did not expect the Hudson's Bay Company charter to cause a rift with France, and certainly had no idea he was giving away almost half a continent and many billions of dollars' worth of resources. He was also illegally handing the lands of several First Nations over to corporate control. Two centuries later, the grant would be used as legal justification for Canadian expansion into the Prairies, with all the disease, displacement, alcoholism, and social destruction that followed for the First Nations who lived there.

For now, the focus was on building and paying for ships and gathering what was needed to build forts—"factories" in Hudson's Bay Company lingo—along the shore of that vast inland sea. Like the French in Quebec, the company had no desire to colonize the land holdings that it laid claim to. All it wanted was furs, at the cheapest price possible. And no competition. There was no real head office. Directors met in private homes and coffee houses—which were also the sites of the fur auctions—and would continue to do so through the next century.[165]

In May 1670, the new *Prince Rupert*, skippered by the ubiquitous Captain Gillam, left England carrying Groseilliers. Radisson went to the bay on the *Wivenhoe,* along with an odd character named Charles Bailey, whose previous residences included Virginia, several London jails, and the Tower of London. His crimes were political: he was locked in the Tower for sedition, though his real offense was probably religious and social non-conformity. He liked to give unsolicited advice to various kings. Charles II had been a childhood friend, but Bailey now nagged him about "rioting and excess, chambering and wantonness," all of which were Charles' favourite pasttimes.[166]

Bailey was a strange-looking man with a beard longer than Groseilliers'. He was a Quaker who supposedly tried to convert the Pope, and he'd been jailed a few times in Europe while on the run from the English government. Bailey was also something of an organizational genius with a talent for business. When the *Wivenhoe* arrived in Hudson Bay, it was Bailey, acting as a local governor, who chose the sites of the company's forts and ran the trade. Radisson wanted to go into James Bay to find a big river that would take him to Lake Superior and back to the upper lakes, where he and Groseilliers had made so much money a decade ago. Radisson claimed an English canoe flotilla could reach Green Bay on Lake Michigan in a week, which is absurd. He also told the English that it was only 150 miles from the south end of Lake Michigan to the Gulf of Mexico. Luckily for Radisson, his geography was never tested.[167]

This trip was not just about finding a northwest passage or a fast route through the interior of the continent and the Gulf of Mexico. Bailey wanted to trade from the shore and couldn't care less where the rivers came from, so long as the Cree could find his factories. The main fort was to be at the mouth of the Nelson River, a fantastic choice, since it lay at the end of the Saskatchewan River-Lake Winnipeg canoe route. At the last minute, the 1670 expedition left the Nelson for the nearby mouth of the Nemisco, which they renamed Rupert River. Bailey had brought bricks and wood to build a comfortable fort. His men loved him because he looked after them, bringing barrels of beer on the trip and the ingredients to make more, and giving them time off to hunt ducks and caribou. At times, he even got along with Radisson, to whom he gave a prized possession: a fine, expensive manuscript atlas.[168] The old jailbird was nevertheless determined to make Radisson redundant. Bailey took over the negotiations with the Cree, even though he knew nothing about them, at least at first.

Despite the work Bailey did on their behalf, the men of the expedition faced a hard winter. Capt. Newland of the *Wivenhoe* died of scurvy just before Christmas. Capt. Gillam pulled the *Wivenhoe* ashore and had its crew build strong tents out of sail canvas, while his men lived in two cabins that they made from building materials brought from England. Rather recklessly, Radisson left in the dead of the brutal, dark winter to trade with Cree at the mouth of the Moose River, hundreds of miles away at the bottom of James Bay. Knowing they would be short of food, he brought dried peas, for which the Cree were willing to pay dearly. The Cree, at what's now Moose Factory, promised Radisson they would come north to the Rupert River in the spring. In their reports to England, Bailey and his second-in-command, Gorst, gave Radisson no credit for any of this.

In the summer of 1671, Bailey and Gorst explored and mapped James Bay before leaving for home on July 24 with the ships' holds stuffed with furs worth one pound sterling for every two pounds of fur. For the first time, Radisson and Groseilliers found themselves shunted aside. They were now tourists on their own expedition, foreigners among the xenophobic English, Catholics among Protestants. They didn't have enough money to have a stake in the ownership of the company. Now the English

Contemporary engraving of James, Duke of York (later James II). His bad luck rubbed off on Radisson, whose career ended with James's downfall in the Glorious Revolution of 1688.

were becoming experts in cold-weather survival and in diplomacy with the First Nations. The two Frenchmen had come up with a great idea, but once they shared it, it was no longer theirs. When they got back to England, they were given a measly bonus of £5, while the Duke of York got a full share of the company, worth £300, just because he was next in line for the throne. The duke's share also came with the promise of a big dividend.

At about the same time, the company's leaders decided to enforce a rule against its employees trading privately with the First Nations. This had been the real gravy for the two Frenchmen, who, between them, had made £162 by moonlighting with their own stock of trade goods, diverting furs that would otherwise have gone to the company. This was far more than their base salary of £50 a year. Even with the profits of private trading, they were making nowhere near the money they'd pulled in from their Lake Superior expedition to the Sioux and the Cree. Radisson and Groseilliers stayed in London to help put together a third expedition to Hudson Bay, but their pay, and even the now-official title of "Captain Gooseberry," did not keep them happy as they watched the Hudson's Bay Company investors making a 50 percent return on their investments. In Quebec, they dealt with just one greedy governor. With the English scheme, there were the calloused hands of sailors and the soft hands of eighteen investors waiting for gold.

Radisson may well have seethed with jealousy when he saw that it was the English sea captains, and not him, who were invited by the Royal Society to give lectures on their Hudson Bay adventures. Radisson was no longer the centre of attention or the go-to man on Arctic exploration, which must have really hurt. Soon, the company would be able to run its Hudson Bay trade without him.

FRUSTRATION AND DEFECTION

Radisson was given opportunities to pad his pay with kickbacks when the company put him in charge of buying trade goods, but he preferred to track down the same hardware that he'd traded at Lake Superior, and that meant doing business with the same French blacksmiths and coppersmiths who supplied the St. Lawrence trade. Most were in northwestern France and were willing to ship their wares to England. These were big purchases: two thousand hatchet heads in 1673; and two hundred shotguns, along with powder horns, gunpowder and shot, and two hundred brass cooking pots, about a thousand knives, and boxes of metal arrowheads.[169]

The French administration in Quebec knew about Radisson and Groseilliers' trip to the bay. Jean Talon, the intendent, or business manager, of Quebec, sent an expedition of three Frenchmen and eight Indigenous guides north in the fall of 1671 to deal with the threat to the colony's fur business. Among its members was Fr. Charles Albanel, a tough old Sault Ste. Marie-based Jesuit who'd been pushing Quebec merchants to open the northern trade. But the French missed Radisson and Groseilliers by a few days and had to head back to the St. Lawrence Valley.[170] After Fr. Albanel and his companions arrived in Quebec, the colonial administration decided to try to push the English out of Hudson Bay, even if it meant arming the Cree's enemies with guns and starting a new version of the brutal warfare that had wiped out the Huron trading empire.[171] The French started by sending a group of traders to open a post on James Bay, at Moose Factory Island. Soon afterwards, a dynamic, war-loving man, Louis de Buade, Count Frontenac, was appointed governor of New France. Quebec's fur trade and its kickbacks were his last hope of fending off the mob of creditors who were after him for spectacular amounts of money.

In 1673, Radisson and Groseilliers set out from England on what was to be a miserable two-year trip. Groseilliers seems to have alienated almost everyone who ever worked with him, but he took control of part of the expedition. They couldn't find any Cree, and Groseilliers showed, through his ineptitude, that he couldn't navigate to the Severn River from James Bay, even with the help of a map. Then the Hudson's Bay Company men came across the French fur traders sent north by Frontenac but decided to ignore them and move on to another river. When the English did find Indigenous people, many of them refused to trade or had already sold their furs to the French, and the Hudson's Bay Company men managed to get only 250

Contemporary engraving of a 17th-century London coffee house. Business owners would spend much of their day in these coffee houses, making deals and meeting clients. The first business meetings of the Hudson's Bay Company were held in coffee houses.

beaver pelts. Groseilliers, who had tried to be tough with the Cree, was blamed for that, too. At almost the last minute, Bailey found a group of Cree at the Moose River who had brought 1,500 pelts to trade and were willing to deal with the English.

That spring, Radisson sailed back to London without Groseilliers and went to work undermining the company's faith in Bailey. Then, back on the Bay, either by accident or as part of a conspiracy, Groseilliers ripped open the scab that had grown over relations between the Catholic Frenchmen and the violently Protestant English merchants and sailors. In the spring of 1674, the Hudson's Bay Company traders caught the ubiquitous Fr. Albanel, who had made another overland trip from Quebec to James Bay to "accidentally" meet Groseilliers and return him to the French fold.[172] The priest's cover story was that he had escaped an ambush by Cree warriors and needed charity. This was believable, since Fr. Albanel had, in fact, been beaten and robbed by some Cree men just days before the English found him.

In England, harbouring a Jesuit was treason, and Jesuits were put to death when caught. The English searched the Jesuit's baggage and found letters addressed to Groseilliers from Frontenac and, more bizarrely, to Bailey. After reading the letters, the Hudson's Bay men realized Fr. Albanel was on a secret mission to lure Groseilliers back to the French. French spies in England must have sent reports to Quebec about the expedition. It was clear to the English that the French had a mole in their expedition, and that Groseilliers might still have a back channel from London to Paris, or maybe even Quebec. Groseilliers very likely already knew Fr. Albanel from his days in New France. The priest had been there since 1649, and may have been the one who met Radisson and Groseilliers at Percé Rock in 1661. Frontenac had taken special care to write a kind, generous letter to Bailey, who was well known for his hatred of Catholics and the Pope. Bailey seems to have been somewhat touched by Frontenac's letter because, at first, he treated the old Jesuit with remarkable kindness.

A few days later, Cree traders reported how Fr. Albanel had been to James Bay a couple of times, had visited an empty trading station at the mouth of the Rupert River in 1672, and had pulled down Charles II's coat of arms. The English sailors, already unhappy about having a "papist" on board, tossed the priest in the brig on one of their ships until they could get him back to London and into the hands of the English secret service.

While the English company men had the Jesuit locked up and were eyeing Groseilliers for arrest, fighting broke out at the English trading stations between Indigenous groups over who would act as middlemen. One shaman, who set up his tent next to the English fort at the Rupert River, warned the Cree not to trust the English. Bailey, on the advice of Groseilliers, bought off the Cree traders by paying more for their beaver pelts. The Cree gave Bailey credit for that and refused to trade with Radisson, but when the expedition finally returned to England, Bailey, who stayed behind until 1679, was accused of wasting about £830 worth of trade goods by overpaying for furs.

As Bailey was trying to shake off these accusations of waste, word leaked out that Radisson had eloped with Mary Kirke, who came from a family of French-English Protestant pirates and whose father was an investor and

The Royal Charter of the Hudson's Bay Company. Granted by Charles II on May 2, 1670, it gave millions of acres of Indigenous land to the Hudson's Bay Company.

director of the Hudson's Bay Company. The Kirke brothers, ruthless sea dogs, had left their home in Dieppe in 1629, sold their services to the English, illegally captured Quebec, and arrested Champlain, along with Jesuit Paul Ragueneau, Groseilliers' mortal enemy. The English loved this kind of swashbuckling, but the Kirkes' fate was tied with those of the Stuarts during the Civil War. Because of what the French saw, with some justification, as treason and piracy, the Kirke brothers, scions of a marriage between an English merchant and a French Protestant woman, became outlaws in France and favourites of Charles I of England. Mary's uncle, David Kirke, had been knighted by the king but died in jail after Charles I's execution.

The Kirkes got their property and influence back when Charles II was restored to the throne. The Kirke family and their Canada Company never gave up on claims that they owned New France and Nova Scotia.[173] For decades, they kept up the pressure on the French by smuggling furs sold to them by French Canadian bootleg traders. In 1666, while Quebec was staggering from yet another humiliating defeat by the Iroquois, the Kirkes made a blatant raid up the St. Lawrence and left with a boatload of furs.

We know a bit more about Mary than about the other women in Radisson's life. She was very much in love with him, and he seems to have shared that affection. However, Mary's father, Sir John Kirke, an investor in the Hudson's Bay Company, was enraged when Radisson eloped with his daughter. He threatened to cut off her allowance, £200 a year, which was more money than Radisson ever made in England. Not only had Mary married beneath her class, she had also, Sir John believed, secretly converted to Catholicism. Most likely, the pair were married by a fringe clergyman in a ceremony in someone's house, without the banns—church announcements—that were mandatory for a decent marriage in those days. There would be no dowry and some shame attached to the union. Still, it was a legal marriage.

The marriage did, however, became very strange as time went by. In the 1670s, a husband was supposed to have absolute legal power over his wife, a non-person in law who could not make a contract on her own. Nor could she make a will without her husband's approval. A husband could also beat her, as long as he didn't cause serious bodily harm, as part of "lawful and reasonable correction."[174] Radisson never got control over his wife. At first, the couple lived together, the £200 per year allowance from Mary's father ensuring Mary and Pierre did what Sir John wanted. Mary moved back in with her father whenever Radisson was away at sea. Later, when she bore Radisson a daughter, the child would also remain under Sir John's thumb.

The rest of the Hudson's Bay Company insiders were not enthusiastic about the match either. Rupert's secretary, Sir James Hayes, who was effectively the chief executive officer of the company throughout Radisson's early career, later summed up the feelings of the company's backers, writing how Radisson "deluded and privately married a daughter of Sir James Kirke (A Gentleman of His Majesty's band of Pensioners and a member of the Hudson's Bay Company)."[175] Instead of benefitting by marrying into a powerful merchant family, Radisson had made himself more of an outsider.

Mary's feelings were often utterly ignored by her husband and father. She must have known Radisson would be away a lot. His whole purpose in London was to organize expeditions to the subarctic. Still, time would show she would do almost everything for him except risk estrangement from her father.

Just after Hayes wrote his assessment of Radisson's marriage, the vehemently anti-Catholic, troll-like Earl of Shaftesbury took over the reins of the Hudson's Bay Company and began to undermine both Kirke and Radisson. Shaftesbury was a holdover from Parliament's side of the Civil War who believed—and with some good reason—that the king was secretly Catholic and his brother, the Duke of York, who was now open about his "Popery," would restore the Roman Catholic Church if he became king. (In fact, while Radisson was in Hudson Bay, Charles had taken a huge bribe from Louis XIV, with a new mistress thrown in as a bonus, to return England to the Roman Catholic Church.) Despite being an aristocrat, Shaftesbury was no great friend of monarchs, especially half-Bourbon princes like Charles II and James, who seemed to want to impose a Versailles-style absolute monarchy in England. He probably engaged the liberal ideas of his personal secretary, John Locke, one of the age's greatest thinkers, who believed in a government of reason, laws, and binding contracts, which have turned out to be capitalism's greatest protectors.[176]

Despite being an economic liberal, the Earl of Shaftesbury was a xenophobe who refused to buy trade goods from foreigners. This meant Radisson and Groseilliers, who'd been dealing with French merchants for their trade goods, were sidelined and probably lost a lucrative stream of kickbacks and secret commissions. Hudson's Bay Company employees and suppliers were now ordered to take an oath of allegiance to King Charles. Under Shaftesbury, the company launched lawsuits against Capt. Gillam and other employees for trading privately, and Gillam was fired. The organization was a mess, and many of the original investors unloaded their stock. The new investors had very little knowledge of the origins of the company or Radisson's role in its creation, and when they finally did learn of it, they showed little gratitude. There would be another sell-off a decade later, when Shaftesbury fell from power at the company and in politics. The new investors, people like the architect Sir Christopher Wren (who rebuilt London and designed the church where Radisson would be buried many years later), would have even less corporate memory and gratitude.[177]

By the mid-1670s, Radisson had the reputation of a seducer and a rogue whose knowledge of the Hudson Bay fur country was no longer needed. His days of intriguing the king and Prince Rupert with tales of life among the Indigenous people of Canada were over. Rupert was now engrossed in running the Admiralty and in his experiments. The king was having a tough time holding the Restoration settlement together while rebuilding London, going on benders, gambling, and fathering an ever-growing army of illegitimate children whose descendants are among the dukes and earls of Great Britain today (they include Prince William and Prince Harry).

Groseilliers sailed into this snake pit in the winter of 1675, on a company ship with his Jesuit friend locked in the hold. London was in the grip of violent "No Popery" demonstrations and was, again, losing a war with the Dutch. Radisson and Groseilliers' boss, the Earl of Shaftesbury, was whipping up anti-Popery demonstrations. Despite the mob violence against London's Catholics, Charles II had Fr. Albanel released and graciously received him at court, much to the disgust of the Hudson's Bay Company directors. Charles also made the company executives write a letter to Fr. Albanel's superiors in France and Rome explaining why and how he was in England. They were also ordered to pay for his passage and expenses to France. This was a lot of crow for Shaftesbury to eat, but he wrote the letters and came up with the priest's travel money.

The Albanel mess, the pro-Catholic stigma that was sticking to the restored Stuarts, and the backlash on the Hudson's Bay Company executive committee may be among the reasons Rupert withdrew from company affairs and sulked in his Windsor Castle apartment and laboratory for the rest of his life. He had come full-circle since the Civil War, being now a firm ally of Parliament and the merchants of the city, but he was tired of fighting.

Radisson and Groseilliers were, at least temporarily, finished in England. The leaders of the Hudson's Bay Company made it clear that its future did not include the two Frenchmen. The Jesuit was the last in their series of embarrassments and miscalculations. Shaftesbury and Bailey had effectively squeezed them out, their dreams were broken, and France, now back on its feet and glorious with aggressive young Louis XIV in absolute control, began to look pretty good. Fr. Albanel's trip had been a roaring success.

Radisson had to break the news to his new wife that he was no longer working for the Hudson's Bay Company, which he told her was run by ingrates. He didn't want to go back to France, and was loyal to England, but the company had left him with no other option but to make peace with Louis XIV. He would do what he had to and make sure they were together again soon, in France

"[A]ll my friends know the tender love I felt for my wife, and that I declared unto them how much I was troubled in being reduced to the necessity of leaving her," he wrote years later. And he seems to have meant it: of all the women in his life, Mary Kirke was the one that Radisson worked hardest to make happy. He wanted her in France with him as soon as he had a job. Her father, who made sure she rarely left his house without someone watching her, kept that from happening.

Book Five:
Radisson in the Caribbean (1675–1677)

When Radisson and Groseilliers arrived in France in 1675, Louis XIV's government paid their debts and gave them a little money, but there were no jobs waiting for them. If the brothers-in-law harboured dreams of a life at Paris or Versailles, or thought they might be important players in a French version of the Hudson's Bay Company, they were quickly disabused of that notion.

For one thing, the French government insisted Radisson had shown his true colours by not bringing his wife to France. What kind of man was not master of his own wife? Radisson could not give an explanation that preserved his honour or his masculinity. His new French masters wanted to know if Mary was still in England because Radisson was just visiting France. First minister Jean-Baptiste Colbert and the aristocrats who ran the court were not impressed to learn Radisson had so little money that he couldn't match the allowance his wife received from her much-despised father. And, just after Radisson and Groseilliers defected, the Hudson's Bay Company petitioned Charles II to call in the French ambassador to warn him that the two fur traders couldn't be trusted.

By the summer of 1676, Radisson and Groseilliers were back in New France, where they met the senior merchants and government leaders at Quebec City. All the big stars of New France were there: Count Frontenac, René-Robert Cavelier de La Salle, members of the Le Moyne family, Louis Jolliet, and Charles Aubert de la Chesnaye. La Chesnaye ran the Compagnie du Nord, which took furs to Russia for processing. Radisson hoped La Chesnaye's company could be adapted into a French version of the Hudson's Bay Company.

The meeting, however, went nowhere. The merchants still seethed about Radisson and Groseilliers' involvement in helping to create their English competitor. They also probably knew of the outrageously boastful letters

French man-o'-war running down a pirate galley at about the time of Radisson's Caribbean adventures. (Contemporary print)

Groseilliers had sent from England to New France. Marie de l'Incarnation, the well-connected nun, heard that Groseilliers claimed to have discovered the route to Hudson's Bay, found many people along its lovely shores, and made so much money for his backer that the king had given him twenty thousand ounces of silver and made him a Knight of the Garter. He further claimed to have become a very rich man and to have been written up in London's leading newspaper. Yet, here he was, just a few years later, hungry for a job and a second chance in New France.[178]

Frontenac, the governor, had different plans for New France. Advised by Jolliet, the first European to travel from the Great Lakes region to the mouth of the Mississippi, and by his friend Ourehouare, a Cayuga chief and former galley slave, Frontenac and La Salle had opened a route to the Illinois country. They hoped to rake in huge profits from a monopoly on furs, buffalo hides, and exotic woods. In the far future, once they had picked off the easy profits by fleecing the Indigenous people, they would make a fortune selling Mississippi Valley land to settlers. At the same time that New France's leaders were coming up with a plan for the Mississippi Valley, Louis XIV's government froze the number of fur-trading licenses that could be issued in Quebec. Only a few years had passed since Frontenac sent Fr. Albanel north to snatch Groseilliers and Radisson. Now the turncoats were in Quebec but were redundant because there was no work.[179]

Radisson, desperate for a role or job, pitched the idea of a fishing company, something the Hudson's Bay Company had tried to create on islands in the North Atlantic.[180] This, too, was shot down. The best he could get was the exclusive right to hunt seals on Anticosti Island in the Gulf of St.

Lawrence. Disgusted, Radisson left Quebec for France, while Groseilliers stayed behind.

Groseilliers went back to his wife and children at their farm near Trois-Rivières after more than a dozen years away. He would stay there, growing his gooseberries and smuggling furs with his son Jean-Baptiste, who learned a lot from his father. There seems to have been no legal or marital repercussions to his being an absent, deadbeat father. Marguérite had lived in poverty and was barely able to keep her creditors from seizing her store and blacksmith's forge, but she still took her husband back. She was eventually able to pay her accounts with the money from her husband and son's smuggled furs, but the team of "Radisson and Groseilliers" was out of business, at least for a while.

PIERRE JOINS THE MARINES

Once he got back to France, Radisson started looking for a way to make some quick, easy money. Instead, he ended up on a Caribbean cruise from hell.

Tobago is a beautiful island in the south Caribbean that's popular with tourists. Europeans like it so much that, since Christopher Columbus first landed on the island in 1498—when it was still called Kairi by the people who lived there—it changed hands thirty-three times before Britain became the final colonizer in 1814. Almost every European power with warships on the seas had tried to grab it over the years. In 1677, Tobago was in the hands of the Dutch, who were fighting to carve out an American empire to match their holdings in Asia. The island produced cotton, sugar, and indigo dyes. By and large, the island fits the Western ideal of a tropical paradise, with palm-shaded beaches lying at the foot of steep green hills, sparkling clear water alive with colourful fish and sea turtles. Inland, rivers tumble over waterfalls on the rugged landscape. While out of the main hurricane track, it does get hit from time to time. Tobago was just the kind of place where the great powers of the age would want to wage war, defoliate the landscape, enslave locals, and plunder resources.

In 1676, France and Holland were at war. The Comte d'Estrées, scion of one of France's most ancient and noble families, was made vice admiral of France and dispatched to the Caribbean to wipe out the Dutch colonies. He sailed to the French-held island of Martinique early in the winter

Drawing of Jean II, Comte d'Estrées, commander of the ill-advised 1678 raids on Dutch colonies in the Caribbean. The cover-up of the fiasco was so complete that almost no scholarship exists on the Las Aves disaster that cost France a fleet.

of 1677, resupplied his ships, and headed to Tobago on February 11 with ten men-of-war, two smaller ships, and a fireship. A week later, he arrived at Tobago, where the Dutch admiral Jacob Binckes waited with fourteen ships: nine men-of-war, one thirty-gun frigate, another with eleven cannons, two smaller warships, and a fireship—a hulk full of combustibles that was to be set loose among the enemy fleet to break up its formation. There was also a Portuguese ship nearby, crowded with sailors and officers watching the action unfold.

On his second day at Tobago, d'Estrées's fleet landed 750 men on shore. There was no resistance to their invasion, so their commander, Fontaine, marched them inland. D'Estrées arrived on shore the next day and ordered Fontaine to launch a night attack on the Dutch fort, which had been hastily built near the modern-day town of Scarborough. At the same time, the French fleet was supposed to send out small boats called shallops to create a diversion in the bay below the fort. The boats were put out, but the army stayed put. D'Estrées decided to land more men ashore, probably to put some spine into the first landing force. At the same time, he made the mistake of sailing his main fleet into the teeth of Binckes' armada. The Dutch ships outgunned the French fleet. Binckes also had thirty cannons on shore and was a much better commander than d'Estrées.

Binckes was part of a generation of spectacular sea captains that emerged from the Netherlands at the time of Rembrandt. He prowled the coasts of North America and the Spanish Main fighting whomever the Dutch were at war with. He'd been a ship captain in the two Dutch raids on England in 1667. He'd even taken New York back from the English in 1673—though the Dutch handed it back after a year during negotiations for the Treaty of Westminster, knowing they couldn't hold it, or believing it wasn't worth the money and effort to defend it. Binckes was rewarded for this success by being appointed commander of a Caribbean fleet that protected the Dutch West India Company's trading posts. The WIC was trying to push its way into the Caribbean and tap the vast profits in slaves and sugar that the Spanish, French, and English were making. Some of the small islands had the most expensive real estate in the world. One, the French island of Guadeloupe, made ten times more profit for France than all its mainland North American holdings. Binckes, whose fleet was being bled by disease and desertion, began fortifying Dutch holdings, including Tobago.[181]

The first fight for Tobago, waged in Rockley Bay, lasted from seven in the morning until five at night. One big French ship, the *Marquis*, was locked in a struggle with a Dutch man-of-war until both ships caught fire. Only one man survived. Another sixty-six gun Dutch ship went up in flames and exploded, spewing fire onto d'Estrées's flagship, *Glorieux*. Both ships became masses of fire. The French commander escaped in a small boat with two of his officers while the men on *Glorieux* were left to burn. Dutch sailors and soldiers fired at the little boat as it headed for shore, but it was France's bad luck that none of the bullets hit d'Estrées. The little boat did sink and the Count had to swim the last hundred feet to shore but, unlike so many of the men who served under him, he survived.

While d'Estrées was ashore, the two big fires spread through the Dutch fleet and part of the French line of battle, sinking almost all the Dutch ships and all but four of the French warships. At the same time, the island's heavily outnumbered Dutch troops crushed the French landing force, killing most of its fighting men and officers. Rather than pursue a pyrrhic victory over the Dutch fleet, d'Estrées ordered his captains to collect the survivors of his little army, then set sail for France.[182]

Within months, d'Estrées was gathering a new force for a second run at Tobago and the rest of the Dutch-held Islands. Louis XIV, the Sun King, was willing to provide more ships but d'Estrées had to find the crews and the soldiers, and pay for the cannon. It's reasonable to conclude that this expedition was as much a profit-seeking privateering raid as it was a government-run military operation. Radisson invested in the trip, handing over two thousand livres in return for a spot on the ships. It's likely Radisson hoped to keep himself out of harm's way; at thirty-eight, he was getting a bit old for war, but still collected his share of the prizes.

L'abbé Claude Bernou, a well-connected cleric in the French court who also backed La Salle's voyages and colonies in North America, was one of Radisson's few important friends. Bernou was also a journalist who wrote for the official newssheet, *Gazette de France*, as well as a fundraiser who, in the name of Christ, was able to pull together donations for various missionary and not-so-bloodless projects. Bernou believed, at first, in a French empire anchored on Quebec and the fur trade, and he used letters from Radisson to flesh out ideas and proposals that he put in front of more powerful courtiers. Bernou was patronized by the d'Estrées family, and that was probably the "in" that allowed Radisson aboard d'Estrées's second expedition to Tobago.[183]

It wasn't much of a favour, but for a man who loved adventure and had spent more than a decade swept up in other people's plans and politics that usually left him cooling his heels in a strange, unpleasant city, it was a chance to feel some of the adrenalin that he surely must have been missing. He also needed the chance to rebuild his finances and maybe even to outbid his father-in-law for his wife's affection.

On September 27, d'Estrées's new fleet of eleven ships of the line, the biggest warships of their time—and far out-gunning Binckes, who received no reinforcements after so much of his fleet burned off Tobago—left Brest.[184] The timing meant that the fleet would dodge any hurricanes. (Tobago is outside of the normal hurricane zone, but d'Estrées would have to cross the main storm track to get there.)[185] The next day, they were forced back into the harbour. On October 3, they set sail again, tacking off the coast of France in a headwind. By October 18, they were at the Portuguese island of Porto Santo, off the coast of Morocco, and the next day they sighted Madeira. Soon, they reached at El Hierro in the Canaries.

D'Estrées sent a fireship ahead to Martinique with a message to order the French ships there to set sail for Barbados and await his fleet. When they passed the Tropic of Cancer on October 28, those who had never crossed it before—including Radisson—were given the traditional sailors' mock baptism by King Neptune and the rough hazing that went with it (a tradition that continues in many navies today). Radisson's ship was detached from the main fleet to reconnoiter a strange sail they'd seen on the horizon, but the ship turned out to be English and, for a change, France and England were at peace. The two ships saluted, and Radisson's warship rejoined the fleet.

It was a lovely cruise to a part of the world where Radisson had never been. As his ship cut through the warm water, flying fish surrounded it, and at least one landed on deck. By the beginning of December, the French were at Cape Verde, where the Dutch ran a slave-trading station. While d'Estrées approached the Dutch harbour at Gorrée, his men stripped the masts of

French flags and replaced them with English or Dutch ones. Gorrée is a small island, only about three miles across, but the Dutch had built two forts that commanded the sea approaches from the north. One on higher ground provided artillery cover to a lower fort. The Dutch saw through the false flag ruse and opened fire on the French from both forts, but the cannonballs missed the French fleet because the ships quickly moved out of artillery range. That night, the leaders of the French expedition met on d'Estrées's flagship and decided to try to terrify the Dutch into surrendering. Officers, under a flag of truce, went ashore the next morning and told the Dutch that the French would give no quarter if the Dutch opened fire again. The Dutch garrison hurrahed its loyalty for its leader, but at the same time sent its rather terrified surgeon to the French flagship to feel the French out about surrender terms.

The talks didn't go well. For two weeks, the French fleet waited offshore, then d'Estrées dispatched five hundred armed men in small boats to try to storm the island. Radisson claims to have tried to join the fighting troops—French marines—before leaving Brest, but to have been turned down because the leaders of the expedition had more important work for him. He stayed aboard his ship and guarded it against a Dutch assault while his ship's guns pelted the Dutch with cannon fire. The Dutch abandoned the lower fort. The guns of the upper batteries continued their fire on the French fleet, but when one of the French shells landed on the Dutch powder magazine and almost set it off, the Dutch flag came down from both forts. The enemy commander was rowed out to the French flagship to hand over his keys. The garrison would get quarter after all, even though they had ruined forty of their own cannons and wrecked all their gunpowder, probably by mixing it with water or sand. D'Estrées assured the Moorish merchants who ran the fort's slave pens that they wouldn't be harmed or sold, but the French did take sixty Africans and two-and-a-half tons of merchandise worth 200,000 ecus, then blew up everything the Dutch had built.

Within a few days, the French fleet had passed Fogo and Radisson watched nightly as its volcano belched flame and lava. Then, for weeks, there was nothing but sea as the fleet slowly crossed the South Atlantic. At Barbados, the son of the governor of St. Kitt's met the officers of the French fleet at the island's main wharf, but the French didn't bother to salute. That left the English wondering if, again, they were at war with France. For three days, the French tried to calm their English hosts' nerves. Even more important, they watched to make sure that none of the English slipped out to alert Tobago that the French were coming. Someone did get away, however, and the Dutch, now warned, shipped all their rum, cloth, and everything else of value to the Spanish colony of Mexico.

When the French arrived at Rockley Bay, the Dutch weren't taken by surprise. Again, d'Estrées put five hundred marines ashore on Tobago. This time, Radisson was among them. The next day, another three hundred men followed, so the French now outnumbered the healthy members of the Dutch garrison. The French set up camp out of sight of the Dutch fort and sent fifty men to scout it, looking for ways to attack it from the landside while their ships bombarded it from the sea. They found the Dutch working hard to strengthen its walls. Some Dutch prisoners who were caught outside the fort walls assured the French that the Dutch garrison would not be intimidated as easily as their colleagues back on Cape Verde.

Radisson stayed in the main camp, where the French gunners assembled two siege mortars, and made notes of what he saw. For two days, nothing happened, even though the Dutch could clearly see the French preparing their assault. The French sent trumpeters to summon the Dutch commander to a parley. Binckes would not surrender. He would rather be killed than give up. But, he said, if he did win, he would treat the French with kindness and honour, feed them and clothe them. And he had advice for d'Estrées: the rain would be constant, the climate of the island was unhealthy, and d'Estrées could expect his men to start dying of disease and fatigue in about four days. As the son of a marshal of France, such a disaster would bruise d'Estrées's honour. It would be better to break camp and leave now. With that, the trumpets sounded and Binckes went back into his fort.

Cannonades opened from both sides within minutes. Radisson was close enough to see the action. D'Estrées's chief gunner, Landouillette, said he would hit the fort with his third shot. When the first two French mortar rounds fell short, the Dutch waved their beaver hats in mock salute. Landouillette tweaked his range. Binckes wasn't worried. He ate dinner with his men and was finishing desert and drinking to the health of his prince when a flaming French mortar round fell directly on the fort, penetrated the tile roof and three storeys of its ammunition magazine, and set off eleven tons of gunpowder.[186] The explosion obliterated Binckes, all but one of his officers, and much of the fort.

Radisson saw the bomb fall and claims to have cried out "God Save the King" as the blast blew the place apart. He could see pieces of Binckes and his men as they flew into the sky and fell back onto the ground. Somewhere between two hundred and five hundred Dutch were killed in the blast, with the best estimates being at the lower end. It was difficult to know how many people died since everything within nearly a mile was blown away. "It was a terrible dessert," Radisson wrote. "They had never been served such fruit before. Two thousand grenades and all the cannons taking fire, the air seemed like the abyss of hell for a quarter of a league. [We could see] nothing but arms, heads, legs, huge [numbers of] bodies flying about. The flames roasted many of these wretches. When the smoke cleared there was no longer a fort to be seen."[187]

The 250 survivors, mostly men stationed in trenches far from the blast, staggered out of the wreckage and wandered toward the seashore, afraid the French would massacre them. "Our lives, good Frenchmen," some cried out as the French approached in battle array. The French, as shocked perhaps as the Dutch, took pity on the survivors, fed them, and stayed with their captives as a Jesuit and a White Father (the nickname for Dominican friars) visited and tried to comfort them. Radisson, who still knew some Dutch, was in the middle of this ghastly scene and translated for the priests. Meanwhile, some of the French troops went into what was left of the fort to pillage anything that was left. The ruins were still hot, and the heat set off hand grenades that killed two French soldiers. The French got some satisfaction, however, when the Dutch prisoners handed over a French deserter who had left d'Estrées's fleet on its first night in Tobago, and Radisson watched as the man was hanged.

Radisson shared all this good news with Abbé Bernou, but he left out a few details. D'Estrées had made some mistakes. The worst was when famous pirate Jan Erasmus Reyning—someone worth catching—escaped from the harbour on a stolen ship to exact his revenge on the French for the next twenty years.[188] The following May, much of d'Estrées's fleet was destroyed. D'Estrées sailed off from Tobago to more comfortable quarters in Grenada and St. Kitts, where his men enjoyed the best of buccaneer culture for several weeks, then shipped out to attack the Dutch island of Curaçao. Its governor sent three ships to reconnoiter the big French fleet that was moving toward his island.

D'Estrées's fleet was strengthened with about an equal number of French pirate ships out of what's now Haiti. Just because most of the captains and crews were French doesn't mean the pirates had any loyalty to the French crown. And there may have been pirates in this fleet who were outlaws of other nations, people like the Dutch captain Laurens de Graaf, a ferocious sea robber. Pirates were, by nature, independent of all states and for sale to the highest bidder, and admirals like d'Estrées had to keep them happy or risk losing them to their opponents. With four major powers in the region—France, Spain, England, and Holland—and smaller players like Sweden and Portugal also trying for toeholds, the pirates could auction themselves or go freelance. They could also, it turned out, be very unlucky sailors.

STRANDED WITH THE BOOBIES

D'Estrées's fleet set out from St. Kitts to take Curaçao with twelve men-of-war, three fire ships and two transports, a hospital ship and a dozen pirate and privateer ships called *filibustiers*. The pirates, with their smaller ships and, allegedly, better knowledge of these waters, led the way, with the big navy ships following a few miles behind. On May 11, d'Estrées's fleet was destroyed on the Las Aves Archipelago. The pirates should have known about this place. The shipping charts showed it as little more than a few islands in an obscure corner of the Caribbean off the coast of South America. But below the surface of the warm, tropical waters lay a network of coral reefs fringing the desert islands. These islands and reefs, eighty miles off the coast of Venezuela, are straight out of the set of a Hollywood castaway movie, and they would soon be a temporary home for Radisson, a few French military men lucky enough to survive the disaster, and a lot of pirates.

The disaster happened on an overcast, moonless night. Like most shipwreck stories, it's a tale built on mistakes adding to mistakes. The pirates, sailing blind, got over some of the reefs along the edge of Las Aves before they reached shallower water and their ships' bottoms were ripped out by coral. A pirate captain ordered a cannon to be fired as a warning to the rest of the pirate fleet and d'Estrées's men-of-war. This brought d'Estrées battle charging what he thought was a Dutch force coming from Curaçao. He ordered his flagship's captain to raise every stitch of sail, with the five hundred men running for battle stations on their seventy-cannon ship, and *Le Terrible* made straight for the reefs. The rest of the ships' captains, following close behind, also hoisted as much canvas as they could and plowed full-speed into rocks and sand. Within minutes, almost all the French navy ships were wrecked on reefs along a half-mile arc. It remains one of the worst French naval disasters in history.[189] Radisson somehow survived when his ship was wrecked, but he didn't have time to grab his hoard of cash. Radisson didn't believe in banks. Everything he had was aboard that ship.

Nicholas Lefèvre de Méricourt, captain of *Le Terrible*, later testified that d'Estrées had lost his nerve as his ships were torn open on the reefs on that hot, damp, moonless Caribbean night. He was the first to get off his ship and flee to a safer place. Other survivors were more generous, saying the admiral, while keeping himself ignorant of the hazards, was accidentally lured onto the reefs by the pirate ships, which were smaller and drew less water. Radisson kept a discreet silence in his letters to Bernou, who was also a friend of d'Estrées. Whatever happened, d'Estrées, even if he saw the danger in those moments when he was making for the phantom Dutch fleet, simply didn't have time to turn his ships around before they were on the rocks. A few of the ships ran aground on sand and could be re-floated, but most of them, with their hulls already honeycombed by wood-eating worms, were finished. So many details of that night are missing from the historic record, but we do know Radisson was one of the French mercenaries who made it to shore. But he had little reason to feel relieved, knowing he was now utterly broke and marooned on a rock thousands of miles from home with a bunch of pirates.

The record is very hazy about the number of French who died in the wrecks or starved over the next few weeks. Even at the time, some observers in the Caribbean thought the French casualties were light. A closer look at the facts suggests many French sailors and probably a fair number of soldiers died, since all the survivors from the thirteen big navy ships returned to France on just two men-of-war. The pirates' losses are a complete mystery, but were likely very low.

The stranded French military men and the tough pirates fought over the barrels of salted meat and wine in the wrecked ships. The pirates usually won. The buccaneers also knew how to live off the land, so the French were at a disadvantage. Radisson, though, was used to surviving in the wilderness, so probably had an easier time of it. (He didn't complain about the food, which is usually a sign that things were going well for him.) Radisson was probably still in good shape at forty-one, with few scruples when it came to preserving himself. He had already broken many European survival taboos, including those against cannibalism.[190] He could get by on fish if he had to, and pirate if necessary.

Stuck on Las Aves, Radisson seems to have suffered little except anxiety over his money. The pirates who were marooned with him were men of a similar worldview, survivors who could make the best out of what was, for ordinary, more scrupulous people, a disaster. William Dampier—a Caribbean freebooter who pirated his way around the Spanish Main before making his name as an explorer of Australasia—wrote, twenty years after d'Estrées's catastrophe, that some five hundred men drowned on the night the fleet was lost. The rest of the five thousand men on the naval and military expedition were marooned. Dampier says one thousand of them were killed by thirst and hunger.

Dampier wrote:

> Many of those [French navy sailors and soldiers] that got safe on the island, for want of being accustomed to such hardships, died like rotten sheep. But the privateers who had been used to such accidents lived merrily ... For they kept in a gang by themselves and watched when the ships broke up to get the goods that came from them.
>
> They [the pirates] lived there about three weeks ... in which time they were never without two or three hogsheads of Wine and Brandy in their tents and barrels of beef and pork.

One pirate survivor later told Dampier that he couldn't have had a better time in Jamaica with thirty English pounds in his pocket.

After about three weeks, d'Estrées returned and picked up Radisson and some of the rest of the survivors from the reefs and islands. He also carefully mapped the location of all the wrecked ships.[191] In the 2000s, a marine archaeology company licensed by Venezuela used these charts to find the wrecks and discovered that the old maps were quite accurate.[192] They found d'Estrées's flagship, along with most of the rest of the lost fleet, but they didn't find Radisson's money. Over the years, the lost fleet had been picked clean of almost everything of any value, including by privateers who stripped the warships of mast and rigging to use on their own ships.

Back in France, d'Estrées was exonerated of personal responsibility for the disaster in what some historians see as a cover-up. After a short stint back in the Caribbean, where he worked to salvage his lost fleet instead of attacking the Dutch, d'Estrées became a land general, and, eventually, reached the top position in the French army, Marshal of France.

Radisson, as soon as he reached dry land, petitioned the government to pay him the money he lost on the Curaçao expedition, plus the income he'd given up—boldly claiming the annual pension from his father-in-law of £200 sterling that really belonged to his wife—when he patriotically left England. In another plea, he said his wife's father, Sir John Kirke, had cut off Mary's allowance because he believed she had become a Catholic. His patrons, still determined to make Radisson prove his loyalty by severing his English connections and settling his wife and daughter in France, gave him 1,000 livres to go back to England to try to patch up the marriage.

This did not go well. Radisson arrived in London at the beginning of July 1679, and was able to see Kirke, who asked him to collect an old debt for him from traders with businesses in Canada. When Radisson completed that task, Kirke reneged on his promise to let his daughter and her child go to France. Fairly soon, Radisson's 1,000 livres were gone, and he was reduced to spending cash and selling jewels that his wife sent him. He even had to part with the portrait of Charles II that the king had personally given to him back in 1665, and his gold chain necklace, another gift of the king. He finally resorted to begging the Hudson's Bay Company for work and, when that failed, gave up and sailed back to France in mid-October. He arrived penniless and without any important patrons.

Radisson was able to convince the Marquis de Seignelay, Colbert's son, to listen to his tales of woe. Seignelay was hardly sympathetic. Instead, he berated Radisson for failing to control his wife. He raised the idea that Radisson left her in England because he planned to move back there as soon as he had some money. Radisson, the marquis said, was very likely a traitor who was still loyal to the English. He would nevertheless put in a word with his father to see if some use for Radisson could be found. In his petition to Louis XIV, Radisson grovelled and pleaded: "I beg His Majesty to have pity on my family in order that I may prove my fidelity to God and to him, praying to God for the rest of my life that he will give him blessings."

He got nothing.

Book Six:
True and Absolute Lords and Proprietors (1681–1685)

In the fall of 1681, Groseilliers was back in New France and Radisson was on his way west across the sea for the seventh time. The Quebec census taken that year shows Groseilliers, now sixty-three, owned nothing more than a gun. Radisson, forty-five years old, was penniless, and spent that winter either in a Quebec rooming house or in a camp somewhere on Canada's Atlantic coast. This was a long fall from their days as the most successful fur traders in New France and their time spinning yarns with kings and princes. Groseilliers was now an old man by the standards of the time, but still had at least one adventure left in him. At first, it seemed he might take part in one of La Salle's expeditions to the Mississippi (which eventually ended in mutiny and La Salle's murder). Instead, he, his son Jean-Baptiste, and Radisson crept away again to that old smuggler's rendez-vous, Percé Rock, to meet with "illegal" French traders. Their destination was Hudson Bay, and the two old fur pirates were promised a big piece of the profits if they showed the way.[193]

New France needed furs desperately. The Iroquois were challenging the French again for control of the Ottawa River canoe route and the upper lakes trade, so a Hudson Bay trade seemed to be the last hope until French soldiers could be shipped over to crush the Five Nations. France in the 1680s was something of a police state, and there was very little that happened without Louis XIV's government or the Jesuits knowing about it. It seems certain Colbert, through intermediaries, including banker Charles Aubert de la Chesnaye, was behind the expedition. La Chesnaye and Quebec merchants now decided to use the Compagnie du Nord for the Bay trade.[194]

The French government and its ministers were playing a complicated game. They had granted a monopoly to the traders of New France (for a price) to gather beaver from the Great Lakes country. This agreement was supposed to keep the price of beaver skins high in the European market by preventing competition, at least among the French. But they also knew Hudson Bay could generate far more profit without the expense of defending a colony against the First Nations and the English colonists to the south. Owning New France required France to have a North Atlantic naval squadron capable of turning back an English or Dutch fleet headed toward the St. Lawrence, an expense that was to drain the French treasury until 1763. (This was one of the reasons the French unloaded Canada after the Seven Years' War and Napoleon refused England's offer to return Canada to the French in 1803.) The king and his advisors also liked La Salle's Mississippi project because the French Caribbean fleet could protect the new colony at no extra cost to the treasury. A Hudson Bay ship-based fur trade would be protected by its isolation or be so fleeting that its ships could evade any hostilities from Indigenous people and European enemies. Quebec, that drain on France's finances, could finally be abandoned or sold.

Sometime in the previous couple of years, someone in France finally realized Radisson was right in his twenty-year-old claim that the Nelson River and the nearby Hayes River were the key to the trade in furs of the Canadian Shield and could supply much of Europe's felt hat materials. The rivers seem obscure now, but they are the eastern end of a canoe route through Lake Winnipeg and the Saskatchewan River that reaches all the way to the Dakotas and the foothills of the Rockies. It was the main highway of the Hudson's Bay Company's fur trade for more than two centuries.

It Was Hard not to Think of the Bay

Meanwhile, from wherever he was, a sad room in Quebec or a snow-covered tent in Acadia, Radisson was still communicating with his friends in New England, the Gillam family of sea captains he had met half a lifetime before. Young Benjamin Gillam was also ready to claim the Nelson River gateway, and members of his family may have been making trips to the bay in the five years after the company fired Zachariah, the family patriarch. Gillam's wonderfully named *Bachelor's Delight* was being fitted out in New England for a voyage sponsored by Boston merchants.

Whatever sleaziness, back-channel plotting, and double-dealing had transpired, Radisson and Groseilliers, along with the latter's son, Jean-Baptiste,

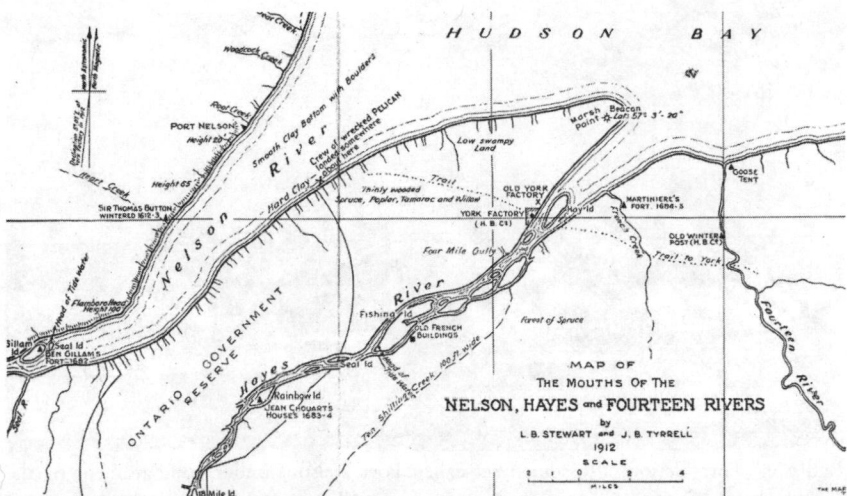

Government of Canada map of the mouths of the Hayes and Nelson Rivers showing Jean-Baptiste Groseilliers' house and other settlement sites used during mapping expeditions and the fur trade.

were hired by the Compagnie du Nord to make the trip that Radisson had begged for when he met the main merchants after his previous defection. Back then, he'd been fobbed off with a seal-hunting license and had sulked back to France and joined the Tobago expedition. This new expedition always had an element of sleaze. Radisson and Groseilliers left Percé on the small, old, unpleasant schooners *St. Pierre* and *Ste. Anne*, ships that were probably used more for smuggling than for honest transport.

Somewhere off the north coast of Newfoundland, the sailors aboard Groseilliers' ship mutinied, but the old trader used threats and promises to get them back to work. Near Baffin Island, they stopped to trade with the Inuit for sealskins, which they could sell in Europe as fancy furs. Along the north shore of Hudson Bay, men aboard Radisson's *Ste. Anne* shot a big polar bear as it walked along an ice floe. Some of them ate meat that had mixed with blood and bile from the bear's liver, which was so poisonous that it almost killed some of the men. (Polar-bear livers contain a toxic amount of Vitamin A and cadmium that would have attacked the sailors' bodies.) The victims' hair fell out in great clumps. Their skin sloughed off too. They tried to cope with brutal headaches, dizziness, blurred vision, joint pain, and dry mouths. It must have been terrifying to men at the edge of the known world, without medical care of any kind, and at the mercy of leaders who expected to lose some of them as part of the cost of doing business. It seems the stricken sailors recovered enough to keep going. So

Radisson's Fort Nelson, also sometimes called Port Nelson, under bombardment by the French about 50 years after it was built. Built at the Hudson Bay end of a canoe route that stretched to the Rocky Mountains, the post was vital to the fur trade until York Factory was built on the Hayes River.

far, the voyage had been miserable and the chance of returning alive, let alone making money from this subarctic wasteland, seemed slim. After yet another abortive mutiny, the two French ships set sail for the west side of the bay. The latter and the *Bachelor's Delight*, skippered by Benjamin Gillam with a crew of fourteen New England bachelors, arrived at the mouth of the Hayes River at almost the same time.[195] The French moved off to the Nelson River and Groseilliers started building a fort, while Gillam and his men stayed at the Hayes.

Near the end of August, Radisson and his nephew found a Cree hunting party on the Hayes River. Radisson was, as usual, the key go-between with the First Nations. He spoke Cree, which impressed the local chief when Radisson visited his camp. Radisson told the Cree of France's great power and described his own vast importance and courage. He knew how the Cree family and clan systems worked, and he had his own adoptive pedigree to add to the mix. The French had come to help the Cree, not exploit them. "I know the whole land," Radisson told the leading chief. "Your friends will be my friends, and I have brought you weapons to destroy your enemies. You will not die of hunger, neither your wife nor your children, because I have brought you merchandise. Take courage. I want to be your son, and I have brought you a father [old Groseilliers]. He is down there having a fort built, where I have two big ships. You must give me two or three of your canoes so your people can visit your father."

Radisson passed pipes around to the Cree. When one of them took out a small iron blade to cut some tobacco, Radisson snatched it and threw it into the fire. At the same time, he pretended to cry, then wiped away his tears and said it saddened him to see his new brothers so poor. He would make sure they never lacked anything. Radisson took the dagger from his belt and gave it to the man whose iron he had taken, then unwrapped a packet of smaller knives and passed them around. He smoked from a pipe with the men, then served them some food. Radisson told the chief that the Cree leader was now his father, an adoption sealed when the chief covered Radisson with his robe. The Frenchman answered by taking out a blanket and telling some of the Cree men to take it to Radisson's new mother, the chief's wife. When that ceremony was over, the Cree men gave Radisson every scrap of fur that they wore, then began searching their canoes, packs, and lodges for any other skins. When the meeting was over and Radisson was getting ready to leave, the Cree promised to gather more furs and bring them to the French camp.

None of the French—certainly not Groseilliers, whom Indigenous people never seemed to like and, rightly, never trusted—could put on a show like that, nor could their English and New Englander competitors. A few days later, Radisson impressed Cree visitors to the French settlement by ordering the cannon aboard his two ships to fire a broadside. They were likely even more impressed when they started trading guns inland and realized the fantastic profits they could make as middlemen. Writing a century later, after all the inland Indigenous people were familiar with guns, which were likely much cheaper, Hudson's Bay Company trader Samuel Hearne said the usual mark-up for guns and other trade goods was 1,000 percent each time they changed hands. Something that cost ten beaver furs at a European post on the sea became worth a hundred when carried inland. And guns needed powder and shot, which kept the inland people dependant on the Swampy Cree who lived in the Hudson Bay Lowlands until competing Europeans built posts inland.[196]

On September 17, as winter closed in, the French, in canoes, and Gillam's men, in rowboats, encountered each other on the Hayes from a distance. The New Englanders thought Radisson and his companions were Cree. Capt. Gillam, using an English-Cree dictionary, tried to make a deal with the Indigenous traders. Radisson, showing off, answered in Cree, then French, then English, and claimed the whole country for France. Radisson demanded to know who the New Englanders were and who gave them permission to trade on the bay. He warned them that he had a fleet of heavily armed ships. Then, as he got closer, he recognized his old friend and co-conspirator, Benjamin Gillam, who was glad to see him. Once the ice was broken, they agreed not to fight, and Radisson even promised that the French would protect the New Englanders from the Cree, if need be. Radisson very strongly suggested the New Englanders build some houses, but no fortifications, and rely on him for protection.

Then, a few days later, another ship arrived, this time from England. This was the old *Prince Rupert*, again commanded by Zachariah Gillam, the family patriarch, who had settled his quarrels with the Hudson's Bay Company after Bailey died. Radisson and Groseilliers had known and travelled with Zachariah Gillam since 1661.

Small world.

The senior Gillam was transporting John Bridgar to be governor of a new colony that the company planned to establish at the mouth of the Nelson. Radisson knew the older Gillam had become his sworn enemy for going back to the French, but he went on the ship and dined with Gillam and the Hudson's Bay Company expedition's leaders anyway. He warned Bridgar and Gillam they were on French territory, and that the French traders had the men and firepower in their fort upstream to defend themselves. Radisson was bluffing. "He took all at face value," he wrote, "and it was well for me travelling forty leagues [120 miles] through the woods and sleeping on the cold, hard ground to make my discoveries, he would soon have learned my weakness. I had reason to conceal it, and do what I did; moreover, not having sufficient men to resist openly, it was necessary to use trickery."

He also didn't tell them Benjamin Gillam was setting up his bootleg trading camp just one river away. Radisson made his goodbyes, pretended to be heading back to the French base, then spent two days lurking in the scrub pine, watching the English. When he got back to the French camp, Groseilliers kept working on the construction of the fort while Radisson manipulated the two camps of Englishmen. First, he made sure neither camp knew the other existed. Then, when Zachariah Gillam got sick, he let his son Benjamin in on the secret and smuggled him into the Hudson's Bay camp without Governor Bridgar knowing. Radisson was collecting IOUs that he would need later.

It took weeks before Bridgar started to understand what was going on. Even then, when he sent spies out to watch the French, his men went to the New Englanders' camp by mistake. Then, in late fall, things got serious:

The *Prince Rupert* was dragged out to sea by the ice and crushed, taking with it old Zachariah Gillam. The Company men were now stranded, and young Benjamin's ship was their only way out of the bay. But Radisson pre-empted that by inviting the New Englanders into his camp. They thought they were visitors, but, in fact, they were prisoners. He let them know it when they tried, in the early winter, to go back to their own camp. He also seized the *Bachelor's Delight* along with the bachelors. Benjamin Gillam wanted to kill Radisson, but his men believed the old turncoat was their only hope of getting home. Soon afterwards, the hungry, stranded Hudson's Bay Company men learned of the New Englanders' arrest and threw themselves on Radisson's good graces as winter's cold and darkness took hold. After he had taken them in, Radisson uncovered a few plots, including a plan to blow him up. He dealt with those threats by calling on the Cree to menace his prisoners. And since Radisson had promised to be an enemy of the Cree's enemies, they felt they were obliged to reciprocate. They were willing to kill all the English, but Radisson said that wouldn't be necessary, at least not yet.

So, in April 1682, at the first sign of spring, Radisson was master of the bay, dominating the French expedition, the two English trading crews, and Groseilliers, who was under his brother-in-law's control. Radisson was also

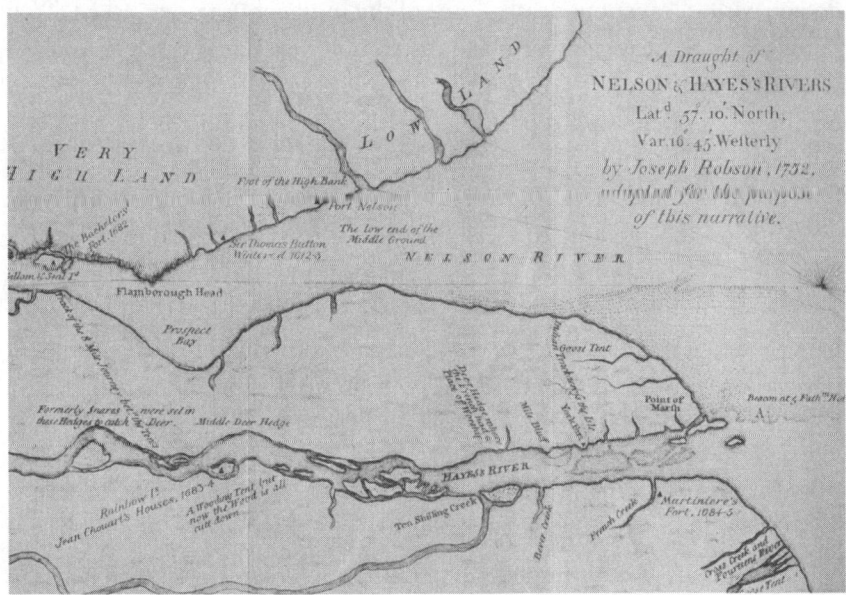

English map of 1752, drawn by Joseph Robson. The ruins of many of the scenes of Radisson's Hudson Bay adventures were still visible seventy years after Radisson's time.

the go-to trader for the Cree, who now saw him as a father rather than a son. He was exactly where he had wanted to be in the previous ten years. But his fortunes shifted again when eight-foot-thick blocks of sea ice blew into the river and crushed the French ships, which turned out to be rotten. Now only the *Bachelor's Delight* was left. The English and French traders worked together to chop it out of the thick blue ice and push it over the snow to shore, but Radisson was still in charge.

Radisson used his new powers harshly. He warned Bridgar, who had lost four men to starvation and two more to poisoning (they drank what they thought was alcohol, which they'd stolen from the surgeon's sea chest), to get out of the bay in spring, and to leave any furs behind in his camp. Bridgar, believing he had the law on his side, refused the ultimatum, so Radisson arrested him. He did, however, save the rest of the Hudson's Bay Company men by giving them fresh meat. The whole miserable party hunkered down for months until the ice on the river and the bay had broken up. Once the snow melted, Radisson burned the English settlements.

But the Cree had suddenly turned into tough customers. Somehow, likely from the English, they learned Radisson had been underpaying them for their furs, offering them less than what traders normally gave Cree on James Bay. They confronted Radisson: "You men who claim to give us life, do you wish to cause our deaths?" one of the Indigenous traders asked. "You know what the beaver is worth and the trouble we take to catch it. You call yourselves brothers but you don't want to give us what those who are not our brothers offer us. Accept our gifts," the headman said as his men laid out beaver tails, tongues, cured caribou bladders, and moose, bear, and deer fat, "or we will no longer come to visit you, and we will go to the others."

Radisson took so long to speak that one of the Cree yelled out, "answer him!"

"To whom do you wish me to respond?" Radisson asked. "I heard a dog bark. When a man speaks, he will see that I know how to defend myself, that we love our brothers and deserve to be loved, having come here to save your lives."

Then he drew his dagger and grabbed the Cree chief by the hair.

"Who are you?" Radisson asked.

"Your father," the chief replied.

"Well good," Radisson said. "If you are my father, if you love me, and if you are the chief, speak for me. You are the owner of my merchandise. This dog has just spoken, what has he come here to do? Let him go away to his brother the English, at the bottom of the bay. But I am mistaken. He does not have far to go, since he can see them [here] on the island." Then he let the Cree know the English were his prisoners.

Radisson continued with the hardball negotiations.

"I know what the woods are, what it is to abandon one's wife, to run the risk of dying of hunger, or to be killed by one's enemies. You avoid all these misfortunes by coming to us, so I see clearly that it is more advantageous to you to trade with us than with the others. Nevertheless, I want to take pity upon this wretch so that he may yet live, even if he wishes to go to our enemies."

Louis XIV of France. The most powerful man in Europe, Louis played a complicated game with Radisson but eventually wanted him dead.

Then he handed a sword blade to the man who complained, telling him to go to the English and warn them Radisson was coming.

It was a great show, and somehow it worked. The trade alliance forged between Radisson and the Cree of the Hayes and Nelson River regions held for years. Later, Radisson wrote to King James II to explain why he had been so tough with the Cree: "It was necessary for me to speak like that in this encounter or our trade would be lost, because once one has yielded to the wild men, they will never come back."

He further cemented his friendship by mediating a near-fatal dispute between two Cree clans. Radisson's adoptive father had killed a man from the marten clan who had tried to steal his wife. The marten clan had come after him and his own clan, which was why Radisson's adoptive clan was unexpectedly at the ocean shore the previous fall. Radisson organized the ritual payment of gifts between clans to settle the dispute.

The trading season was wrapping up. Bridgar, John Outlaw, and nine other men were, like Henry Hudson, forced into the bay in a small boat with nothing but some salt beef and oatmeal. They would have to row six hundred miles to the empty post at Fort Severn, on what's now the Quebec side of James Bay. (The enraged men would be rescued later and would try to sue Radisson.) Radisson left young Jean-Baptiste Groseilliers and a handful of men at the French post.[197] The older Groseilliers, Radisson, and the New Englanders—who were still prisoners—sailed on *Bachelor's Delight* to Quebec, where all them were freed by La Barre, the governor.[198]

Radisson, ever the narcissist, didn't understand what was happening around him. He thought La Barre was just tidying up loose ends. In fact, the governor, who had some business sense and political morality, wrote to Louis XIV: "It does not seem to me that Radisson had any justification for the seizure of this [Gillam's] vessel… Thus, without speaking of justice or of formalities, I shall try to reconcile them by having Captain Gillam compensated with the sum of one thousand pounds for the detour from the mouth of the river [St. Lawrence] to here [Quebec City], as I do not believe His Majesty would have found it advantageous had I started a war in this country with the English."[199]

Once it was clear Gillam was going home at the French government's expense, Radisson took him aside and told him that the two old fur traders were loyal to England, and that he would soon be back in the services of Charles II.[200]

Meanwhile, the French smuggling ship *Black Eagle* arrived at Percé to rendezvous with what its captain expected to be the two French ships from the bay. Instead, tax collectors met the *Black Eagle* and grabbed it. The whole mess was settled in Quebec, where the governor decided the tax collector had no authority over furs taken from Hudson Bay. The French investors would be able to sell all their furs and the king's court in Paris would decide what they owed, and whether the colonial administration or Versailles would get the money. Radisson and Groseilliers' dream of French traders working out of France, bypassing New France, and cutting it out of the northern fur trade, appeared to be coming true. There would be no more Iroquois raiders, no more Odawa middlemen, no Quebec governors. Jean-Baptiste Groseilliers was still at the Nelson River, buying furs from the Cree at what seemed like a permanent French colony. But, back in Versailles, the king's right-hand man was very worried that his minions on Hudson Bay were starting a war with the English. A couple of weeks after Radisson sailed into Quebec with the New Englanders, a navy ship from France brought a letter from Colbert. Radisson, it said, had some explaining to do.

In person. At Versailles.

Now.

THE TEMPTATION OF PARIS

Finally, France had a sea trade with Hudson Bay. It was all too good to be true.

When Radisson and Groseilliers arrived in France in the middle of January, after two months at sea, they learned that Colbert was dead. He had been somewhat sympathetic to Radisson over the years and had been able to deflect English complaints against Louis XIV's troublesome subject. With Colbert gone, James, Duke of York, governor of the Hudson's Bay Company, cousin of Louis XIV and heir to the British throne, was free to vent his rage about Radisson directly to the French king. The English made it clear they would not sit on their hands while renegade, traitorous Frenchmen bullied Charles II's subjects on Hudson Bay. Lawyers in England and New England were gathering evidence from the Hudson's Bay Company men and the Boston fur traders for lawsuits and petitions. Stacks of affidavits, many of them full of quite believable lies and half-truths about Radisson's recklessness and cruelty, were circulating in Versailles and the Court of St. James.

The two bootleg traders were now being tossed by forces they had no chance of resisting, if they even understood what was going on. First, the Hudson's Bay Company began an aggressive quasi-military campaign to sweep all interlopers—French and New Englanders—out of the bay, which made Jean-Baptiste Groseilliers a marked man. The Hudson's Bay Company let the world know that it would seize any unlicensed ship entering Hudson Bay. The vessels and cargoes would be sold and the money they fetched split evenly between the king and the company.

France, at the moment, wasn't interested in shedding blood over a few acres of tundra and some beaver pelts. So, despite the success of Radisson's raid, the old fur trader was sidelined at the court of

René-Robert Cavelier, Sieur de La Salle, bankrupt French nobleman who swayed France to invest in Louisiana, rather than compete with the English on Hudson Bay.

Versailles. La Salle, of nobler blood and with better friends, like the Prince of Conti, a member of the royal family (to whom he owed an awful lot of money), was the face of North American adventure in Paris. It didn't seem to matter that everything he touched seemed doomed to fall apart. He had already lost his first full-sized sailing ship on the Great Lakes. His plans for a new colony in what's now the American South, centred on the Gulf of Mexico, was an invitation to war with Spain, with all the risks and costs that went with it, and with no obvious chance of profitability. Still, he was younger, more dashing and stylish, and had a better bloodline than Radisson. Versailles saw no value in the tough, wind-burned, buckskin-wearing man who always seemed to have no money and was always eager for a better deal. No one would back Radisson as he tried to put together a new expedition, and the government seemed ready to toss him to the wolves, in the guise of English lawyers.

Richard Graham, Viscount of Preston, a friend of the Duke of York, led the legal lynch mob. He brought several letters to Louis from the Duke of York complaining that Radisson had "most brutally abused the English, robbed, stolen and burnt their habitations." Preston wanted cash compensation and demanded Radisson be jailed or flogged. The English envoy was gently but firmly told nothing of the sort would happen. The king would wait until he heard from his people in Canada, content that his cousin Charles, who was still secretly taking massive bribes from the French, would do nothing serious.

Preston soon realized the French plot against the Hudson's Bay Company went much deeper than Radisson and Groseilliers. There were still people at Versailles who wanted to keep the Hudson Bay option open, although probably without Radisson. Some could look at a map and see New France lying strategically between the hammer of an English colony in Hudson Bay and the anvil of the established English colonies of New York and New England. Jesuits in France were making money from the fur trade and wanted to be part of a new French trading operation on Hudson Bay. There, they would win the souls of Cree and buy the skins of beavers—though the Jesuits still lobbied for this to be done overland from Quebec, so they could run missions to the Iroquois, Odawa, Ojibwe, and other Upper Lakes nations.

Under Quebec governor La Barre, the Jesuits were back in their Canadian missions after being sidelined by Frontenac, who hated them. The price of beaver furs had temporarily collapsed, so no one was eager to stake money on another northern expedition. Meanwhile, the well-connected Abbé Bernou, the man who got Radisson his post on the Caribbean adventure, now needed Radisson's help with a new project, the creation of the most accurate globe in the world, which Bernou wanted to give to the king. At the same time, he was trying to undermine Governor La Barre. Bernou, like La Salle and Frontenac, believed in an agricultural, continental New France encompassing the Mississippi Valley and Great Lakes, not the little one-industry colony centred on Quebec and Montreal. Politics in the age of the Louis XIV were both complicated and duplicitous, and there's really no need to keep this all straight.

Radisson's case was simple: the English had never set up a colony at the Nelson River. They had abandoned the posts they'd built. Charles II may have given the gentlemen adventurers a charter endowing them with vast territories, but the men of the company had to use it, or it was, in law, *terra nullius*, empty land that could be taken by anyone. (The rights of the Cree, who did live there and therefore prevented it from being empty, were ignored.) And it was fitting for the French to seize the English vessels since, just a few years before, Capt. Zachariah Gillam and Governor Bailey had snatched poor Fr. Albanel and dragged him off to England. As for damages, Radisson and Groseilliers claimed, again, to be broke.

In the end, Louis XIV ordered the almost-empty fort at the mouth of the Nelson River to be returned to his cousins Charles and James. It was hardly worth fighting for. At the same time, all furs collected in eastern North America were to be taxed at Quebec, and all traders would need a license issued by the authorities in New France. There would be no compensation to the English and New Englanders for Radisson's kidnappings and arson.

Meanwhile, the wheels were turning again in England. Governor Bailey, the ex-convict, died suddenly after being recalled to England to face embezzlement charges. Shaftesbury, the ultra-Protestant English earl who had been so suspicious of Radisson, had been arrested in 1681 for opposing James, Duke of York, as heir to the throne. Though he'd been one of the few men of his time acquitted of treason, he was now sidelined politically. James would take Shaftesbury's place as the man in charge of the Hudson's Bay Company. The company's long-term future seemed to have been mapped out for the next few decades as the English king grew old and his brother waited. No one knew Charles II would die young, James would quickly show himself to be a poor king, and just three years after he came to the throne, there would be a revolution.

In 1682, anti-Catholics plotted to kill Charles and James in what came to be known as the Rye House Plot. Two lords, members of the Whig faction that spoke for Parliament, Protestantism, and city merchants, went under the axe. The Sheriff of London, along with a member of the House of Commons, and five other men, were hanged, drawn, and quartered, two were hanged until dead, and a woman who sheltered some of the conspirators was burned at the stake. The Earl of Shaftesbury, Radisson's nemesis on the company's board, was lucky not to be among the executed, as he was probably one of the plotters.

The destruction of Charles' Whig enemies didn't solve the country's political problems. The Popish Plot—a fantasy concocted by sociopathic liar and Anglican priest, Titus Oates, and fanned by the Whigs, especially Shaftesbury— had created a wave of anti-Catholic hysteria from 1677 to 1681. The "plot" was a bizarre conspiracy theory invented by Oates when he and an insane minister wrote a draft of a book alleging an all-pervasive plot among English Catholics to kill the king. The "Popish Plot" was invented at the same time that a real murder scandal, the Poison Affair, broke out in France. In Paris, poisoners, alchemists, and abortionists had provided various illegal and sometimes murderous services to various members of Louis XIV's court, including to his mistress. At the court of his cousin, Charles II, there was no real plot, but Oates convinced the London rabble and several high-ranking courtiers that one existed.

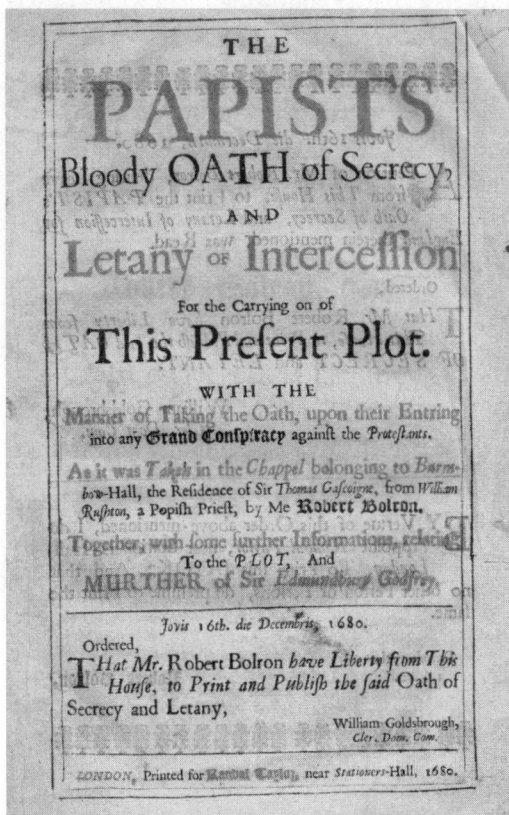

Propaganda handbill from the "Popish Plot," a spectacular hoax that cost many English nobles their lives and forced Catholics like Radisson out of commercial and public life.

All of this fuelled mob hysteria against Catholic foreigners like Radisson. It also unleashed xenophobic politicians and business leaders who set out to destroy all Catholics, especially James, Duke of York, head of the Hudson's Bay Company and heir to the throne, and anyone connected with him. This wave of anti-Catholic bigotry and violence would, in the end, ruin Radisson's career.

Anti-Catholic parliamentarians and agitators seized on Oates' claims that more than five hundred Jesuits and many Catholic noblemen were plotting to kill Charles II. The net caught some strange birds, including Samuel Pepys, who worked for the Duke of York at the admiralty. The diarist was sent to the Tower. During the flurry of accusations, arrests, and denials, someone murdered an anti-Catholic Member of Parliament. Charles, who never believed the plot existed, had to be seen to be investigating, and more Catholics and people close to James were rounded up. Five English lords were arrested, and one was convicted and beheaded. By the end of 1678, every Catholic in London was forced out of the city and ordered to stay at least twelve miles away, and most people at court and Parliament went about armed. James escaped exclusion from the throne by just a handful of votes, and the House of Commons voted to exile the queen, who was also Catholic. Refusing to throw his wife or his brother to the political wolves, Charles dissolved Parliament and began letting the purged people out of jail.

Charles had interviewed Oates, found him to be a liar, and wanted to arrest him for perjury. But Protestant diehards in Parliament—who were also taking over the Hudson's Bay Company and replacing its board of directors—blocked Charles.

Even after Charles ordered new elections that brought in a less extreme Parliament, the politically motivated panic—which concealed a huge transfer of political and economic power from Catholics and conservative Anglicans into the hands of Protestant extremists—continued. Priests were hunted down across the country. Nine Jesuits were hanged and another twelve died in jail. It took three years for the hysteria to die down and arrests to stop. By then, the country was seething with rumours of plots and counter-plots and the Restoration settlement hammered out by an exhausted nation in 1660 was coming apart. Oates had opened the great national sore of religion and shown how easy it was to turn Englishmen against each other over matters of faith. There would be a reaction, a clampdown that would finally crush the Cavaliers, members of the Royalist old nobility with their closet Catholic supporters, and bring in a simple, very English Protestant capitalist regime. It was this revolution that would take Radisson and other dubious foreigners down.

"I Durst Not Indeed Trust Them"[201]

While all this was happening in corridors of political power that were off-limits to Radisson and the rest of the people of France and England, people with financial power were making decisions that would, yet again, cause Radisson and his now elderly brother-in-law to change sides. Hudson's Bay Company managers knew that, while Radisson was back in France lobbying for a French version of their corporation, young Jean-Baptiste Groseilliers was still in the forlorn fort at the mouth of the Nelson River, with no idea that Louis XIV had given away his little bit of subarctic real estate. Here was some very low-hanging fruit for the first person strong enough to rob Jean-Baptiste.

There never seems to have been a time in Radisson's adult life when he wasn't playing off various factions and listening to clandestine offers. Now, the Hudson's Bay Company, grudgingly impressed by Radisson's new moves in the bay and knowing he could finish off their business if he were let loose there again under the French flag, wanted him back. And Radisson, who could never crack the rigid, closed court life of the new Palace of Versailles, knew he had reached the end of the road in France. He would never get close enough to the throne to be able to tell stories of his wilderness adventures to Louis XIV. The king's grandfather, Henry IV, may have listened to Champlain's tales of adventure, but there had been two attempts at revolution and civil war since then. Louis' reaction, to neuter the aristocracy by turning them into court fops whose social standing and access to the king depended on winks and nods, created an artificial world of rigid class structure that put a man like Radisson on the bottom and kept him there.

At the same time, France was lacking in "gentlemen adventurers," since nobles, who held most of the money, were traditionally forbidden to engage in trade or any other kind of non-military work. Those city merchants who did dirty their hands bought or lobbied the government for monopolies like the one held by Pierre Duguay Sieur de Mons, who paid for the founding of Quebec. Radisson would never get the chance to be one of those insiders with government licenses; he would be seen, instead, as a peasant labourer who had to be satisfied with what was given to him by his "betters."

To people like Abbé Bernou, ignoring Radisson's plans for a Hudson Bay fur empire was a terrible mistake. After he heard of Radisson's last defection to the English, Bernou wrote to the man who told him the news:

> What you tell me about Radisson does not surprise me, I have long noticed and regretted the slight notice that the French Court pays to its colonies. If a little attention had been paid, we could easily have made ourselves masters of the entire fur trade of North America, which would have amounted to at least three million a year, without reference to the other advantages it would have given us. But we are not the masters of it and the people who know best and have the least at stake in it are not consulted in these matters.

Bernou knew who'd been consulted: the Jesuits, who had always opposed using sea trade on the bay to circumvent New France and their missions, and who had thwarted all those rendezvous at Percé Rock. Radisson, Bernou wrote, should not have been lured back to France and then left with no meaningful work.

So, instead of leaving France with a bag of cash from the French court for the damage Radisson caused to the Hudson's Bay Company, Lord Preston left France with Radisson himself. Or he at least knew that the company's chief lawyer, William Yonge, was secretly pointing Radisson in the direction of London. The old trader, now creeping up on fifty, was burning his last bridge when he left France with Gédéon Godet, one of Lord Preston's flunkies. Godet was a lawyer and a Protestant who had fallen on hard times, not for his religion but because he was both indiscreet in his speech and writings and reckless with money. Godet had belonged to Henry Savile, Preston's predecessor, who warned Preston about Godet's big mouth and his over-familiarity with debtors' prison. Savile had bailed Godet out several times. "Some people look upon him only as a Protestant and forget he is a knave," Savile wrote to Preston. Still, the new ambassador hired Godet anyway.

Godet, who, at the time, spoke little or no English, found Radisson on the third floor of a house in the Faubourg St-Antoine and cooked up a plan to flee France with him.[202] Godet took his daughter Charlotte with them to England and left his wife and younger daughters behind in Paris, with the intention of bringing them over when he had raised some money. Hopefully Radisson and Godet learned to enjoy each other's company, since they spent the next few weeks on the road together and Radisson would, a few years later, marry Godet's daughter. Radisson knew there was no going back now: France would not pardon him twice. Radisson left without Groseilliers, who stayed behind to go with La Salle on his disastrous Mississippi adventure, though he, too, was flirting with the English.[203]

Radisson made this deal with the Hudson's Bay Company: £50 a year in wages, plus £200 worth of company stock. If Groseilliers came over he was to get a bit less: 20 shillings a week, or £52 a year, but no stock. The company also gave Radisson a silver tankard worth £10 and fourteen shillings. In return, Radisson had to take an oath of allegiance, not to England or Charles II but to the Hudson's Bay Company. Jean-Baptiste Groseilliers was also supposed to be paid well if he joined in this treachery, and the Frenchmen who were still on the bay thinking they were trading for the Compagnie du Nord were to get the wages due to them.

Loyalty Is for Dogs

Within days of arriving in England, Radisson was presented to Charles II and the Duke of York, to whom he told the stories of his latest adventures in the subarctic.[204] Soon, he was on a boat back to Hudson Bay to find Jean-Baptiste Groseilliers and the rest of Louis XIV's the loyal subjects, who had no idea their king had already given them away to his cousin Charles I, and that their former leader, Radisson, was now a turncoat. Radisson wanted young Groseilliers' furs, a haul he expected to be comparable to that fabulous cargo he and old Groseilliers had shepherded to New France from Lake Superior nearly fifteen years before. It didn't seem to matter that Jean-Baptiste Groseilliers was his nephew. Family never counted for much with Radisson, except in his dealings with Groseilliers.

The trading ships were loaded with 247 hogsheads of Brazilian tobacco, 15 grosses of pipes, 390 blankets, assorted household items like pots and pans, 10,000 knives and hatchets, powder, ammunition, and 300 guns.[205] As much as this was a fur trade, it was also an exercise in arms dealing. Not only were the guns potent weapons that changed the way First Nations made war (and hunted big game), they were also a means of making Indigenous people dependant. The need for ammunition and repairs locked the Cree into a permanent relationship with European merchants. The English also brought 834 gallons of French brandy, starting a trade that would ravage the Cree for generations and cause them, through addiction, to be even more dependant on the English. This was the fur trade's cruellest legacy.

There was a lot of intrigue on this trip. William Bond and the wonderfully named John Outlaw, one of Radisson's former prisoners who'd been marooned on Hudson Bay with nothing but salt beef and oatmeal, skippered the ships. Either Outlaw was a very forgiving man, or he was paid very well. The captains had secret orders written by Sir James Hayes, Rupert's former private secretary and now effectively the company's manager, which they were not to open until they were inside Hudson Bay: "We do therefore require you to treat him [Radisson] with respect and to cause all others under your command to do the like, he now being sent upon this Expedition by the order of His Royal Highness [James, Duke of York] and the allowance of His Majesty." Another letter, to John Abraham, the new governor at Port Nelson, warned Abraham to "treat him [Radisson] with all respect as one in whom we have entire confidence and trust and that you will follow his advice in reducing the French Factory and in making our settlement in and about Port Nelson." Abraham was ordered to put Radisson on the governing council of the new colony. The company made sure Radisson wouldn't get sidelined again by someone like Bailey.[206] The English also came ready to fight: cannon for a new fort had been loaded into the ships for ballast. But the sailors, out of loyalty to John Outlaw, spite for the French or for Radisson's slights to the crew, hated him.

This brief trip, just five months long, was not just about reasserting English control over the Hudson Bay fur trade. The real motivation, at least for Radisson, was robbery: relieving young Groseilliers of all the pelts he'd gathered over the past two years. Jean-Baptiste had earned those furs. Unlicensed English traders had arrived two summers earlier, just after Radisson, his crew, and prisoners had left, and started trading with the Cree. They offered one of the Cree bands bribes to massacre the French.[207] Young Groseilliers beat his would-be assassin in hand-to-hand combat, which impressed all the Cree and shifted their trade back to the French. Then the Cree attacked the English trading camp and killed some of the men living there. Jean-Baptiste made the smart choice of moving the French trading camp farther up the Hayes River to avoid all the violence and to intercept Cree and Assiniboine coming to the bay.

It took a while for Radisson and his expedition to find Groseilliers, who was unpleasantly surprised to see his uncle turn up on an English ship. Radisson believed it was "of utmost importance to win them over with mildness or surprise them with cunning before they knew what plan I had in mind," according to the report that he gave to the Duke of York two years later. First, though, he had to deal with the local Cree. He proved who he was by showing them some kind of identifying mark, perhaps a clan tattoo, then explained: "I made peace with the English for love of you. From now on, you and I, with them, we should be but one… Go without delay and bear him [young Groseilliers] this news and the signs of peace. Tell him that he should come and see me while the men of your company go and wait for me at the mouth of the river." At the same time, Radisson told the Hudson's Bay Company men to stop giving presents to the Cree. The Indigenous people, he said, should show their gratitude by giving gifts to Radisson instead.

All this manoeuvring and the obvious power brought to bear on young Groseilliers and his men was effective. As they reached Radisson's old trading house on an island in the Hayes River, Radisson took his nephew aside and explained the situation.

> You will undoubtedly remember having heard your father talk about the troubles and difficulties that we have experienced serving France for many years. You have also learned from him that the recompense for it we expected turned out to be black ingratitude, as much from the court as from the company of Canada, and that when we were reduced to the necessity of seeking to serve elsewhere, England received us with expressions of joy and satisfaction.
>
> You also know that the motives which obliged your father and me to quit the English after thirteen years of service, the necessity of survival, and the refusal to satisfy us of those in the Hudson's Bay Company who are our enemies, gave rise to our separation and the establishment that we created, and which I placed in your hands when I departed for France. But you surely do not know that the prince who rules in England has repudiated the company's proceedings, and has had us recalled to his service in order to receive the effects of his royal protection, and full satisfaction for our discontents.

Old Groseilliers was back in England, Radisson lied, getting some well-earned rest, and enjoying the money the company gave him. "You are of my blood," he said, while promising to let his nephew step into his place as the brains behind the English trade in Hudson Bay. This warm family talk took on an edge of menace when he added, "but above all do not

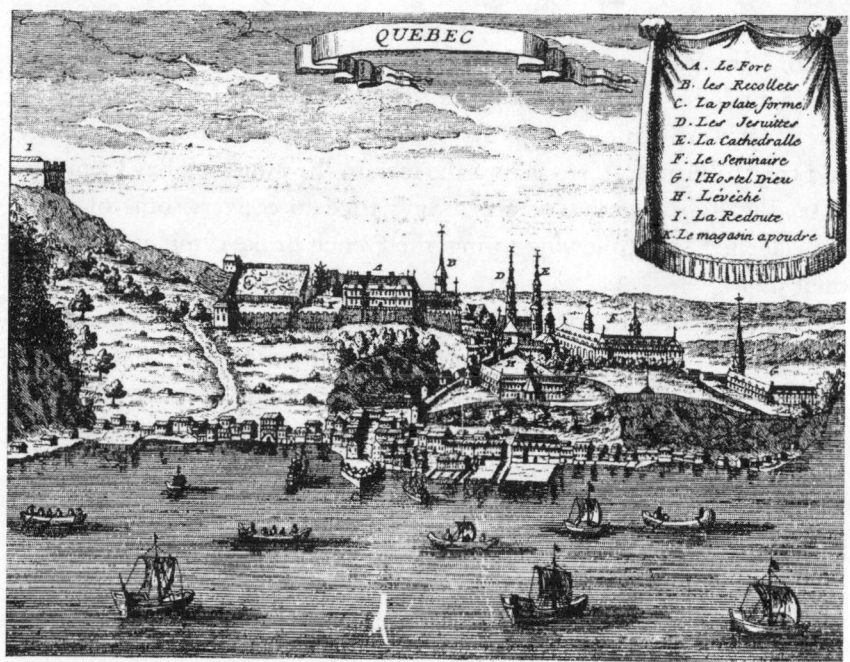

Contemporary print of Quebec City a few decades after Radisson left it for the last time.

forget the injuries of the French to the one who gave you life, and that you are in my power."[208]

The French traders had tons of furs but very little food, and Radisson made their choice very clear: hand over the beaver skins and submit to him, or starve. The traders started digging out their caches of about 20,000 furs and loading the English ships. The Cree knew there was dirty dealing going on and were sure they were being underpaid, but they, too, finally handed over their beaver skins, albeit grudgingly. Young Groseilliers, who must have enjoyed this cold, bleak, insect-plagued post on the edge of the known world, was willing to stay yet another winter, but Governor Abraham ordered him and the rest of the French camp to board the English fleet. The expedition set sail, leaving behind a few men, some cannon, and an English flag that was spotted by a French relief expedition from Quebec when it arrived a few days later.

The French were shocked to see this strange flag flying over buildings at the mouth of the Nelson River, and disgusted when they learned what had happened to the Compagnie du Nord's traders. A bilingual trader left behind by Radisson was sent out to parley with the French commanders. Fr. Antoine Silvy, chaplain of the French expedition, summed up their rage: "We then said it was a manifest robbery, and that Radisson was a traitor." The English envoy had trouble disagreeing with that assessment, but reminded the French that Louis XIV and Charles II were at peace.[209] The French expedition set up a post nearby, traded through the winter, and tried to turn the Cree against the men in the Hudson's Bay Company post. This didn't work. And when Silva tried to convert some of them, they laughed. The following spring, the French broke camp and boarded their ships.

The strong westerly winds of autumn brought the little English fleet home on October 23, and Radisson travelled quickly from the coast to London to tell the king of his trip and hand him a long manuscript dedicated to James, Duke of York. This was his second account of his subarctic adventures—the first had been a letter describing the founding of the Hudson Bay posts—and it opens with Radisson defending himself against accusations of disloyalty and "fickleness." Radisson wrote both accounts in French, bound them, and gave them to the king, who put them in the library of Windsor Castle. Dr. Jean Radisson, a Belgian relative of Pierre's, found these documents in 1996, when the Queen allowed him to use the library.

John Churchill, 1st Duke of Marlborough. Conqueror of Louis XIV's armies, third governor of the Hudson's Bay Company and friend to Radisson, Churchill's fame is eclipsed by his wife Sarah's notoriety.

The accounts of his early 1680s voyages to the bay are nothing like his stories of life among the Iroquois and Odawa. The journals are Radisson's attempt to defend himself from rumours at the king's court and in the city that he had ruined and abandoned Mary Kirke and betrayed everyone he'd ever done business with. James almost certainly knew these stories, and Radisson's manuscripts are a blatant attempt to curry some royal favour. It's no wonder the document is in French. He makes it clear that he supports an absolute monarchy and the restoration of the Catholic Church, positions that would have horrified the Whigs who ran the company.

Radisson argued that he had been short-changed and let down by ingrates on both sides of the Channel. Every move he had made was in reaction to dirty deeds done by Hudson's Bay Company management, corrupt courtiers in Versailles, and sleazy colonial officials in Canada. According to Radisson, he had, in fact, been an island of honesty in a seething sea of ingratitude and sharp practice. His respect for North America's Indigenous people vanished as the memories of his life among the Iroquois faded away. No longer a man of two cultures, Radisson was now just a greedy European with some valuable language skills and insights about how to use Indigenous peoples' manners and law to manipulate them. Any Mohawk that had survived in Radisson during the early Hudson's Bay Company years had been purged out of him. Now, at least in these pages, he was just another unscrupulous European exploiter of the North American Indigenous people.

But the winds of change were sweeping through England, and shiploads of beaver pelts weren't on most people's minds. Whigs and Tories were still fighting over claims of treason and papistry. In February 1685, Charles II died at the age of fifty-four. His openly Catholic brother, James, had gone from being governor of the Hudson's Bay Company to King of England. John Churchill, Earl (later Duke) of Marlborough, whose loyalties were as elastic as Radisson's, was now head of the company—when he wasn't plotting revolution.

At first, Churchill seemed loyal to James. His sister, Arabella, was mother to one of James's illegitimate sons, and they had other important social and business connections. Churchill took a shine to Radisson, who, like him, was a man who needed adventure. Still, they were very different men. Winston Churchill, writing about his ancestor, described him as the kind of cheapskate who was a lousy host and friend, a man who put no effort or money into socializing. This, Churchill wrote, "puts all his admirers to shame." The great wartime prime minister, a man who put a lot of thought, time, and effort into the steady consumption of good food, fine alcohol, and the best cigars, seems truly appalled by his ancestor's stinginess and hunger for money (the one fault never attributed to Winston, who was always short of cash despite the high fees and fat royalties he collected from his writing). Rupert would be Radisson's first patron. James, Duke of York, would be his second, and Marlborough would be the third—and least helpful.

Marlborough embraced managing the Hudson's Bay Company, tapping into the same energy as when he fought the French and crushed Louis

XIV's dreams of dominating Europe. In the tumultuous year of 1688, as Marlborough and his cronies overthrew James II, the Hudson's Bay Company declared a dividend of 50 percent. The next year, it paid 25 percent, but made up for that disappointment the following year, 1690, with a 75 percent return for its shareholders, all paid out in cash. That year, it tripled the holdings of its investors—except for Radisson, whose stock was deliberately left out—with a three-to-one stock split. Many of the investors, either shrewdly or because they'd seen the company books, quietly unloaded their stock at premium prices, expecting to cash out at the top of the market. Partly as a response to this fabulous profit and the share price windfall that followed, the company named a major river in what's now northern Manitoba after Churchill. But the flow of money was not to last. In 1692, Churchill temporarily fell out of favour at court. He was thrown out of the army, and the ingrates on the Hudson's Bay Company board of directors stripped Churchill of his position and elected Sir Stephen Evance in his place. It was a mistake that would cost the shareholders dearly, since Churchill turned out to be as good a businessman as he was a general, and Evance was a non-entity. Dividends would be rare over the next few decades.[210]

Young Groseilliers, with his father's elastic loyalties, quickly assumed the role of Hudson's Bay Company employee while his former trading friends lingered in London, waiting to see what would become of them. Radisson went back to work gathering a cargo of cheap trade goods for the next voyage.

He also found time to marry his second wife. Mary Kirke's death in 1685 was only a slight setback, since it seems she never came back to him after his return to England, perhaps because Radisson had found someone else. Either in France, or soon after he arrived in London, Radisson began an affair with Charlotte Godet, daughter of Gédéon Godet, Preston's flunky who'd spirited him out of Paris. Radisson and Charlotte already had a son, Peter, when they were married in 1685. The wedding was in St. Martin-in-the-Fields, which meant Radisson, despite his earlier professions of loyalty to the Roman Catholic Church, must have converted to the Anglican faith at some point. It was a rush job: a bishop's license dispensed with the customary church banns, which would have delayed the wedding by three more weeks.[211] It was obviously a love, or at least a lust match. There was no dowry. Old Godet hadn't been able to find a full-time job with the Hudson's Bay Company or anywhere else when he arrived in England, but Radisson got him some freelance work writing the Hudson's Bay Company's official reply to French claims that Radisson had robbed its northern fur trade.[212]

Godet's French legal training was of no use to him in England, and he finally succumbed to the reality of his financial situation by lapsing into journalism. The newssheet business was politically risky and relatively unprofitable, and Godet probably wasn't very good or very lucky. If fortune and talent had smiled on him, he would have published Radisson's manuscripts about his North American adventures, rather than the sleazy sheets that were sold on the streets of London. It's not much of a stretch to imagine that the old deadbeat father-in-law, who outlived his daughter and lingered on until 1693, was another strain on Radisson's always-stressed finances.[213]

Meanwhile, there was more civil strife and growing ugliness in London. The Duke of Monmouth's rebellion, waged by Charles II's oldest illegitimate son, took the shape of a sloppy invasion of the West Country and was cruelly crushed by Marlborough. Monmouth's peasant supporters were strung up on trees throughout southwest England, the result of a series of trials called the Bloody Assizes. The young duke, who claimed Charles II had legally married his mother, was brought to James II to beg for his life. He received no mercy: Monmouth was publicly decapitated in one of the most notoriously botched executions in English history—the headsman, after hacking away at the popular young man's neck for some time, finished the work with a knife. By that point, the city of London was filled with disgust, conspiracy, dread, and hatred of James and all papists and foreigners.

This fear and hatred started showing up in the Hudson's Bay Company's decisions. Radisson, one of King James' men, was told he would have to serve under his old prisoner and enemy, John Bridgar, if he went back to the bay. Radisson's trouble caused some of the Compagnie du Nord traders picked up the previous summer to balk at working for the English and go back to France. Then Radisson's pay was cut. But the big dispute, which would fester in Radisson until he died, centred on all those furs he'd stolen from young Groseilliers and his men on the 1684 expedition. The company decided to keep them, without giving Radisson his 25 percent share. This was worth £1,800, or about $500,000 in today's money.[214] The company was willing to give Radisson a small pension if he would just fade away. Predictably, Radisson told the company's directors what to do with their offer, but, in the end, he had very few options. He could take his chances as a foreigner in an English court of law, but he would likely have lost because he had no contract regarding the furs and appeared to be a well-paid employee at a time when wage earners had few rights and little respect.

Marlborough tried to break the deadlock with the promise of a £300 life-insurance policy payable to Charlotte if Radisson did not make it back from his next trip to Hudson Bay. She could choose to convert that money into stock and collect dividends as a sort of pension. But there was no offer for the furs, which the company appears to have believed were its property.

All the Frenchmen still in England were being watched and tested. Young Groseilliers wanted to get back to North America, preferably to New France, and didn't care about the furs he'd risked his life to collect in those years on the Hayes River. He put together a plan to travel on Hudson's Bay Company ships, then desert the expedition to go overland to the new French fort on Lake Nipigon, which was easily accessed from the Albany River canoe route. Like his father, he had quickly found French agents in London who helped him with his plans, and who told him he would be welcomed by Daniel Greysolon, Sieur du Lhut, who was trying to take over the Cree trade by building posts north and west of Lake Superior. The British secret service was on to young Groseilliers, however, and twice caught him trying to leave for France without a passport. There were no such overtures to Radisson. Instead, the governor of Quebec put a price of fifty pistoles—about £50—on Radisson's head.

In May 1685, Radisson, young Groseilliers, and some of the remaining kidnapped French traders left England as part of that year's Hudson's Bay Company trading expedition. Morale must have been terrible, since the management committee, having already cut Radisson and Groseilliers' pay, had also clawed back most of their on-ship perks, including free claret, and taken away all of Radisson's authority.

Near the entrance to Hudson Bay, the two French ships that had been sent from Canada to Port Nelson and were on their way home after their miserable winter at the Hayes River captured the company ketch *Perpetuana Merchant*. The French, Fr. Maria de Silva, chaplain of the French expedition, later wrote, were looking for Radisson, but he wasn't on board. Another HBC ship—which also wasn't carrying Radisson—escaped capture after a short running fight. Finally, Governor Bridgar's ship arrived. He wanted the English ketch back, and boarded the Quebec vessels to remind their captains that France and England were not at war. The French captains replied they were acting as police, not navy, and that seizing the English ships would simply make up for some of the losses caused by Radisson's double-cross.[215] Capt. Pierre Allemand said Radisson was "a traitor and a thief" and swore he "would kill him wherever he should find him." Not being able to mount much of an argument in Radisson's defense, Bridgar saluted and went back aboard his own vessel.

When the English ships arrived at Port Nelson, the Hudson's Bay Company men arrested a few French traders from the Compagnie du Nord who had overwintered nearby and stayed to see if events would turn their way.

Radisson, whose ship evaded the French blockade, seems to have relished the price put on his head, and at the same time appears to have been unconcerned about the fact that there were people sailing around the bay hoping for a chance to kill him. At York Factory, he renewed his contact with the Cree and Assiniboine and started trading. In his letters to his corporate masters, Radisson seems obsessed with getting the best possible deals. Young Groseilliers was sent inland to drum up business. All seemed to be going well until a French military force under the command of Chevalier de Troyes arrived overland from Quebec and began picking off the English posts on James Bay. De Troyes may have been the biggest threat that summer, but an even more menacing figure, Pierre Le Moyne d'Iberville, was itching to go north. Le Moyne d'Iberville had no qualms about massacring English and Irish women and children in Newfoundland fishing outposts, let alone English traders and French turncoats on the shores of Hudson Bay.

Meanwhile, France and England were at peace and negotiating a treaty that would make their colonies neutral in times of war. Both sides in Hudson Bay thought they were acting legally, even when their actions seemed hostile. The French believed Radisson and old Groseilliers, both subjects of Louis XIV, had "discovered" the Hudson Bay fur country and, despite the truth of various reasons, that the discoveries made the territory a colony of France. The English, on much better legal footing (at least in Europe, if not in the Cree councils), could point to Henry Hudson and the other English mariners who, though usually ignorant of the fur potential (Capt. James being the valuable exception), had been the first Europeans in the region. They also made the remarkable claim that Radisson, as a supposed native of Avignon, was never a Frenchman at all, but a subject of the Pope (the city, medieval home of the popes, was a papal state until the French Revolution and therefore legally not part of France). If that argument failed, they would claim Radisson had discovered nothing and was no more than an interpreter. In a letter that Radisson certainly never saw, the company also said he was simply a pirate who, after his latest betrayal, had to beg Charles II for his life.[216]

Radisson stayed on the bay until the summer of 1687. His fortunes were improving: in July 1687, the company's directors promised him another cask of claret "as a present" and the use of the captain's cabin on his next trip to the bay.[217] But revolution was in the air in England. Catholic King James II—Radisson's old friend, the former Duke of York—had offered freedom of worship to all Christians in his country, which infuriated diehard Protestants of all denominations. At the same time, he had issued edicts threatening imprisonment, mutilation, and crippling fines to anyone who spread "false news." Marlborough and the Whigs (including many of the city investors in the Hudson's Bay Company) made overtures to William of Orange, the Dutch sovereign, who was married to James' daughter, Mary. James reacted by tightening the screws, raising an army, and forcing Anglican clergy to announce Catholic emancipation from their pulpits. He arrested bishops, stacked the law courts with judges who would do his bidding, and purged the university faculties. Then, when his wife gave birth to a male heir and these changes looked as though they would be permanent, the aristocrats of England embraced treason. James realized the danger in the summer of 1688 and back-peddled on some of his edicts, but it was too late. In the early fall, William of Orange landed with Dutch troops in southwest England. James fled his capital, was caught at a Channel port, brought back to London, and allowed to escape again, this time to France. History remembers this as the Glorious Revolution.

Rebellion was also brewing on the bay. Small-group politics can be the ugliest of all, and factional fighting had broken out between Radisson and some of the other Hudson's Bay Company managers in the posts on the shores of James and Hudson Bays. Radisson was back in England by the fall of 1687, swearing out charges against some of the men he had bickered with on the bay. Radisson was given a raise and the company sponsored the naturalization of Radisson and his nephew, who was still trading in North America. The next year, war broke out between England and France, where James had taken sanctuary at the court of Louis XIV. Again, London mobs saw Catholics and foreigners as seditious conspirators. Not only was Radisson foreign and, therefore, Catholic, he was also very friendly with James II.

Radisson would never leave England again. He was a wanted man in France. It was unsafe for him to go back to the bay, where he was loathed by many of the English traders and was a dead man if captured by the French. During the war with France that broke out after the English coup, d'Iberville, probably the most ferocious soldier ever to come out of New France, picked off all the Hudson's Bay Company forts and would certainly have shown Radisson no mercy. As for the Groseilliers—father and son—they disappear from the historical record. The old man may have lasted until the mid-1690s, when he is supposed to have died at Sorel, not far from Trois-Rivières. The fate of his son is even more mysterious. He stayed on at the bay until well into the war. Hudson's Bay Company records show him being owed more than £200, a serious amount of money that he never tried to collect. He may have finally fled south from Hudson Bay and rejoined the French, finishing out his days as a frontier trader, or he might have ended up in an unmarked grave, dead of disease or killed by his former countrymen.

Book Seven:
Decayed Gentleman (1688–1710)

More than anything else, the coup against James II finished Radisson's career. He was fifty-two years old when James was ousted, so he probably lost, at best, about ten more years of trading. Not only had his Catholic Francophile patron been unceremoniously removed from the throne, the royal expulsion started a war that quickly spread to North America, despite peacetime promises of colonies being off-limits. Radisson's great value to the Hudson's Bay Company lay in his knowledge of the Cree's language and customs, but by the end of the 1680s, English traders were catching up. He was no use to the Hudson's Bay Company in England; he was in fact, being French and possibly Catholic, a liability. It had been more than twenty years since Radisson and Groseilliers had shown up in England, and the first generation of friends, supporters, and investors, people like Prince Rupert, were retired, dead, or out of favour. Marlborough, who seems to have liked Radisson, fought to regain influence at court but would not succeed until Radisson was a very old man. The person who had used charm to win over the Mohawks, ferocity to thrive in the Great Lakes wilderness, and guile to convince English and French capitalists to bankroll what he hoped would be his fur-trade empire, had run out of tricks.

The signs were already there before the revolution. At the end of 1687, Marlborough had extended Radisson's pay until James II could find some job for him in government service. The pay kept coming until 1689, along with the dividends that Marlborough issued on Radisson's stock. It was more than enough to live comfortably. Radisson, along with a new wife—Charlotte having likely died in childbirth—moved into a rented home in Westminster. In 1690, the company started chipping away at Radisson's salary, claiming it was losing money and couldn't afford the £50 "gratuity" that was, to be fair, supposed to be short-term. By 1692, Marlborough was out as the company's governor but was still a director. He and Yonge, the lawyer who had coaxed Radisson out of France, fought for Radisson's pay.

Through the records of this dispute, we get one of very few glimpses of the Radisson family. They show that Radisson, now fifty-three, had four or five children—the uncertainty came from second-hand reporting, not by Radisson losing track—with another baby on the way. He paid £24 a year for rent and had servants, but he also lived payment-to-payment and was one payout away from bankruptcy. The company agreed to keep paying him £50 a year as a pension, if he signed away all claims against his former employers. Radisson refused. His supporters said the pay cut would force Radisson to toss his wife and children onto the charity of the parish and force him to flee, presumably back to France. London was an expensive city, and it was, they said, impossible on £26 to "maintain a wife and servants and four or five children in London with meat and drink and clothes... his debts are so great, through necessity, not ill management..."[218]

The dispute dragged on through 1693. We do not know what Radisson did with his time, since, by then, his pen had fallen silent. It is clear, though,

Westminster Hall. This building was the scene of some of England's most famous trials. Radisson's case against the Hudson's Bay Company was argued at the far end of the hall, while booksellers, relocated from burned-out St. Paul's Cathedral, sold volumes under the watchful eyes of censors.

that he obsessed over money and still felt he was owed £1,800 just for the furs taken from the French traders in 1684–85. In 1694, the company gave him a little money to pay his debts, but the old explorer had had enough. On May 22, he filed suit in the Court of Chancery.

England, in the 1600s (and until the last century), had two kinds of courts that heard civil suits, along with a Church court that mainly judged moral cases. Courts of law decided cases using the Common Law, the accumulated wisdom of hundreds of years of judicial rulings. These courts had several built-in failings: they could only award damages, rather than make people change the way they behaved; and, if old case law went against a party, it was binding, even if the decision was patently unjust. Courts of Chancery were supposed to use the power of the king, delegated to the Lord Chancellor, to correct failings in case law that generated unconscionable decisions. A Court of Chancery could also use its powers of equity to order people to do things. (An injunction issued during a strike is grounded in equity, not law, and is a remedy that would have been available only to a Court of Chancery.) Radisson needed the court to order the company to keep paying his salary.

The Court of Chancery sat in Westminster Hall, part of the parliamentary complex, and Radisson's case was heard in the same space used for the trial of Sir Thomas More and Charles I. Almost certainly, Yonge drafted Radisson's pleadings, which have survived. In them, he described how he had delivered Hudson Bay into the hands of Charles II and been the driving force for the creation of the Hudson's Bay Company. He argued that he and his brother-in-law had brought with them unique knowledge of the First Nations people of Hudson Bay, expertise that gave the Hudson's Bay Company a strong advantage over any competitors. The pleadings describe how Radisson's shifting loyalties in the early 1680s had cleared the French out of Hudson Bay while making the company an awful lot of money. He had given up all allegiances to France, and had lost track of his dear brother-in-law, who, as far as he knew, was dead. In return for this faithful and sometimes painful service, he was supposed to be paid until (or if) he was given a better-paying government position. And, by the way, the company still owed him his share of the value of the 12,000 pelts.

The lawsuit was served on the company in June 1694. The board of directors decided to fight it. By the time the case got to court half a year later, Radisson was registered as a pauper. Deep-pocketed litigants are always advantaged by the passage of time, and the company ran the clock by claiming many of its witnesses were in Hudson Bay and would need to be summoned back to England. They also said Radisson exaggerated his claims of importance to the company's founding and couldn't prove the promises that he claimed were made to him. Rupert, Hayes, and so many of the early investors were dead and, in those days, litigants did not have to submit to examination for discovery by opposing counsel or disclose documents to the other side. If they had, the company records would have shown it collected £100,000 worth of furs just from the Nelson River between 1684, when Radisson had seized the place, and 1692.[219]

Radisson thwarted his former corporate masters by having someone he trusted go through the company ledgers. His spy missed the profit figures but swore evidence that no company ships had left England in more than two years and none of the supposed witnesses was overseas. Through this ordeal, Radisson had been arrested several times for debt but had been bailed out by loyal friends. The company tried to settle, offering a one-time payout, but Radisson refused. He was as tenacious a litigant as he was a fur trader, and he seems to have had no fear of the company or its lawyers. Finally, the case was heard in Westminster Hall in November 1696 and a decision rendered the following March: Radisson was to have his "gratuity" continued as a pension. From then on, he was paid his £50 annual pension in four payments, plus the £50 gratuity each November. There was no mention of the twelve thousand furs, something Radisson obsessed over for the rest of his life. Since the court had simply ignored that part of the pleadings, Radisson believed the issue was unresolved. More likely, the judges saw the lawsuit for a one-off unpaid claim as an issue of law, not equity, because it was an old debt, and Radisson was in the wrong court.

There was one "fact" in the company's pleadings that was definitely true: it was not doing well. The big profits had dried up two years before. As Radisson and his company moles learned during the lawsuit, it hadn't even been sending ships to the bay, probably because of the effective military campaign run out of Quebec by the Le Moyne family. In 1696, d'Iberville had captured York Factory, on the Hayes River, for a second time. The slump was long-term: the Hudson's Bay Company did not pay a dividend from 1691 to 1718.

The company may have been lucky both in the timing of the lawsuit resolution and the way the war was working out. The French and English governments were putting out feelers for a truce, or even a full treaty, and they were gathering information about the validity of various colonies' claims to rightful ownership. Radisson was not only a key player in the English claim to the Hudson Bay fur trade, he was also the reservoir of the Hudson's Bay Company's corporate memory, things he had shown to his ungrateful former employers when he made his case in Westminster Hall.

It was fortunate for the company that Radisson didn't hold a grudge, because, just weeks after he won his court case, the company's very future turned on the evidence he gave about the first trading in Hudson Bay. Certainly, in terms of right of conquest, the French were on solid ground: the country's troops and men from Quebec had taken many of the important Hudson's Bay Company posts, though the English had managed to take a few back. The company needed to prove it had a solid claim to the region (again, ignoring the fact the Cree owned the land). In mid-August 1697, the Hudson's Bay Company board swallowed its pride and asked Radisson for help. Executives sent a coach around to Radisson's house to fetch him, and, after dinner in the company's boardroom, got down to business. The board wanted to know the story of all Radisson's voyages and, not having the manuscripts that were given to Charles I and James II, they made him recount the trips from memory. All of this was written down and given to the French peace envoy.

The discussions lasted through the next day, then Radisson swore an affidavit describing his time in Hudson Bay. The history was important, but the key argument in this thousand-word document—whose survival, like so many of the court records and Radisson's manuscript accounts, is a testament to British recordkeeping—was simple. Radisson had tried twice to hand the Hudson Bay fur trade to France, and twice he had been tossed aside. And both times, the Gentlemen Adventurers, who were intermingled with the English court and were practically an arm of the government, had taken up the trade. France, it seemed, wanted it only because England had it. The French delegate knew Radisson was telling the truth: Versailles' envoy was the banker Charles Aubert de la Chesnaye, who had been one of Quebec's business leaders and founder of the Compagnie du Nord. He seems to have had no hard feelings for the cheating he'd received from Radisson in 1685, when the old trapper had made off from Hudson Bay with Jean-Baptiste Groseilliers and the fruits of two years of the Hayes River fur trade, costing the company 120,000 livres.[220]

The English peace commissioners let down both the Hudson's Bay Company and the government. One had concocted a scheme with Louis Hennepin, La Salle's fabulist priest, to betray the French colony in

Louisiana, and decided, for what he saw as the greater good, to bargain away some of the Hudson's Bay Company posts. (D'Iberville was able to thwart the Hennepin scheme.) Even after the Treaty of Ryswick—which ended the war—was signed, talks dragged on for another year between the French government and the Hudson's Bay Company. Its managers acknowledged, in a letter to Yonge, Radisson's friend and lawyer, the key role played by Radisson: "As for taking Mr. Radisson's advice in our affairs, you need no doubt for we do apprehend his particular evidence in the premier occupancy of those places [in Hudson Bay] to be substantial, and hope will prove convincing. And notwithstanding any former misunderstanding between the Committee [the directors of the company] and Mr. Radisson, the company will not be ungrateful for any service he shall do them to the utmost of his merit, which he may assuredly depend upon."

Not only was Radisson's claim to be the real founder of the company vindicated, but Yonge was also reappointed to the board of directors.

The French, who had also been trying to show their occupancy of the bay, were on shakier ground. It seems none of the Jesuits who had been to Hudson Bay were around to testify. Their *relations*, the letters they sent back to be published in France to raise money for the missions, showed they knew of the canoe routes to the bay, but they were coy about whether they or their traders had ever made the trip before 1668. Only one man employed by the French (other than Radisson) claimed to have been to the bay and realized its potential. That was van Heemskerck, the Dutch sailor who had stolen Radisson's story. He was of no real use. D'Iberville, an honest if cruel man, had admitted that everywhere he went, he saw signs old and new of English settlement and trading on Hudson Bay. The legal issue wasn't solved until the Treaty of Utrecht in 1713, when the posts were handed back to the Hudson's Bay Company and France recognized its charter.

By then, Radisson had managed to alienate the company one last time. In 1698, the company's charter was up for renewal. Its competitors wanted the monopoly cancelled by Parliament. After all, it had been granted by a long-dead king and had benefitted his brother, who'd been kicked out of the country by many of the same men who sat in the House of Commons and the House of Lords. Radisson petitioned Parliament to allow the company to keep its charter, but only if clauses were added acknowledging his role in its founding and the company promised to keep paying his pension to his heirs. This, Radisson said, was for the benefit of his four children, all born in England. (There was no mention of his new wife, who had probably died, or of his other two children.) This was one of the very few times Radisson showed any public interest in his offspring. Parliament renewed the charter without changing it.

A year later, Radisson, still strained for cash, applied for the job of Hudson's Bay Company warehouse keeper. He didn't get it. After all those years of service and work on behalf of the company, Radisson's application was put up against another man's, and the company decided the issue by drawing lots. Radisson, who seemed to repel money, lost. By now, he was sixty-four years old, still living on Clare Court, near Drury Lane in Westminster, a street that was lost when the London School of Economics was built. This was a fashionable neighbourhood in the late 1600s. The Radissons could have moved to a less expensive part of the city, but Radisson clung to his social pretensions. Most of his children were now teenagers, and Radisson claimed to have found them work as tradesman's apprentices.

Meanwhile, the world was changing without Radisson's help. In 1709, the Schuyler brothers of upstate New York convinced four Iroquois civil chiefs to travel to England to see Queen Anne and ask for more help against the French in Quebec. Peter and Abraham Schuyler owned big tracts of land that had been in their family since the days of New Netherland, and their property was no longer safe from French troops and Indigenous warriors operating out of Montreal. The chiefs each represented one of the nations allied to the English in their fights against the French. (The Seneca did not send a chief because they were neutral.)

Theyangouin, a Mohawk who was fluent in English, spoke for the Iroquois delegation. The four chiefs boarded HMS *Reserve* in New York City on February 20, 1710, arrived in Portsmouth, England, on April 2, and were in London about a week later. On April 19, the Iroquois leaders

The "Iroquois Kings" who visited Queen Anne shortly before Radisson's death. From left to right: Nicholas Iro, the Mahican delegate, John of Canajoharie, Hendrick, and Brant.

were picked up at the Crown and Cushion, where they were staying, packed into two royal coaches, and taken to St. James's Palace, where the "Indian Kings of Canada" were presented to the queen by her Lord Chamberlain, the Duke of Shrewsbury. The Iroquois, speaking though Theyangouin, got down to business, telling the queen they had made this long trip for her good, as well as theirs. The Iroquois had lost their best warriors fighting the French and protecting English settlements in the Hudson River valley. The English had promised a fleet and soldiers for an attack on Quebec, but they never came. Driving the French from the St. Lawrence was vital to protect Iroquois hunting rights and the Europeans in New York and New England. At the very least, the queen could pay for a big, strong fort.

They presented the queen with several large, gorgeous wampum belts. In return, she gave them a set of silver church plates that are still prized possessions of the Mohawks. They are curated by leaders of the community of Tyendinaga, near Napanee, Ontario.

Once this business was over, the queen ordered Shrewsbury to show the Iroquois chiefs a good time at her expense. The chiefs went on the eighteenth-century version of a London pub crawl. Being skilled politicians, they told their hosts they preferred English ale to French wine. They gave interviews to journalists, who described them in the most glowing terms, writing about their fabulous health and physiques. The chiefs, who, like most Iroquois, were taller and stronger than a typical European, stood out everywhere they went with their painted faces, gorgeous clothes that combined English fashion with Iroquois crafts, and their bead-covered moccasins, described in the press as "yellow shoes."

A royal barge took them to Greenwich, where they were shown the most modern astronomical devices. Then came a trip to the Theatre Royal on Drury Lane, just a few blocks from Radisson's house, where they stood while the audience gave them a standing ovation before the play started. The chiefs had a business meeting with the Board of Trade, and a house party at the home of a duke. In Hyde Park, they reviewed the men and horses of the queen's Life Guards. One of the city's best engravers took their portraits. The queen saw them one last time, at Windsor Castle, before the Iroquois delegation left London for Southampton and the long trip back to America.[221]

Radisson would have heard about these remarkable visitors and the sensation they had caused in London. He might have even wanted to speak to them in their own language. But the old scoundrel was on his last legs.

He had lived about seventy-four years, a ripe old age for that time. It's not clear how he spent the last decade of his life. Did he again adapt to the customs of the locals and affect the image of a well-off pensioner? Or did he, like so many Londoners of the time, spend the last years of his life drunk? Whatever happened, he was no longer a friend of kings, princes, and city powerbrokers.

Years before, he had set aside a small bag of gold coins to pay for a monument that was to be built if he didn't return from one of his Hudson Bay expeditions. That money was long gone. There would be no monument, no big funeral with a crowd of rich men in silk clothes and long wigs.[222]

Radisson must have known the end was coming soon, as he drew up a new will just a few weeks before he died. It was a very political document. In it, he memorialized his own service to Charles II and James II and stated flatly that he had pried from the French a vast fur empire "to the great advantage of the English Nation and particular of the Society or Company of Hudson Bay." The full extent of his efforts "is in the memory of his Grace the Duke of Marlborough to whose care I have been recommended by the late King James before the Revolution." He was owed money on his pension—probably just the last payment, as the company had been paying it promptly—but there was still that debt of £1,800 for the furs he had seized on Hudson Bay nearly thirty years before. He had never let that debt go, and now he was leaving the claim to his best friend, James Heanes, a wine-barrel maker in the city of London, and Radisson's new wife, Elizabeth. Neither of them pursued the claim.

By the end of 1710, he was dead. Despite the ill will between them, the Hudson's Bay Company chipped in £6 for Radisson's funeral. It never made good on the old fur debt, but, twenty years later, it started paying Elizabeth £10 a year out of pity for her poor health and miserable poverty. She lingered on until 1732.

Pierre Radisson, who had seduced the Mohawks, outsmarted the Onondaga, changed the lives of the Odawa and the Cree, bedevilled and perplexed the most powerful kings of Europe, sought glory and booty from Lake Superior to Tobago, was buried at his parish church, St. Clement Danes in Westminster. A pretty little church built just off the Strand by Sir Christopher Wren, St. Clement Danes was originally built as a mission to the Vikings living outside the city wall, and was blasted during the last and worst raid of the Blitz on the night of May 10, 1941. It was eventually restored by the Royal Air Force and is now its official church. Whether

St. Clement Danes, a church on the Strand built by Christopher Wren, is Radisson's burial place. It was rebuilt after being bombed on the last day of the Blitz, the German air campaign against London in 1940–1941.

Radisson's old bones survived the bombing is, and probably should remain, a mystery. The man who had fretted so much about his looks while living as a Mohawk and who had chased wealth through so many forests and seas was listed in the parish register as "a decay'd gentleman."[223]

Even in his lifetime, Radisson was forgotten as the founder of the Hudson's Bay Company. He had never broken through the boundaries class placed on him. He was never a rich man, nor was he ennobled, commemorated, or celebrated for almost two hundred years. He would have ended up among those great, anonymous skeleton heaps in Paris's catacombs, the millions who were born, lived, and died without leaving any footprint. That all would have happened were it not for his fabulous pen. We know his life story, at least the parts he wanted us to know, and we can piece together much of the rest. And it leaves us to wonder about all the exceptional people through history who didn't write their own story.

Epilogue

Despite Radisson's determination to find jobs for his children, not all of them came to a good end. A James Radisson claimed to be the explorer's son at his 1713 trial on some minor charge that led to the usual death penalty. In his petition for mercy, he said he spent ten years in the navy, a career that his father would has approved of. Unfortunately, the rest of the records are lost, and James' fate is a mystery.[224] We don't know what happened to Peter and William, the other sons for whom we have names. If they left descendants, they're not known to historians. While they left no historical footprint, they may well have lived out middle-class lives in London without generating work for hangmen and bureaucrats, which was fine for them but frustrating for researchers. Because some of Radisson's daughters took their husbands' names, it is even more difficult to track his descendants through the female line. At least one, Constance Radisson, who was likely a daughter of Charlotte Godet, came to a grim fate. She was murdered in London in 1721 and Robert Bembridge, her killer, testified she was "an old St. James whore." It seems likely all of Radisson's children with his last wife were girls; if any sons lived to adulthood, they either died without male children or the Radisson line in England was extinguished soon afterwards. His previous wife had three girls, and they were all still alive in 1710, so it is quite likely Radisson has many descendants still living in the United Kingdom and places colonized by that country. As well, if the genealogical stories and records from Michilimackinac are accurate, Radisson almost certainly has thousands of descendants among the Ojibwe and Odawa, as well as the mixed-race people descended from them who live in Michigan and in Penetanguishene, Ontario, where many of them settled after the War of 1812. Radisson's sisters also left thousands of descendants in Quebec, among them the Jutrat and Lavallée families. Calixa Lavallée, who wrote Canada's national anthem, had some Radisson genes.

Radisson himself was barely remembered until the 1880s, when the manuscript of his first four voyages, squirrelled away by Pepys, was discovered in an English library and published in the United States. More have turned up over the years, including manuscripts of the two Port Nelson "relations," which were found recently at Windsor Castle by Dr. Jean Radisson of Brussels, a distant relation. Local American historians embraced Radisson and falsely framed him as the "discoverer" of Minnesota and Wisconsin. The owners of a hotel chain may have inadvertently come closer to the reality that Radisson was always a guest when he visited these places. They began the chain in Minneapolis and have used a version of Radisson's signature as their logo. In French Canada, Radisson has morphed in popular culture from a traitor to a man of action cheated by corrupt government officials. The myth that Radisson was forced to constantly shift loyalties because of the actions of crooks and politicians has always been easy to believe. Radisson and Groseilliers are now inextricably linked to the founding of the Hudson's Bay Company, a fact that would have been lost to history, or been just an oddity mentioned in passing, if Radisson hadn't told his own story, or if these writings had been lost. Streets, parks, and a Canadian coast guard cutter have been named after him. Two of his best biographers, Grace Lee Nute, in the 1930s, and Germaine Warkentin, who published a brilliant reprint and reassessment of his writings in this century, were women. Likely the old rogue would have enjoyed that fact.

Yonge, Radisson's friend on the Hudson's Bay Company board, died in 1709. He was kind enough to write a clause into his will forgiving a £60 debt owed to him by Radisson. By that point, only the Duke of Marlborough was left from the old days, and he had moved on to more important things. Marlborough won the decisive Battle of Blenheim against the forces of Louis XIV in 1704. A grateful nation gave him Blenheim Palace, where his descendant Winston Churchill was born. Marlborough was also an ancestor of Diana Spencer, Princess of Wales. In time, his descendants will sit on the British throne.

After the first few expeditions brought Hudson's Bay Company investors big profits, the Quebec and First Nations fur traders found ways to drain away its trade. Radisson had planned for a few coastal operations, with the Indigenous people doing all the work collecting and transporting furs. The Quebec-based fur companies countered by building posts along the big rivers around the bay, forcing the Hudson's Bay Company to match these posts and set up a transportation system that eventually reached the foothills of the Rockies and the headwaters of the Mississippi. This extra overhead caused dividends to dry up, sometimes for decades. The struggle over the North American fur trade continued until 1821, when the St. Lawrence traders, now working for the Northwest Company, based in Montreal, merged with the Hudson's Bay Company. The latter company, one of the oldest in the world, is still in business, mostly as a department-store chain that, at the time of writing, was owned by an American hedge fund. Its vast territories were transferred to Canada at Confederation, though it still retained ownership of large parcels of city and farm land that it sold over the last century and a half. Still, it is no ordinary company, and its vast archives are the single most valuable collection of documents related to northern Canada's history.[225]

The Indigenous people, whom Radisson knew and sometimes loved, have struggled for centuries in the face of colonialism. The Mohawks, split into Roman Catholic and Anglican factions, fell apart during the same war in which d'Iberville grabbed the Hudson Bay forts and, by the early decades of the 1700s, the canoe routes to the north and west were no longer menaced by Iroquois war parties.[226] French massacres in the Mohawk Valley convinced many of the Catholic Mohawks to settle around Montreal. The Anglicans came to Canada as United Empire Loyalists after the American Revolution, bringing Queen Anne's silver with them. The Iroquois worked in the fur trade until the fur convoys ended, travelling on brigades to the Arctic and Pacific.[227] When the canoe brigades were shut down for lack of profit, the Iroquois became one of the most entrepreneurial Indigenous groups in Canada. Many still make their living as steelworkers building skyscrapers in Manhattan.

Many members of the Great Lakes First Nations who stayed in the United States were pushed onto reservations west of the Mississippi. Huron-Petun refugees, part of the mass of people forced out of the Great Lakes country by the American government, now live as the Wyandots in Oklahoma. The Cree, once they were sold hundreds of guns, vastly expanded their territory at the expense of their neighbours, and some bands became buffalo hunters living as far west as Saskatchewan. They were an important force in the resistance to Canadian colonization and now live on small reserves on their ancestral lands in Canada.[228] The Ojibwe, once armed, also expanded their lands to include those emptied during the Iroquois wars, taking almost all Southern Ontario before the influx of British settlers after the American War of Independence put an end to their expansion. Like many other First Nations, the Cree and Ojibwe are struggling with the consequences of the destruction of their economy and culture, substance abuse rooted in poverty, racism, bureaucratic neglect, and attempts by the Canadian government to assimilate them.

As for the beavers, they've made a comeback in North America and are being reintroduced to Europe. They are settling in nicely in England. Now, they're not only a pest, building dams that cause flooding and road washouts in some rural parts of the United States, Canada, and Europe, their ponds have been identified by scientists as an important source of climate-changing atmospheric gases.[229] But, so far, they're still safe from hatters.

Appendix: Maps

Radisson's 1652–1653 Expedition

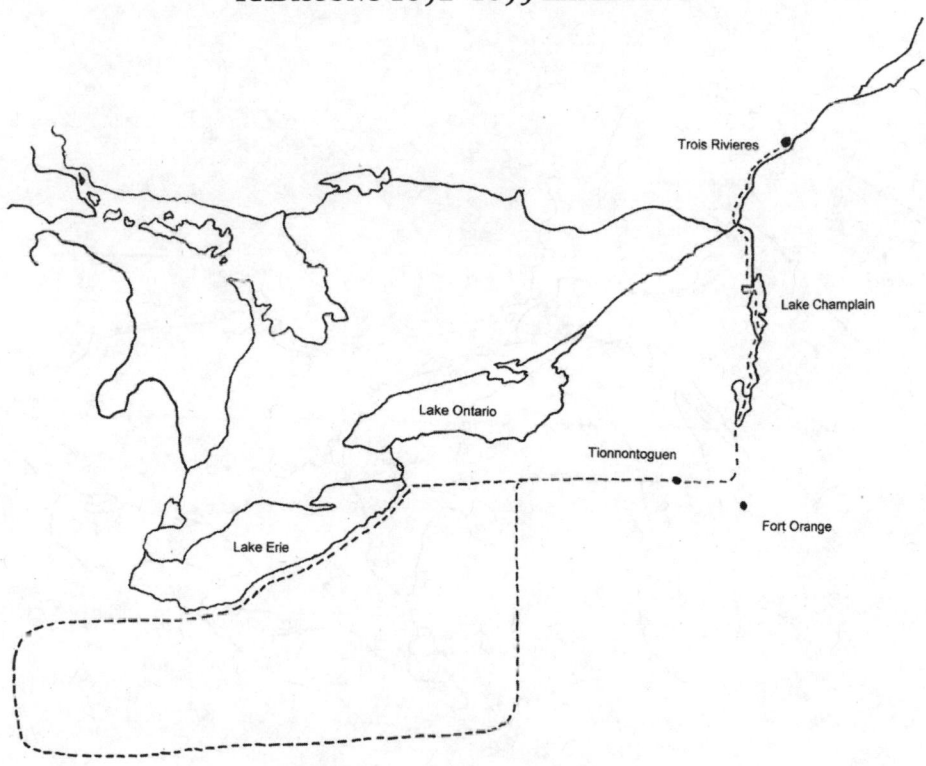

The dotted line follows Radisson's journey to
Mohawk County and the route of his raid.

RADISSON'S 1658–1660 EXPEDITION

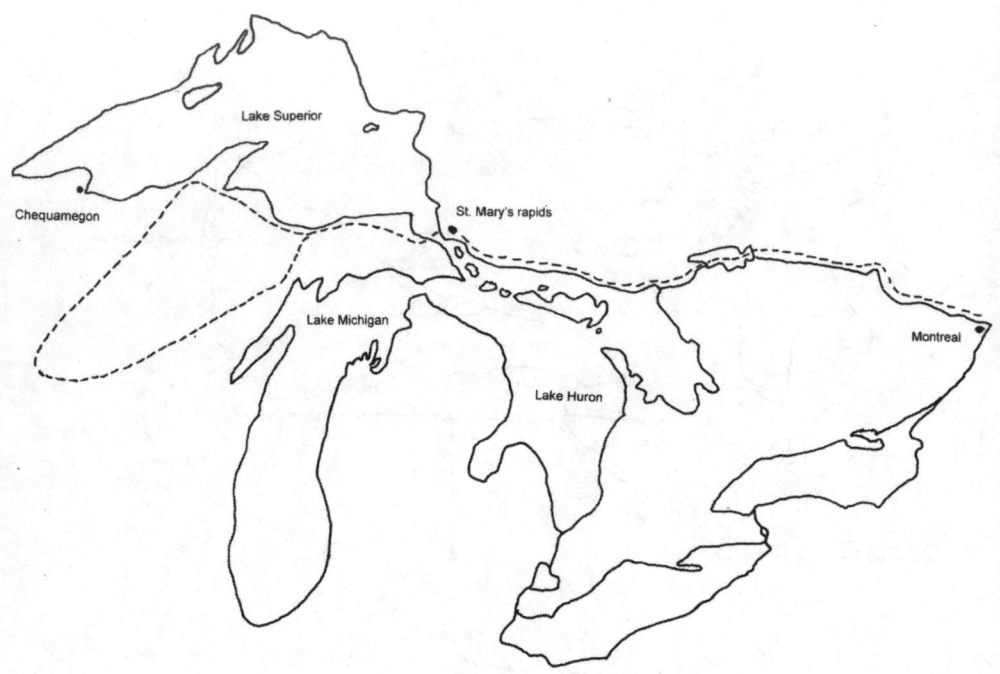

The dotted line follows Radisson's journey south
of Lake Superior to the Cree and the Sioux and into
what's now Wisconsin, Illinois, and Minnesota.

ENDNOTES

1   This claim should be taken with a grain of salt. It was made in a document drafted by the Hudson's Bay Company in April 1687 to try to prove the French had no claim on Hudson Bay. The memorandum contains great stretching of the truth and statements that are demonstrably false. E.E. Rich, ed., *Copy-Book of Letters Outward &c 1679–1794* (Toronto: Champlain Society, 1948), 226–226.

2   This brutal childrearing wasn't confined to Paris, nor was it limited to the seventeenth century, as any reader of Charles Dickens will quickly realize. For a short description of cities' need for young bodies, see Fernand Braudel, *The Structures of Everyday Life*, (New York: Harper & Row, 1981), 489–490. See also David I. Kertzer, ed., Marzio Barbagli, ed., *History of the European Family*, Book 1. (New Haven: Yale University Press, 2001).

3   Outside of the Church, the bureaucracy, and the small merchant class, New France was a spectacular wasteland when it came to reading and, especially, writing. For example, from its permanent founding in 1608 until the British conquest in 1760, the colony did not have a single printing press. Every book and newssheet was imported from France.

4   See, for example, Mima Kapches, "The Auds Site: An Early Pickering Iroquois Component in Southeastern Ontario," *Archaeology of Eastern North America*, Vol. 15 (Fall 1987): 155–175.

5   Olive Patricia Dickason, *The Myth of the Savage and the Beginnings of French Colonialism in the Americas* (Edmonton: University of Alberta Press), 1984, 118–119.

6   Author Michael McDonnell, in *Masters of Empire: Great Lakes Indians and the Making of America* (New York: Hill and Wang, 2015), argues the Odawa were simply members of the Ojibwe Anishinaabeg working in the fur trade, and that their name is a corruption of the Ojibwe word for traders, rather than a separate political entity. Trying to parse this out may lead us into the mistake of trying to apply European-style political and national structures to the Anishinaabeg. The Anishinaabeg First Nation was very decentralized and fluid, reliant on kin structures and consensus-building while holding (and expanding) its territory and trade as a cohesive ethnic group. It does appear, however, that the Odawa were a distinct group of clans or families who originally lived in the Beaver Valley on southwest Georgian Bay, where they were visited by Champlain, and who moved northwestward to take over Huron canoe routes after 1650.

7   The sections of the *Jesuit Relations* that claim the Huron were so desperate that they had to resort to cannibalizing their dead has been backed up by recent archaeological research. See Michael W. Spence and Lawrence Jackson, "The Bioarchaeology of Cannibalism at the Charity Site," *Ontario Archaeology*, Vol. 94 (2014): 65-80.

8   McDonnell, *Masters of Empire*, 32.

9   Radisson often describes Indigenous people using "hatchets," which, even when he wrote in English, was misinterpreted as "tomahawks." The iron trade axes used at this time had full-sized or slightly smaller axe heads on fairly short handles. These axes could be used for wood cutting as well as for weapons, while the trade tomahawks that were later sold to Indigenous people, with their long, slim, straight handles, were strictly weapons of war.

10   Bruce Trigger, *The Children of Aataentsic* (2 Vols) (Montreal: McGill-Queen's University Press, 1976), 83–85.

11   Radisson's description: "(T)hey tooke at the same instance the heads of those that weare killed the day before, and for to preserve them they cutt off the flesh to the skull and left nothing but skin and haire, putting of it into a litle panne wherein they melt some grease, and gott it dry with hot stones."

12   Germaine Warkentin ed., *Pierre-Esprit Radisson: The Collected Writings, Vol. 1: The Voyages* (Montreal-Toronto: McGill-Queens University Press/Champlain Society, 2012), 29.

13   The author has eaten many kinds of wild game and agrees with Radisson that bear is almost inedible, no matter how it is cooked and seasoned. Other opinions may differ.

14   For an examination of how Eastern Indigenous peoples saw Europeans, see Cornelius J. Jaenen, "Amerindian Views of French Culture in the Seventeenth Century," *Canadian Historical Review* 55:3 (September 1974): 30–62.

15   For an excellent study of the power structures in a closely related society, see William C. Noble, "Tsouharissen's Chiefdom: An Early Historic 17th Century Neutral Iroquoian Ranked Society," *Canadia Journal of Archaeology* 9:2 (1985): 131–146.

16   This type of communal work would also have been familiar to most Europeans, who were required to work on major projects and to maintain roads and bridges as part of their feudal obligation to their lords (and, through them, to the community at large).

17   Arthur C. Parker and William Fenton, ed., *Parker on the Iroquois* (Syracuse, NY: Syracuse University Press, 1968), 29.

18   Ibid, 90.

19   Father Gabriel Sagard and George Wrong, ed., *Long Journey to the Country of the Hurons* (Toronto: Champlain Society, 1939), 267.

20   Conrad Heidenreich, *Huronia: A History and Geography of the Huron Indians, 1600–1650* (Toronto: McClelland & Stewart, 1971), 70–171. The same land system was used in the Five Nations country.

21   Ibid, 52.

22   The Jesuits surveyed the country and calculated a population of about 30,000 in the 1630s. Writers in the 1970s and 1980s calculated the population to have been

around 20,000. The looting of archaeological sites, their quiet destruction by plowing and development, and the lack of a published comprehensive site survey make population calculation difficult. However, excluding the town of Midland, the modern, year-round population of this territory is less today than the low estimates of writers like Heidenreich and Bruce Trigger. Modern theorists believe Indigenous populations were much higher before contact with Europeans than twentieth-century historians believed. Champlain called the region "a land of meadows" and the European authors of the period wrote of regularly meeting people on their river and overland travels.

23 This was noticed by Champlain, the Recollet missionary Sagard, and the Jesuits in the first half of the seventeenth century, and has been confirmed by archaeology. See Heidenreich, *Huronia*, chap. VI, and Bruce Trigger, *The Huron: Farmers of the North*, 2nd edition (Fort Worth: Harcourt Brace, 1990), 83.

24 The literature shows drought was a problem for the Wendat and their neighbours. Corn crops were also lost to late frosts and pests. See Heidenreich, op cit., 66–67.

25 Ibid, 198.

26 Ibid, 200.

27 Anthony F. Wallace, "Political Organization and Land Tenure among the Northeastern Indians, 1600-1830," *Southwestern Journal of Anthropology* 13:4 (Winter 1957), 301–321.

28 Ibid, 311.

29 Franklin B. Hough, *Proceedings of the Commissioners of Indian Affairs Vol. 1* (Albany: State of New York, 1861), 274–280.

30 Pickering MS (reproduction of memorandum book containing extracts of commissioners' proceedings in 1784–1785), (Massachusetts Historical Society (ND), 121.

31 Radisson describes them as slaves. It's something of a misnomer. At this time, the Iroquois did not have chattel slavery, and the Huron were more like members of a low caste, without full political and social rights, eager to ingratiate themselves and assimilate. A century later, the Iroquois did have both Black and Pawnee slaves. Many of the refugee bands that "disappeared" after the wars of the mid-1600s may well have fled south and had members picked off as chattel slaves by the Iroquois and Indigenous people trading with the English, and these slaves ended up on plantations. Pawnee slaves taken from their villages in the Mississippi Valley began showing up in Quebec in the 1670s, sold to the French by the Odawa and Iroquois. They are specifically mentioned in the Capitulation of Montreal of 1760, in which the British promised to allow owners of "panis" and African slaves to keep their "property." Iroquois leader Joseph Brant owned more Black and Indigenous slaves than anyone else in British North America when he moved to the colony after the American Revolution. Partly in response, one of Upper Canada legislature's first acts was to ban the import of slaves, and those held in the province were freed in 1834 when the British parliament banned slavery throughout the British Empire.

32   Adam Stueck, "A Place Under Heaven: Amerindian Torture and Cultural Violence in Colonial New France, 1609–1729" Phd diss, Marquette University, 2012, epublications.marquette.edu/dissertations_mu/174.

33   Scott Manning Stevens, "The Historiography of New France and the Legacy of Iroquois Internationalism," *Comparative American Studies An International Journal*, 11:2 (2013): 148–165.

34   See cbc.ca/news/indigenous/the-orenda-faces-tough-criticism-from-first-nations-scholar-1.2562786.

35   See peggyblair.wordpress.com/2013/12/31/iroquois-torture-canadian-history-part-ii/.

36   Roger Carpenter, "Making War More Lethal: Iroquois vs. Huron in the Great Lakes Region, 1609 to 1650," *Michigan Historical Review* 27:2 (Fall 2001): 33–51.

37   Iroquoian villages had no outhouses or other toilet facilities. Waste was collected in earthen pots and dumped outside the village, along with trash such as meat bones, broken tools, pottery, and pipes, and anything else cluttering up the longhouses.

38   The story of wampum is probably worth a book of its own. Wampum was made by Algonkian people living on Long Island and the nearby mainland from shells harvested in the warm months and cut in the winter. The people who made these shell beads were always left in peace. The arrival of steel, which they made into tiny drill bits, allowed wampum makers to make consistent tubular purple and white beads with long, thin holes in a hard shell. What had been a small trade in disk-shaped beads quickly evolved into a mass trade in uniform-sized shell beads that make for breathtaking embroidery. Everyone wanted wampum, but the Iroquois had a lock on the trade and used it to draw the furs from northern hunters. To the Huron, 1,200 wampum beads—what the Jesuits gave to one Huron nation—was a fortune. The Iroquois could afford to dress diplomats from head to foot in wampum-covered clothes and belts. In one archaeological site, 250,000 wampum beads and eight belts were excavated. It is very hard to calculate the buying power of seventeenth-century currencies and compare them with modern money. We do, however, know that, at about this time, six white wampum beads were worth one English penny. This calculation was more than just academic: the Pilgrim Fathers got into the wampum trade and used the profits to pay off their debt for the Mayflower. So if all of the beads left behind at that one archaeological site were white, we end up with a value of nearly 40,000 English pennies, or 3,000 shillings, or 150 pounds sterling, or 30 ounces of gold. And this is based on an exploitive exchange rate set by Europeans. Among the First Nations, the value would have been much higher.

39   Dickason, *The Myth of the Savage*, 120–121.

40   European farmers in the 1600s subsisted on wheat or oats ground into flour and cooked with water to make gruel, which was usually eaten with the hands from a large communal dish. From time to time, and depending on the region in Europe, farmers also had some cheese, poultry, pork, beef, or mutton for protein, but most meals were meatless. Middle Easterners had hummus, yet another subsistence dish of ground seed and water. Asian farmers lived on rice, along with a little meat and fish.

41 Robert D. Kuhn, and Robert E. Funk. "Boning Up on the Mohawk: An Overview of Mohawk Faunal Assemblages and Subsistence Patterns," *Archaeology of Eastern North America* 28 (2000): 29–62. See page 34.

42 Until the mid-1800s, Atlantic salmon runs in the rivers and creeks flowing into both sides of Lake Ontario were spectacular. Over-fishing, the accidental and deliberate introduction of new species, and pollution have destroyed the original fish populations of the Great Lakes. In Lake Ontario, salmon and steelhead have been introduced to replace the lost Atlantic salmon fishery. In the upper lakes, steelhead and various kinds of Pacific salmon have replaced lake trout in their environmental niche. Lake herring were displaced by alewives and smelt, which entered the lakes through the St. Lawrence Seaway. Carp have filled the niche of fished-out sturgeon, which all of the Indigenous people valued, and which lived to be over 200 years old and grew to six feet. The despoiling of the Great Lakes fishery is one of the great untold ecological disaster stories of our time.

43 Radisson's obsession with palatable food comes through in all his writings. He almost never mentions sex or alcohol, and doesn't appear to have gambled or indulged in any other serious vice.

44 This is one of the few times he mentions his (French) family, and there's nothing in the record to suggest that any of his blood relatives were, in fact, killed by the Iroquois. This may, in fact, have been a slip into the Mohawk social view that great swaths of unrelated people were, through clan and moiety connections, "relatives."

45 Any descendants of non-Indigenous North Americans who feel a sense of superiority when reading about Iroquoian executions and what would seem now like wartime atrocities, needs to pause and reflect on the of their own ancestors and culture. Normal rules of war allowed for the slaughtering of the garrison of a besieged town, without quarter, once a city or castle wall was breached. Hanging, and drawing and quartering, the English penalty for treason, was as much a ritual as any North American Indigenous killing. Each aspect, from dragging the victim along the ground, hanging, castration, gutting, and dismembering, had both civic denunciation and religious overtones. Officially sanctioned violence has evolved from public, hands-on actions to fake clinical executions (men in white coats using sterile needles to inject lethal drugs into the condemned), but violence inflicted from a distance—out of sight and so put into the abstract—has increased dramatically. Torture occured in Eastern North America in the shadow of horrendous plagues, massive cultural disruptions caused by new technology, and a concerted attack by Europeans on the religion and governance of the First Nations. Still, in all of this fighting—from the time of Champlain in the first decade of the 1600s to the end of the Beaver Wars almost one hundred years later, it's likely fewer Indigenous people were killed than Allies on the first day of the Battle of the Somme, when the British and French lost some 20,000 dead, most blown to bits by artillery or mown down with machine guns. Aerial bombing from drones and planes and artillery fire has

made us better killers, though less personal ones. At least the Iroquoians gave some war victims a chance at adoption, and those that were killed had been allowed the opportunity to prove their courage. At the same time, the Iroquois did not use corporal or capital punishment on their own people, nor did they employ any kind of imprisonment or exile. The reasons for that will be described later in this book.

46   The gauntlet was a common way to brutalize prisoners in all the Iroquoian countries and probably symbolized the power the community had over those who entered the town, whether they were adopted or killed.

47   Compensation for murder and other crimes was not unique to the Iroquois. Before the Norman conquest, Anglo-Saxon justice used fines to settle disputes. This idea survives in Common Law, where, in civil cases, damages are almost the only means open to a court to settle disputes. (Specific performance orders are rare. Injunctions and other types of court orders arose later, as the concept of "equity," when some courts were allowed to share the king's power to make orders to set things right.)

48   By then, Radisson had been living in the Mohawk country for about a year. Radisson's account of his capture at Trois-Rivières strongly suggests he won the hearts of his captors because he was a precocious boy. When he was put in a fight at one of the Mohawk camps, he was pitted against another boy, not a warrior. Radisson's mother's concerns that he was not ready for war may have been very well founded.

49   Radisson called them "slaves" but they were more likely new arrivals who were just beginning to be integrated into Mohawk society. Very few started with the privileges afforded to Radisson.

50   Iroquois canoes were much heavier and more cumbersome than the birchbark canoes used by the northern people. They were also easy to build. For a description of how they were made, see C.E.S. Franks, *The Canoe and White Water* (Toronto: University of Toronto Press, 1977), 17.

51   Radisson appears to be describing a hellbender salamander. Radisson overestimates the salamander's length, but it's still a spectacular creature that grows up to thirty inches long, making it one of the largest salamanders in the world. Its range does not include the Iroquois country, so the members of Radisson's war party would likely rarely or never have seen one. Radisson's description of this animal has sometimes been used as evidence of his exaggerations—at least one writer claims no such animal existed in America—but, in fairness, the creature had just fallen into a moving canoe, which was soon also beset by a terrified squirrel. Radisson had no time to measure the creature, even if he had been inclined to touch it, and he described seeing it some ten years after the event.

52   The farmers were probably in as good shape as Radisson. His account was written in the mid-1660s, for an English audience, when England and Holland were at war. More likely, the settlers knew that resistance would only generate more problems that could lead to a war that the Dutch would not have won.

53   A French punitive expedition, led by Alexandre de Tracy, did lay waste to the Mohawk

country in 1666, but most people had evacuated the towns and returned after de Tracy's troops withdrew.

54 Radisson's silence regarding his romantic life as a Mohawk is quite deafening. The Mohawk tended to make teenage attachments and to have views about sex that would fit modern norms but that would be scandalous to Europeans (despite the open secret of streetwalkers and brothels, symptoms of class being used to validate hypocrisy). Radisson, who comes across as an attractive, physically fit, personable young man, never mentions any romantic or sexual interactions with Mohawk women. Some remarks about his "sisters" show an intense intimacy with them, but this was probably limited by social rules against incest. Later, Radisson exposes a Dutch housewife for her sexual approach to him. It might be important to the real story that nothing came of it, and Radisson may have told of the encounter to make another dig at the Dutch.

55 She may have been the sister of a half-Dutch Mohawk chief the French called "The Flemish Bastard" who hated the French. He turns up later in this story as an opponent of a Jesuit mission in the Onondaga country.

56 A comment made by his mother in the spring, before he went to war, suggests the Mohawks believed Radisson was not particularly good at navigating in the forest. Having been in North America for just a couple of years, it's quite likely Radisson wasn't particularly good at the difficult art of orienteering in forests in which the canopy blocks out most of the sky.

57 It seems most Dutch farmers in the upper Hudson Valley had their fingers in the fur trade to the point that they could undermine a short-lived ban on the trading of guns to the Mohawks. Farmers in the Fort Orange area were tenants of the Van Rensselaer family, ancestors of Eliza Schuyler Hamilton.

58 Unlike the Neutral and the Tobacco Nation, the Mohawks did not tattoo their bodies, so the only permanent reminder of this adventure was one crushed index finger and a scar where Radisson's foot was pierced.

59 Russell Shorto, *The Island at the Centre of the World* (London: Doubleday, 2004), 71, quoted in Charles Spencer, *Killers of the King* (London: Bloomsbury Press, 2014), 275.

60 Only one piercing remains. When Jacques Cartier visited the region in the 1530s, there were three holes through this cliff. Radisson saw two. The second one collapsed in 1845.

61 Chouart was the man's real last name, while des Groseilliers, or Sieur des Groseilliers, was a sort of fake title implying Chouart was a member of the minor nobility. Since he's known to history as Groseilliers, that's what he'll be called in this book. His son, Jean-Baptiste, was always known as Chouart, which adds to the complications caused by Groseillier's attempt at social climbing.

62 Like her new husband, Marguérite was very litigious. In fact, the couple's astounding number of court cases—mostly what we would call small claims, along with lawsuits against Groseilliers for assault and battery—have left us with a far better paper trail in Quebec than we have for Radisson, who usually avoided lawsuits.

63 Ragueneau to Colbert, 7 November 1664, Melanges Colbert, 125 f 181. Transcribed

in LAC MG7-IA6, 231-2. See also Germaine Warkentin, ed., *Pierre-Esprit Radisson: The Collected Writings, Vol. 2: The Port Nelson Relations, Miscellaneous Writings and Related Documents* (Montreal-Toronto: McGill-Queen's University Press/Champlain Society, 2014), 40.

64   Ragueneau to the Comte d'Estrades November 7, 1664, accusing Chouart of whipping up the Iroquois to destroy New France BN Melanges.

65   Letter of July 28, 1655. Guyart, *Correspondance*, letter ccxv, 742. Warkentin, *Pierre-Esprit Radisson: The Collected Writings, Vol. 2.*

66   For example, his description of southern Georgian Bay and the Bruce Peninsula, including Huronia, is so utterly wrong that I have left it out of this story and incorporated the obvious eyewitness detail of the trip into the chapter about Radisson's voyage to the south shore of Lake Superior. As an example, Radisson says he paddled past the Huron country and could not see the fort of the Jesuits. In fact, Ste. Marie II, site of the 1649–1650 famine, is on the channel between Christian Island and the mainland, which is the only route for canoes along that stretch of Georgian Bay. Radisson could not have missed it.

67   In popular culture, the Sioux are always seen as a horse culture on the Great Plains, but many of the Sioux bands were relative latecomers. The Yankton Dakota, the First Nation that Radisson met, lived in the forests of Minnesota and along the west shore of lake Michigan, with settlements as far west as Iowa. See James H. Howard, "Notes on the Ethnogeography of the Yankton Dakota," *Plains Anthropologist*, 17:58, part 1 (November 1972): 281–307.

68   From the intro to the Prince edition of Radisson's *Voyages*: "The Abbe Cyprian Tanguay, the best genealogical authority in Canada, gives the following account of the family: Francoise Radisson, a daughter of Pierre Esprit, married at Quebec, in 1668, Claude Volant de St. Claude, born in 1636, and had eight children. Pierre and Claude, eldest sons, became priests. Francoise died in infancy: Marguérite married Noel le Gardeur; Francoise died in infancy; Etienne, born October 29, 1664, married in 1693 at Sorel, but seems to have had no issue. Jean Francois married Marguérite Godfrey at Montreal in 1701. Nicholas, born in 1668, married Genevieve Niel, July 30, 1696, and both died in 1703, leaving two of their five sons surviving. There are descendants of Noel le Gardeur who claim Radisson as their ancestor, and also descendants of Claude Volant, apparently through Nicholas. Among these descendants of the Volant family is the Rt. Rev. Joseph Thomas Duhamel, who was consecrated Bishop of Ottawa, Canada, October 28, 1874."

69   In the Autoxiat Voyage, Radisson's likely imaginary account of his trip to the Mississippi River.

70   Champlain had joined with Algonkian and Huron warriors in a raid near Lake Champlain against the Mohawks. The French explorer believed a military alliance would strengthen trade relations with the Huron and Algonkians.

71   Eventually, the Jesuits armed the people under their control, drilled them as infantry and cavalry soldiers, and created what amounted to a Jesuit-run nation in defiance of

the colonial administrations of France and Portugal. The reductions began in 1609 (at about the same time the first Jesuit missionaries arrived in Canada) and were crushed by Spanish troops in the mid-1700s. In 1648, according to the *Jesuit Relations*, the Christian Huron offered the Jesuits political control of their country, but the Huron were destroyed before the Jesuits could begin their rule. Indigenous people later settled near Quebec City, Trois-Rivières, and Montreal, but the Jesuits were unable to exert political control over them. See Manfred Barthel, *The Jesuits: History and Legend of the Society of Jesus* (New York: William Morrow, 1983), part X. The theme of Volume 2 of Trigger's *Children of Aetaentsic* is the collapse of Huron independence in the face of the Jesuit assault on their culture.

72   Penny Petrone, ed., *First People, First Voices* (Toronto: University of Toronto Press, 1983), 13.

73   Ibid.

74   Now called Christian Island, just north of the Penetanguishene Peninsula. It is now home of the Beausoleil First Nation, an Ojibwe group that moved south after the dispersal of the Huron.

75   See David S. Brose, Robert C. Mainfort, C. Wesley, eds., *Societies in Eclipse: Archaeology of the Eastern Woodlands* parts 1400–1700 (Washington: Smithsonian Institution Press, 2001), 62–64.

76   Paul Ragueneau, in Reuben Gold Thwaites, *The Jesuit Relations and Allied Documents: Travels and Explorations of the Jesuit Missionaries in New France, 1610–1791: the Original French, Latin, and Italian Texts, with English Translations and Notes* (Cleveland: Burrows, 1897) 1658 volume, 157.

77   In fact, according to Radisson, the Jesuits were making 20,000 *livres tournois* a year from the Hurons' agriculture and fur trading when the refugees were being shunted around the Quebec area. Not all Huron left in 1654. The descendants of those who stayed behind live at New Lorette, just outside Quebec City.

78   These are now tamed by the Beauharnois Dam near Valleyfield, Quebec.

79   These rapids, except for the Lachine Rapids near Montreal, were drowned by the St. Lawrence Seaway in the 1950s.

80   Stanley Island, which has not changed much despite the construction of the St. Lawrence Seaway and the dredging of a ship channel on its north side, is about the right size and shape to fit the events Radisson describes. It is small enough for the Jesuits and Hurons to be controlled, large enough for the Huron and French to be separated, but not so large that any of the Iroquois' intended victims, or the French, could get away into the forest (which could have happened on a larger island like Cornwall Island). Stanley Island also has two distinct parts, separated by what would have been a gully. It is clear from the descriptions that there was some sort of natural barrier between the French and the Huron at the time of the massacre. As well, Radisson says the French, on the return trip, weren't sure which island was the site of the massacre until it was identified by a Huron survivor, which would not have been

the case if it had happened on Cornwall Island, which is much bigger than those downstream. Stanley Island would have been somewhat indistinguishable from its neighbours, especially in winter.

81 This is one of many instances in which renowned warriors were exempted from the horror of Iroquoian war because of previous conduct in battle. A famous Huron warrior was allowed to leave the captured stockade of St. Louis, in the Huron country, after a battle on March 18, 1649. The same warrior warned some Iroquois leaders not to visit Gahoendoe with the Onondaga in 1650. This opens the possibility of chivalrous societies among the Iroquoians that cut across tribal and clan loyalties.

82 This made no sense in Iroquoian law, as murder, which could be punished either with a demand or payment, or, if that failed, revenge, seems to have required intent. It would have been a stretch for the Onondaga to argue that the death of their men was the fault of the Huron. Ragueneau, who had lived among the Huron a long time, probably knew this. In his *Relations*, he blames the murders on an incident in which a Huron woman supposedly rejected the sexual advances of an Onondaga chief, a claim that makes almost as little sense as Radisson's. Trigger (*Children of Aataentsic*, Vol. 2, 813) blames long-simmering rage over the Gahoendoe treachery for the massacre.

83 The Iroquois often placed these pictograph-covered posts along trails and water routes to mark special occasions and to communicate with people who came by. Stories of successful raids were quite common. Unfortunately, none of these posts have survived. Pictographs drawn by people in the Canadian Shield still exist, some with quite vibrant and clear pictures. One, at Agawa on Lake Superior, north of Sault Ste. Marie, tells the story of a raid by local warriors against people living in what's now northern Michigan.

84 Trigger, *Children of Aataentsic*, Vol. 2, 263, quoting Lescarbot (1907–14, 5:22).

85 The Iroquois were quick to trade for Dutch livestock and, within a couple of generations, had become self-sufficient in meat within their own county, but these pigs appear to have been brought by the French. The introduction of European livestock was likely a vector for some of the diseases that caused so many thousands, perhaps millions, of deaths in eastern North America from the time the Spanish explorer brought pigs on his exploration of the American south-east.

86 For a description of the salt springs and their later uses in industry, see pubs.usgs.gov/fs/2000/0139/report.pdf. Onondaga Lake now gets 20 percent of its water from the Syracuse sewer system. The site of the main Onondaga town is now one of the most polluted places in America.

87 Trigger, *Children of Aataentsic*, Vol. 2, 853.

88 Ibid, 852.

89 William N. Fenton, *The Great Law and the Longhouse: A Political History of the Iroquois Confederacy* (Norman, OK: University of Oklahoma Press, 1998), 248–252.

90 Apparently, humans taste remarkably like pork, which may be the real punchline of this joke. The author has not tested this observation.

91 Iroquoian ideas of liability and damages seem to mirror those of Anglo-Saxon and Norman England, where the idea of compensatory damages evolved to prevent families from feuding over accidental negligence. The Iroquois extended this idea to deliberate acts of violence, with damages for wounding and murder set so high that the assailant's entire extended family and clan would feel the financial sting of settling disputes. By making extended groups, rather than individuals, responsible for the conduct of members of Iroquoian society, the clans were able to exert a powerful grip on people who were raised to cherish their standing in society. The Iroquois had no capital punishment except for treason and sorcery, no jails, and no corporal punishment. Presumably, sociopaths and others who were prone to violence could simply join a raiding party and indulge their sadism on people of other nations. Habitual thieves, rapists, and other antisocial people appear to be rare or non-existent in seventeenth-century Iroquoian society.

92 The Jesuits said a young Frenchman, who had been captured and adopted by wealthy Iroquois, organized the plan. This young man also ran the feast. It would stretch the imagination to the breaking point to believe the description might fit anyone other than Radisson. It is the only mention in the literature of Radisson playing the guitar, but he was an intelligent man and, during his long, tedious sea voyages and his time in Europe, certainly had time to buy one and learn how to play it.

93 Ragueneau, in Gold Thwaites, *Jesuit Relations and Allied Documents,* 1658 Volume, 157.

94 This was a fairly common practice, and it was lethal. Of fifty-one Cayuga warriors kidnapped by the French near Cataraqui (Kingston, Ontario) in 1687 and shipped off to France to be worked as galley slaves, only thirteen were still alive two years later, when the French government realized the folly of its action and sent them back to Canada.

95 *Jesuit Relations* 44:312.

96 They did so even if they walked around barefoot and in rags the rest of the time. See Braudel *Structures of Everyday Life* Vol 1 (New York: Harper and Row, 1981), 11.

97 Pepys paid 4 pounds, 10 shillings for a beaver hat to replace one that was ruined when he dropped it in the filth of a London street. It is very difficult to calculate the buying power of money in the seventeenth century, especially since so many people had none at all and subsisted on barter. The figure used here is based on calculations made at uwyo.edu/numimage/currency.htm. The story of Pepys' hat purchase comes from Lisa Picard, *Restoration London* (London: Phoenix Press, 1997), 123.

98 Personal communication with Colleen Cox, owner of Cowboy Up Hatters, Denver, Colorado (cowboyuphatters.com). Ms. Cox made the estimate after seeing Rembrandt and Vermeer paintings.

99 Henri IV was Champlain's personal benefactor and wanted him around the Louvre whenever he was in France. There may have been a personal reason. There's speculation Champlain was Henri IV's illegitimate son. Henry IV had a busy sex life and was almost literally the father of his country, so the idea is not as far-fetched as it might

seem. See David Hackett Fischer, *Champlain's Dream* (Toronto: Vintage Canada, 2009), chapter 1.

100 For a good description of the role of the beaver hat in seventeenth-century fashion and the beginning of the beaver felt trade, see Timothy Brook, *Vermeer's Hat: The Seventeenth Century and the Dawn of the Global World* (Toronto: Viking Canada, 2008), especially chapter 2. See also J. F. Crean, "Hats and the Fur Trade," *Canadian Journal of Economics and Political Science* Vol. XXVII, no. 3 (August 1962): 373–451.

101 Beaver musk glands, "castoreum," were believed to have medical value and, by the 1800s, the Hudson's Bay Company exported tons from North America. See Lorne Hammond, "Marketing Wildlife: The Hudson's Bay Company and the Pacific Northwest, 1821–49," *Forest & Conservation History*, Vol. 37, Issue 1, (January 1993): 14–25.

102 The role of women hunters in the Great Lakes region Indigenous communities could use much more study. Although women were responsible for the big cornfields at Iroquoian villages, they were also harvesters of wild food and game. European descriptions of fishing and hunting parties from this period invariably mention the presence of women. Very likely, European writers either didn't understand or didn't care that Indigenous gender roles differed from those of their culture.

103 Radisson's movements at this time are utterly confusing. He claimed to have made an earlier trip with Groseilliers, but evidence seems to point to solo travels to Lake Huron area, or that he stayed in the Ottawa Valley-Montreal-Trois-Rivières area where he traded and helped transport Jesuits. For an alternative interpretation that has little modern support, but should be noted, see Arthur T. Adams, "A New Interpretation of the Voyages of Radisson," *Minnesota History*, 6:4 (December 1925): 317–319. While Adams' theory, that Radisson and Groseilliers made two trips together that were later written up by Radisson with rather scrambled dates and details, seems far-fetched, Adams was the foremost Radisson scholar of the late nineteenth and early twentieth century and was the first person to edit and publish Radisson's accounts of his North American voyages.

104 He may have been the trader who accompanied Chouart on his first trip into the interior. Groseilliers had business dealings with the Le Moyne family, whose sons would carve out their own reputations as soldiers and adventurers and make the family rich. It was unlikely, however, that the governor of Trois-Rivières would throw such a well-connected man in jail for illegal trading. Whoever this man was, Radisson went out of his way not to name him, and we'll likely never know the reason why.

105 This tolling by French officials bears more than a superficial resemblance to the Kitchisspirini's tolling operation on Morrison Island, run by the hereditary chiefs who had the name Tessouat.

106 Had the Europeans lived under Iroquoian law, Radisson would have been a much wealthier man after opening the sea route to the Hudson Bay fur trade.

107 H.P. Biggar, ed., *The Works of Samuel Champlain*, Vol. 2 (Toronto: Champlain Society, 1922), 166.

108 This section examines the Kitchisspirini toll operation on the Ottawa River. The Montagnais of the lower St. Lawrence River also collected tolls. See Ragueneau, in Gold Thwaites, *Jesuit Relations and Allied Documents,* Vol. 8, 41; Vol. 12, 187–189.

109 The Nipisserians were a group of Algonkian-speaking people who lived on Lake Nipissing. After Iroquois attacks began in the winter of 1649–1650, their grip on their homeland had become quite tenuous.

110 This is an accurate description of the small islands just above the falls, which were formed by a geologic fault that crosses the river.

111 For a description of the sacredness of this site, which has been despoiled by factories and is about to be redeveloped as a condominium project opposed by some Indigenous groups, see Dr. Julie Comber, "Spotlight Hiding a Dam Shame: Controversial Mìwàte Show Continues at Akikodjiwan (Chaudière Falls)," *The Media Co-op*, accessed Oct. 13, 2017 mediacoop.ca/story/spotlight-hiding-dam-shame-controversial-m%C3%A Cw%C3%A0te-sh/36614.

112 Oral and written history of this period is vague about how the Ojibwe and their allies defeated the Iroquois, but some type of battle likely took place in the early 1660s in central Ontario. Most traditions place the battle just south of Georgian Bay. While the Iroquois rarely allowed one defeat to force them to change their own strategy, the communities they founded along the north shore of Lake Ontario on the Humber, Rouge, and Ganaraska rivers and at the Bay of Quinte after the dispersal of the Huron were abandoned and their people seem to have moved back to the Five Nations heartland. From about this time, the Iroquois changed the focus of their attacks to the Lake Michigan region and further west, where they waged war on the Pawnee and the Sioux until those people obtained horses and moved west.

113 The writer, familiar with placer and vein gold deposits on the north shore of Lake Superior, the astounding wealth of Silver Islet, near Thunder Bay, where a foot-wide seam of nearly pure silver bisected an island, and who has knowledge of copper deposits on the south shore of Lake Superior, which Indigenous people shared with the French, going back to Champlain, is left wondering what the history of eastern North America might have been if the French had dispatched geologists and miners to New France, along with fur traders and soldiers.

114 See gennick.com/the-box/rock-collapses-at-grand-portal-point.

115 These were named in 1820 by geologist and naturalist Henry Schoolcraft and Michigan governor Gen. Lewis Cass, who explored the region during that period. Cass was an ancestral cousin of the author.

116 A vast amount of this copper was mined and made into tools. It was traded throughout eastern North America. See, for example, specimens found at the Morrison Island site in the Ottawa River, which is dated from 3500 BCE. Seeottawariver.org/pdf/04-ch2-2.pdf.

117 For a description of this resource, see geo.msu.edu/extra/geogmich/copper.html. See also Louise Phelps Kellogg, "Copper Mining in the Early Northwest," *The Wisconsin*

Magazine of History, 8:2 (December 1924): 146–159. For a discussion of the peoples living in the now-Canadian side of this region at the height of the exploitation of these resources, see Charles A. Bishop and M. Estellie Smith, "Early Historic Populations in Northwestern Ontario: Archaeological and Ethnohistorical Interpretations," *American Antiquity* 40:1 (January 1975): 54–63.

118 Much of the study of the fur trade centres on the flow of weapons and, later, liquor into First Nations communities. Many authors miss the impact of the trade on women, who could now get good cooking pots, cloth, scissors, needles, and other very useful household items. The labour savings would have been impressive. For example, the pots were far more efficient than their old pottery and bark vessels. Needles would previously have been made of bone and required many, many hours to carve and drill. (A few were made of native copper in archaic times.) Beads, an integral item in cultures that valued style, were also in great demand.

119 While the Petun and Huron had been neighbours and had fled west together in the face of Iroquois attacks, the two peoples had also been at war in living memory. During the Huron-French fur trade that collapsed in 1649, the Petun had been prevented by the Huron from trading with the French and had faced other humiliations. Radisson's account of discord among the band of "Wendat," the name adopted by these people, suggests cleavages and old scores based on ethnicity, history, and, perhaps, clan politics that were still fresh. Eventually, this group would fuse into a single people who lived in the Lake Huron, Detroit, and northwestern Ohio regions before some of them were forcibly removed from their American territory by the US government and forced onto a reservation in Oklahoma as Wyandots. A few on the Canadian side settled near Windsor, Ontario. The main Huron-Wendat group in Canada lives in Quebec. Most Huron eventually ended up joining the Iroquois, and their descendants assumed the identity of their adopted nation and identify as members of the Six Nations.

120 McDonnell, *Masters of Empire*, 8–12.

121 Historian Bruce M. White has argued convincingly that marriage into Indigenous communities was mandatory for successful trade. See his paper "The Woman Who Married a Beaver: Trade Patterns and Gender Roles in the Ojibwa Fur Trade," *Ethnohistory* 46:1 (Winter 1999): 109–147.

122 Chouart was not a victim of French fashion. His beard was also out of style in Europe, and would be for almost two hundred years. See Braudel, *Structures of Everyday Life* Vol. 1, 332.

123 There are still unanswered questions about the Feast of the Dead. Multiple burials from the Archaic period have been found in southern Ontario, including several graves in Little Lake Park in Midland, Ontario, in what was the centre of the Huron country, that contained native copper offerings and may pre-date corn agriculture. Many of the big burial ossuaries in Huronia and throughout southern Ontario were found and looted early in the last century. The large ossuary where Brébeuf watched the 1636 Huron Feast of the Dead was excavated in 1954 by the Royal Ontario

Museum. It contained about one thousand bodies and a vast amount of Huron crafts and French trade goods. The bones were reinterred in 1999 and the site now belongs to the Huron-Wendat of Quebec. Another large ossuary found in Little Lake Park, Midland, not far from the Archaic graves, was found in this century. It was covered in concrete to protect it from looters. For an examination of the short-lived phenomenon of the Feast of the Dead in the Upper Lakes, see Harold Hickerson, "The Feast of the Dead Among the Seventeenth Century Algonkians of the Upper Lakes," *American Anthropologist* 62:1, new series (February 1960): 81-107.

124 Radisson is among those credited with "discovering" the Mississippi, a river that most First Nations people in the Great Lakes region would at least have heard about, if not seen. It's not clear whether he actually saw it. Chouart might have in the mid-1650s, without Radisson. It doesn't really matter much. Radisson has received a lot of study from Minnesota historians as one of the state's more important European "explorers." He did visit part of the land that became that state, as well as what's now Wisconsin, and probably went into northern Illinois. He had travelled with the Mohawks in the early 1650s in Ohio, Indiana, Pennsylvania and probably entered Kentucky and West Virginia.

125 Radisson says the Indigenous people he travelled with snared hundreds of moose, a figure that seems ridiculous. However, another French trader who lived with Algonkian hunters on Manitoulin Island gave similar figures for moose kills using snares. Moose are large animals that require a considerable range and that produce just one or two calves a year, and it's unlikely Manitoulin Island and the Upper Peninsula could have supported that kind of over-hunting without the quick extirpation of moose.

126 Radisson uses this phrase in his manuscript. They are the same words Cromwell used when describing the killing of Royalist prisoners at Drogheda, Ireland, in the fall of 1649.

127 Radisson was rather coy about his sexual relations with the Indigenous women. In his discussion of the sturgeon harvest, he does write about travelling and getting back to "our wives." At least one major Franco-Ojibwe family based at Michilimackinac, the Langlades, claimed descent from Radisson. Their descendants later settled in the Penetanguishene area. Anything written by seventeenth-century Europeans about Indigenous women should be looked at with some skepticism, though it appears Indigenous women in the Great Lakes region had considerable sexual freedom until they were married. See McDonnell, *Masters of Empire*, 2015.

128 Radisson dismisses all of these rumours, but we do know that at least seven hundred Iroquois warriors, a huge fighting force for that time, were moving around the Ottawa Valley in May 1660. We know they found Adam Dollard and his men, but that was an accident. It seems that about two hundred of these men had been on fur raids in the upper Ottawa Valley or even around Lake Huron, while the other five hundred had mustered for a big attack somewhere in the St. Lawrence Valley. News of the band of two hundred could easily have made it to the Cree leadership and the Ojibwe, making their intelligence far better Radisson and Chouart's.

129 The Battle of Long Sault is commemorated with a monument below the dam that was built to harness the rapids' hydro power. Some historians believe it was fought upstream from these rapids, probably on the south (Ontario) side of the Ottawa River. Radisson is very clear in his description that the forts were above the rapids. He says so outright, then, after describing the battle site and the fight itself, says he and his fur brigade shot the rapids and headed toward Montreal. This supports the theories put forward in Thomas Lee's "Lost Battleground of the Long Sault," *Genus* Vol. 16:1/4 (1960), 116–157.

130 This amount was, coincidently, the cost of running the entire colony for a year. Martin Fournier, *Pierre-Esprit Radisson, Merchant Adventurer, 1636–1710* (Sillery, QC: Les editions du Septentrion, 2002), 128. The conversion was made at uwyo.edu/numimage/currency.htm.

131 Patricia Simpson, *Marguérite Bourgeoys and Montreal, 1640–1665* (Montreal: McGill-Queens University Press, 1997), 174.

132 Their plans included an expedition up the Saguenay River to James Bay the following year. This expedition of traders sent by the colonial administration and Jesuits failed, as did several others over the next five years. Radisson and Chouart's plan would have seriously hurt New France because furs and trade goods would have been shipped directly in and out of France, making the colony, with all its expensive problems with the First Nations, redundant.

133 J.B. Tyrrell ed., *Documents Relating to the Early History of Hudson Bay* (Toronto: The Champlain Society, 1931), 3–7. See also Peter C. Newman, *Dreams of Empire* (Toronto: Penguin, 1998), chapter 2.

134 This was the work that infuriated Marie l'Incarnation, the nun who believed Groseilliers was responsible for the English seizing New Netherlands. The transfer was completed in the Treaty of Breda in 1667, at the end of the second Anglo-Dutch war, though the Dutch temporarily seized New York City again a few years later.

135 In any European treaty negotiation, all lands were in play. For example, while the Dutch won the First Dutch War, they were willing to give up their relatively meagre North American holdings for a better deal. For the social impact of Carr's bad reputation in Boston, see E.E. Rich, *The History of the Hudson's Bay Company* (London: The Hudson's Bay Record Society, 1959, Vol. 1) 27.

136 Grace Lee Nute, *Caesars of the Wilderness* (New York: D. Appleton-Century Company, 1941), citing affidavits made in later claims for the lost cargo, including the Winthrop Papers, part IV, in the Collection of the Massachusetts Historical Society, 5th Series, 8:104 (Boston 1882) 129–137.

137 Adrian Tinniswoood, *By Permission of Heaven: The True Story of the Great Fire of London* (London/New York: Riverhead Books), 2003.

138 "Documentary History of Maine" 3: 201, 202, 299, from Nute, *Caesars of the Wilderness*, 95.

139 Mood Fulmer, "The London Background of the Radisson Problem," *Minnesota History* 16 (December 1935): 391–413; Nute, *Caesars of the Wilderness*, 9.

140 Not only was the climate colder, but the Thames was shallower and the current was undisturbed above London Bridge. New bridges and dredging are among the reasons why the river does not freeze, even in abnormally cold weather.

141 Tinniswood, *By Permission of Heaven*, 2003.

142 Trigger, *Children of Aetaensic*, Vol. 1, 263–264. Savignon later became a vocal critic of European settlement and missionary work among the Iroquoian nations.

143 Quoted in Roy Porter, *London: A Social History* (London: Penguin Books, 1994), 83.

144 Quoted from Evelyn's diary in Margaret Willes, *The Curious World of Samuel Pepys and John Evelyn* (New Haven: Yale, 2017), 39.

145 See Grace Lee Nute, "Radisson and Groseilliers' Contribution to Geography," in *Minnesota History* 16 (December 1935): 418.

146 James Scott, Duke of Monmouth, was about sixteen at the time Radisson and Groseilliers arrived at court. In 1685, he made a play for the throne, trading on public hatred and suspicion of his uncle, James II. His rebellion was put down swiftly and with much brutality. His execution completed a strange pattern in the Stuart family: Monmouth's grandfather, Charles I, had been beheaded by Parliament, and Charles' grandmother, Mary, Queen of Scots, had been beheaded by Elizabeth I. The headsman had collected from every second generation of Stuarts over the course of a century.

147 Charles' arboreal experience is commemorated by several hundred thousand real and fake Royal Oak pubs scattered throughout the world. The owners who know the origin story post signs showing the king peeking through oak leaves.

148 See Grace Lee Nute, "Two Documents from Radisson's Suit Against the Company," in *The Beaver* (December 1935): 41–49 quoted in Nute, *Caesars of the Wilderness*.

149 John Stubbs, *Reprobates: The Cavaliers of the English Civil War* (New York: Norton and Co, 2011), 395.

150 For descriptions of Rupert's inventions and experiments, see Charles Spencer, *Prince Rupert: The Last Cavalier* (London: Weidenfield and Nicholson, 2007), especially chapters 20 and 21.

151 Spencer, *Prince Rupert: The Last Cavalier*, 340. See also Anne M. Carlos and Stephen Nicholas, "Agency Problems in Early Chartered Companies: The Case of the Hudson's Bay Company," *The Journal of Economic History*, 50:4 (December 1990): 853–875.

152 Rich, *History of the Hudson's Bay Company*, Vol. 1, 39.

153 For the role of the Protestant Reformation in the development of credit and the rise of the corporation, see R.H. Tawney, *Religion and the Rise of Capitalism* (London: Peter Smith, 1962.) See also Max Weber, *The Protestant Ethic and the Spirit of Capitalism* (New York: Scribner, 1958.)

154 This prediction appeared in the August 30, 1666 edition of the semi-official *London Gazette*, which was in circulation four days later when the city began to burn down. Touret's arrest put Groseilliers—"Mr. Gooseberries" in some of the plot records—in a bind. He got out of it his usual way, by betraying Touret, claiming he had known all along that Touret was a spy, and insisting he was duping the agent.

155 Tinniswood, *By Permission of Heaven*, 29.

156 De Witt was killed and partially eaten by a mob of his constituents in 1672, in what must be one of the most bizarre political assassinations in European history. See Jill Stern, "Poison in Print: Pamphleteering and the Deaths of Concini (1617) and the Brothers De Witt (1672)," *Pamphlets and Politics in the Dutch Republic* (Brill, 2010) 119–142.

157 P. Clement, *Lettres, instructions et memoires de Colbert*, 3:239 (Paris 1865) quoting Archives de la Marine, Depeches concernant le commerce, 1670, f. 181, cited by Nute, *Caesars of the Wilderness*, 109.

158 Possibly because Colbert had already opened a new backchannel to Radisson and Grosseilliers and confidently expected them to betray the English.

159 Liza Picard, *Restoration London* (London: Phoenix Press, 1996), 89.

160 While many scholars have tried to tackle Radisson's timelines, sometimes in very complicated ways, the most convincing interpretation was made by Arthur T. Adams, "A New Interpretation of the Voyages of Radisson," *Minnesota History* 6:4 (December 1925): 317–329.

161 Spencer, *Prince Rupert*, 341. Spencer has footnoted this quote to Sir John Clapham, *Minutes of the Hudson's Bay Company 1671–1674*, 131, quoted in Morrah, *Prince Rupert of the Rhine*, 383.

162 Nute, *Caesars of the Wilderness*, 119.

163 Statistics for Churchill, Manitoba, one of the closest communities to Radisson's Fort Nelson camp: theweathernetwork.com/api/sitewrapper/index?b=%2Fstatis-tics%2F&p=%2Fforecasts%2Fstatistics%2Findex&url=%2Fstatistics%2Fsumma-ry%2Fcl5060600%2Fcamb0033%2F%2F%3F.

164 This despite apparently being personally stuck with a bill for over £100 for repairs to the *Eaglet*. Nute, *Caesars of the Wilderness*, 120.

165 Michael Bliss, *Northern Enterprise: Five Centuries of Canadian Business* (Toronto: McClelland & Stewart, 1987), 80–81.

166 Newman, *Dreams of Empire*, 85. Bailey's name is spelled several ways by historians. This is not unusual, as he lived in a time when spelling was very fluid. Radisson's name is spelled many different ways in the historical record, while people simply gave up on Groseilliers and called him Mr. (or Capt.) Gooseberries.

167 Radisson's belief that Lake Superior was drained by rivers flowing to Hudson Bay is added proof that he had not made a trip to the bay in the 1650s, or that he knew much about the geography of the north shore of Lake Superior, which he had probably also never seen.

168 Warkentin, *Pierre-Esprit Radisson: The Collected Writings, Vol. 1*, vii.

169 Harold A. Innis, *The Fur Trade in Canada* (New Haven: Yale University Press, 1962), 123.

170 E.R. Osler, *La Salle* (Toronto: Longmans, 1967), 39.

171 Ibid, 41.

172 The Jesuits were playing their own political game. They wanted to establish northern missions while René-Robert Cavelier de La Salle sought a new empire in the west and south, headquartered at the mouth of the Mississippi. La Salle favoured the Franciscan Recollets, especially his friend Fr. Louis Hennepin, the man who first brought a highly embellished description of Niagara Falls to the world. The Jesuits had been trying to push the Recollets out of New France for some forty years. For a description of Fr. Abanel's mission and the politics behind it, see W.J. Eccles, *Frontenac: The Courtier Governor* (Toronto: McClelland & Stewart, 1959), 91.

173 These claims were not fully extinguished until the Treaty of Breda in 1667. Rich, *History of the Hudson's Bay Company* Vol. 1, 17.

174 Picard, *Restoration London*, 225.

175 Nute, *Caesars of the Wilderness,* 153. There's some question of whether Mary was her actual name. The record is remarkably thin about her, though she certainly did exist. There is no parish record of the marriage. She was Protestant and Radisson was nominally Catholic, so it's not clear who performed the ceremony. At least two of Radisson's wives were Protestants, but Radisson does not seem to have contemplated converting.

176 For an examination of Locke's role in the Enlightenment, especially in the lead-up to the American Revolution, see James MacGregor Burns, *Fire and Light: How the Enlightenment Transformed Our World* (New York: St. Martin's Press, 2013), chapter 2.

177 Bliss, *Northern Enterprise*, 81.

178 Nute, *Caesars of the Wilderness,* 146.

179 Osler, *La Salle*, 80–81.

180 The HBC plan failed because the islands, supposedly just south of Iceland, did not exist.

181 In the late-eighteenth century, the British government retained ownership of the land on the main ridge that runs north-south on the island and set it aside as a nature preserve. This was in contrast to the denuding of most of the smaller islands in the Caribbean, and the defoliation of large tracts of big islands such as Hispaniola (Haiti and the Dominican Republic) for monoculture plantations. The fortuitous decision by the British has made Tobago an important ecotourism destination. It's also popular with wreck divers.

182 threedecks.org/index.php?display_type=show_battle&id=58.

183 Warkentin, *Pierre-Esprit Radisson: The Collected Writings, Vol. 2*, 69–71.

184 The list of ships can be found in David F. Marley, *Wars of the Americas: A Chronology of Armed Conflict in the New World, 1492 to Present*, Vol. 1, 2nd ed., (New York: ABC-Clio, 2008), 185–186.

185 A freak hurricane in 1847 ended sugar-plantation agriculture on the island, and Hurricane Flora ravaged the island in 1963.

186 Marley, *Wars of the Americas*, quoted in Warkentin, ed., *Pierre-Esprit Radisson: The Collected Writings, Vol. 2,* 193, note 30. Other writers have claimed the Dutch were sloppy with their gunpowder and had spilled it on the path leading to the magazine,

leaving the kind of trail that was a common feature of Looney Tunes cartoons of the twentieth century. Supposedly, the third shot missed the magazine but set off this powder, which then ignited the magazine. Even so, it was a fine shot.

187 Warkentin, *Pierre-Esprit Radisson: The Collected Writings*, Vol. 2, 195.

188 Binckes was a superb commander, but might have devoted more effort to the safe storage of explosives, as will be seen later.

189 Some have even credited Nostradamus with foreseeing it. See Reading, Mario, *The Complete Prophecies of Nostradamus*. Digital: Watkins Publishing; reprint edition, 2015.

190 While the loss of the French fleet was disastrous, d'Estrées's attacks on the Dutch convinced the United Provinces to curtail their colonial expansion into the Caribbean because of the cost and risk. As for Tobago, the French held it until the end of the Seven Years' War in 1763, when they ceded it to the British. The French did almost nothing with the island during the decades they held it. For d'Estrées, it took more than incompetence and bad luck to ruin a French noble's military career in the age of Louis XIV. He eventually became a Marshall of France, the highest rank in the French army.

191 D'Estrées, under orders from the French crown, returned months later to salvage the cannon from these ships.

192 See bbc.co.uk/history/ancient/archaeology/marine_wreck_01.shtml.

193 Radisson was supposed to get 25 percent of the profits. Warkentin, *Pierre-Esprit Radisson: The Collected Writings, Vol. 2*, 15.

194 The company survived Radisson's betrayal and became a Quebec-based entity that conducted its own trade and wars in Hudson Bay until 1713, when France, settling the War of the Spanish Succession, ceded Hudson Bay to the British in the Treaty of Utrecht. Still, its investors ended up with a substantial loss on their investment.

195 Certainly, the Hudson's Bay Company and the English government thought all of this was no coincidence. The powers that be believed the scheme was dreamed up by Radisson and Zachariah Gillam years before and put into action after all the key plotters had been sidelines by their various governments and the better-connected merchants in their home countries. See "The Committees Answer to Esqr Yonges Letter," March 8, 1693/4, HBC Archives, A/6/2, quoted in Nute, *Caesars in the Wilderness*, 188.

196 Bliss, *Northern Enterprise*, 89.

197 This is the only voyage in which a surviving account by des Groseilliers survives. In it, he claims to have made most of the decisions. See Médard Chouart des Groseilliers: "Letter Concerning the Events at Port Nelson," 1682–83, reproduced in Warkentin, *Pierre-Esprit Radisson: The Collected Writings, Vol. 2*, 207–211.

198 Bridgar, unlike Hudson, made it back to England. He would be Radisson's lifelong enemy.

199 Cornelius J. Jaenen, ed., *The French Regime in the Upper Country of Canada During the Seventeenth Century* (Toronto: Champlain Society, 1996), 144.

200 Ibid, 139.

201 Preston, quoted by Nute, *Caesars of the Wilderness*, 213.

202 In *Company of Adventurers,* Peter C. Newman quotes Godet describing Radisson wearing "apparel more like a Savage than a Christian. His black hair, just touched with grey, hung in a wild profusion about his bare neck and shoulders. He showed a swart complexion, seamed and pitted from frost and exposure in a rigorous climate. A huge scar wrought by the tomahawk of a drunken Indian, disfigured his left cheek. His whole costume was surmounted by a collar of marten's skin; his feet were adorned by buckskin moccasins. In his leather belt was sheathed a long knife." I have several issues with this quote. Newman did not cite it. If Radisson told Godet he'd been wounded in the face with a small axe, he would have called it a hatchet, not a tomahawk. There is no evidence that Radisson, either in the Great Lakes country or Hudson Bay, traded liquor to Indigenous people. (That ugly business started, for the most part, in the next century). Radisson was always a stickler for the way he looked, and, even when he was with the Mohawks, was very fussy with his hair. No one else describes Radisson as adopting a wilderness costume in France or England, and his detractors would certainly have mentioned it.

203 Peter C. Newman, *Company of Adventurers* (Toronto: Penguin Canada, 2003), 99.

204 Rich, *Letters Outward,* 131.

205 Newman, *Company of Adventurers,* 99. The company insisted to Radisson that the trade goods were the very best quality. See HBRS-11: 180 and 195, quoted in Fournier, *Pierre-Esprit Radisson, Merchant Adventurer 1636–1710,* 262.

206 Terms, Nute, *Caesars of the Wilderness,* 220; secret orders, Nute, *Caesars of the Wilderness,* 221.

207 The man was later murdered by Groseilliers' adopted Cree brother, a member of another Cree band.

208 Warkentin, *Pierre-Esprit Radisson: The Collected Writings, Vol. 2,* 115–117. Radisson, whose sloppiness with dates and time frames has long vexed historians, was wrong in his claim that he and the senior Groseilliers had worked for the English for thirteen years, It was, in fact, ten years from the time they arrived in London until Radisson abandoned his wife and fled, and just eight years during which he worked for the merchants who established the Hudson's Bay Company (1667–1675).

209 Journal of Father Silvy, reproduced in Tyrrell, *Documents Relating to the Early History of Hudson Bay,* 1–52.

210 Winston S. Churchill, *Marlborough: His Life and Times,* US edition (New York: Charles Scribner's Sons, 1968), 206–208. He writes about Radisson and Chouart: "In 1666 two French-Canadian Protestants [sic] who had opened up the fur trade around Hudson Bay, but had found no support from their own Government either in Quebec or Paris, came to England..."

211 Parish register of St. Martin-in-the-Fields, March 3, 1685, cited by Warkentin *Pierre-Esprit Radisson: The Collected Writings, Vol. 2,* 88. The wedding was in an earlier version

of the church. The gorgeous building at Trafalgar Square was built some thirty-five years later.

212 Rich, *Letters Outward*, 342.

213 Warkentin, *Pierre-Esprit Radisson: The Collected Writings, Vol. 2*, 92.

214 See measuringworth.com/calculators/ukcompare/result.php?year_source=1682&amount =1800&year_result=2017.

215 Journal of Father Silvy, reproduced in Tyrrell, *Documents Relating to the Early History of Hudson Bay*, 71–73.

216 Rich, *Letters Outward*, 222–227.

217 Ibid, 237–238. Radisson's supply of claret seems to have been a barometer of his favour and disfavour with the company.

218 Rich, *Letters Outward*, 171–172, quoted in Warkentin, *Pierre-Esprit Radisson: The Collected Writings, Vol. 2*, 95.

219 Rich, *History of the Hudson's Bay Company*, 293, quoted in Fournier, *Pierre-Esprit Radisson, Merchant Adventurer*, 266.

220 That figure is for the Quebec merchants' losses on their investments in the Compagnie du Nord. Eccles, *Frontenac*, 172.

221 Fenton, *The Great Law*, 369–377.

222 British Library, Add 63773, Preston papers, 157–158, Hayes to Preston, May 22, 1687, quoted in Warkentin, *Pierre-Esprit Radisson: The Collected Writings, Vol. 2*, 87.

223 St. Clement Danes burial record Vol. 6, June 21, 1710, cited by Warkentin, *Pierre-Esprit Radisson: The Collected Writings, Vol. 2*, 4.

224 Warkentin 91, quoting Old Bailey online. We can hold out some hope of mercy, since many death penalties were commuted.

225 Many, many authors have used this company's archives as the basis of their research. For an explanation of their value to history, see John B. Davenport and Dan Rylance, "Archival Note. Sources of Business History: The Archives of the Hudson's Bay Company," *The Business History Review* 54:3 (Autumn 1980), 387–393.

226 For a discussion of the causes of the Fourth Iroquois War, which lasted from 1657 to 1696, see Raoul Naroll, "The Causes of the Fourth Iroquois War," *Ethnohistory* 6:1 (Winter 1969), 51–81.

227 Keith J. Crowe, *A History of the Original Peoples of Northern Canada* (Montreal: McGill-Queen's University Press, 1974), 70.

228 For a discussion of the fur trade's impact on Cree society and the expansion of Cree territory, see Crowe, *A History of the Original Peoples of Northern Canada*, 74.

229 "Beaver Ponds a Growing Source of Greenhouse Gas," *The Science Teacher* 82:2, (February 2015), 16.

SELECT BIBLIOGRAPHY

BOOKS

Ackroyd, Peter. *Rebellion: The History of England From James I to the Glorious Revolution.* New York: St. Martin's Press, 2014.

Barthel, Manfred. *The Jesuits: History and Legend of the Society of Jesus.* New York: William Morrow & Co., 1984.

Bliss, Michael. *Northern Enterprise: Five Centuries of Canadian Business.* Toronto: McClelland & Stewart, 1987.

Braudel, Fernand. *The Structures of Everyday Life: Civilization and Capitalism, Vol. 1.* New York: Harper and Row, 1981.

Brook, Timothy. *Vermeer's Hat: The Seventeenth Century and the Dawn of the Global World.* Toronto: Viking Canada, 2008.

Brose, David S., Robert C. Mainfort, and C. Wesley, eds., *Societies in Eclipse: Archaeology of the Eastern Woodlands, 1400–1700.* Washington: Smithsonian Institution Press, 2001.

Burns, James MacGregor. *Fire and Light: How the Enlightenment Transformed Our World.* New York: St. Martin's Press, 2013.

Churchill, Winston. *Marlborough: His Life and Times.* New York: Charles Scribner's Sons, 1934.

Crowe, Keith J. *A History of the Original Peoples of Northern Canada.* Montreal: McGill-Queen's University Press, 1974.

Davies, Godfrey. *The Restoration of Charles II 1658–1660.* San Marino, CA: The Huntington Library, 1955.

Dewdney, Selwyn and Kenneth E. Kidd. *Indian Rock Paintings of the Great Lakes.* Toronto: Quetico Foundation-University of Toronto Press, 1962.

Dewdney, Selwyn. *Dating Rock Art in the Canadian Shield Region.* Toronto: Royal Ontario Museum, 1970.

Dickason, Olive Patricia. *Canada's First Nations: A History of Founding Peoples from Earliest Times.* Toronto: Oxford University Press, 1997.

Dickason, Olive Patricia. *The Myth of the Savage and the Beginnings of French Colonialism in the Americas.* Edmonton: University of Alberta Press, 1984.

Dunning, R.W. *Social and Economic Change among the Northern Ojibwa.* Toronto: University of Toronto Press, 1959.

Eccles, W.J. *Frontenac: The Courtier Governor*. Toronto: McClelland & Stewart, 1959.

Ellingson, Ter. *The Myth of the Noble Savage*. Berkeley: University of California Press, 1991.

Fenton, William N. *The Great Law: A Political History of the Iroquois Confederacy*. Norman, OK: University of Oklahoma Press, 1998.

Fischer, David Hackett. *Champlain's Dream: The Missionary Adventurer Who Made a New World in Canada*. Toronto: Vintage Canada, 2009.

Fournier, Martin. *Pierre-Esprit Radisson, Merchant Adventurer, 1636–1710*. Sillery, QC: Les editions du Septentrion, 2002.

Franks, C.E.S. *The Canoe and White Water*. Toronto: University of Toronto Press, 1977.

Green, L.C., and Olive P. Dickason, *The Law of Nations and the New World*. Edmonton: University of Alberta Press, 1989.

Handover, P.M. *A History of the London Gazette*. London: Her Majesty's Stationery Office, 1965.

Heidenreich, Conrad. *Huronia: A History and Geography of the Huron Indians*. Toronto: McClelland & Stewart, 1971.

Hough, Franklin B. *Proceedings of the Commissioners of Indian Affairs Vol. 1*. Albany: State of New York, 1861.

Hunter, Douglas. *Half Moon: Henry Hudson and the Voyage That Redrew the Map of the World*. New York: Bloomsbury Press, 2009.

Innis, Harold. *The Fur Trade in Canada*. Toronto: University of Toronto Press, 1962.

Jaenen, Cornelius J., ed. *The French Regime in the Upper Country of Canada During the Seventeenth Century*. Toronto: Champlain Society, 1996.

Jaenen, Cornelius J. *Friend and Foe: Aspects of French-Amerindian Cultural Contact in the Sixteenth and Seventeenth Centuries*. Toronto: McClelland & Stewart, 1973.

Jennings, Francis. *The Ambiguous Iroquois Empire: The Covenant Chain Confederation of Indian Tribes With English Colonies*. New York: W.W. Norton, 1984.

Kertzer, David I. and Marzio Barbagli, eds. *History of the European Family: Book 1*. New Haven: Yale University Press, 2001.

Kishlansky, Mark. *A Monarchy Transformed: Britain 1603–1714*. London: Allen Lane-Penguin, 1994.

Lajeunesse, Ernest J., ed. *The Windsor Border Region: Canada's Southernmost Frontier*. Toronto: Champlain Society, 1960.

Marley, David F. *Wars of America: A Chronology of Armed Conflict in America, 2nd ed.* New York: ABC-Clio, 2008.

McDonnell, Michael. *Masters of Empire: Great Lakes Indians and the Making of America*. New York: Hill and Wang, 2015.

Morison, Samuel Eliot. *Samuel de Champlain, Father of New France*. New York: Little Brown/Atlantic Monthly, 1972.

Newman, Peter C. *Caesars of the Wilderness*. Toronto: Viking Press, 1987.

Newman, Peter C. *Company of Adventurers: How the Hudson's Bay Empire Determined the Destiny of a Continent*. Toronto: Viking Canada, 1985.

Nute, Grace Lee. *Caesars of the Wilderness*. New York: D. Appleton-Century Company, 1941.

Ollard, Richard. *Pepys: A Biography*. London: Hodder and Stoughton, 1974.

Osler, E.B. *La Salle*. Toronto: Longmans, 1967.

Parker, Arthur C. *Parker on the Iroquois*. Syracuse, NY: Syracuse University Press, 1971.

Petrone, Penny, ed. *First People, First Voices*. Toronto: University of Toronto Press, 1983.

Picard, Liza. *Restoration London*. London: Weidenfeld & Nicolson, 1997.

Porter, Roy. *London: A Social History*. London: Penguin, 1994.

Rich, E.E. *The History of the Hudson's Bay Company* (2 Vols). London: The Hudson's Bay Record Society, 1959.

Rich, E.E., ed. *Copy-Book of Letters Outward &c 1679–1794*. Toronto: Champlain Society, 1948.

Sagard, Fr. Gabriel and George Wrong, ed. Pierre. *Long Journey to the Country of the Huron*. Toronto: Champlain Society, 1939.

Schmaltz, Peter S. *The Ojibwa of Southern Ontario*. Toronto: University of Toronto Press, 1991.

Schoolcraft, Henry Rowe. *The Literary Voyager or Muzzeniegun*. Ann Arbor, MI: Michigan State University Press, 1961.

Simpson, Patricia. *Marguérite Bourgeoys: Montreal 1640–1665*. Montreal: McGill-Queens University Press, 1997.

Spencer, Charles. *Killers of the King: The Men Who Dared to Execute Charles I*. London: Bloomsbury Press, 2014.

Spencer, Charles. *Prince Rupert: The Last Cavalier*. London: Weidenfeld & Nicolson, 2007.

Steele, Ian K. *Setting All the Captives Free: Capture, Adjustment and Recollection in Allegheny Country*. Montreal: McGill-Queen's University Press, 2013.

Stubbs, John. *Reprobates: The Cavaliers of the English Civil War*. London: Viking, 2011.

Tinniswood, Adrian. *By Permission of Heaven: The True Story of the Great Fire of London*. New York: Riverhead Books, 2003.

Trigger, Bruce. *The Children of Aataentsic* (2 Vols), Montreal: McGill-Queen's University Press, 1976.

Trigger, Bruce. *The Huron, Farmers of the North*. Toronto: Holt, Rinehart & Winston, 1969.

Trigger, Bruce. "The Jesuits in the Fur Trade." In J.R. Miller, ed., *Sweet Promises: A Reader on Indian-White Relations in Canada*. Toronto: University of Toronto Press, 1991.

Trudel, Marcel. *The Beginnings of New France, 1524–1663*. Toronto: McClelland & Stewart, 1973.

Tyrrell, J.B. *Documents Relating to the Early History of Hudson's Bay*. Toronto: Champlain Society, 1931.

Vastokas, Joan M., and Romas K. Vastokas, *Sacred Art of the Algonkians: A Study of the Peterborough Petroglyphs*. Peterborough: Mansard Press, 1973.

Warkentin, Germaine, ed. *Pierre-Esprit Radisson: The Collected Writings, Vol. 1: The Voyages*. Montreal-Toronto: McGill-Queens University Press/Champlain Society, 2012.

Warkentin, Germaine, ed. *Pierre-Esprit Radisson: The Collected Writings, Vol. 2: The Port Nelson Relations, Miscellaneous Writings and Related Documents*. Montreal-Toronto:

McGill-Queens University Press/Champlain Society, 2014.

Wilkinson, Clennell. *Prince Rupert, the Cavalier*. London: George Harrap & Co., 1934.

Willes, Margaret. *The Curious World of Samuel Pepys and John Evelyn*. New Haven: Yale University Press, 2017.

ACADEMIC PAPERS

Adams, Arthur T. "A New Interpretation of the Voyages of Radisson." *Minnesota History* 6:4 (December 1925): 317–319.

Bishop, Charles A. and M. Estellie Smith. "Early Historic Populations in Northwestern Ontario: Archaeological and Ethnohistorical Interpretations." *American Antiquity* 40:1 (January 1975): 54–63.

Carlos, Anne M. and Stephen Nicholas "Agency Problems in Early Chartered Companies: The Case of the Hudson's Bay Company." *The Journal of Economic History* 50:4 (December 1990): 853–875.

Carpenter, Roger. "Making War More Lethal: Iroquois vs. Huron in the Great Lakes Region, 1609 to 1650." *Michigan Historical Review* 27:2 (Fall 2001): 33-51.

Crean, J.F. "Hats and the Fur Trade." *Canadian Journal of Economics and Political Science,* Vol. XXVII, No. 3 (August 1962): 373–451.

Davenport, John B. and Dan Rylance. "Archival Note. Sources of Business History: The Archives of the Hudson's Bay Company." *The Business History Review* 54:3 (Autumn 1980): 387–393.

Hammond, Lorne. "Marketing Wildlife: The Hudson's Bay Company and the Pacific Northwest, 1821–49." *Forest & Conservation History* 37:1, (January 1993): 14–25.

Hickerson, Harold "The Feast of the Dead Among the Seventeenth Century Algonkians of the Upper Lakes." *American Anthropologist* 62:1, New Series (February 1960): 81–107.

Howard, James H. "Notes on the Ethnography of the Yankton Dakota." *Plains Anthropologist* 17:58, part 1 (November 1972): 281–307.

Jaenen, Cornelius J. "Amerindian Views of French Culture in the Seventeenth Century." *Canadian Historical Review* 55:3 (September 1974): 261–291.

Kapoches, Mima. "The Auda Site: An Early Pickering Iroquois Component in Southeastern Ontario." *Archaeology of Eastern North America*, Vol. 15 (Fall 1987): 155–175.

Kellogg, Louise Phelps. "Copper Mining in the Early Northwest." *The Wisconsin Magazine of History* 8:2 (December 1924): 146–159.

Kuhn, Robert D., and Robert E. Funk. "Boning up on the Mohawk: An Overview of Mohawk Faunal Assemblages and Subsistence Patterns." *Archaeology of Eastern North America* 28 (2000): 29–62.

Lee, Thomas. "Lost Battleground of the Long Sault." *Genus* 16:1/4 (1960): 116–157.

Mood, Fulmer. "The London Background of the Radisson Problem." *Minnesota History* 16 (December 1935): 391–413.

Naroll, Raoul. "The Causes of the Fourth Iroquois War." *Ethnohistory* 6:1 (Winter 1969): 51–81.

Noble, William C. "Tsouharissen's Chiefdom: An Early Historic 17th Century Neutral Iroquoian Society." *Canadian Journal of Archaeology* 9:2 (1985): 131–146.

Nute, Grace Lee. "Radisson and Groseilliers's Contribution to Geography." *Minnesota History* 16 (December 1935): 418.

Nute, Grace Lee. "Two Documents from Radisson's Suit Against the Company:" *The Beaver* (December 1935): 41–49.

Spence, Michael W. and Lawrence Jackson. "The Bioarchaeology of Cannibalism at the Charity Site." *Ontario Archaeology* 94 (2014): 65–80.

Stern, Jill. "Poison in Print: Pamphleteering and the Deaths of Concini (1617) and the Brothers De Witt (1672)." *Pamphlets and Politics in the Dutch Republic.* Brill (2010): 119–142.

Stevens, Scott Manning. "The Historiography of New France and the Legacy of Iroquois Internationalism." *Comparative American Studies An International Journal* 11:2 (2013): 148–165.

Stueck, Adam. "A Place Under Heaven: Amerindian Torture and Cultural Violence in Colonial New France, 1609–1729" (2012). Dissertations (2009), Paper 174. Available at epublications.marquette.edu/dissertations_mu/174.

Trigger, Bruce. "The Woman Who Married a Beaver: Trade Patterns and Gender Roles in the Ojibwa Fur Trade." *Ethnohistory* 46:1 (Winter 1999): 109–147.

Wallace, Anthony F. "Political Organization and Land Tenure among the Northeastern Indians, 1600–1830." *Southwestern Journal of Anthropology* (1957): 301–321.

Index

ACKNOWLEDGMENTS

First and foremost, this book would not exist without the support, encouragement, and hard work of my friend and editor, Janice Zawerbny, who held on to this proposal for thirteen years and three jobs before convincing Dan Wells at Biblioasis that Radisson would make a good biography topic. I was impressed by Biblioasis's fiction and its success as an independent Canadian publisher, and I welcomed the opportunity to work with Dan and his team. It turned out to be a good decision, at least from my point of view.

I have to acknowledge the work of Radisson himself, and of the scholars who have researched and put it into perspective. Grace Nute's *Caesars of the Wilderness*, published in 1943, mined Radisson's own writings and added extensive archival work to them. Nute was part of a cluster of American Midwestern (Minnesota) scholars who adopted Radisson as a sort of mascot and were determined to give him credit for being the first European to describe the Upper Mississippi.

Germaine Warkentin took this scholarship even further. In her scholarly two-volume Champlain Society edition of *Pierre-Esprit Radisson: The Collected Writings*, she has weeded out much of the conjecture and taken Radisson scholarship to a much higher level. Martin Fournier's 2002 academic biography, *Pierre-Esprit Radisson: Merchant Adventurer, 1636–1710*, provided some psychological insights on Radisson.

My hope is that I have added value to Radisson scholarship by contextualizing it amid the events and political culture that had so much influence on his life. There's a bibliography at the end of this book, but I want to single out the works of Conrad Heidenreich, a scholar who was very kind to me when I was a student; Bruce Trigger, whose work on the Huron (Wendat) culture is invaluable; Indigenous writers Scott Manning Stevens for his work on anti-Iroquois propaganda, and Olive Dickason, not only for her friendship but also for her book *Canada's First Nations*, and, as important, *The Law of Nations and the New World* and *The Myth of the Savage and the Beginnings of French Colonialism in the Americas*.

I'd also like to acknowledge the kindness of Charles, 9th Earl Spencer, who answered my queries on 17th-century Stuart history and for his biography of Prince Rupert. I'd also like to thank my Canadian historian friends, among them Dr. James McKillip, Dr. Tim Cook, Constance Backhouse, Dr. Robert Englebert, Dr. Michael Osmann, Dr. Nick Clark, Dr. John Maker, Dr. Douglas Hunter, and others in the odd little world of Canadian non-fiction writing who gave encouragement to me and to this project.

Above all, I'd like to thank my wife, Marion, and our three kids for putting up with the piles of books around the house, the long hours of neglect, and the snits. They have as much of an investment in this book as I do. I would also like to thank Marion for drawing the original maps in the book.

I would also like to acknowledge the support of the Ontario Arts Council's Writers Reserve program for their financial help with this project.